RALLYCOURSE

THE WORLD'S LEADING RALLY ANNUAL

HAZLETON PUBLISHING

PAVAROTTI IN THE CHARTS.

◆

TINTORETTO ON POSTCARDS.

TUSCANY ON TELEVISION.

◆

AT LEAST THERE'S

ONE PIECE OF ITALIAN CULTURE

YOU CAN KEEP TO

YOURSELF.

Martini Brut cuvée speciale. An elegantly dry yet
fruity sparkling wine from Martini & Rossi.

Publisher
Richard Poulter

Editor
David Williams

Executive Publisher
Elizabeth Le Breton

Art Editor
Julian Bigg

Production Manager
George Greenfield

Production Controller
Peter Lovering

Advertising Co-ordinator
Jocelyne Bia

Results and Statistics
Paul Fearnley

Chief Photographer
Reinhard Klein

Rallycourse

Published by
Hazleton Publishing
3 Richmond Hill, Richmond
Surrey TW10 6RE

Typeset by
Bigg Sense Design
25 Calvin St, Spitalfields
London E1 6NW
on Apple Macintosh™

Colour Reproduction by
Adroit Photo Litho Ltd
Birmingham

Printed in England by
Ebenezer Baylis & Son Ltd
Worcester

ISBN: 0-905138-89-9

Distributors

United Kingdom
Reed Illustrated Books
Michelin House
81 Fulham Road
London SW3 6RB

North America
Motorbooks International
PO Box 2, 729 Prospect Ave,
Osceola
Wisconsin 54020, USA

Australia
Technical Book & Magazine Co. Pty
289-299 Swanston Street
Melbourne
Victoria 3000

Universal Motor Publications
c/o Automoto Motoring Bookshop
152–154 Clarence Street
Sydney 2000
New South Wales

New Zealand
David Bateman Ltd
'Golden Heights'
32–34 View Road
Glenfield
Auckland 10

Once again, Lancia left its opposition flat-footed to win a sixth consecutive manufacturers' title (dust jacket). **Photograph** Reinhard Klein
Toyota had its successes, though, including Mats Jonsson's Swedish Rally victory. **Photograph** Pascal Huit

Contents

rallycourse

Acknowledgements

Photographs appearing in *Rallycourse 1992-93* have been contributed by: Reinhard Klein (Chief Photographer), Michael Chester, Pascal Huit, LAT Photographic, Gavin Lodge and Brian McLean. Maps supplied by Castrol.

The Editor of *Rallycourse* wishes to thank the following for their assistance, resourcefulness and tolerance during the compilation of the 1992-93 edition: Julian Bigg, Hugh Bishop, Liz Le Breton, Amanda Campbell, David Campbell, Michael Chester, Charles Coates, Kay Edge, Paul Evans, Paul Fearnley, Mike Greasley, George Greenfield, Malcolm Griffiths, Pascal Huit, Reinhard Klein, Gavin Lodge, Peter Lovering, Brian McLean, Brian Patterson, Liz Patterson, Martin Sharp and Steve Small.

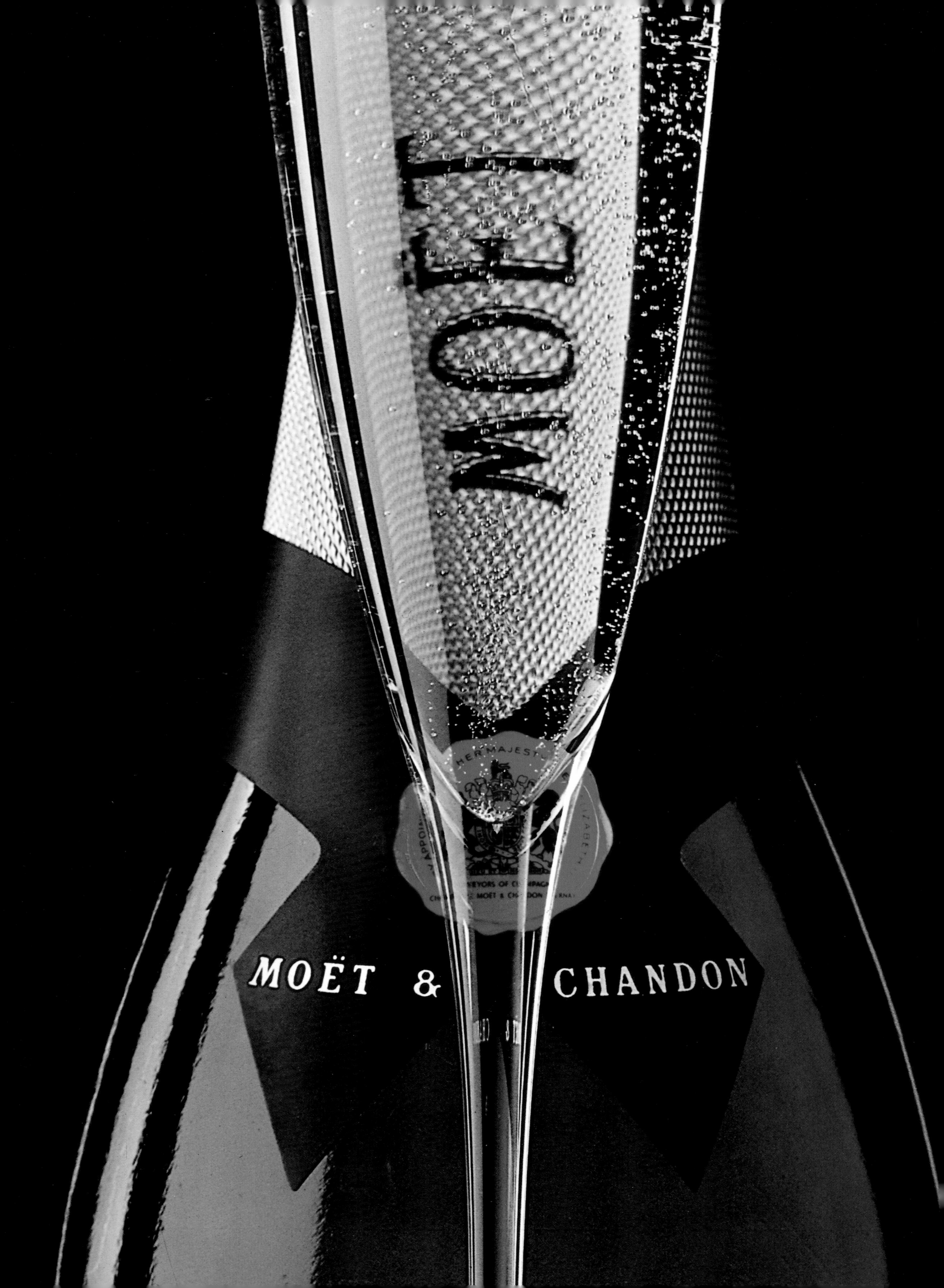
MOËT
MOËT & CHANDON

FOREWORD
by Carlos Sainz

I can hardly believe that I am Champion again. It has been an incredible season, and it has been a really big fight with the Lancia drivers. We have had some problems, but we have never given up, and I want to say a special thank you to Mr Andersson and everyone at Toyota Team Europe. It makes up for the disappointment of last year. Now I will be able to read about it in *Rallycourse*.

THE NEW VAUXHALL CAVALIER. NOW IT'S CRUNCH TIME FOR THE COMPETITION.

Here's the first body-blow to the Vauxhall Cavalier's competition.

The new Cavalier has arrived.

A few of the changes we've made, the competition might have expected. Like the new front and rear body-

colour bumpers. The new bootlid panel. And the new, sleeker-looking headlights. The new trims inside. The three new colours available. The new body-colour grille.

And, on many Cavaliers, the new alloy wheels.

But what the competition will certainly not have anticipated, and which might well put them in a state of shock, are the remarkable new safety improvements which make the Cavalier as much a cocoon as a car. Every Cavalier comes equipped with new twin side-impact protection bars in all doors.

The bars greatly reduce the risk of injury in the event of a side-impact.

And a steel safety cage and reinforced B-pillar are there to increase protection still further.

What are also standard on every Cavalier are 'body-lock' front seat-belt tensioners.

Tests have shown that these tensioners can reduce the severity of head and chest injuries by as much as 20%.

From March, available on all Cavaliers will be the added protection of the 'airbag',* a safety device designed to significantly lessen the impact on a body thrown against the steering-wheel.

The 'airbag' also cushions a large area of the chest. This significantly reduces the risk of fractured ribs and other chest injuries.

The ABS (Anti-lock Braking System) is now available on all Cavaliers.

These, and many other, advantages make the new Cavalier one of the safest, and most stylish, cars in its class.

And with three new engines (including the narrow-angle 24-valve V6** and the 2-litre Turbo), you'll find absolutely nothing lacking in the Cavalier's performance.

Indeed, you might care to know that, in the 1992 Esso RAC British Touring Car Championship, the Vauxhall Cavalier 16-valve walked off with both the Team Championship and the Manufacturers' Championship.

Now isn't that the final body-blow to the Cavalier's competition?

For more details, call 0800 444 200. Or visit your local Vauxhall dealer.

THE NEW CAVALIER.

VAUXHALL

Once driven, forever smitten.

THE ELEMENT OF SURPRISE

In many ways, it was not a vintage rallying season. All the warnings that the ruinous expense of the World Championship needed curtailing came home to roost with a vengeance and, for much of the year, the news consisted of an impressive but not particularly enthralling stream of Lancia victories on the one hand, and a dismal succession of cutbacks and closures on the other, as the big Japanese teams came to terms with reduced economic circumstances.

The staggering cost of international rallying for a factory team or even a privateer still requires further attention, but it is heartening — even surprising — to record that 1992 produced the closest, most dramatic finish in the 14-year history of the World Championship for Drivers. For the first time, three drivers from rival teams entered the final round with a chance of winning. Carlos Sainz's victory was against the run of play certainly, but it demonstrated a phenomenal capacity for performing flawlessly under pressure, as well as the blistering speed in any conditions that one has come to expect from the Spaniard. It was an audacious feat that will pass into motor sport legend. That said, it was impossible not to feel a large measure of sympathy for Didier Auriol, who won a record number of World Championship rallies in a season, yet only came third in the points table. His fate looks certain to trigger demands for a change in the points-scoring system. In spite of financial restrictions and the gloomy economic outlook, the World Championship has never been so closely fought, nor so dramatic. Whether FISA stirs itself to arrange the kind of television coverage that the manufacturers want remains to be seen, but there has been some evidence that the excitement that a World Championship rally can provide is attracting national television networks regardless. The flood of publicity surrounding Colin McRae, and the live satellite link between Carlos Sainz and Spain during the Lombard RAC Rally were encouraging signs for the future. In Britain, meanwhile, rallying has become a popular feature of television's coverage of motoring and the nature of the sport has become an attribute, not a hindrance.

A year ago, Colin McRae's success in the British Championship deserved commendation. He is now beginning to generate the same excitement in the World Championship arena. Accordingly, it seems an appropriate moment to take a closer look at the flamboyant British Champion and analyse what makes him different from his predecessors.

This year's edition of *Rallycourse* also considers the wider concerns facing the sport and the general belief that it must continue to evolve. Martin Sharp provides expert technical analysis of the impending 'Formula 2' regulations, delving into the secrets of the current contenders and the potential impact of a two-wheel drive category on international rallying. Elsewhere, the views of three of the sport's most thoughtful figures, Miki Biasion, Andrew Cowan and Juha Piironen — a mixture of detachment, commonsense and outspokenness, if you like — provoke unexpected and controversial hints as to where rallying might be heading.

Amanda Campbell looks into the world of the service co-ordinator, an indispensable member of a factory team who rarely steps into the limelight. She examines the contrasting public and private personae of Rob Arthur, the former co-driver who plays a leading role at Mitsubishi Ralliart.

These are hard yet intriguing times for British rallying. *Rallycourse* prides itself on the breadth and depth of its coverage, and the latest edition dwells at length on the British scene, Paul Evans stating forthright views on the Mobil l/*Top Gear* and Mintex championships. The best rallies have always developed personalities of their own regardless of championship status, and we therefore celebrate the restoration of the Circuit of Ireland to something like its former glory. There is a final, irreplaceable factor: the remarkable photography of Reinhard Klein.

David Williams
Camden
London

December 1992

Lancia's partial withdrawal made little enough difference to the Italian firm's dazzling run of success. Didier Auriol and Bernard Occelli are pictured on their way to victory on the Acropolis.

The new Peugeot 405 will take you from 35 years to 4 years in an instant.

Its ultra responsive roadhandling rekindles memories of how you handled your favourite toy car.

PEUGEOT A feat due largely to the 405's very grown-up

sounding Integrated Chassis Design (ICD). A unique configuration of suspension layout, weight distribution and bodyshell rigidity.

Put more simply, it sticks to the road like chewing gum to a school desk and handles with the sensitivity of... well, of a hand.

FOR FURTHER INFORMATION ON THE PEUGEOT 405 RANGE PHONE 0800 800 405. CAR SH

REMEMBER THAT FEELING OF TOTAL CONTROL?

Fortunately, whilst sharing that feeling of total control with your toy car, the new 405 doesn't share its child-like feel, inside.

A completely new interior and instrument layout, remote control in-car entertainment with RDS* and cocoon-like sound insulation pander to the needs of us adults.

Ask your local Peugeot dealer about the new range of petrol and diesel 405s. And you could be taking a test drive down memory lane.

THE NEW PEUGEOT 405

JAGUAR WERE SO IMPRESSED WITH OUR OIL, THEY DESIGNED SOMETHING SPECIAL TO PUT IT IN.

Castrol Formula RS is, without doubt, the most advanced fully synthetic oil ever made.

It's stable enough to withstand the red hot temperatures of a combustion chamber without evaporating.

It's viscous enough to leave a thin protective coating on vital moving parts even after the engine is turned off.

Yet it's thin enough to circulate rapidly on cold starting, the time when maximum engine protection is needed.

It also contains specially blended additives which keep the engine cleaner and keep catalytic converters more efficient.

Above all, Formula RS dramatically reduces engine friction, thereby minimising fuel consumption and maximising power output.

It's this kind of performance that enabled JaguarSport to develop

their incredible XJ220 engine to its full potential.

In fact, if you have the opportunity to glance at the oil-filler cap,

you'll notice it says 'Use only Castrol Formula RS.'

For more information regarding availability or suitability to your

car, please call our External Affairs department on 0793 512712.

FULL SYNTHETIC ENGINEERING.

THE CAR IN FRONT IS –USUALLY– A LANCIA

By David Williams

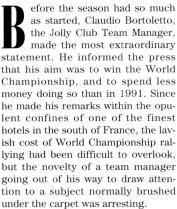

Before the season had so much as started, Claudio Bortoletto, the Jolly Club Team Manager, made the most extraordinary statement. He informed the press that his aim was to win the World Championship, and to spend less money doing so than in 1991. Since he made his remarks within the opulent confines of one of the finest hotels in the south of France, the lavish cost of World Championship rallying had been difficult to overlook, but the novelty of a team manager going out of his way to draw attention to a subject normally brushed under the carpet was arresting.

It was typical of Bortoletto's direct manner — if there is an Italian equivalent of a northerner, he is it — but his pronouncement signalled that the wind had changed direction abruptly and set the tone for the season. A year ago, *Rallycourse* dwelt on the scale and extravagance of manufacturers' PR operations. Much of that was swept away by the grim, commercial realism of 1992, but the season was marked not only by withdrawals and cutbacks, but by a loss of confidence in the current format of the World Rally Championship and an unprecedented debate about the sport's future. When Lancia's competitions chief, Giorgio Pianta, declares that rallying has become too expensive, the situation is bordering on the critical. Many of the developments springing from this crisis are addressed elsewhere in this book, but it is safe to say that, while the suggestions covered the spectrum, agreement was patchy. Carlos Sainz stated that endurance was dead in rallying — and he should know, having won the Safari at a gallop — whereas Didier Auriol bagged most of the wins and the fastest stage times in 1992, and said that it was time that stages grew longer and that an element of endurance was restored.

Times need to be very hard indeed before the Italian commitment to motor sport wavers and, on that basis, Lancia's continued run of success under the Martini Racing/ Jolly Club banner should come as no surprise. Yet there were surprises in Lancia's sixth consecutive manufac-

turers' title. The sheer scale of the Turinese firm's success until the very end of the year was astonishing, for it won most of the rallies that mattered, and it did so by comfortable margins. For most of the season (particularly if Auriol was still in the running), there was none of the fighting for seconds that recently made the World Rally Championship more closely fought than Formula 1. In the end, the most extraordinary aspect of Lancia's campaign was that the drivers' title managed to slip from Auriol's grasp.

Unusually, this dominance wasn't achieved by outspending the opposition. On the contrary, the Jolly Club men sometimes took on the role of the underdogs; they would point out how many extra mechanics Toyota had in Argentina, or vans in Australia. Indeed, Bortoletto sometimes gave the impression that saving money was as important as winning in the first place. Lancia bailed out the Jolly Club on both those visits to the southern hemisphere in fact, as they weren't particularly attractive to Martini, but in other respects, Bortoletto collected another makes' championship with some ease, thanks largely to the merits of the latest Integrale HF. It eliminated virtually all of its predecessors' faults, while setting new standards for Group A performance in spite of the 38 millimetre turbo restrictor. It is hard to conceive of a better front-engined rally car without starting with a clean sheet of paper and no production minimum. The changes to the Integrale are well known: crucially, bigger wheel arches and a wider track finally gave it suspension travel to match any of its rivals, along with bigger tyres under all conditions. Coupled to a stiffer, strengthened bodyshell prepared by a small Turinese firm called Cecomp, it banished the handling deficiencies that have been apparent since four-wheel drive Deltas first appeared. It isn't necessarily straightforward to pinpoint the improvements though. If asked, the drivers merely said that the car was easier to drive. On stages, it was clear that the old instability and twitchiness on bumps had been banished. It rode uneven surfaces like a

Galant or a Legacy, while retaining the compact dimensions and manoeuvrability that have always weighed in the Delta's favour. Combine that with the lightest bodyshell, an engine as good as anyone's and Lancia's customary reliability, and it starts to look like an irresistible combination. In fact, its superiority was generally so pronounced that even the team's most jaundiced rivals ceased to whisper about Integrale engines, and the Jolly Club was able to run its cars at the 1993 minimum weight — 1200 kilogrammes — and still win hands down in Australia. Towards the end of the season, the Italians were even boasting that they didn't test as much as the opposition, an unthinkable development at Lancia. The lack of testing coincided with the appearance of heavily revised Celicas, and may have cost Lancia a repeat of the clean sweep it unexpectedly took in 1991.

Only the Safari exposed the Delta's age. Since handling was of secondary importance, the Celica was very much on the pace — which was something of a novelty at that stage of the season — and, if there was a difference between the cars, it was the ease with which major components could be swapped on the Toyota. When Sainz replaced a blown turbo, driveshafts and shock absorbers in barely ten minutes, the Jolly Club men recognised that the rally was as good as lost. Repairing an Integrale that swiftly is out of the question, and the Jolly Club's defeat owed as much to the Safari's relentless time schedule as to Sainz and Toyota. Of course, the 1993 rules may well handicap the kit cars in any case, assuming an effective means of policing transmission changes can be found.

Improbable as it seems, there had been considerable room for improvement in a design that was already the most highly developed in international rallying. Lancia still retains the capacity to take the Group A rules a stage further than any of its adversaries, and it has an unrivalled power to get the production line to turn out what the competitions department wants. It remains to be seen if any of the wing-and-wheel-arch specials taking shape elsewhere will be quite so effective. None of the team's rivals seemed to think that the venerable Delta could be written off for 1993, even if Lancia reduces its support further.

Due tribute should be paid to Bortoletto for stitching a new team together so effectively that the seams were rarely visible from the outside. Many of the old faces still appeared, doing the same jobs and wearing the same clothing as they had when Lancia put its own name to its rally team: Ninni Russo co-ordinated operations, Vittorio Roberti was the engineer on the spot, and Rino Buschiazzo was chief mechanic, but there were plenty of new recruits, and a gradual increase in Milan-registered service vehicles provided a hint that the balance of power was shifting. Reputedly, there were disputes between the old Abarth hands and some of the Jolly Club men early in the season (they would sit at different tables in restaurants and the like), but this never spilled over in public. It was equally hard to tell that the team was being run from two centres, the cars still being prepared in Turin, and management based largely in Milan.

With respect to Didier Auriol, this was a year when the excellence of the car in terms of both performance and reliability mattered more than driving skill. At first, the 'Deltona' was so far ahead of the opposition that Juha Kankkunen earned a new reputation as a tarmac expert, beating François Delecour on the Monte and at Sanremo, and finally winning in Portugal. The inexperienced Andrea Aghini scored an unexpected yet thoroughly deserved victory at Sanremo, even though he was usually the slowest of the top four on the gravel stages that made up over half the route; an affinity for tarmac and the Integrale's matchless performance more than compensated. While Auriol did most of the winning, it was usually another Lancia driver in second place, and that driver was usually Kankkunen. In terms of results and finishing record, the 1991 World Champion had a marvellous season, and Auriol paid him a fulsome compliment, saying that those who thought that his wins had come easily had no idea how hard it was to beat the Finn.

The Frenchman's record-breaking run was ultimately scant recompense for the disappointments of 1991, when he was frequently quickest, yet rarely the winner. His luck changed out of all recognition for most of 1992 and his confidence soared to such an extent that it wasn't until Sanremo that the gnawing pressures of an impending world title began to leave their mark. Wins in Corsica and on the 1000 Lakes put him on a par with Sainz as one of the few genuine all-rounders, equally at home on almost any event and any surface. It was this ability to adjust that shattered the old record of five wins in a season. There were no events where Auriol was better left at home, nor obliged to drive for points from the start. Accordingly, a points system

Lancia focused on the essentials, the new Integrale giving Juha Kankkunen an enviable finishing record (left). Ford smartened up its operation no end, but didn't quite manage to take a victory with the Sierra Cosworth 4x4.

As a spectacle, Group A cars now bear comparison with Group B, as power outputs escalate and reliability continues to improve. Carlos Sainz (top), Jorge Recalde (centre), and Joaquim Santos put the proposition to the test.

that put him third in the championship, behind two men who had won fewer rallies between them, must be regarded as in serious need of revision.

His success, allied to Aghini's win at Sanremo, contributed to a further marginalising of the Finns. Kankkunen's superb consistency kept him in contention for the drivers' title to the end, but without concealing his abiding weakness on dry asphalt. Sanremo exposed it cruelly: Aghini improved spectacularly on loose surfaces during the season, and his vulnerability on gravel was more than outweighed by Kankkunen's on tarmac. Although Juha at least was in no danger of losing his job, Ari Vatanen's rising stock at Subaru was the only other bright spot for the nation that used to dominate the sport. The elder Finns — Hannu Mikkola, Timo Salonen and Markku Alén — were either sidelined or fired, and even Tommi Mäkinen's future looked far from rosy once Nissan announced its withdrawal. Increasingly, team managers are looking elsewhere for new blood.

Telling the Japanese that it was important to maintain a presence for the future, and that they wouldn't contemplate doing something between a couple and half a dozen Grands Prix would have fallen on deaf ears in 1992. The watchword was jam tomorrow, only Toyota made any real effort to have jam today, and even Japan's largest and most successful car maker didn't support the series with its customary enthusiasm. A combination of the decline of the domestic economy and the impending arrival of new cars for the 1993 rules prompted most of the Oriental teams to cut their losses, quite literally.

It would be misleading to say that Toyota's season fell into two halves. In fact, it could be divided into sixth-sevenths and one-seventh, for the car that won the last two rounds of the championship and gave Sainz his second world title performed in a manner that made the 'sixth-sevenths' Celica look like a Group N car. Until then, TTE's willingness to throw money at the problem had been singularly unproductive. Good as the Delta was — as a comparison with cars that had been competitive in 1991 shows — the Jolly Club's run of success was in part a reflection of TTE's failure. The one team with the experience and the resources to match the Italians duly finished runner-up in the makes' contest for the fourth year running, but mid-way through the season it looked as if Köln might lose second to Ford, which never set out to contest the full championship. It is

Photo Pascal Huit

17

possible to overstate Toyota's troubles. At the half-way mark, it had won three rallies to Lancia's four, which was three more than any other team, and a fine reliability record kept Sainz in the running for the title when all seemed lost.

There were times when it was tempting to suppose that the old Celica would have been as effective, if not more so, for TTE's problems centred on the new car. In fact, testing times showed that it was quicker than its predecessor, but the drivers often struggled to find much else to say in its favour. In theory, the ugly Celica Turbo 4WD rooted out the GT4's weaknesses as thoroughly as the Integrale HF tackled the 16V's. Greatly improved cooling and under-bonnet ducting were allied to a new turbo intake, and Karl-Heinz Goldstein's trump card, infinitely adjustable suspension. The alloy hub and strut assemblies were ingeniously linked by brackets that made it possible to change anything from camber angles to roll centres in minutes. TTE made the old-fashioned business of altering springs or toe angles look prehistoric. If a journalist asked what the current suspension tweak was intended to achieve, he was quite likely to be told that it was changing the axis of the roll centres in relation to the centre of gravity. In Australia, above all, the mechanics must have felt that the range of adjustments was truly infinite, as a frustrated Sainz demanded change after change. Never mind the centre of gravity, this was more like a quest for the holy grail.

The number of accidents would have made it plain that the Köln team had a problem even if it hadn't been honest enough to admit it. As Armin Schwarz put it, the Celica was 'a real fighter car'. Not for the first time, the Acropolis was the low spot, all three cars ending up some distance from the road, in varying states of disrepair, but the measures to rectify or even identify the problem revealed that TTE was in desperate straits. Resorting to a locked centre differential brought some predictability to the handling, but at the

price of unremitting understeer. That was only to be expected from a crude solution that Audi abandoned in 1985, and even Mitsubishi dropped in 1990. It was a startling change of policy from the team that had pioneered the Xtrac system in World Championship rallying and paid for much of the development. Arguably, the car was eventually persuaded to work by making it *less* sophisticated, by swapping to a conventional viscous coupling centre differential, slackening the bodyshell, and reverting to old suspension settings. There was some truth in Juha Piironen's remark that it was Lancia's solution fitted to Toyota's car.

The difficulty in sorting out the car reflected the turmoil bubbling within TTE. Goldstein's abrupt departure for Volkswagen soon after the Monte Carlo Rally, taking a number of other engineers with him, destroyed TTE's best hope of getting to the bottom of its problems swiftly. No rally engineer has a higher reputation and, if there was a fundamental geometry problem, which allegedly there was for both the Monte and the Rally of Portugal, he should surely have been able to cure it. Opinions varied as to whether his successors, headed by Dieter Bulling, were left with an impossible task, given that the season was already under way, whether they were up to the job, or even if they were keen to make the existing solution work at all. Take your pick, but the range of opinion suggests that TTE tackled 1992 with something less than a common purpose. Eventually, TTE's old stager, Gerd Pfeiffer (universally known as 'Pepper'), assumed greater responsibility, while TTE attempted the awkward compromise between making fundamental engineering changes and maintaining its commitment to an extensive programme: a withdrawal for a few months was out of the question. Sainz's title was won in the teeth of adversity; it was a breathtaking achievement.

The personality clashes within TTE extended to the drivers, Sainz

and Schwarz falling out publicly in Portugal, when the latter slid off the road near the finish while driving in the former's dust. Schwarz argued that Sainz should have known that he was being caught after blowing a turbo, and that a good team-mate would have pulled aside. Sainz pointed out that he could see nothing behind him but dust, and Schwarz rapidly fell from favour. Since the Toyotas were hardly neck and neck with the Lancias until November, the intense pressure on Sainz that had prompted Andersson to hire and use a third driver never arose. The Spaniard remained TTE's undisputed number one, but the need for another star driver was sufficiently pressing for TTE to snap up Auriol as soon as Lancia's commitment to 1993 was seriously called into question — a move that didn't necessarily find favour with Sainz himself.

Signing another of the sport's undoubted stars, Miki Biasion, was a momentous, dramatic step for Ford, and, sure enough, it had dramatic effects. Employing the double World

Champion was only one of an array of far-reaching changes at Boreham, but it was perhaps the most important. Miki is a popular member of the team, which isn't always the case where his co-driver, Tiziano Siviero, is concerned, but he served a crucial purpose irrespective of results. For all the carping in some quarters that he is past his best and that François

Delecour is a better bet, Biasion provided a benchmark. If the car was drastically off the pace, there was clearly something badly wrong with it. Ford could no longer blame the drivers if the Sierras weren't up to scratch.

Signing a piece of paper changed nothing: Ford's trip to the Monte was an unqualified disaster. The cars were disgracefully unreliable, and both the drivers were embroiled in damaging public rows, in which they allegedly criticised the machinery. In Delecour's case at any rate there was some truth in the allegations, and he subsequently had an emergency meeting with the Chairman of Ford France. Testing in Portugal wasn't much better. No one thought to tell Biasion where it was, and he spent much of the first day driving round Arganil, looking for the test team. Bearing his salary in mind, that alone wasted several thousand pounds.

Under the circumstances, one might have expected Colin Dobinson, Ford's new Director of Motorsport, to sanction wholesale bloodletting. Surprisingly few heads rolled in fact, and some would argue the case for dispatching a few more. Nevertheless, Portugal marked a turning point. At the start of the rally, the Sierra was still far from sorted out, and Biasion coolly treated the event as an extended test session. By the finish, he had soundly beaten Sainz and demonstrated that reliability was vastly improved. There were no embarrassing repeats of 1991, when the cars were sometimes slower than they had been the year before, and by the Sanremo, the Cosworths were as close to the Deltas as they had been all season — in Italy, of all places.

The change owed a good deal to a concerted attempt to devote more resources to engineering. The establishment of an Escort test team under Steve Ridgers had direct benefits for the Sierra, since many components were in common, and longstanding weaknesses, ranging from the front differential to limited suspension travel were systematically tackled. Hiring Melvyn Hodgson from Motor Sport Developments greatly augmented the strength and experience of the management team, yet certain traditional features of Ford policy remained, as changeless as the boom and bust cycle. Somehow, while there was plenty of money to be ladled out on drivers or aircraft, the budget didn't quite stretch to an engine development programme, even though both drivers were insisting that it was vital from the Tour of Corsica at least. At times, one has to remind oneself that Ford is the second largest car maker on earth, not the 22nd.

Engines weren't mentioned often at Subaru, and with good reason. Wresting control of engine tuning from Japan for the 1991 RAC Rally made a world of difference to the Legacy. The Prodrive-tuned motors performed consistently and reliably in hot conditions, giving the team its best Acropolis result by a long way and, while engine trouble struck down all three cars in New Zealand — a humiliating defeat on an event the team should have won — they were isolated failures and the faulty components were reputedly Japanese. In common with the other Japanese teams, Subaru's World

was well matched, a good deal cheaper than some, and became more effective as the season passed. Vatanen had little luck, but his confidence returned as he covered more stages and the times improved. He drove superbly in the latter part of the season. McRae followed an upward path for rather different reasons. He is still taking part in events for the first time and has plenty to learn, although there is abundant evidence that he learns quickly. A stirring RAC drive, on terrain where he wasn't handicapped by inexperience, suggests that a World Championship victory cannot be far off.

For varying reasons, neither Mitsubishi nor Nissan made much use of cars that were quite capable of achieving good results. The former had a disappointing Monte, the Galants predictably off the pace in largely dry conditions, and that set in motion a bizarre train of events that

Championship competition.

Nissan's ham-fisted attempts to run a rally team combined irony and idiocy in equal proportions. A carefully executed development programme turned the Sunny GTi-R into an effective car on forest events such as the 1000 Lakes and the RAC, the performance increase being in inverse proportion to the number of people employed at Milton Keynes. The demise of the team always seemed likely once Charles Reynolds himself was dismissed, as well as many of his men, in April, some weeks after the Tour of Corsica had been scrapped. A skeleton staff then produced two cars capable of setting fastest times on the 1000 Lakes, which would have been unimaginable 12 months previously, and NISMO responded by pruning their number to such a degree that mercenaries were needed for the RAC.

In its existing form, the Sunny

level in 1992 (even Rod Millen didn't score points, and the Brussels team failed to appear at all thanks to a wheel manufacturing problem that obliged it to cancel the Swedish entries at the last minute), but because it scrapped its team towards the end of the season. While doing so made a certain amount of sense, considering the factory's lukewarm commitment to rallying, it also indicated the depth of Japanese fears about the recession in general, and the cost of Group A rallying in particular.

Cost lay behind most of the significant decisions of 1992, whether it was the way Lancia went about defending its world titles, or the decision of the Sanremo and Catalonia organisers to cut their events to three days, in line with recommendations for 1993. The lack of money to hand extended to the Group N Championship and the two-wheel

Championship assault turned out to be nothing like as adventurous as planned, the promised build-up at the end of the season quietly falling prey to the recession. A limited programme was only one of the factors that kept the team off the winner's rostrum: in performance terms, the Legacy must now be treated as a match for any car apart from the Delta, at least on gravel, but reliability is still a trifle suspect, transmission problems afflicting Vatanen in Greece and Australia, while there were also niggling faults with things like intercooler pumps. In addition, tarmac development (which was shelved after Corsica in 1991), must be re-started if the team is to be competitive under all circumstances.

Subaru's driving team had a second division look to it at first, and it is a tribute to Vatanen and Colin McRae that it appears a good deal more impressive now than it did 12 months ago; either of the two might have won the RAC. The combination

confined the team to barracks on all but two more events in 1992. The Swedish — which both Kenneth Eriksson and Timo Salonen were quite capable of winning — was shelved to punish the engine department in Japan for its failures in 1991, and then senior management abruptly cancelled everything bar the Acropolis and the RAC. Given a little enthusiasm from Japan and, perhaps, more fire from Europe, there is no reason why the team shouldn't have done at least as well as it had in 1991. Instead, Mitsubishi was coaxed or bullied into giving the lion's share of the competition budget to Ullrich Brehmer's cross-country operation. While millions of yen were spent to limited purpose coming second on Paris–Peking, there was every chance that Ralliart Europe would fall behind at World Championship level, new car or no. Winning the Ivory Coast with Kenjiro Shinozuka did nothing to keep Mitsubishi at the forefront of World

GTi-R was never a potential World Championship winner. However, a drastic shedding of weight, improvements to the cooling system, and the use of the same kind of chemical brew in place of pump petrol as every other team proved that the basic design wasn't beyond redemption. A limited, carefully chosen programme of the type Mazda once pursued could be cost-effective and quite successful. Nissan's motor sport policy has veered wildly in recent years and, to that extent, the sudden fall of the rally team follows a pattern of sorts. It is some consolation that a workshop in Milton Keynes has been retained with an eye on future developments, but the crowning irony is that the money withdrawn from the World Rally Championship was diverted into a sports prototype engine, of all things.

Mazda needs mentioning not because of anything the team achieved at World Championship

Andrea Aghini rocketed to prominence as he came to grips with the Lancia (far left), whereas John Bosch endured a miserable year in his Group N Sunny (below left). Lancia drivers took wings (above), whereas Armin Schwarz (overleaf) parted acrimoniously from Toyota.

drive runners, for although there were a number of serious contenders in the former, there were no works teams; Renault's only World Championship foray was the Tour of Corsica, and the Finnish driver, Eija Jurvanen, succeeded in winning the Ladies' title merely by driving over the start ramp and retiring from most of her events. It wasn't the finest advertisement for the sport; luckily, it was overshadowed by an unexpectedly dramatic conclusion to the overall drivers' championship.

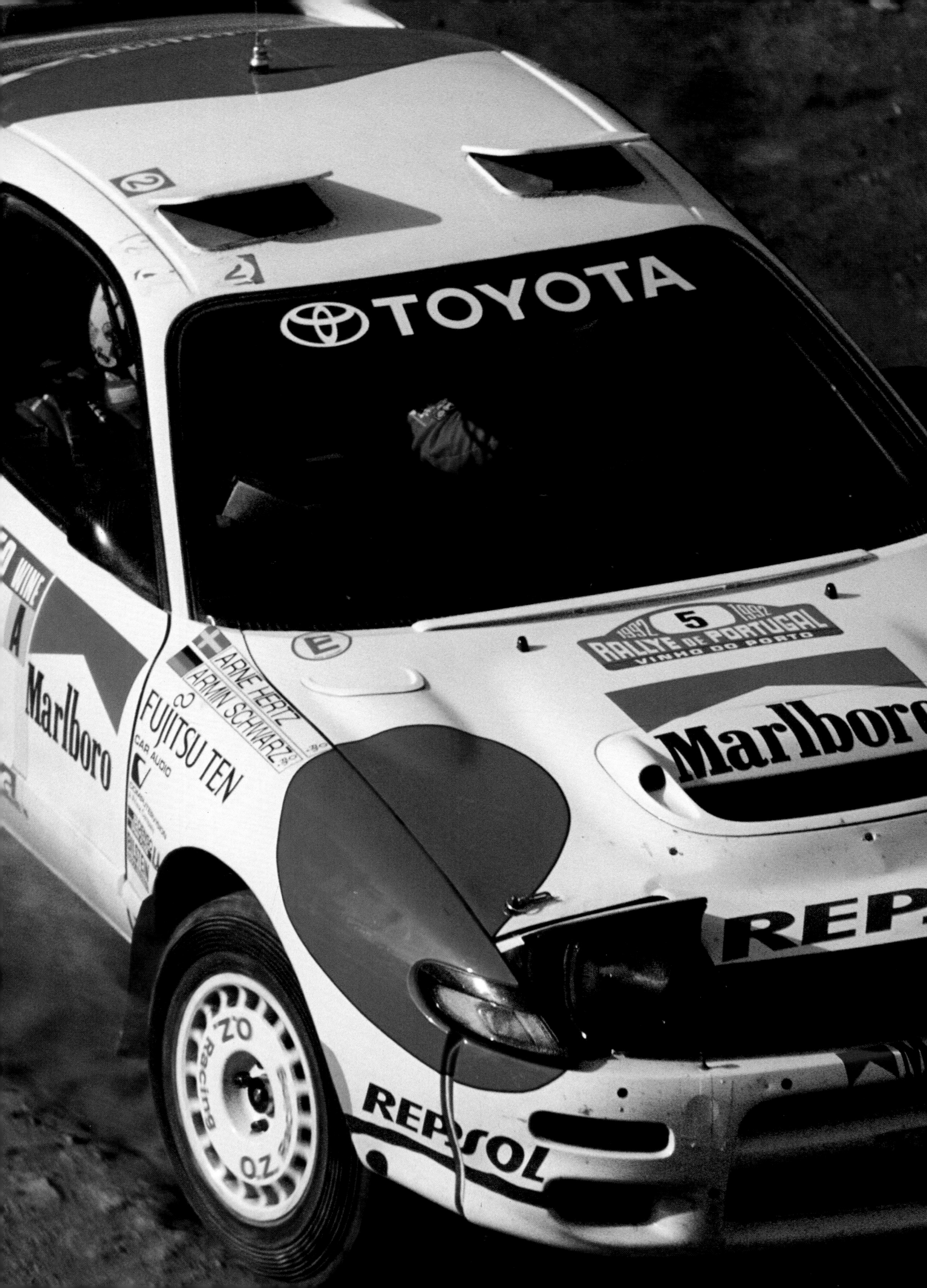
TOYOTA
1992 5 1992
RALLYE DE PORTUGAL
VINHO DO PORTO
ARNE HERTZ
ARMIN SCHWARZ
FUJITSU TEN
CAR AUDIO
Marlboro
Marlboro
REP
REPSOL
OZ Racing

Photo Pascal Huit

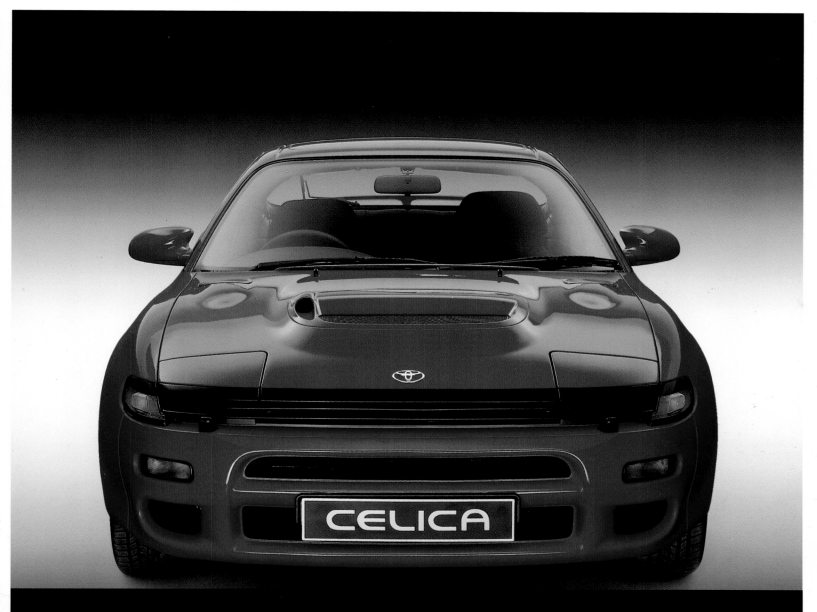

ON THE ROAD, IT WILL ONLY REACH 440.

Two litres, 16 valves, fuel injected, turbo charged. Under that bulging snout, the Carlos Sainz Celica GT Four rallies 205bhp of muscle.

Between 3,200 and 4,800rpm, it produces a constant 203lbs. ft. of torque.

With four-wheel drive, 60mph is 7.6 seconds in an arrow-straight line from zero.

And with Toyota's standard warranty, the adrenalin is guaranteed to keep flowing for three years or 60,000 miles.

For more information, call **0737 768585.**

The Carlos Sainz GT Four is bred from our class-leading Celica GT coupe. However, only 440 of this out-and-out rally version will ever reach British roads.

Is it any wonder that this car's going fast?

THE CAR IN FRONT IS A TOYOTA

A colourful, exciting record of Nigel Mansell's heroic progress to win the coveted 1992 Formula 1 World Championship for Drivers. One of the most popular sporting heroes Britain has ever produced, he achieved an almost unprecedented stranglehold on Formula 1 racing, winning five of the first eleven races of the season to take the title with five rounds remaining.
96 pages, over 90 colour photographs
ISBN: 1 874557 00 4 Price: £9.99

His long career in Formula 1 brought two World Championships with Brabham, followed by a third in a Williams four years later in 1987.
ISBN: 0 905138 81 3
112 pages Price: £12.95

From 1962 until his tragic fatal accident at Hockenheim in 1968 he was absolutely the standard-setter of his time, twice winning the World Championship.
ISBN: 0 905138 77 5
112 pages Price: £12.95

AUTOCOURSE DRIVER PROFILES

Each volume contains approximately 20 colour and 80 black and white photographs.

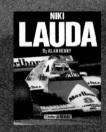

The remarkable career story of the 1992 World Champion up to the end of the 1989 season describing the fierce ambition which was eventually rewarded with Grand Prix victory and universal recognition.
ISBN: 0 905138 67 8
112 pages Price: £11.95

One of the most pragmatic men ever to drive a racing car, this volume reflects the shrewd mind, iron determination and wry sense of humour of this three-times World Champion.
ISBN: 0 905138 68 6
112 pages Price: £11.95

Winner of three World Championships in a McLaren, Alain Prost holds the record for the greatest number of Grand Prix wins.
ISBN: 0 905138 69 4
112 pages Price: £11.95

His pure genius for driving, with no apparent sense of fear, inspired the adulation which has made him a legend.
ISBN: 0 905138 70 8
112 pages Price: £11.95

The youngest World Champion in history at 25, he won a second title in 1974 before deciding to build and race his own Formula 1 cars. Still a major force in Indy cars.
ISBN: 0 905138 78 3
112 pages Price: £12.95

His tempestuous career ended in tragedy when he was killed during practice for the Italian Grand Prix in 1970, thus becoming the only posthumous winner of the World Championship.
ISBN: 0 905138 79 1
112 pages Price: £12.95

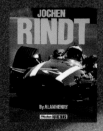

Hailed as the greatest Formula 1 driver of all time, his single-minded approach to racing has produced three World Championships in four years.
ISBN: 0 905138 92 9
112 pages Price: £12.95

During a Grand Prix career that spanned 17 seasons he twice became World Champion and also won the Indianapolis 500 and the Le Mans 24 Hours.
ISBN: 0 905138 86 4
96 pages Price: £12.95

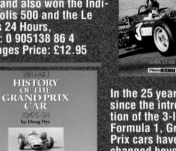

In the 25 years since the introduction of the 3-litre Formula 1, Grand Prix cars have changed beyond recognition. This detailed, illustrated history spans the era from the 350 horsepower tube-framed cars to the 650 horsepower, computer designed, carbon composite cars of 1991.
352 pages, approx. 32 colour and 200 black and white photographs
ISBN: 0 905138 94 5 Price: £40.00

Beginning with the post-war racing revival and the new regulations establishing the Formula 1 and Formula 2 categories, it describes all the cars of the era including the many legendary cars and engines of the 2 ½ litre formula, followed by the multi-cylinder rear engines and monocoque chassis of the 1960s.
Approx. 272 pages, 40 colour and 200 black and white photographs
ISBN: 0 905138 93 7 Price: £40.00

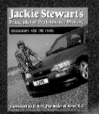

This best-selling title has now been extensively revised and updated by three-times World Champion Jackie Stewart whose ability to analyse driving skills and car performance gives him an unrivalled authority in describing the techniques of car control.
240 pages, 36 colour and 119 black and white photographs
ISBN: 0 905138 91 0 Price: £16.99

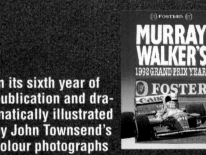

This eleventh edition once again combines the writing talents of Editor David Williams with the exciting and evocative photography of Reinhard Klein to provide the definitive record of the 1992 World Rally Championship. Top journalists contribute a range of interesting and informed features on the technical advances, the drivers and the future of the sport. This luxury book is completed by comprehensive results and stage times, plus colour coverage of the European, British and National Championships.
176 pages, over 140 colour photos
ISBN: 0 905138 98 8 Price: £25.00

In its sixth year of publication and dramatically illustrated by John Townsend's colour photographs of the race action and personalities, this popular annual captures all the excitement, incidents and emotion of Nigel Mansell's championship-winning season. Murray Walker writes with infectious enthusiasm on every round of the Grand Prix season, supported by his own profile of the new Champion and detailed results.
160 pages, over 160 colour photos
ISBN: 0 905138 99 6 Price: £9.99

Profile: Colin McRae

MOVE ON UP

By David Williams

If there was any doubt that Colin McRae had arrived, the 24 Hours of Ieper extinguished it. At one point, a commentator told his expectant audience that the next car would be driven by Jimmy McRae — the father of Colin McRae. The fact that Colin himself was contesting a World Championship event on the far side of the globe, rather than fol-

lowing the well-worn trail across the Channel to Flanders was a more tangible indication that the 24-year-old Scot has moved into a different league. The Subaru's engine failure in New Zealand may have deprived him of a possible victory, but it made no difference to his career: he has gone beyond the point where one rally can be make or break.

Becoming a star means shouldering a burden, even if it's just the constant attention of the media. Colin McRae has to take on rather more than that. He is a phenomenon, not merely because he is quick, but because he is British. One of the striking features of international rallying is that the British have achieved consistent success in most areas, be it co-driving, building cars, or organising events, with the conspicuous exception of driving. For a multitude of reasons, talented British drivers have progressed so far up the ladder, but no further. This state of affairs is not just a British preoccupation and, as a result, McRae's current successes have already brought him an expectant following.

In his case, the sense of expectation wells up very close at hand. In part, he is making up for the perceived injustices inflicted on his father. There is a determination in the McRae family that Colin will not be waylaid by the prejudice that

always afflicted Jim, the championship winner who spent a decade being 'too old' before the charge began to carry any justification. Say what you like about Colin McRae, but he certainly isn't too old.

There is no longer any questioning his ability either. There was a time when it could be argued that his talent was fairly evenly divided between getting round corners at breakneck speed and hurling cars into the scenery at much the same velocity. In 1989, Pentti Airikkala, his rival for Group N in the British Open Championship, publicly offered tuition for the 21-year-old youngster, an offer the family declined. McRae is still the kind of driver who can be guaranteed to be on the limit — the sort of man capable of changing the look of a rally in a couple of stages — and that approach can still lead to a good deal of panel damage, as it did on the 1000 Lakes. Prodrive's boss, David Richards, says that he is no longer surprised by anything his young recruit does, whether that's challenging for the lead in Sweden, or rolling at 100mph in Finland and getting away with it.

Other rallies have given him more satisfaction, but if there was an event that made McRae's reputation, it was the 1992 Swedish. It was always likely to offer richer pickings than his other overseas appearances, since it is a rally he had already contested twice, and the entry was less formidable than it was on the 1000 Lakes or the Acropolis. He reckoned that a top three finish was possible. In the event, he finished second and exceeded the wildest expectations. Unlike Michèle Mouton, the other non-Nordic driver to be runner-up, his car gave him no perceptible advantage, and yet there had even been a moment when it looked as though he might challenge for the lead. He had not only driven quickly, but coolly: finishing second had been an exercise of judgement as much as raw speed.

The entry had included most of the winter experts anyway, former winners such as Stig Blomqvist and Markku Alén amongst them, and their praise for him was generous and unqualified. Alén had already stated his respect for the Scot when they were team-mates on the previous year's RAC, whereas Blomqvist

went a stage further: he regards Colin as the best British driver since Paddy Hopkirk — possibly even better than the Ulsterman. For his part, McRae got more satisfaction from leading the RAC, or finishing fourth and recording a string of fastest times against all the top drivers on the Acropolis: percentage driving brings points, but not necessarily pleasure.

While some maintain that he is admirably consistent, and never the sort of driver to be panicked into changing the car or tyres if his first stage time isn't on the pace, he admits that he remains vulnerable to over-exuberance, that it is sometimes hard to accept that more experienced drivers can be so much quicker on roads they know well. He attributes his first, fifth-gear accident during the 1000 Lakes to that sense of frustration, but his recollection hints at the commitment needed even to hold a place towards the bot-

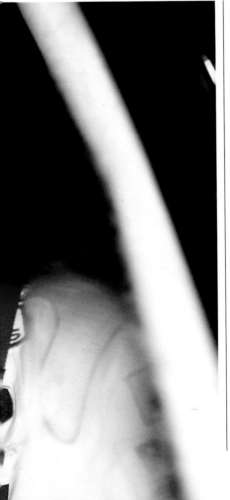

tom of the top ten: 'It was just another, maybe five inches wider at the outside of the corner, it would have been OK.' The occasional rush of blood aside, he has no apparent weaknesses. Like most of the great drivers, he has no strong preference for surface or format. He likes tarmac as much as gravel, he already has a reputation for making accurate pace notes quickly, and his remarkable Swedish performances show that he has a Scandinavian affinity for snow, yet he would like nothing more than the chance to tackle a long, blind Circuit of Ireland. That wish is an indication of the respect he has for his father and the older McRae's achievements, amongst which a record number of wins on the Circuit ranks prominently.

If Prodrive released its grip, it is unlikely that McRae would be on the market for long, but that hasn't always been the case. Ford's support in 1989 and 1990 was simultaneously generous and grudging — he was loaned the neglected Corsica-winning Sierra for the 1990 Ulster for instance — yet there was no sense that Boreham had spotted one of the brightest stars on the horizon. Peter Ashcroft reckoned that Colin could well match his father's results, given another seven or eight years of experience; the fact that the 22-year-old had torn through the ranks of British

rallying like a hurricane, leaping from a scruffy road rally Sunbeam to a Group A Cosworth in just four years, seemed to have passed him by. Stuart Turner went on the record as saying that the young McRae needed more experience before he could expect full scale works backing.

The lack of recognition seems the more short-sighted when Prodrive men assess his ability. David Lapworth, the Engineering Director, says that the Scot is a 'fairly to very perceptive' test driver, and that the capacity for describing what the car was doing was already highly developed when he joined the team, even though there had never been much money for testing at RED. He gives the impression of having enough talent to drive to the car's limit and spare a little thought for analysing its behaviour, not just escaping the impending accident. He is smooth, and no harder on machinery than any quick driver.

It is tempting to compare McRae to some of the great Finns, perhaps to his team-mate, Ari Vatanen, or even the late Henri Toivonen. With or without famous rallying fathers, they soon displayed an exceptional and spectacular gift for wringing the utmost from a car, if not the knack of staying out of trouble. Like them, McRae made his mark at an age

McRae has leapt from driving a 1300 Nova (opposite, on the 1987 Manx), to a factory-prepared Subaru (above) with dizzying speed.

when many successful rally drivers are struggling to find the money to compete at all, and he has endured his share of mishaps and reverses after his ability had been brought to the attention of an expectant public. Along with Alex Fiorio, McRae is the only contemporary driver who stood a chance of beating Toivonen's record as the youngest winner of a World Championship rally. The difference is that Toivonen's win on the 1980 RAC came like a bolt from the blue, whereas a victory for McRae seems to be only a matter of time. The other obvious difference is crucial: Toivonen's progress wasn't impeded by his nationality. McRae has had to surmount the prejudice and the statistics weighted against any British rally driver.

There was never much question in his own mind that he was going to be a rally driver. If his father could make a living from an exciting job like this, Colin could of course do the same. He pestered Jim for a motor cycle, and thinks he took up competition at the age of 12. With a schoolboy trials title behind him, he turned to autotesting in a Mini when he was 16, and won the West of Scotland Championship. This wasn't his first experience of cars, since he had been obtaining them from scrapyards, welding in roll cages, and driving them on waste ground since he was 14 or 15. The wonder is that he waited until he was 17 before doing a rally.

The Sunbeam ended its first rally against a tree, and was rebuilt as a 'proper' stage rally car over the winter. It gave way to a Nova and a string of class wins. By the end of 1988, McRae had proved that he could handle much quicker and more demanding machinery, and that he could adapt to almost anything. He was the quickest of Peugeot's three

Even the accidents weren't a lasting setback. He shares his father's easy-going temperament and, if he was upset by the numerous excursions in RED's Group N Cosworth, it wasn't obvious from the outside. Some of his friends honestly believed that he didn't care in the slightest. 'Nonchalant' is the word that springs to mind.

The talent may be hereditary, but it owes nothing to tuition. Colin has come to tolerate the attentions of the press, but one of the few questions that irritates him mildly is the suggestion that he must have had lessons from his father. Indeed, he now goes out of his way to dismiss the idea without waiting for the question to be asked. He maintains that sitting in cars at test sessions as a

more. His father's advice and contacts had carried him a long way very quickly, steering him away from a potentially unreliable BDA-powered Avenger when he was 17, introducing him to SMT when he was driving the Nova, and putting together the deals to go to Sweden or Ieper, for instance. Shell and Pirelli — staunch McRae supporters over the years — had offered sterling assistance, and Colin had taken his first international victory. Yet the immediate outlook remained bleak. McRae rarely expresses anger — at least in public — but he was puzzled and frustrated as 1990 drew to a close: he accepted that he needed more experience, and spoke enthusiastically of competing abroad more often, but how was he to fulfil this

chance. Rather than throwing him in at the deep end and leaving him to fend for himself against much more experienced team-mates, Richards has brought on his investment gradually. In addition to mopping up the final Open Championship, McRae attended a good number of 1991 World Championship qualifiers as a chase car driver. Doorhandling an Isuzu Trooper instead of a Group A Legacy was at times a frustrating exercise, but it gave him an insight into the big time. As a result, he hasn't been overawed by the scale of the operation when put behind the wheel of a rally car.

Subsequently, Prodrive has resisted the temptation to expose McRae to too much World Championship rallying too quickly, no matter how

'young lions' in a Group N 309, won the Scottish Championship in a Group A Cosworth, and appeared in anything from a Nissan 240RS to a rear-wheel drive Peugeot 205, in which he scored his first victory. Only the Nissan and its cobbled-together steering rack posed him any problems, and those weren't apparent from the outside. His capacity to get the measure of new cars was instinctive: left-foot braking in the Nova seemed the most natural thing in the world. When he tested Donald Milne's Metro 6R4, he was said to have been quicker than his father, instantly. True or false, the story shows that the McRae legend had taken wings. More to the point, he had amassed a breadth of experience that few drivers can call on at his age.

boy was more a case of enjoying the ride than picking up tips, and there is plenty of evidence that Jim McRae isn't the world's finest passenger. Colin hasn't forgotten that his father navigated when he first got the Nova, on the Galloway Hills. 'We got on OK. There were an awful lot of "slow downs, watch this!"' he recalls. Jim didn't ride with his oldest son in a rally car again until a Sierra test session just before the 1990 RAC.

Despite winning the Cartel Rally in Yorkshire (which was one of Ford's few British successes in 1990) and taking an excellent sixth on the RAC in a four-wheel drive RED Cosworth, during which he set fastest times on home territory in southern Scotland, McRae had evidently failed to persuade the works teams that he deserved anything

requirement without some kind of motor industry support?

Just when it looked as though he had completed the first lap of the vicious circle, and that he would be consigned to the British Open Championship for the rest of his days, David Richards stepped forward with a bold yet inspired proposal. He offered a three-year contract to drive works Subarus, starting with another season in Britain, but advancing in carefully graded steps to a full World Championship programme, assuming he was good enough. While it is fair to say that Richards got a very good driver very cheap (McRae himself doesn't talk about figures), he cannot justly be accused of exploitation. As Colin admits, the Prodrive man was taking a risk and he has given his charge a more than fair

promising the results. He has been given a manageable programme, and put under no pressure to do anything but finish. There was a degree of friction at the 1000 Lakes service point after stage six, when McRae chalked up his second accident of the week, but then that pressure was self-imposed. 1993 should continue the path, emphasising the worth of being given time to adapt. Malcolm Wilson for one is a trifle envious of the kind of introduction the Scot has had. McRae is in no doubt what he owes Richards: 'If it wasn't for him, I don't know what I would be doing now — maybe still struggling on in the British Championship, looking for sponsors.'

Richards has given him an opportunity, not turned a sow's ear into a silk purse. Before he had attained

anything in the way of international recognition, McRae had absolute self-belief. It wasn't a question of arrogance: put it to him that many people would argue that he had got so far so fast purely on his name, and he would reply, with his usual deadpan manner, that he would understand if, 'I wasn't good or I wasn't on the pace, but I know I am quick enough, and I think I'm worthy of what I'm getting'. There isn't the slightest doubt in his mind that he has the talent to be World Champion and — rather like Toivonen — he sets targets. He believes he can win the title by the time he is 27. He brings to mind the old saying that all modesty must be false modesty, otherwise it wouldn't be modesty.

Success may have strengthened his self-confidence, but it hasn't altered his personality. He still lives at home in Lanark with his parents, and he remains approachable and good company; teams like working with him. He probably has more time and money to go water ski-ing or quad racing these days, for he remains fascinated by almost anything with an engine, but he is still one of the lads, and he will happily go down to the local motor club for a chat, or test a friend's rally car. He isn't above getting his hands dirty at McRae Motorsport once in a while either. If he does have a weakness, it is for mobile telephones; he rarely travels anywhere without one, an affliction he may have acquired from Vatanen. It's still a long way from a flat in Monaco or a helicopter licence.

It would be inconceivable that two years of being a works rally driver had left no mark, and there have been changes to the packaging, if not to the product. When he was given a prize as a promising youngster at the annual Shell awards evening, the contrast between the shambling, monosyllabic McRae and the spruce, articulate racing driver — his fellow countryman, Allan

McNish — was embarrassingly obvious. McRae quite likes the idea of going on a public speaking course, out of curiosity as much as anything, but then both that and the suggestion that he might learn a foreign language have been kicked around for years, and in the meantime he has developed a style of his own that would have been unrecognisable two years ago. After the 1000 Lakes, he told a press conference that he had now seen the country from all angles, and that he was most impressed. Journalists have come to appreciate a dry wit.

His view of his chosen profession has become much more sophisticated — even detached. He expresses none of the passion for rallying of a

Delecour or a Sainz. In part, it's a matter of possessing a north European rather than a Latin temperament, but it is striking nevertheless to hear a 24-year-old calmly say that he can understand that the pressures of a full World Championship programme cannot be sustained by an individual driver for more than two years at a stretch. He can envisage a situation where he might compete flat out for two years, then accept a smaller programme for 12 months before launching another all-out attack. One expects a driver of his age and experience to believe that he is invincible and inexhaustible.

McRae has also developed an acceptance of criticism, and of his limitations at his current level of experience. He agrees that he was driving too sideways on the 1000 Lakes, explaining that it was safer — despite appearances — bearing in mind that he did not know the stages as well as most of his rivals. On the other hand, he rejects the charge that he was pushing his luck in Sweden, and his views have support at Prodrive. Lapworth comments, 'He's not reckless in the lines he chooses. I think he's been slightly maligned in the amount he uses ditches.'

His first 1000 Lakes has given him a taste for Finland, and he is eagerly looking forward to his next attempt, while accepting that he won't win in 1993 either. He laid his finger on what he felt he had learnt. He believes he has come to terms with the fact that more experienced drivers will gain time on such an event, on the narrow back roads where there isn't much choice of line as well as the wide, smooth, roller coaster tests for which the rally is famous. Put in that position again, he promised that he would throttle back and settle for as good a position as he could get without chasing

the likes of Didier Auriol. He wasn't swayed by all the hype of being the local favourite in the run-up to the RAC, coolly assessing his prospects of beating the flying Frenchman: 'If he does come to the RAC, I would put my money on him winning the rally no problem, just because of the results he's had this year and the way he's been going. He still hasn't got anywhere near the experience that Kankkunen had in Finland, and he beat Kankkunen in Finland, so why shouldn't he beat me in the RAC?' If the opposition set off at an uncatchable rate, he insisted he would aim for third, which he regarded as readily attainable. Like François Delecour, he sees more experience as being the key to progress.

Outwardly, McRae has never betrayed stress. The weight of expectation does not appear to concern him and, in getting and keeping a full factory drive, he has already surmounted an obstacle that has felled most British drivers. Yet the greatest challenges may lie ahead. Having a works drive and being stupendously talented don't automatically lead to overnight success at the highest level. He is now competing against equals, not inferiors, and he may have to swallow a good deal more disappointment before his ability gets the reward it deserves. Even works drivers can be caught out by a fickle sport and the unexpected turn of events. Despite all the evidence to the contrary, it may take time.

McRae has a knack of turning a setback to his advantage. He was the top British driver on the 1990 RAC in his battered Sierra (opposite), while his gripping battle with the Finnish countryside on the 1992 1000 Lakes (left and below) made him the talk of the rally.

WHEN THE GOING G

HARD, WET, OR

IMPOSSIBLE - THE T

1986 Unipart Himalayan Rally Challenge Team. From left to right Philip Young, Janet Sherwood, Nina Sutcliffe, Hywell Thomas.

They say that Formula One is the toughest test of car components there is...there are a number of drivers (and navigators) who may disagree: Philip Young, Hywell Thomas, Mark Ianson, Rev. Rupert Jones, Nina Sutcliffe, Janet Sherwood, Brian Culceth, Chris Bruce, Michelle Mouton, John Watson and Tony Pond, for starters.

Over the past 20 years these famous names have crewed Unipart sponsored cars in the toughest UK and some of the world's most gruelling international rallies.

The Unlimited Guarantee Samson Battery from Unipart.

Not only did the cars bear the Unipart name but, never being a company to miss the opportunity to put its products through their paces in the most testing

conditions, they were also equipped with Unipart components. In fact, our own Engineering Department reconstructed the Unipart sponsored 1985 Paris-Dakar entry Land Rover 90 V8 for the following year's Himalayan Rally.

Fitted with a Gold Seal engine unit, Unipart shocks, up-rated Unipart

Unipart Shock Absorbers and Steering & Suspension Components - from a Himalayan Rally heritage.

steering, clutch and exhaust components, Samson Batteries, Unipart lights and lamp units, in addition to many other standard parts - all of which per-

Our Land Rover 90 V8 and ex-works Rover SDI - 12th and 11th respectively in the 1986 Himalayan Rally

formed without any major problem. Crewed by the first European all-woman team; our Land Rover took the Ladies Prize, and came a reputable 12th overall - one place behind our Rover SDI, also fitted with a wide range of Unipart items - leads, hoses, filters, belts, wipers, bearings, brakes and consumables.

And if that wasn't enough, it was also the first time Unipart semi-synthetic oil was used on an international rally - having already proved itself on the Formula One circuit.

Unipart components were fitted and carried because of their

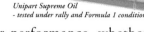

Unipart Supreme Oil - tested under rally and Formula 1 conditions.

reputation for performance, whether slewing out of hairpin bends on mountain roads at 15,000 ft.; crawling through mud, sand or rivers with boulders the size of footballs, or flying down dusty tracks, complete with pot holes, craters and sump-ripping ruts.

Reliability and stamina are the pre-requisites of components in rallies where endurance is the key word, as a breakdown can leave a team stranded literally

1983. The Unipart ex-works Triumph TR7 V8.

ETS TOUGH...ROUGH, UST DOWNRIGHT OUGH FIT UNIPART...

in the middle of nowhere.

If the Himalayan or Paris-Dakar Rallies weren't colourful enough testing grounds for Unipart components, the nature of entrants Unipart has backed has also

Durable and reliable: Unipart Brakes and Clutches endured the worst terrain.

added to the challenge.

Besides the Land Rover 90 and Rover SDI, there has been a Range Rover, a TR7 V8, and the first Austin Healey 3000, (Chassis No.1), which, after being entered in 1960, returned to the Himalayas in 1981, and despite being the oldest car ever entered, led until the

Chassis No.1 - the first Austin Healey 3000 , a dual entrant in the Himalayan in 1960 and 1981 in Unipart colours.

The famous 1967 Morris Minor - with its "one careful owner".

final day.

But probably the most famous Unipart entrant was a very special Morris Minor. The 1967 1098cc 4-door Minor, which once belonged to The Archbishop of Canterbury, was sponsored by Unipart in the Himalayan Rally in 1980. Besides achieving a phenomenal 15th place out of 67 entries, against works teams and Safari experts, it won its class by miles, and is still probably the only rally entrant to have the blessing of the

Unipart Oil & Air filters - performance above and beyond the call of duty.

Church of England!

Even in the early days of the 1970s, when the Unipart range of products, despite being the all-makes market leader, was tiny compared with today's

coverage, the Unipart name appeared on a variety of class and competition winning vehicles for the BL Works Team in UK rallies, including: the RAC, Welsh, Scottish, Forest of Dean, Granite City, Avon Motor Tour of Britain and Hackle. We even provided a Team Unipart promotional coach!

1992 sees us as Britain's largest independent aftermarket parts distributor, and it

The 1967 Lotus Cortina - Unipart sponsored and equipped - our entry in the 1993 London - Sydney.

also heralds our return to the international rally scene. Once again it's one of the toughest endurance events in the rallying calendar - the London - Sydney, and once again we will supporting a rally veteran - a 1967 Lotus Cortina.

And when faced with the gruelling challenge of the 1993 London-Sydney Marathon, are drivers still choosing to fit Unipart products...

The Answer is YES.
Now What's the Question?

HOT NOT BOTHERED.

As any motoring journalist will tell you the Renault 5 GT Turbo was a hot act to follow.

But when its natural successor the Clio 16 Valve came along, we confidently offered it up for evaluation. And this for example is what Car Magazine had to say.

"Overall victory then goes to the Clio... it's not just the best hot hatch you can buy, it's also the best driver's car for the money."

The press were well impressed. Hardly surprising, the 137bhp Clio achieves 0 to 60mph in 7.8* seconds and has a top speed of 130mph.

But it's also a bit of a smoothie. Not just in the ride, which is superb, but in terms of equipment too. Metallic paint and ABS brakes** aside, everything else comes as standard.

It has power steering, that rare item which is usually a costly option. An anti-theft device, which can be a costly omission. Then, mounted right by the steering wheel itself are controls for a superb, six speaker Hi-Fi system.

Electric windows and door mirrors are also included, as are remote control central door lock-

RENAULT
A CERTAIN
FLAIR

ing and a catalytic converter.

We pay healthy attention to economy too. At a constant 56mph the Clio 16 Valve returns 45.6mpg.† Insurance premiums are also good news. Despite its performance qualities the Clio falls into group 11, whereas the Fiesta XR2i and the Peugeot 1.9 205 GTi would cost dearly in group 14.

It has an eight-year anti-corrosion warranty and the option of Renault Cordiale our budget maintenance scheme where a regular monthly sum covers repairs and servicing for up to three years.

Are you warming to it? Then test drive the Clio 16 Valve.

It's hot but not the slightest bit bothered.

To Renault UK, FREEPOST, PO Box 21, Thame, Oxon OX9 3BR. For more information about the Clio 16 Valve fill in the coupon or call Renault Freephone **0800 525150**. CRRC0512

Mr/Mrs/Miss (please delete) _____
BLOCK CAPITALS

Address _____

_____

Town and County _____ Postcode _____

Telephone _____ Age (if under 18) _____

Present car make and model _____
(eg Renault 5 GTX)

Registration Letter ____ Month/Year you expect to replace ⌊_⌊_⌊_⌊_⌋
(eg "F")   M M Y Y

RENAULT CLIO 16 VALVE

SURVIVAL RATIONALE?

Group A rules have always included an up to two-litre category. So what's all the fuss about? Martin Sharp, Deputy Editor of Cars and Car Conversions, discusses whether a revolution is rumbling, or whether 'Formula 2' is just another category to make rallying even more complicated.

Contesting the World Rally Championship demands awesome levels of commitment. Only vehicle manufacturers capable of funding volume production cars of extremely high specification can compete. Yet, in early 1992, before Lancia won its sixth consecutive Group A World Rally Championship, Giorgio Pianta, Fiat Group's Director of all competition activities except Formula One, stated publicly that in world rallying: 'The costs must be reduced immediately.'

In May 1992, the FISA Rallies Commission met representatives of 11 vehicle manufacturers, three tyre

that trend.

In 1986, the last World Rally Championship year under Group B regulations, six apparently determined teams started the season, yet by mid-season only three were left, and just two fought the season through to the end. When Group A arrived as the premier formula the following year, Lancia's four-wheel drive, turbocharged Delta dominated, and continues to do so six years later. It is encouraging that the rule makers have now followed steps that take this precedent into account, and included in the latest regulations an opportunity to avoid a similar situa-

doned. It is, therefore, perhaps not surprising that the initial impetus to create a 'Formula 2' category came from France.

Although this initiative was generated from a genuine desire to do something to aid the survival of rallying, it also generated cynical observations such as: 'Well, they would wouldn't they, not having turbo four-wheel drive cars.' It's a malign slur on a prophetic initiative. Vehicle manufacturers involved in rallying met at Heathrow Airport in February 1992. Here, Patrick Landon, Director of Renault Sport Rallye, explained his concern for the future

the best one — because of the car — is two-litre, front-wheel drive. Now, for five years maybe. And then? We don't know; we must then adjust. We can't change one more time the rule stability. If you are talking without stability, if you change something now, you kill rallying, because you cannot one more time throw out cars the factories have made year after year.'

It may be a minor misnomer, but in this edition of *Rallycourse* we use the term 'Formula 2' to describe the new normally aspirated, two-wheel drive rallying category, precisely because of the thinking behind its introduction. As it stands, 'Formula 2' represents both a stepping stone and an insurance policy.

Categorising these two-wheel drive Group A cars in their own structured battles within championships elevates their status and provides opportunities for teams to go rallying more cheaply. It also means that young drivers might have more opportunity to drive Group A cars, to learn about dog gearboxes and decent brakes, rather than struggling along nursing Group N cars and never getting fully across the bridge to a full-blown, four-wheel drive Group A car. Not only are two-wheel drive, normally aspirated rally

manufacturers and the organisers of each World Championship rally. It was a historic meeting: for the first time in rallying the manufacturers helped shape the future, and FISA listened. A series of measures towards cost saving were drummed up and subsequently written into the rallying regulations for 1993.

As a category of rally cars develops, the law of diminishing returns escalates costs. At the top end of Group A, a trend could be discerned which in part must have been influenced by world-wide economic difficulties. In its 1992 season the World Rally Championship lost the regular participation of Mitsubishi, Mazda and Nissan. The latest regulations, by halving the minimum Group A homologation quantity, shortening rallies, and cutting tyre and service costs, are expected to help reverse

tion recurring. Structuring a rally category accessible to the majority of vehicle manufacturers not only allows more manufacturers to go rallying, but also provides an alternative platform should — for whatever reason — the turbocharged, four-wheel drive Group A cars go the way of their Group B predecessors.

Front-wheel drive, non-turbo, two-litre Group A rally cars have been exclusively contesting the Manufacturers' category of the French Rally Championship for two years. Indeed, with no volume production, turbocharged, four-wheel drive cars in their model ranges potentially suitable for rallying (until Peugeot launched the 405T16 road car in October 1992), French manufacturers have effectively been absent from the top of the World Rally Championship since Group B was aban-

of rallying. Landon foresaw a deepening 'crisis' in rallying as economic climates grew ever more cloudy; fewer teams able to afford the costs of running 4x4 turbo cars in rallies from national to world level, fewer sponsors; in reality, the danger of a similar situation to that in 1987, yet brought about through economic circumstances rather than a knee-jerk rule change.

At that time Landon expressed his opinions: 'At the moment we are really in a crisis — I don't say we have to stop with four-wheel drive. I never say that; it must remain, and they must have big cars, fast cars with technology, etc. etc. Or you must have a situation like a war, and everybody is ready to stop! Something very hard. I say we need stability rules. And I say rallying wants another organisation of rules, and

cars pretty quick these days, when driven competitively they're also spectacular, and provide a good learning curve.

The 'Formula 2' concept was made official in June 1992, allowing six months for teams to decide on and plan strategies. Here there is a distinction: manufacturers committed to front-running four-wheel drive cars in the World Championship have decided which direction they're going, have regulation stability for the next five years, and will keep a watching brief on the development of 'Formula 2' rallying. Evidently, if such manufacturers wish to retain rallying as part of their promotional activities, there will be a time during that watching brief when a decision about the configuration of their future rally cars will have to be taken. Here, the manufacturer blessed with foresight and a wide model range will have the advantage.

Other manufacturers, without a potential front runner under the current rules, will clearly look to 'Formula 2' as a way to compete. This could include some new to the sport, but teams such as Renault and GM, with established experience in two-wheel drive machinery, will be able to put much more weight behind convincing the bean counters on their boards that their previous experience with front-wheel drive cars can be a major asset to the company fortunes.

Some national championships, and the European Cup, allow rear-wheel drive in their 'Formula 2' regulations. It is a physical law that under acceleration, a car's mass is transferred to a rear-driven axle, while it is transferred away from a front-driven axle. Rallying wisdom suggests that, on tarmac surfaces, a well-prepared and driven rear-wheel drive rally car could romp away from a well-prepared and driven front-wheel drive opponent, although a well set-up front-wheel drive car would probably not be disadvantaged on gravel against rear-wheel drive. In 'Formula 2' categories outside the World Cup, it is foreseeable that a well-prepared rear-wheel drive car could run far enough ahead of the

however, the vast majority of manufacturers have suitable, potentially competitive, front-wheel drive cars in their model ranges; of likely contenders, just BMW and Mercedes-Benz have no such machines, yet they do have rear-wheel drive vehicles which could compete in an unrestricted two-wheel drive category.

Each level of the various 'Formula 2' rallying categories will be under deep scrutiny in their 1993 debut year. The drive axle location issue, however, must be given some serious thought by FISA. The 'Formula 2' rules are not technical regulations, *per se*, but a sporting regulation which controls a championship, or cup. So part of the issue must be whether it is better to have, say, six or eight manufacturers battling for honours, or risk having this sector of rallying dominated by a minority of manufacturers.

A suggested option is to employ a weight penalty in the regulations for rear-wheel drive cars, similar to that applied in the British Touring Car Championship. This could, however, be fraught with potential problems, as already proven in British racing.

Of the cars currently being prepared for 'Formula 2' action in 1993, the established manufacturer teams with front-wheel drive experience are

normally aspirated Group A two-litre power units from other manufacturers will be close in output, unless they have a much better inlet manifold arrangement, which, in mass production, transverse-engined terms produces some significant packaging problems in engineering ideal tuned-length, multi-throttle body systems and compatible exhausts into the available area.

It would appear, therefore, that the initial level of genuinely competitive 'Formula 2' cars will have power outputs which vary from some 210-220 bhp, as expected by Citroën Sport with its ZX 16-valve Group A car being developed for the French Rally Championship, to the GM two-litre's 230-240 bhp, while the maximum expected from a Group A development of a current production two-litre engine is in the 250 bhp region.

The team most experienced in engineering and running front-wheel drive rally cars is Renault, which has dominated the Manufacturers' category of the French Rally Championship with its Group A Clios. The Clios' current 1794 cc Group A 16-valve engines produce around 200 bhp officially, but Renault is planning to produce a two-litre 16-valve Clio, which it is hoping to have

By ratifying rally championships and cups for non-turbo, two-litre, two-wheel drive Group A cars, FISA has formalised additional areas of opportunity in World and European rallying, at the same time providing a direction for similar moves in national championships.

From 1 January 1993 there will be an FIA World Cup for Manufacturers. This is reserved for Group A cars with two-wheel drive, though on the front wheels only, and fitted with two-litre normally aspirated engines. Points for this Cup will be awarded only in rallies which count towards the World Rally Championship, providing that there are 10 eligible cars at the start of a rally. The winner of the Cup must have taken part in at least seven events, and points will accrue from the eight best results.

FISA has guaranteed five years' stability for the Group A technical regulations from 1 January 1993, subject to at least four manufacturers continuing to compete in the World Rally Championship. Accordingly, while the normally

Already, there's a wealth of machinery in rallying's second division, including (left to right), the Opel Calibra, the Peugeot 309, the Renault Clio, and the Citroën AX. Plenty more could build similar machinery.

front-wheel drive cars on tarmac events that teams running the latter configuration would see no point in entering such rallies. Equally, it is also foreseeable that a well-developed front-wheel drive car could have the legs of a rear-wheel drive car on gravel.

The essential difficulty in this particular question is that the specific drive location rule in the 'Formula 2' World Cup precludes some manufacturers from contesting it. In reality,

preparing their vehicles, initially, with conventional solutions. Group A engines are restricted in output essentially by the regulations concerning their induction systems and bottom ends. As a current Group A normally aspirated two-litre engine, the GM 16-valve unit is very competitive. In its present configuration, however, a benchmark output is 230 bhp, and with a specially heat-treated — yet standard — bottom end, 8000 rpm is the safe maximum; although it is expected that teams might run engines over that maximum, where the standard connecting rods risk breakage.

A high specification GM motor of this kind will cost between £12,000 and £15,000, but a 'clubman' specification, running slightly less maximum rpm and 'a fraction' less power can be built for around £8000. Similarly

homologated on 1 April 1993, in time for the Tour of Corsica.

Renault's new two-litre is a development of its existing 'F7' 1764 cc Clio unit (1794 cc in Group A trim), the extra capacity being achieved by lengthening its stroke. While some considerable effort has been expended on producing a two-litre national touring car racing development of this engine by French engine specialists Sodemo Octane at Magny-Cours, the production unit does not benefit from this work, having been developed by production engineers in the conventional way.

The national touring car racing engine regulations are much less restrictive than those of Group A and permit optimising the bore/stroke ratio, and induction and exhaust efficiency. The Sodemo touring car racing development will produce

aspirated two-litre, two-wheel rally cars can contest the Formula 2 Manufacturers' Cup in the 1993 World Rally Championship, it will still be the turbo four-wheel drive Group A cars which compete for overall Championship honours.

Additionally, a European Rally Cup for 1993, again for the non-turbo, two-litre, single-drive axle rally cars, is being introduced. The drivers score the points in this Cup, however, and its regulations allow two-wheel drive, two-litre Group A or Group N cars with either front-wheel, or rear-wheel drive. All European Championship rallies count towards the Cup, and a driver can contest every event in the Championship, but again his eight best results will be counted for classification towards the trophy.

some 270 bhp, while Sodemo's Group A rally version of the two-litre Renault unit is expected to achieve some 25-30 bhp more than the 1.8-litre engine's 200 bhp and, with a longer stroke, a significant torque improvement can be expected. Renault Sport will not need to make any significant changes to its — already optimised — Group A Clio chassis, but some 'clever' design in the two-litre rally car's differential (currently a 75 per cent locking plate type) is expected for the future.

From the level of manufacturer interest shown so far in the 'Formula 2' category, and depending on the fortunes of the formula through 1993, the possibility of homologation special two-litre engines — and even cars — must not be underestimated. Here, though, we must heed the sage words, uttered in early 1992, of Landon: 'I think that if the four-wheel drive rally cars are going for five or six or seven years more, we can stop the two-litre, two-wheel drive cars getting too much technical development — stop them getting too expensive.

'Later they can have more, but when we are talking about future rules I think it cannot be 2500 cars, but a minimum of 10,000; if you want to come back to the everyday car, you must come back to a minimum of 10,000 cars per year.'

There won't be an official works Group A Peugeot 309 GTI 16V in 'Formula 2' next year. Peugeot Talbot Sport is working on the 1360 cc 106, for the up to 1600 cc rallying class, but its 309 replacement — the 306 — will be arriving around the middle of 1993, and this will be available for 'Formula 2' rallying for 1994. PTS's Jean-Claude Vaucard, the chassis engineer whose work was mainly responsible for making the Group B 205T16 into a World Champion, is currently undecided whether we shall be seeing homologation special production cars for 'Formula 2': 'Maybe. Yes it can happen, but with 2500 there is always a problem; if you make a too-special car and sell it, the customers will not be happy with it. A big company like us doesn't want to do that, because you lose the customer after that...it's too stupid to do that; you kill the market.'

There is an argument from certain informed quarters that, as it develops, 'Formula 2' rallying is going to become very costly; some consider, as expensive as four-wheel drive turbo Group A rallying. As a guide, currently all the necessary hardware — and software — to build a new, works 'Client' specification 1794 cc Group A Clio 16V costs 630,000FF, and a less competitive five-speed version can be had for 500,000FF. The 'pukka' works front-wheel drive 'Formula 2' Astras have a performance edge over the customer versions, but because these works cars are unique vehicles at the forefront of development, this edge is achieved at greatly increased cost.

Putting things in perspective, however, in 1992 a highly respected independent preparation expert quoted 12 months' investment to develop a manufacturer's normally

aspirated front-wheel drive Group A rally car to be competitive in Group N and Group A rallying. At a cost of £1 million; a mere bagatelle in Group A World Championship four-wheel drive terms.

With one notable exception — which happens to be based in Antony near Paris — all teams which have run front-wheel drive, two-litre Group A rally cars have been unable to pare their competition machines to the 1992 minimum weight of 860 kg. For 1993, the minimum weight for the 1600 cc to two-litre Group A category is increased a further 60 kg to 920 kg — about the weight most two-litre Group A hatches manage to achieve. There was initial concern when, in June 1992, it was announced that tyre sizes would be coming down across the classes for 1993. But this has been revised, and tyre size status quo remains in every class up to three litres, which means that the 'Formula 2' cars can still run with their eight-inch wide rims.

David Whitehead of Motor Sport Developments has great experience of high-powered front-wheel drive rally cars from his years engineering the Group A Opel Kadetts/Vauxhall Astras, and at press time was readying the latest Astra for 'Formula 2' battle: 'That's a good move, because of the problem of tyre wear with front-wheel drive. I think reduced tyre sizes would have made a nigh-on impossible situation with these 220 bhp cars...we suffered two years ago from tyre wear, whether it be slick tyres which have overheated or whether it be gravel tyres that wore themselves out. The degree of wheelspin with a two-litre front-wheel drive car is quite excessive, so I'm glad we haven't gone down on tyre sizes.

'There's always been stages on a World Championship event which were the equivalent of 30-35 km, and we've had to get through those. The driver had to drive accordingly, and the tyre durability was getting better and better. Our biggest problem was on asphalt; once you had overheated the tyre and it had gone off, you had

a problem, and we did struggle on some of the longer stages. I would say that a mixture of traction control, and the tyre manufacturers going a stage further with durability, will allow us to do constantly stages of that kind of length.

'You've also got to remember that they're grouping stages togeth-

er, and that effectively allows the tyre coming off a stage to cool down. So it's not as if you're doing constantly 35 km without stop: sometimes it's three 10 km stages. Well, that won't be a problem. The dilemma there is what compound do you put on, assuming it's going to recover before you start the second stage, and likewise for the third?'

Reverting to prophetic reverie, *Rallycourse* dreamed of a scenario in which tyre coolers could be a competitive contribution to 'Formula 2' rallying. Whitehead: 'We've never struggled to get tyres warm, and they warm up exceptionally quickly; the rear ones take a bit of warming up. But, sure, tyre warmers are a good thing for the start of an asphalt stage without a doubt — for the rear and the front; you might as well have your tyres working for the first couple of corners. I mean, maybe you're talking a couple of kilometres in a four-wheel drive car; you're talking 1/2 km in a front-wheel drive car.'

The most critical contribution to the competitiveness of a 'Formula 2' rally car is the amount of tractive effort which it can generate at its driving wheels, and a particularly significant component in making a front-wheel drive rally car work well is the slip limiting abilities of its drive axle. Being able to control those abilities dynamically, and thereby the torque at each wheel, can contribute to aiding traction, and can be harnessed to optimise the car's handling, but, as Whitehead explains: 'Handling's important, of course, but traction is the biggest single thing, that's where you struggle more than anywhere else. You've only got to watch these cars going up an uphill hairpin — they can dig holes. The degree of wheelspin relative to a four-wheel drive car is phenomenal; you can sit there in third gear at a stage start if you wanted to in a 230 bhp front-wheel drive car on gravel with the speedo reading 60 mph — with a four-wheel drive car you'd never reach that situation unless you had 800 bhp.'

There must be a benefit in a dri-

ver being able to keep both hands on the steering wheel of any rally car, but arguably more benefit when it's front-wheel drive. So this characteristic — and the speed of selection — in semi-automatic gearboxes may also be particularly useful. The advantages in this for a front-wheel drive car, coupled with the traction-

optimising benefit of a closed loop-controlled slip limiting mechanism in its differential and 'active' damping characteristics, may mean that if a high level of manufacturer interest develops into this secondary category, electronic control systems could well bite deeper into the top 'Formula 2' cars before the 'Formula 1' rally cars.

Whitehead: 'You can get away with this formula — like with all formulae — relatively cheaply; it depends on the level of competition, and how each manufacturer has got to respond to that competition. For sure there will be more sophisticated systems, as there are in the road cars, coming in all the time — traction control, controllable differentials, semi-active suspension — all to escalate the costs...if they become necessary.

'The thing is that you won't get the same degree of increase in performance by increasing the power levels over a certain threshold, wher-ever that threshold may be, in a front-wheel drive rally car. It will manifest itself as wearing out tyres, poor traction return. But, it's like anything; once you get above the 40 mph state, or wherever it may be, then the additional power is going to get you going that bit quicker when you go into the higher gears, when traction ceases to be that much of a problem.'

It does seem, therefore, that there's a clear case here for some form of traction control. But the camp is divided. Vaucard argues, 'If you want to stop wheelspin you lose performance, so maybe you improve the endurance of the tyres, but the car goes slower because you are far from the limit. If you want to stop destroying the tyres you have to go down to an engine with 40 bhp less, so I think the stopwatch would lose something. Traction control helps a little, I think, in the control between the left and right front wheels and in a straight line. But it doesn't make up the difference we see between a front-wheel drive car and a rear-wheel drive car, because when you accelerate with a rear-wheel drive car you put the weight at the back; that is automatic and you can do nothing about it.'

Whitehead believes that traction control systems will not be necessary immediately in front-wheel drive rally cars, but that they will have to be incorporated in the longer term. Prodrive Engineering, currently running the Group A Subarus in the World Championship, is studying front-wheel drive rally cars. Already, the Banbury team has worked with Hewland to develop a sequential-change six-speed gearbox in a front-wheel drive Group A package. Not only can this be arranged to fit many alternative front-wheel drive cars, it is also designed to accommodate any future requirement for semi-automat-ic gearchanging, or 'active' differen-tial technology.

David Lapworth, Managing Direc-

At the moment, the Clio is the standard by which others are judged. It's a mixture of simple rear suspension (far left), quickly repaired transmission (left), and a 1.8-litre naturally aspirated engine. Only the latter would need drastic improvement to make it competitive against stronger opposition.

tor of Prodrive Engineering, believes in the future of traction control sys-tems in front-wheel drive rally cars: 'You may well find that you need a lot of bhp — maybe 250 bhp — before you see a big advantage from traction control if you do a one-kilo-metre test. But, I think if you did a 30- or 40-km test, which is what you're going to be looking at next year with the new regulations about combining stages, then if you could have a tyre which, at the end of 40 km, is still in good condition and not worn down to the canvas, you could perhaps run a compound or two softer into the bargain. There is a significant advantage.'

Xtrac has also designed a gearbox for 'Formula 2' rally cars, to be released in January 1993. This is the first time Mike Endean's company has produced a two-wheel drive gearbox from a clean sheet of paper, all previous examples being transverse four-wheel drive designs, 'with a few bits missing'.

The GM Astra GTEs ran with one of these previous Xtrac boxes, and that experience has been particularly useful to Mike Endean in the design of his new front-wheel drive gearbox: 'The components in a front-wheel drive gearbox for a two-litre Group A car have to be as strong as those in a four-wheel drive gearbox. I wouldn't say they have to be stronger, but it depends on traction control, I think. Going back two or three years when we had the Vauxhalls; when Malcolm Wilson was running them, he was running very very hard, as Malcolm does, and he was getting very good results, but we did find that the attrition in his transmission on things like plucking gear teeth off was higher than it is on a four-wheel drive car. That was purely because of the lack of traction — you had enormous amounts of wheelspin, and then suddenly you had grip.'

Recognising the need to stem spiralling costs in rallying, and that 'Formula 2' is one of the measures in that direction, Endean kept this objective a firm priority while conceiving his new gearbox. Xtrac isn't interested in cutting material or manufacturing method costs, but there are economies to be made in areas such as bearing selection; a bearing which might be slightly heavier and last half the life of a specific custom bearing, yet still be adequate for the job, could be as much as 12 times cheaper than the custom bearing, for example.

Another cost saving is in the design of its replaceable adapter plate which enables the gearbox to be fitted to different engines, but Endean pivots his costings on economies of scale. Xtrac has seen a 'quite high' initial level of interest shown in 'Formula 2', and, by making a few modifications involving differential location, this gearbox would suit a two-litre touring car racer. Endean: 'I wouldn't be at all surprised if in a year's time we aren't making 300-400 of these gearboxes a year. At the moment we sell a gearbox for about £12,000, and we're hoping to sell this one for two-thirds that.'

Like the Prodrive development, Xtrac's new six-speed box incorporates sequential gearchanging, similar to a motor cycle gearbox. Endean explains, 'It cuts down on dog wear; it cuts down on the chances of drivers missing gears — more so on bumpy surfaces than on smooth ones.

'We've been running sequential gearchanging now for the best part of this season in various circuit formulae, and the drivers can actually change down quicker on the circuit. The majority of engine blow ups are caused by missed gearchanges rather than anything else, and you're more likely to miss a gearchange on a rough surface than you are on a smooth surface. A sequential change basically stops that problem stone dead.

'The other thing is that we've found that the downshifting is so quick it's just as quick as skipping a gear, and with modern brakes you don't really want to change down too quickly, because you're going to over-rev the engine. I'm fairly convinced that once a sequential change is used by everybody, they're going to say: "I don't know why we ever bothered waving a gear lever sideways."

'We're making it a lot simpler to change ratios. Our current rally box was designed so that you changed the whole box on a rally, because you were allowed to carry as many spares as you liked. The new regulations state that you can only carry one spare, so we're designing the box so that you can pull it apart even quicker. We pull the box off the side the same way as we do on the normal transverse, but we're trying to look at making the box possibly oil-tight so that it's basically a cassette rather than half a gearbox.'

To facilitate the sequential selection, significant changes have been designed into the shape of the dogs in this gearbox, which Endean stresses is a different gearbox altogether, and not modifications designed into an existing gearbox. The new unit will accommodate the conventional Xtrac plate-type limited-slip differential, the cheapest route for an average runner. Xtrac's Hydrolok external electro-hydraulic control system will also fit as an alternative, as will FF Developments' viscous couplings. Xtrac-designed and manufactured semi-automatic gearboxes are already under development by certain racing teams, and the new gearbox is designed to incorporate this technology easily.

Manufacturers go rallying with particular models both because they could win, and because it fits marketing strategies — ultimately, it sells more cars. The vast majority of large volume production cars today are front-wheel drive and normally aspirated.

A properly driven, full-blown, turbocharged, four-wheel drive Group A rally car on the stages is an awesome sight for spectators, and a significant asset to the perception of its manufacturer's image. Rallying, and manufacturers, benefit from the top Group A cars. These specialised top cars, however, are fundamentally different to Group A versions of run of the mill GTi models. The latter, 'simpler' alternative, when structured as a second tier formula seems to promise benefits both for rallying and the manufacturers.

Extracting the ultimate out of any rally car conforms entirely to the law of diminishing returns: the more you put in the less you get out; spend twice the money and you don't get twice the performance. In a 'Formula 2' car there's less there in the first place to put things into.

Nothing has changed; the old adage that good rally cars are simple rally cars is still true today — comparatively. Albert Einstein would have agreed. Reputedly, he once said, 'Everything should be made as simple as possible, but not simpler.'

Renault has always been renowned for its ingenuity: the steel cradle holds the engine during mid-rally gearbox changes.

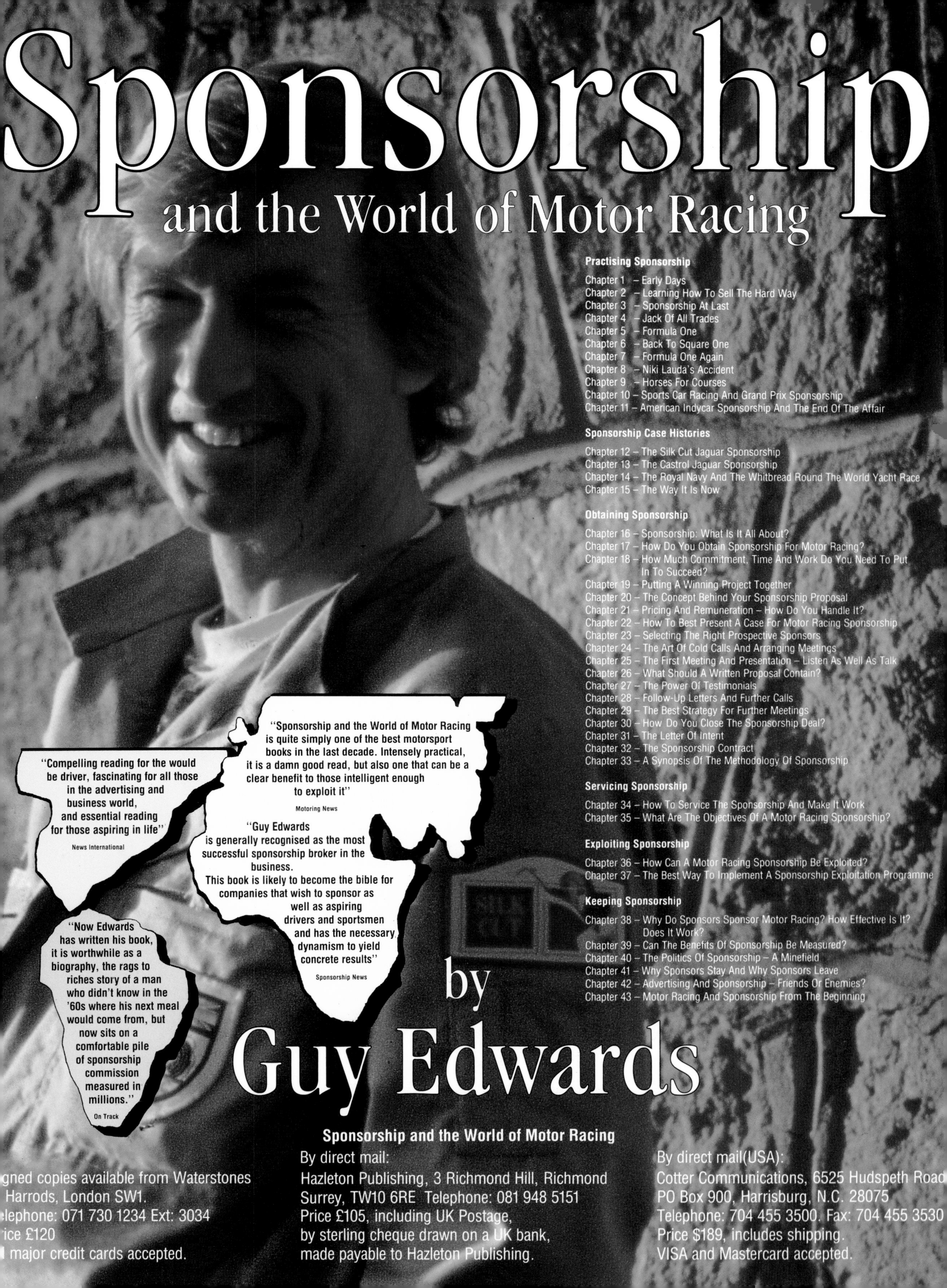
Sponsorship
and the World of Motor Racing
Practising Sponsorship
Chapter 1 – Early Days
Chapter 2 – Learning How To Sell The Hard Way
Chapter 3 – Sponsorship At Last
Chapter 4 – Jack Of All Trades
Chapter 5 – Formula One
Chapter 6 – Back To Square One
Chapter 7 – Formula One Again
Chapter 8 – Niki Lauda's Accident
Chapter 9 – Horses For Courses
Chapter 10 – Sports Car Racing And Grand Prix Sponsorship
Chapter 11 – American Indycar Sponsorship And The End Of The Affair
Sponsorship Case Histories
Chapter 12 – The Silk Cut Jaguar Sponsorship
Chapter 13 – The Castrol Jaguar Sponsorship
Chapter 14 – The Royal Navy And The Whitbread Round The World Yacht Race
Chapter 15 – The Way It Is Now
Obtaining Sponsorship
Chapter 16 – Sponsorship: What Is It All About?
Chapter 17 – How Do You Obtain Sponsorship For Motor Racing?
Chapter 18 – How Much Commitment, Time And Work Do You Need To Put In To Succeed?
Chapter 19 – Putting A Winning Project Together
Chapter 20 – The Concept Behind Your Sponsorship Proposal
Chapter 21 – Pricing And Remuneration – How Do You Handle It?
Chapter 22 – How To Best Present A Case For Motor Racing Sponsorship
Chapter 23 – Selecting The Right Prospective Sponsors
Chapter 24 – The Art Of Cold Calls And Arranging Meetings
Chapter 25 – The First Meeting And Presentation – Listen As Well As Talk
Chapter 26 – What Should A Written Proposal Contain?
Chapter 27 – The Power Of Testimonials
Chapter 28 – Follow-Up Letters And Further Calls
Chapter 29 – The Best Strategy For Further Meetings
Chapter 30 – How Do You Close The Sponsorship Deal?
Chapter 31 – The Letter Of Intent
Chapter 32 – The Sponsorship Contract
Chapter 33 – A Synopsis Of The Methodology Of Sponsorship
Servicing Sponsorship
Chapter 34 – How To Service The Sponsorship And Make It Work
Chapter 35 – What Are The Objectives Of A Motor Racing Sponsorship?
Exploiting Sponsorship
Chapter 36 – How Can A Motor Racing Sponsorship Be Exploited?
Chapter 37 – The Best Way To Implement A Sponsorship Exploitation Programme
Keeping Sponsorship
Chapter 38 – Why Do Sponsors Sponsor Motor Racing? How Effective Is It? Does It Work?
Chapter 39 – Can The Benefits Of Sponsorship Be Measured?
Chapter 40 – The Politics Of Sponsorship – A Minefield
Chapter 41 – Why Sponsors Stay And Why Sponsors Leave
Chapter 42 – Advertising And Sponsorship – Friends Or Enemies?
Chapter 43 – Motor Racing And Sponsorship From The Beginning
"Compelling reading for the would be driver, fascinating for all those in the advertising and business world, and essential reading for those aspiring in life"
News International
"Sponsorship and the World of Motor Racing is quite simply one of the best motorsport books in the last decade. Intensely practical, it is a damn good read, but also one that can be a clear benefit to those intelligent enough to exploit it"
Motoring News
"Guy Edwards is generally recognised as the most successful sponsorship broker in the business. This book is likely to become the bible for companies that wish to sponsor as well as aspiring drivers and sportsmen and has the necessary dynamism to yield concrete results"
Sponsorship News
"Now Edwards has written his book, it is worthwhile as a biography, the rags to riches story of a man who didn't know in the '60s where his next meal would come from, but now sits on a comfortable pile of sponsorship commission measured in millions."
On Track
by
Guy Edwards
Sponsorship and the World of Motor Racing
gned copies available from Waterstones
Harrods, London SW1.
elephone: 071 730 1234 Ext: 3034
ice £120
major credit cards accepted.
By direct mail:
Hazleton Publishing, 3 Richmond Hill, Richmond
Surrey, TW10 6RE Telephone: 081 948 5151
Price £105, including UK Postage,
by sterling cheque drawn on a UK bank,
made payable to Hazleton Publishing.
By direct mail(USA):
Cotter Communications, 6525 Hudspeth Road
PO Box 900, Harrisburg, N.C. 28075
Telephone: 704 455 3500. Fax: 704 455 3530
Price $189, includes shipping.
VISA and Mastercard accepted.

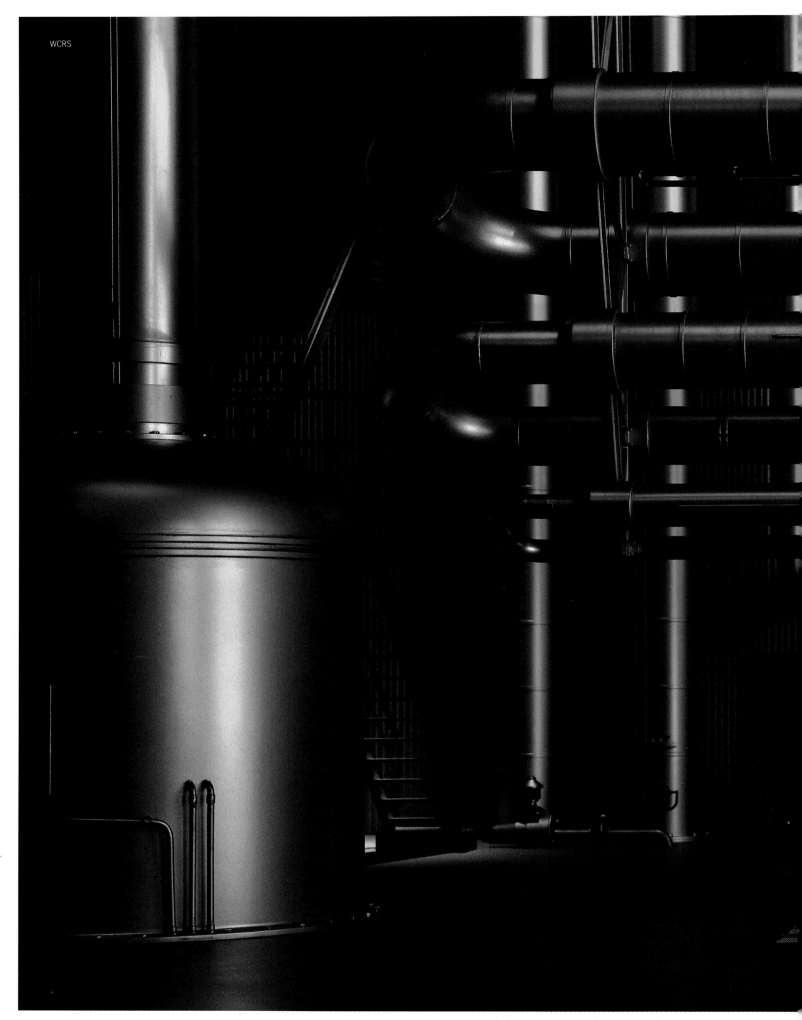

A degree or two lower and wider than the saloon

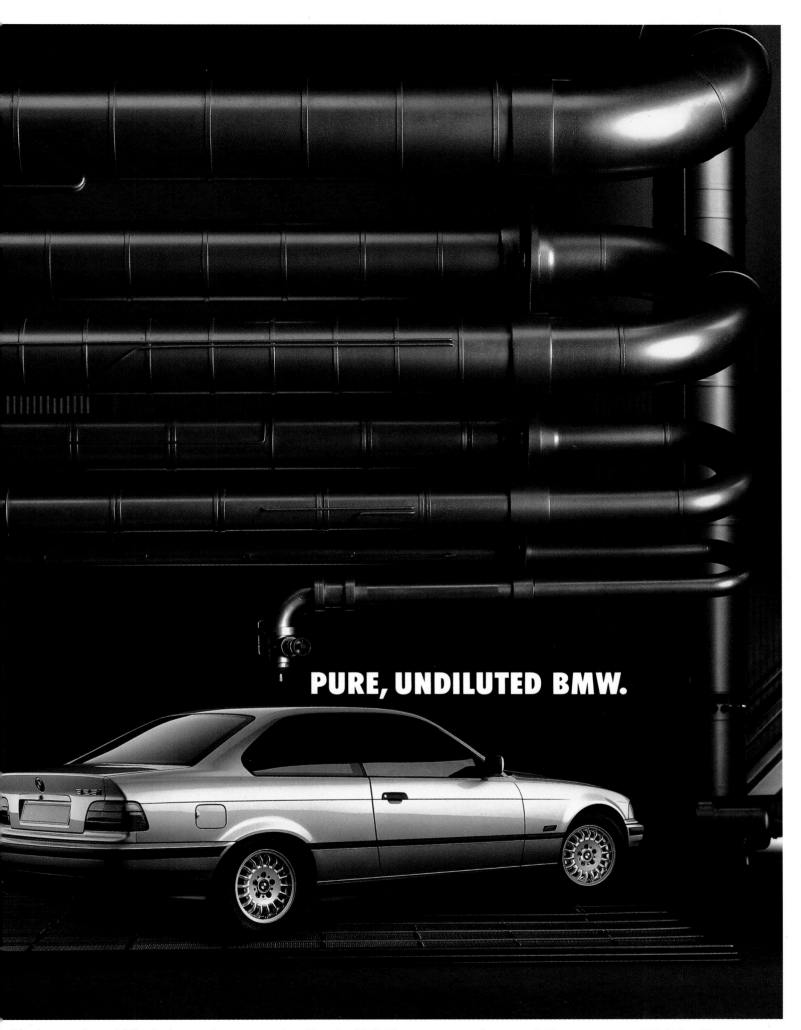

PURE, UNDILUTED BMW.

ultivalve engines. M-Technic sports suspension. Z-axle. ABS. The essence of a coupé. The essence of BMW.

THE NEW 3 SERIES COUPÉ.

Interview: Rob Arthur

THE TEAM PLAYER

By Amanda Campbell

There are few people in British rallying who provide more congenial company than Rob Arthur. He has a wicked sense of humour, a ferocious laugh, and is hard to beat as a raconteur. For fear of painting a pen-picture in imminent danger of sprouting wings and flying off the page, I hesitate to add that he is also warm-hearted.

Given that, it is a surprise to find that spending two hours interviewing him is an uphill struggle; in comparison, selling encyclopedias on the doorstep would be pretty straightforward. Short of wielding a crucifix and wooden stake, Arthur does everything to make the visiting journalist feel that she's just leaving. Sitting behind his desk at Mitsubishi Ralliart, where he has been team coordinator for the past two years, Arthur is all suspicion and profess-

Arthur saw his opportunity and seized it with both hands, giving up his co-driving career for a long-term future with Mitsubishi (opposite). When it comes to servicing the Galants (below), he knows where the buck stops.

ional caution. His resonant gravel-gruff voice — the combined product of his Welsh homeland and abuse by uncounted thousands of his beloved Gitanes — bestows a solemn air on each guarded answer, with every question weighed carefully lest he miss an opportunity of again airing policy straight out of the Mitsubishi manual. As frustrating as it is to be told that he could quite understand the decision to axe the Galant's pro-

gramme literally hours before the team was due to leave for the 1992 Rally of Portugal, when he adds that actually he quite agreed with it, one's immediate reaction is to grab him by the collar of his Ralliart shirt and demand to know how he really felt when yet another programme he was actively involved in was aborted.

Apart from the very practical consideration that there can be few people who have grabbed the fairly substantial figure of Arthur by the throat and not had cause to rue this hasty action, it would be useless: his strict code of professionalism dictates restraint and diplomacy. Besides, he knows only too well how cold it is outside the shelter of professional motor sport, and just how few jobs there are for co-drivers approaching their sell-by dates. While ex-footballers make a good liv-

ing from pubs and old racehorses can earn their keep opening carpet showrooms, the opportunities in top class rallying are few even for the very best, amongst whom Arthur undoubtedly is. Consider the openings at World Championship level: Lancia promotes from within — and its recruits are always Italian; Nissan no longer has a team; TTE and Ford have filled their vacancies with other candidates, also British in fact, but

emphasising that highly specialised openings of this kind are few and far between. They don't get advertised at the local job centre. Arthur knows he is a — never say lucky — fortunate man, and it is this awareness which has made him 'two very different animals' in the words of his long time buddy, Rick Smith: 'The hard exterior stops him being hurt, because of course when you have been a freelance professional co-driver or co-ordinator or whatever, you can be up at the very top and then the next minute you're nowhere.'

Arthur knows the rules and plays to them religiously. He has made the awkward transition from competitor to non-competitor, and the role he has at Mitsubishi fits him perfectly. He needs no reminding that controversy is not something in which a team co-ordinator with hopes of career longevity indulges.

This sense of duty has long been a hallmark of the former Haverfordwest Grammar School pupil who became an auctioneer. It was the same professionalism which brought him such a long and successful partnership with Tony Pond, and again and again, friends and colleagues point to the unflagging devotion to doing the job properly. As Pond observed, 'Rob does everything professionally, whether it's co-driving, chasing women, or whatever.'

A love of the good things in life noted by anyone who knows him well earned him a certain reputation in his bachelor days of travelling the world. Although Jim McRae describes him protectively as 'a bit of a devil', he was adamant about his own reservations. 'He eats garlic and smokes those dreadful French ciggies — I would hate to sleep beside him!', but that didn't seem to stop the women who, in his World Championship days, couldn't wait to meet the 'Oliver Tobias lookalike', according to Pond. 'Personally, I just thought they needed their vision seeing to, but he was a good laugh; he was professional, but we were always good mates as well. I suppose that made it an ideal combination...it's worse than being married — you're in the car all day, together in the restaurant in the evening, then, if you're lucky you get a week away from the bloke. You really have to get on.' He pauses and then pronounces enigmatically, 'There are some pretty weird co-drivers around.'

1982 brought Pond and Arthur together. Following his girlfriend of

the time from Wales to London some five years earlier, he had continued to combine co-driving with his work in the property business, competing with the likes of Terry Kaby in works Vauxhalls and Nissans. An excursion with Nissan to Corsica brought him to the attention of Pond, who was undergoing co-driver problems, changing partners with alarming frequency, and still not feeling really comfortable with any of them. 'Ian Grindrod was actually top of my list, but he was tied up at the time, so I was very impressed with the way he (Arthur) co-drove. He had a clear speaking voice, which was important, and so I contacted him.'

New Zealand was the start of a famous partnership which was to last on and off for six years with Austin Rover, but the invitation to sit alongside Pond posed something of a dilemma for Arthur: 'I had basically run out of holiday at work so I had to think, "Do I stay in the property business or do I take a gamble?" The gamble won, although it was a calculated risk, because I felt confident in myself to be able to do a good enough job to be asked again.' He pauses and then laughs at the memory. 'And then of course, when we came back from New Zealand, there was no rally until the RAC and that's when you think, "Oh no, what am I going to do now?"!'

He can allow himself a fond look back, because of course the rallies did come and the team became the flag-bearers for British rallying, but the partnership was not without its doubters in those early days. 'I was amazed at the number of 'phone calls that said, "He's bad news to work with, he really is a hard taskmaster and this, that, and the other." And I can remember thinking, "I'm not going to listen to any of this, it's up to me to do it, I'm going to make my own mind up and it's up to me to adopt a professional attitude." Obviously some relationships are never going to work, but if you don't go into it with an open mind you don't give it a chance to work.'

He was right to disregard the comments, as the years that followed were the highlight of both competitors' careers, with the 1985 RAC, when they brought a Metro 6R4 home third on its first World Championship appearance, an outstanding moment. 'It was something I'll never forget, because it was like driving around Wembley. There were Union Jacks everywhere on approach roads and in villages as well as on the stages.' If the 1985 RAC was the high, the low followed horribly swiftly the next year.

'We had a good WCR programme, but you could see it coming, something had to happen. We went to Portugal where there was that dreadful accident in Sintra and we were one of the crews that actually refused to go any further, and then of course Toivonen and Cresto were killed in Corsica. That is the only time I've ever walked away from a situation, because when I heard that news we'd just retired with a blown engine, and we'd been back to the hotel, had lunch and then the news came through via our PR people. I then had to go and break the news to Davenport — because he was one of Henri's godfathers — and I left the island that afternoon, because as a direct result of that you had speculation all around you — press speculation, speculation from other competitors, and the fact of the matter in my view was that no one actually knew what had happened, especially at that stage...I didn't really feel it was the place for me to stay around and listen to all this claptrap, so I'm afraid I did an ostrich job and left the island as soon as I could, which was literally within an hour.'

In terms of serious competition the partnership was all but finished; Pond became increasingly disillusioned with the sport and subsequently retired, while Arthur kicked his heels, bound for a further year to a manufacturer no longer interested in top class rallying, and wondering what the future held. Although he went on to win a British Open title and did compete abroad again in the World Championship, in Greece and New Zealand with his new partner, Jim McRae, the effective end of his competitive career was on the Circuit of Ireland in 1990. Ask him how much he misses active competition and he gives a fairly colourless answer — 'Well, obviously having always been a competitor you are going to miss it,' before going on to detail how he was working for Ford and then Ralliart on a casual basis, prior to making the post at Ralliart permanent. Jim McRae is more forthright about Arthur's attitude, insisting, 'Although I know he does a brilliant job (at Ralliart) I can't believe he wouldn't rather be in a rally car.' The occasional call to arms is still met by the old warhorse, as was the case on the 24 Hours of Ieper last June. 'There was no intention for me to do the rally, he'd been there a week with Dougie Paterson and the rally started on the Friday,' recalls Arthur.

'On the Wednesday night Jim rang me up and said "Help! Dougie's had to go back to the office!" So I cleared it with him and drove out on Thursday morning, and we drove 75 per cent of the stages just once over, and I mean it was great, it was really good to be back in the car...and I found it quite laid back, because you just come in at the last minute and you haven't really had time to think about it, so you just jump in the car and get on with it. Actually it was quite a laugh, because as soon as we pulled up on the start ramp, some wag in the crowd enquired as to where we kept the zimmer frames these days. I thoroughly enjoyed it, but it hasn't made me want to do more events.'

For McRae, getting his co-driver to combine his day job with life outside the World Championship can sometimes call for that special brand of Lanarkshire diplomacy. 'It's not frustrating unless you're trying to do things on a budget and you've got only one and a half service vans, and he says you need five, and then he asks how many chase cars you have and you have to tell him

Arthur had as good a relationship with Tony Pond as any of his co-drivers. The Metro 6R4 never quite lived up to its promise, however.

there's just one!'

McRae is just one of the drivers that Arthur and Ian Grindrod have in common, and the pair have undoubtedly been two of Britain's foremost co-drivers. McRae points out that neither suffers fools gladly, Pond to the hard work they would put in: 'I had co-drivers who in the evening just wanted to put their feet up and get back to the hotel — they didn't want to know about practising at six o'clock, but Rob was never like that, nor Ian.' Despite the obligatory leg-pulling which hides a genuine mutual respect, Arthur acknowledges Grindrod's help in saving him from making a disastrous error. 'It was on the Mintex in '85 with the Rover, and it was simply that we'd missed our service and subsequently found there was a slight panic on, and I looked at the road timing and I'd convinced myself that we had ten minutes less than we did... so we drove like hell to the start of the next stage where there was a queue and I told Pondy to go straight past, and I was desperately trying to give this girl my time card, but she just doesn't want to take it, and I presumed the queue was due to a delay in the stage and everybody else had booked in, but of course nobody had booked in, so Grindrod wandered across and sugg- ested that maybe I ought to add it up again — that's the sort of camaraderie you had. We were leading Group A so it would have been a crucial error — an unforgiveable one.'

Despite his close shave, Arthur is adamant that an unforced error is inexcusable and one for which this particular Mother Hen would give her chicks a good pecking. 'I'm the first to accept that there are pressures in modern World Championship rallying, but I don't think those pressures have changed since my day and I don't think any of my then bosses would have been too enamoured if I had booked in carelessly. OK, you try and find out what's happened, they might have gone in late because of a fault on our side, so then you start looking at why that happened...but at the end of the day when the car comes into the service point, whilst I have made an educated judgement as to how long it will have, the co-driver should know; and if the co-driver makes a mistake he must bear that mistake.'

So much for co-driver solidarity; in fact Arthur admits that he is probably harder on co-drivers than he is on drivers, since he feels that if he could manage it, they can also. 'I have a good working relationship with Staffan (Parmander, Kenneth Eriksson's co-driver) but he is at the top of his profession and so you expect certain things,' he says.

There is categorically no crossover between Arthur's philosophy on and off the stages; an almost

puritanical streak creeps into his working practices. In a relationship with Ralliart Manager Andrew Cowan, where it is often the latter painted as the dour taskmaster, Arthur is actually the harder in some cases. For instance, Eriksson retired the lone Mitsubishi well before the end of the 1992 Acropolis and Cowan, aware that his mechanics were disappointed at not going to Finland or Australia later in the year, allowed them to stay on until the end of the rally as a holiday. 'I wouldn't have done that, I would have had them on the first plane back,' con-

tests Arthur. He is also against wives and girlfriends being allowed on events. 'I remember one of my bosses once asking a driver would he take his wife to the office with him, and I think I agree with that. How can you concentrate on the job in hand? It's something I've never done, and my wife is very good and puts up with it.'

In total contrast, he is also more than capable of being one of the lads. When on the last night of the Acropolis he went over to talk to some of the mechanics by the pool in Itea, 'I realised it was a mistake as soon as I went there: they were

going to have me in that water, so I ran around quickly stripping off and jumped in before they could get me!' He is also his troops' fiercest defender when necessary; another poolside incident, again in Greece, was laid wrongly at the door of the Ralliart mechanics, and he ensured that their behaviour was exonerated. In private as well as in public, the mechanics think the world of him. In the space of two years, he has become one of the key players at Ralliart.

The year before on the Acropolis it had been Eriksson and Parmander who had needed his support, when a road traffic accident brought crippling penalties. 'They were devastated. However, he then drove an absolute blinder for the rest of the rally. I then did my utmost to persuade the organisers that they hadn't given sufficient time for that road section, simply because of the time of day and the average rush hour traffic. They had obviously realised there was going to be a problem prior to that, because they'd brought the start forward half an hour, but they kept the timing of that section to 51 or 52 km/h even though there was a report from one of their course cars that the traffic was bad and they should consider changing the allowable time. This year, for example, virtually the identical route was timed at 32 km/h. But still, the driver and co-driver were upset, realised that the penalty was such that they would be fortunate to recoup but, nevertheless...with the thought that maybe they could get it scrubbed, I explained to them on what basis I thought I had a case by giving evidence and backing up the claim that 60 per cent of the field had dropped time.'

The penalties stood, but total disaster had been averted, the team clocking up 30 fastest stage times. 'There's no point in walking into the organisers' office and beating the table. It's got to be done constructively; there's a panel of stewards in charge of that rally and you have to present to them a properly constructed case. You can't go in there bleating; *force majeure*. It's just bad luck.

'You've got to try and remain calm in order to have clear thoughts. Now I think that's a discipline you have when you're competing. I've always tried to have it, but I remember once...' Enter Mr McRae, the driver on that occasion — the 1989 24 Hours of Ieper — and whose account of the incident is less diplomatic than Arthur's. 'We'd had an accident, damaged the rear beam axle on the car, and the only way we could get going again was for Rob to jump onto the boot — he's a bit heavy for a co-driver, but really useful to get some traction. Anyway as we went through the flying finish and then the stop control I heard him shout, "Don't stop, keep going!" so I did. They often have little caravans where they operate the time controls from

play of anger towards marshals — 'We always felt they were there doing a thankless job anyway and should never be abused, it was never his way.' To Arthur, losing control is a sign of weakness and ultimately unprofessional. Even now his patience is slow burn: 'I don't very often lose my rag; you've got to try and maintain a coolness on an event, otherwise it kills clear thought; but if I ask someone to do something over our airwaves I expect them to do it. What I don't need at the time, especially if I'm having to juggle vehicles about, is the smartarse who thinks he knows the event better than I do

ure. I've never, ever seen him flap. We were making pace notes for competitors on the Mazda Winter Rally; we'd been over this particular piece of forest time and time again, but we still couldn't get it quite right. We had it down as a "crest, right 1", but Rob still wasn't happy — he thought maybe we'd missed something. So despite the fact that by now it was getting dark, we decided to do it yet again. Rob was driving, so he backed the Shogun up about half a mile and then shot down this track. At 70 mph this crest looked like Mount Everest, and when you took off you landed in the biggest hole ever! The Shogun

cheque, and really wants to help, he says he just couldn't cope with going there.'

After more than two hours on the rack, Arthur remains impenetrable in his interview persona, a distant relation of the figure that appeared on stage after winning the 1986 Manx with Tony Pond: resplendent in wigs, false noses, moustaches, and glasses, they flung back their gold lamé jackets with a flourish to reveal to a delighted audience a pair of the biggest plastic willies the gleeful Austin Rover crew could find. Pond is succinct when summarising his old partner: 'Rob would never do any-

in Belgium, and when I looked in the mirror he had this guy halfway out of the caravan, saying, "You will give me my f-ing time!"'

Bring in the guilty party: 'This Belgian marshal just looked at my time card and said "Non!" So I said, "What do you mean 'No'? Give me my time please." And he said "Non, you did not stop," and I said, "Well, if I didn't stop, where the hell do you think I came from? Give me the time," and then I picked him up. But I got my time, and then felt so bad about it that I did actually go to the organisers later that night and apologised.'

He has made a huge, conscious effort to control his natural temper and his ability to do so has indubitably contributed to his success. Pond is unable to remember any dis-

questioning it, so then we have this nonsensical debate over the radio, that I won't put up with. If it's wrong, it's not his fault, it's my fault...I haven't had to shoot myself yet.'

Accountability and responsibility have never been greater in his professional life than they are now, and so presumably the pressure has increased in ratio, but he still enjoys his life in motor sport and revels in the new challenges he must meet. He assumes a slightly confessional air. 'Although there was no panic in Greece, I was relieved at the end of the event that it had actually worked, and albeit it was stretched resources in places, we all came through without valium.'

Smith sees Arthur as an 'exceptionally cool customer under pres-

went over on its side in one ditch and then into the opposite ditch on its other side. I don't know how he got out of it — Pond would have been impressed with his technique — but after we stopped, all he said was, "That would have been bloody embarrassing!"'

Arthur would like you to believe that his bite is at least equal to his bark, but Smith knows better. Between them, the two have been responsible for raising over £45,000 for the Tadworth Court Children's Hospital yet, despite his wholehearted support and unflagging work on behalf of the charity, the Ralliart man refuses to visit the hospital. 'He just couldn't cope,' explains Smith. 'Although he will do anything for them, he loves doing the work, seeing their faces when we present the

It's not all Gitanes and garlic: Jim McRae and Arthur head for victory on the 1988 Ulster in an RED Cosworth.

thing dodgy or try and pinch a minute like some co-drivers — he always played it straight.' Asked if there was any particular incident that sprang to mind involving Arthur, he chuckled. 'I think it must have been that first night in New Zealand. In the evening, Rob disappeared with a barmaid and the next morning when he re-appeared I asked him what on earth he saw in her, because as I remember she was rather large.' Arthur had a ready answer for that one but, more to the point, he had of course reported for duty that morning on time. What else would you expect from the ultimate professional?

44

actual reality

Professional rider pictured

At Suzuki, we're turning tomorrow's dreams into today's reality. We've developed a fresh approach to design, backed by innovative refinements in performance and reliability, creating a range of quality motorcycles. With precision engineering and over 70 years experience, we're establishing a new era of total motorcycling enjoyment. That's no idle boast. It's actual reality.

FOR INFORMATION
FREEPHONE
0800 526263
Heron Suzuki PLC, 46-62 Gatwick Road, Crawley, West Sussex RH10 2XF

A Heron International Company

$ SUZUKI

No, it's

First impressions can be deceiving.

But a Rover it certainly is. Your first glimpse of the new Rover 220 Turbo Coupé.

An electrifying cocktail of high-performance, space-age materials, and a twist of leather and walnut.

It's a taut, 2 litre turbo that will reward the skilful with an immensely satisfying drive.

In fact you're looking at the most powerful and, many will say, the most beautiful Rover we've ever put into production.

The new Rover 220 Turbo Coupé heralds a range of models from 1.6 to 2 litres, each with the potential to leave their rivals back at the drawing board.

(For example, 0–60 in 6.2* seconds should put any hazard well behind you.)

An ingenious T-bar glass roof is fitted with titanium coated panels that pack away to produce an open-topped coupé in minutes.

And on the Turbo, the engine's immense power is delicately channelled to the driving

A ROVER.

wheels via a revolutionary Torsen® torque-sensing traction control system.

So a patch of ice or a stretch of mud shouldn't wrest control from the driver by spinning a wheel.

Truly, a car for all seasons.

To find out more about the range just telephone or fill in the coupon and we'll set the wheels in motion.

We predict rather a lot of coupé drivers will soon be saying "Yes, it's a Rover."

Post to: Rover Cars, Freepost, 1399, Slough, Berkshire SL1 4BU.
Fax to: 0753 696005. Telephone free on 0800 52 10 20.

Title: Mr Mrs Miss ⌊⌊⌊⌊⌋   Initials ⌊⌊⌊⌋ BLOCK CAPITALS PLEASE

Surname

Address

Postcode

Home Tel. No. (Inc. STD code)

Current Car (Make/Model)

Reg. No.   Likely to Change
                           (Mth/Yr)

CRC1

THE NEW ROVER 220 TURBO COUPÉ

Rarely, if ever, has international rallying been plunged into a crisis of confidence to compare with 1992's. It differed markedly from the Group B crisis of 1986, say, where the nature of the cars and, to a lesser degree, the length of the rallies themselves were the sole points at issue. In 1992, after years of steadily escalating costs with the minimum of reflection on FISA's part and relatively little grumbling from the factory teams, almost every aspect of the sport was brought into question. Dissatisfaction reached unprecedented levels. As manufacturers slashed pro-grammes or retrenched while they concentrated on new cars, it looked as though rallying might have priced itself out of a shrinking market. Finally, the game was no longer worth the candle.

Accordingly, it seemed appropriate to seek the views of three men closely involved in the sport at the highest level — Miki Biasion, Andrew Cowan and Juha Piironen. Each brought a slightly different perspective, derived from job titles, teams, and nationalities as well as individual personalities. Significantly, none of them was surprised to be asked; indeed they welcomed the opportunity to offer their opinions. Cowan remarked that in the spring he had started to wonder if the World Rally Championship had a future at all, while Biasion believed that a public debate was needed to root out the disease afflicting the sport.

While most of rallying's features or accepted ways of doing things were challenged in 1992, there was a considerable range of agreement amongst the three on what has gone wrong and what needs to be done. In that respect, FISA's policy of listening closely to the manufacturers and acting cautiously on their recommendations has been a wise one, for the views of a dozen representatives are mirrored by individuals who aren't necessarily embroiled in motor sport politics.

Above all, there was a common agreement that the imperative has been economic. Rallying is inevitably an expensive sport, and it was bound to suffer at a time when nearly all the industrialised nations are experiencing economic difficulties, and the motor industry is suffering more than most kinds of manufacturing. In consequence, all three welcomed reducing the duration of rallies to three days, restricted opportunities

Debating the Future

THREE MEN IN SEARCH OF A SOLUTION

Miki Biasion, Andrew Cowan and Juha Piironen consider the future of rallying with David Williams

for servicing, and the adoption of a single source of fuel, the latter with the aim of quietening accusations of sharp practice that have come to a pitch in the last year or so. They were also against the widespread introduction of a two-wheel drive 'Formula 2' category.

Three-day World Championship rallies have of course been perfectly feasible since FISA rushed through its time and distance limits in May 1986, but there has been no particular demand for them hitherto and, once they had overcome their initial terror of obliging competitors to do anything strenuous outside office hours, organisers have been quite willing to send them out after dusk, yet continue to oblige the local tourist board by detaining the World Championship circus for a day or two longer than strictly necessary. Cowan agreed that driving time each day might have to be extended, but saw no real obstacle 'considering the fitness of these crews today', while

Biasion reckoned that rallying from eight in the morning until eight at night for three days would neatly pack a World Championship distance into the designated time span.

This is standard, uncontroversial stuff, and seems to be taking the logic of 1986 to its inevitable conclusion; after all, Carlos Sainz has pronounced that endurance is dead, and that he would not be interested in being a rally driver if it were not. Yet the nature of rallying and the balance between speed and endurance remains a live issue. While Biasion and Cowan argue that a World Championship rally should have 600 kilometres of stages — if you like, that the World Championship mountain has to be a certain minimum height to remain a worthwhile target and to merit the admiration of the outside world — Piironen differs. In one respect, this is the co-driver talking; the driver and the team manager speak airily of compressing rallies and leave the details to others, whereas Piironen has worked out the required amount of recce time to the nearest minute. Biasion reckons that 36 hours of actual rallying, followed by a long time control, allowing the results to be worked out and awards to be presented on the spot will do nicely. Piironen sees no reason why a top level rally shouldn't be compressed into two weeks flat: cut the recce to eight days, perhaps run loops of stages, and change the route every year. The last proposal was less expected from a 40-year-old who has won three World Championships and has not only done very well from the current system, but would profit further from the manufacturers' suggestion that routes should be standardised as far as possible, again with the aim of saving money. Piironen argues that that is unfair on younger drivers and new teams (now that full speed practice is more or less a thing of the past), and that rallying cannot afford to turn away either.

However, he feels an eight-day recce necessitates a much shorter

rally, with 350 or 400 kilometres of stages at the outside. What about endurance then? 'Normally if you calculate the rallies of today, if you cut them in half, it would be solved already in the halfway,' he answers dismissively. This is Finnish reasoning. Long before Timo Salonen's plea for office hours rallying was treated as holy writ, the Finns were arguing publicly that the Circuit of Ireland was too long and that there was no need for 500 or 600 miles (anything up to 950 kilometres) of special stages. It's a little like the argument for one-day cricket rather than test matches: damn tradition and let's have short, sharp, entertaining events that keep spectators and, above all, television interested. Piironen (who is not a noted cricket fan) would be just as impatient with comparisons between the stars of today and Eugen Bohringer as he would with a debate on the merits of Don Bradman as against Viv Richards.

This is not a matter of ignorance: 'We are talking about marathon rallies, and then we are talking about costs which is marathon costs...it's idealistic the thought that you could do it, but the cost would be so enormous that we wouldn't have the roads. Using different roads would be so expensive — it would be so expensive to move the organisation, to move the rally around. It's impossible. It's a beautiful idea, and that's how rallying started, but rallying has to be modern, because in all the rallying it's important that we are the ones who have the advantage of making the new ideas, not that someone tells us to do something. As long as we can still choose what to do and show the lines what we would like to do, that's positive, but if we stick to the old things and say that rallies have to be 600 kilometres long and

nothing new, we are ending up with a cost which is enormous, and then we have the green people — society, community — coming against us.'

The case for longer events is less closely argued. Cowan begins by saying that there must still be an element of endurance — 'It's got to be run in a way for the drivers to take some responsibility for the end result in that they do a good recce, and

that they drive the car at a pace that suits the event' — before conceding that drivers now treat even the Acropolis as a sprint and that endurance by this definition vanished in May 1986. Like Biasion, he has a greater regard for tradition than Piironen.

More persuasively, Biasion maintains that he has nothing against short events, but there should still be a place for tactics. While endurance is more or less a thing of the past for the works driver in Europe, there are still brilliantly successful drivers who have won a good many rallies by picking their moment to launch an attack, rather than charging an event like a bull in a china shop; Biasion and Juha Kankkunen spring to mind.

Differences over event length touch an equally vexed question: the number of rounds in the World Championship. Piironen takes the logic of his position a stage further, saying that he sees nothing wrong with a 14-round World Championship if the rallies are compressed into a two-week period. Under those circumstances, 14 rallies wouldn't pose an unacceptable strain on the crews, and it might be possible to package the World Rally Championship along similar lines to Grands Prix. It could find a regular slot on television, with the same sort of wide-ranging appeal, and the tension and excitement could be sustained and milked much more effectively than from an eight- or

10-round series.

Neither Biasion nor Cowan will countenance 14 rounds. The former regards the present marathon as the unwanted product of political manœuvring, which ought to be scrapped in favour of a 10-round series, in which five rallies are replaced each year as part of a rota. Cowan also views 14 rallies as out of the question, and would slim down the championship by weeding out the rallies with the least concern for safety. When it is put to him that the Monte Carlo Rally comes near the top of any such list, he agrees, 'It's a difficult one'. How does one chuck out such a prestigious event, no matter how mediocre the organisation?

Cowan's attitude to rallies is much less traditional in other respects. Modestly professing that he couldn't offer a detailed plan for a more compact rally to an organiser doesn't prevent him from seeing the need for it. The financial aim is to cut the hotel bill. Staying in one hotel would achieve an impressive saving, regardless of the number of people in the team, on the basis that most headquarters hotels demand full payment for the two or three days that a team may spend elsewhere. This is much more than an administrative point. TTE based itself near Delphi for the 1992 Acropolis, only sending the rally

crews and the minimum number of vans to Athens for the start and finish. It is only a small step to scrapping the start and finish in the capital city altogether and basing the entire rally in Delphi, or some other town in northern or central Greece, such as Itea or Kamena Vourla; Cowan liked the idea of moving the Rally of Portugal to Porto. Suddenly, hotel bills might change the traditional shape of a rally completely, far more than the rule changes of 1986 did.

Servicing is less controversial on first examination, yet a vital area. If the cost of a car is pretty much a constant factor, the various constituents of the support team assume great importance in the ceaseless drive to cut spending. More than tyres, spares or vans, Cowan points out that the number of people retained by a front running rally team makes them the most expensive asset a team has. 'You've got to get them there: it takes four days to get there, and it takes time to get them home, because they've got to take these vans, they've got to stay in hotels; wages — freelance wages — costs are quite high,' he explains, outlining Ralliart's approach to the Acropolis.

Limiting the frequency of gearbox changes is all very well, but no more than a step in the right direction if teams still need 12 or 15 vehi-

cles to cover every service point. On that score, World Championship organisers would be best advised to turn their rallies into a series of loops, rather like a Belgian event, on the grounds that the number of service points (which dictates the number of vehicles and mechanics, and the volume of spares) is the crucial figure. Piironen regards looping as a growing trend, while pointing out that too much of it will destroy gravel roads, In addition, he argues against longer stages, although it is hard to see any way of reducing the number of service points without letting the present 30-kilometre stage maximum fall into disuse. By common consent, a smaller number of stages is the most effective means of cutting the frequency of service points and the range of tyre choice, but all three were keen on enforcing a 30-kilometre stage distance as a minimum between service points, irrespective of the number of stages. Cowan wistfully comments that life would be much easier if everyone adopted the same approach as the Rally Australia.

Surprisingly, no one could offer an effective means of enforcing a service ban if the distance was split into three or four stages, as it is at Fafe in Portugal, or in the Lake District on the RAC, and Cowan wants to know what happens if a driver

gets two punctures, when 1993 rules will probably restrict crews to one spare. In effect, the rule is as open to abuse as servicing restrictions were in the past, and a rule that cannot be enforced remains a bad rule, just as it was in the 1970s and early '80s. There is the economic aspect: Ninni Russo has worked out that making tyres last 30 kilometres would cut a team's tyre bill by around 25 per cent, but there would be nothing to stop the better financed teams drafting in extra service vehicles the moment the budget permitted.

Biasion argues that it might even entail a measure of integrity. 'I think there are many solutions quite easy to find. It is only a question of organisers and the factories, they think to rallysport and not for their own interest. OK, for sure the factories they do this job for interest, but if the rallysport is not in a good light they have no interest, so it is better to work together and to improve much more the popularity of the sport,' he maintains.

If it does work, the accountants will be delighted. Cowan revealed that Group A turbochargers cost £3000 each, and a complete four-wheel drive transmission for a Galant VR-4 is over £30,000. Work out the number of vans and spares kits, and the average Ralliart convoy starts to carry the same financial payload as a

essence, the three felt that, if World Championship rallying is the equivalent of Formula 1, it should be for 'Formula 1' cars, not for two-litre hot hatchbacks.

Their rejection of 'Formula 2' combined sentiment, shrewdness and prejudice in varying degrees. Piironen considers that the lack of spectacle resulting from the re-introduction of front-wheel drive would kill a sport with a following that would fill dozens of football stadia, but then, as an Integrale was fired up in the background, pointed out that speed and noise were joint attractions of a 'Formula 1' car. Watching a front-wheel drive car negotiate a dry, uphill hairpin may not quicken the pulse, but anyone who has heard a naturally aspirated Clio or an Astra on a stage won't need telling that they sound a great deal more appealing than the medium rev, metallic clatter of an Integrale. With a handful of exceptions, turbocharging and restrictors have given the modern Group A car the aural appeal of a racing diesel.

It is less easy to pick holes in Biasion's argument. 'I think it can be a good idea inside the event,' he says, referring to Formula 2. 'But we cannot stop the technology of the four-wheel drives, of the turbocharged engine.' He feels that a development budget would be spent, regardless of the nature of the car. If there is no centre differential, it will be spent on shock absorbers or traction control.

Cowan widens the field of fire. 'The actual build costs wouldn't be a lot less. I would say, for example, that if you're spending £130,000-140,000 building a Group A car at the moment, you'd probably build one of these for £90,000-100,000...I

sophisticated, high-tech stuff involved in rallying, and I wouldn't like to take that away, and I'm sure a lot of manufacturers wouldn't like to take that away.'

He believes that cars are now as standard as the Japanese could wish, and that they well appreciate the need for competition gearboxes and the like. He emphasises the need to stabilise the rules and protect the investment that Toyota, Ford and Mitsubishi, to name but three, have put into new cars. As it stands, the teams regard Group A as a pleasing balance between acceptable performance and, apparently, cost, and the sort of technical sophistication the Japanese are fond of plastering on the doors or the boot lid. Take out the four-wheel steer and the four-wheel drive, and rallying loses some of its glamour. After all, the manufacturers are trying to foster an image.

Piironen feels that power outputs could be reduced a little if necessary, without offering any suggestions for doing so, while Biasion agrees there is a case for South African rules: two-litre engines, four-wheel drive, but no turbochargers. As it stands, the obvious culprit isn't perceived as being anything more than the most peripheral aspect of the problem.

Rallying has indulged in a prolonged bout of collective scab picking. Nevertheless, optimism is unquenchable. If anything, 1992 is starting to look like a blip on the graph — albeit a serious one — rather than the beginning of the end. The driver, the co-driver and the team manager might have sounded plaintive at times, but none of them was in the least disillusioned. The least accessible form of motor sport

Technical sophistication in a car like the Sierra Cosworth 4x4 has a certain glamour, albeit with a cost penalty. Aerial support (such as TTE's Safari jumbo) has reached the point where the cost penalty is starting to outweigh the benefits.

bullion train.

With characteristic shrewdness, Biasion laid a finger on an obvious extravagance during the Acropolis. 'Probably it is possible to limit the services. Everybody is looking for the cost of the cars, but yesterday there were 11 helicopters! Maybe only one helicopter for team, maximum. Maybe the helicopter is for the organisation, for the safety.'

Other measures for cutting costs revealed that the men who sign the cheques know a good deal more about team organisation than the star performers. Piironen feels that much more should be done to cut airline costs, and that teams could save themselves a handsome sum by sending all their personnel out on the same flights, and putting air freight on the same aircraft. Cowan retorts, 'Air travel is not a big percentage of our costs,' adding that airlines are now so desperate for business that they will ring back three or four times to get the work, and that he can get 'super deals' —

and Cowan doesn't have a reputation for being free with Mitsubishi's money. As for air freight, a good deal of equipment can be sent cheaply by sea (a container to Australia costs £1000), and 'one jumbo wouldn't take us anyway'.

Reducing the cost of and scope for repairing cars isn't necessarily controversial. Suggest fundamental changes to the type of cars used, and you have the basis of a quarrel. In

think it's a good idea to have for the sport a class that if there was a catastrophe you could bring in something that would make a fairly major gesture to reducing speeds, satisfying the environmental problems — that sort of thing. It's nice to have that sitting there on a shelf ready, but Formula 1 technology is open-ended. You can't have rally development open-ended, but it's nice to see that there's quite a lot of fairly

still has a spell to cast and, as Cowan puts it, 'I would say now for 1993 it's looking very good. You're going to have at least four manufacturers with a fairly big commitment to a number of World Championship events.' If anything has changed, it is a realisation that every facet of rallying demands planning. The years of untrammelled, unco-ordinated growth have finally pushed costs beyond the bounds of reason.

SPORTS PERSONALIT

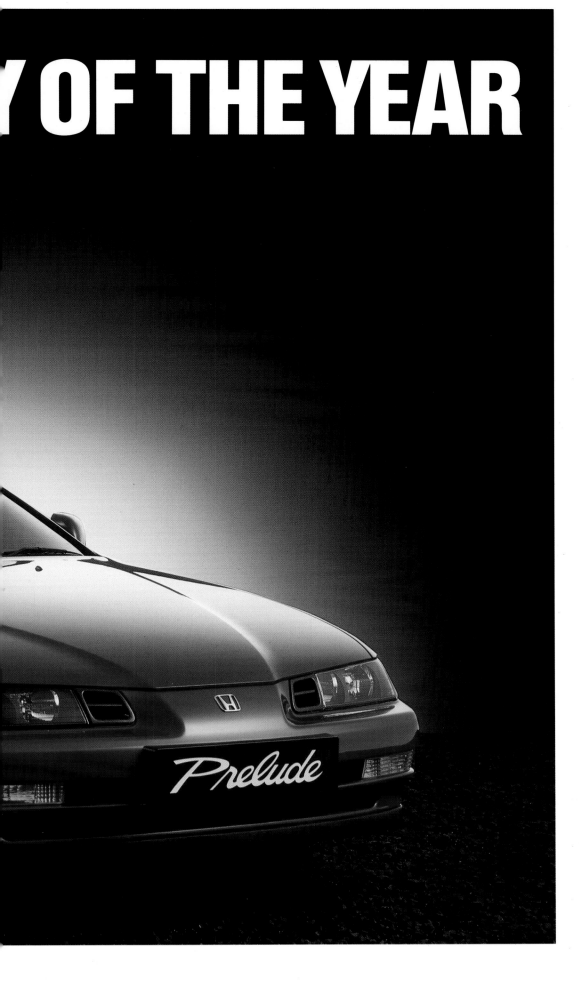

And the winner is...

The new Honda Prelude.

While we're about it, we'd also like to nominate it for best newcomer and best performance.

But does the new Prelude deserve all these plaudits?

We firmly believe it does.

Radically styled to look every inch a sports car, it's also endowed with suitably sporting prowess.

There's a choice of two 16 valve engines; 2.0 litre and 2.3 litre, both fuel-injected and more powerful than ever before. And the 2.3 has electronic four-wheel steering which gives it extraordinarily responsive handling and agility.

But the real beauty of the new Prelude is that it combines all the performance of a sports car with all the reliability of a Honda.

And, unlike many sports cars, it boasts a distinctive and luxurious interior.

With power-steering, ABS and, on the 2.3, a safety SRS airbag, it's no wonder 'World Sports Car' magazine declared: "The Honda Prelude has it all."

But don't take our, or their, word for it.

Visit your Honda dealer and give the new Prelude a personality test of your own.

The new Honda Prelude

To: Honda (UK) Information Service, PO Box 46, Hounslow, Middlesex, TW4 5BR.   27/PR/A/1

| (MR/MRS/MISS/MS) | INITIALS | SURNAME | | | |

ADDRESS

| | | | POSTCODE | |

| TELEPHONE | | | PRESENT CAR MAKE | |

| MODEL | | YEAR OF REG | MONTH EXPECTED REPLACEMENT | YEAR OF REPLACEMENT | AGE IF UNDER 18 |

FROM A FAMOUSLY RELIABLE SOURCE, CONFIRMATION THAT ENGINES RUN BEST ON WASHING LIQUID.

Clearly, Volkswagen can tell when it's Shell. Because Shell Advanced Fuels contain a unique detergent that cleans the engine as you drive.

The dirt it washes away is carbon.

Every engine produces carbon. It's an intrinsic by-product of combustion.

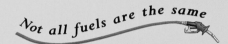

Unless you get rid of it, engine heat bakes it into a hard crust on the fuel injectors and inlet valves. These are the components that constitute your engine's breathing system.

And carbon strangles it.

Not even the most reliable engine in the world can survive unscathed.

Any engine will be harder to start when it's contaminated by carbon.

It will also be lacklustre in performance and rather more greedy for fuel. Not to mention more expensive to maintain.

But independent tests have proved that regular use of Shell Advanced keeps engines twice as clean as any other brand.

With the result that they perform as they were designed to.

You will enjoy the benefit of an appreciable improvement in throttle response. And save money, because less fuel will be consumed and less maintenance required.

In addition, Shell Advanced not only helps prevent freshly· formed carbon sticking to an engine's induction system. It actually has the power to start removing deposits which have already accumulated.

So you can rely on the fact that it's never too late to start cleaning your engine.

Shell Advanced. One of the few things in life that's as reliable as a Volkswagen.

YOU CAN TELL WHEN IT'S SHELL.

An air of expectancy descended over prizegiving as Ernest MacMillen took the microphone. 'The rally's back on the right track. We all thoroughly enjoyed it, and it's one of the finest rallies in the world,' he declared, beaming with pleasure and defying anyone to argue.

No one did. Instead, the ceiling of the Slieve Donard Hotel's ballroom echoed with roars of approval, only in part because MacMillen was preaching to the converted. At the ripe old age of 63, he is entitled to a little respect, and not merely because he has contested events as diverse as the Mille Miglia and the Coppa Dolomiti, quite apart from 29 Circuits of Ireland: far from being an old fogey itching to suggest that it was all much better in the days of

TR2s and autotests, he still drives a modern car — a Suzuki Swift — and had done so quickly enough to win his class by ten minutes and beat some of the 1600 cars to boot. Granted that the prizewinners in the 1992 Circuit of Ireland were naturally disposed to agree with his every word, it was in any case the occasion to celebrate the best aspects of Irish rallying, for the re-launched, rejuvenated Circuit had embodied many of them.

There was no need to draw the route on a map to appreciate the scale of the undertaking, nor to comprehend the 24 finishers' pride at having survived the four-day event at all. There was a sense of achievement in having finished that one gets on few modern rallies — a feeling that has been conspicuously absent

from recent Circuits. Since the fiery deaths of Henri Toivonen and Sergio Cresto barely a month after the 1986 Circuit, the event had been pinned down by FISA's kneejerk decision to slash the length of all international rallies. To some — the 1000 Lakes for example — this had made little enough difference to length or character, but the UAC's event had suffered more than any other in the world. Quite apart from the indignity of being cut from 605 to 190 miles of stages in line with its lowly European Championship status, it was saddled with a name which it could not possibly live up to: a compact series of loops round Belfast would be no circuit, and would merely duplicate the Ulster Rally; a true circuit would have involved an unacceptably high proportion of road

mileage, and the compromise meandering down the eastern side of Ireland was derisively known as the 'Semi-Circuit' or the 'Straight Line of Ireland'. Forced into a corner by the loss of British Championship status for 1992, the Ulster Automobile Club did a very brave thing. It withdrew from the European Championship, voluntarily reduced its event to national status and, with RAC approval, planned a 1100-mile, 375-stage mile route that spanned the whole of Ireland, without a repeated stage. There would be no practising and no pace notes, and the organisers adopted the slogan, 'The way it used to be'.

There were plenty of detractors — one trenchant observer of Irish rallying said, 'It won't be a good rally, because it's being organised by

56

David Williams considers the changing fortunes of the Circuit of Ireland

A DAY ON THE STAGE A NIGHT IN THE BAR

Photography: Brian McLean

the same bunch of eejits as last year' — but the result, flawed or otherwise, was like a freeing of the spirit. The idea of making a rally longer and tougher, of introducing a near non-stop 24-hour run through the night into the sanitised, identikit world of 1990s rallying captured the imagination whether one knew the minute details of FISA regulations and pace note making or just liked watching cars being driven quickly. Spectators thronged the route in their thousands. It was hard to find a corner without a crowd during the Sunday Run, and even in the small hours of the morning, in teeming rain, the hillside above Lough Nafooey was clustered with people, although they didn't fill every nook and cranny in quite the same way as they had crammed the bars of Waterford the

night before. A wistful Colin McRae, the 1991 winner, came over to watch and enjoy the atmosphere. Professional drivers are not allowed to jump in an RS2000 to go and do a rally they like the look of on a spare weekend, but one sensed that McRae would gladly have swapped places with his uncle, Hugh Steel, who teamed up with Ian Porter in his well-used Escort. True, it needed emergency resuscitation between every stage and a new cylinder head by the time it reached Waterford. Other crews were surprised to find that it had got that far and reckoned its driver had no grasp of the word 'terminal', while Porter had the look of a man who had discovered a new dimension to staying calm under stress. Yet the Scottish-Ulster combination took part, and allowing the

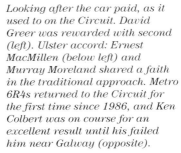

Looking after the car paid, as it used to on the Circuit. David Greer was rewarded with second (left). Ulster accord: Ernest MacMillen (below left) and Murray Moreland shared a faith in the traditional approach. Metro 6R4s returned to the Circuit for the first time since 1986, and Ken Colbert was on course for an excellent result until his failed him near Galway (opposite).

clubman to have a go in out of date machinery had been an important facet of the 'new' Circuit. The engine finally gave up the ghost during the Sunday Run. Spectator interest was mirrored in the press. Sports editors the length and breadth of Ireland woke up to the fact that Easter was once more associated with motor sport; apart from anything else, there was a much better chance that the rally might be venturing into their catchment area once more. Without a works car in sight, the event was capable of generating an hour of coverage on television, north and south of the border.

The route more than lived up to its promise. The longest tarmac rally in the world, and comfortably the longest rally of any kind in the British Isles, it included classic Irish stages that have never fallen into disuse, such as Hamilton's Folly and Sally Gap, and revived others that have lain fallow since 1986 at least — Cooneen Hill, Partry Mountains and Sheeffry Mountains amongst them. It returned to some of the most challenging roads in Ireland and, by spanning such a wide area, competitors took on a varied array of stages that they would normally find only on a World Championship rally, if anywhere. None of the stages were rough, but the run through the night tore the heart out of the entry nevertheless: no fewer than eight of the top 20 runners at the Galway supper halt had fallen by the wayside before the finish in Newcastle the following afternoon. A Galway resident's promise that Partry and Sheeffry Mountains were 'Indian country' had been no idle threat, and the UAC's honour had been satisfied: this was a vintage Circuit.

Even daybreak on the final morning didn't offer the survivors much respite: a pause in Enniskillen was followed by four stages in quick succession, looping through the muddy,

awkward lanes of Fermanagh and Tyrone. The modern works car would take this in its stride (although the factory teams might have been alarmed to find out how little service time was available in places, there being precious few six- or eight-minute road sections left at World Championship level), but to the privateers at whom the rally was primarily aimed, finishing was an altogether harder task: tell your local motor club audience about this rally and it was bound to be impressed. The demise of the four-wheel drive cars gave new weight to the old adage that winning the Circuit required a large measure of mechanical sympathy as well as raw speed. On leaving Waterford, Frank Meagher looked no more likely to win than the last Irish winner, Billy Coleman, had in 1984.

As in the old days, everyone lent a hand. Clerks of the Course of Irish national rallies were to be found marshalling from coast to coast. Bertie Fisher himself journeyed to Waterford after retiring the Tough-MAC Subaru, and was to be found manning a passage control and dispensing Easter eggs during the Sunday Run!

In the teeth of a vicious recession, widespread hostility to the format in Ireland, and the English competitors' reluctance to travel to Ulster, the UAC increased the entry by nearly a third, bolstering it to a respectable 70 odd cars thanks to the historic contingent. In 1992, it is hard to imagine any national rally of this length doing much better than that, since there was no shortage of potential competitors who couldn't raise the money to run a quick car on a rally as long as a World Championship qualifier. The dilemma was that they would probably not have considered it in the first place if it had retained its 1987-91 format. It was the worst entry in terms of quality since 1973, without a single leading

name from England, Scotland or Wales, but the fact that it was a substantial increase on the 1991 entry, despite the lack of professional teams who would have attended a British Championship round as a matter of course, was a fillip for the organisers. If they didn't hit the jackpot, they had at least been rewarded for their gamble. It is open to debate whether many potential winners were missing in any case, for of the top British drivers who can lay their hands on a winning car currently, only Colin McRae was absent.

Those who did enter the rally had been attracted by its length and the variety of stages certainly, but by an event that was different in character to any other. Opting for a secret route was controversial, but made the Circuit stand out compared to any other rally in Ireland, let alone to asphalt rallies elsewhere. Drivers found it hard to adapt to the lower level of commitment required by not knowing what lurked round the next bend, while co-drivers resorted to the neglected skills of map reading, not necessarily just on the stages. Some managed this with more success than others. There were plenty of crews getting lost on road sections, and even the winners, Meagher and Micheal Maher, managed to pick up 90 seconds in road penalties

when they got lost in Tipperary — the driver's home county, of all places — and arrived at a time control nine minutes late. A broken tripmeter had led them astray in the first place; from an early stage, there was no shortage of tetchy co-drivers at the first hint of trouble from the distance recorder.

With a long route, a run through the night, and Escorts and Chevettes in the top ten, it would have been hard not to succumb to a warm glow of nostalgia for Irish rallying 'the way it used to be', particularly as the time schedule had carefully built in enough time to consider the finer points in the bar and still be alert and ready for action the following morning. Unfortunately, the other aspect of 'the way it used to be' was equally prominent: accusations of cheating were two a penny, certain top competitors surreptitiously put the knife into their rivals and, inevitably, there was a good deal more in the way of accusation than proof.

It was most unfortunate that the Bill Connolly affair soon dragged in solicitors, never mind an RIAC tribunal, but the UAC deserves only a limited amount of sympathy. Its desire to eliminate the cost and time spent practising such a large, ambitious route was commendable, but

by banning any form of pace notes, it made a rod for its own back. Weeks before entries had even opened, there were rumours that certain competitors had been out practising, and the pundits accurately predicted what would happen. For a man like MacMillen or Roger Kennedy (who contests the Circuit once every 10 years or so, and finished a commendable eighth overall and won his class in a 205), it was pure enjoyment. Yet Austin McHale was against the new format from the start, contested the rally with some reluctance, and was at the centre of controversy thanks to repeated pace note searches and an extraordinary incident when pace notes were apparently found in the Toyota at a service point, in the absence of the crew. McHale insisted that they had been planted. There wasn't a shred of evidence to prove the notes had been used on a stage, and he was therefore allowed to continue.

The atmosphere was charged to a pitch where it no longer mattered whether one was in favour of notes. One leading co-driver even insisted that officials searched his car after an overnight *Parc Ferme* before he would get into it. Call it paranoia, but it exemplified the sourness that tainted the battle for the lead and the final result.

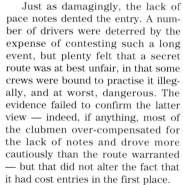

Just as damagingly, the lack of pace notes dented the entry. A number of drivers were deterred by the expense of contesting such a long event, but plenty felt that a secret route was at best unfair, in that some crews were bound to practise it illegally, and at worst, dangerous. The evidence failed to confirm the latter view — indeed, if anything, most of the clubmen over-compensated for the lack of notes and drove more cautiously than the route warranted — but that did not alter the fact that it had cost entries in the first place.

As an illustration of how attitudes have changed since pace notes became universal in Ireland, there were some who argued that a secret route negated driving skills. A glance at the leaderboard at the halfway mark suggested that the animals were going in two by two: the quickest Group A cars naturally led the way, but they were followed by the best two-litre cars — the Escorts and Mantas — the quickest Group N

cars, the two-litre Group N cars, and so on. According to the theory, everyone was tackling blind corners at pretty much the same speed, and the results were being sorted out on brake horsepower. Driving on the maps might have appealed to the handful of British road rally crews, some of whom had travelled from as far away as Kent and Surrey, but it failed to inspire the mass of Irish clubmen. Ironically, the concept had been greeted with real warmth but precious few entries from the eastern side of the Irish Sea (McRae was there, but Malcolm Wilson welcomed the idea with open arms and spoke fondly of his first forays to the Circuit in the 1970s), and a good deal of suspicion from the people expected to make up the backbone of the entry.

The pace note issue had been debated thoroughly and resolved, for better or worse, after an open meeting the previous July, in which Bertie Fisher had argued strongly for secret

stages. The outline of the route had been set at the same time, and yet an opportunity was missed. The Circuit became the longest tarmac rally in the world by default, following the cancellation of the last four stages of the Tour of Corsica in the aftermath of the disaster at the Furiani football stadium. The UAC had never been aware that its rally might even be in the running for such an accolade, let alone that the addition of one or two more stages could have given it the title without dispute, and perhaps a device to drum up extra entries or sponsorship. People like absolutes, and all sports thrive on this kind of statistic. It was rather as though the owner of a cheap reproduction had discovered that it was an old master after all.

For all the arguments, the 1992 Circuit was a step forward. It generated so much passion because it is an Irish institution, and there tend to be decided ideas about how to treat institutions. Whatever the manner of

its revival, the UAC had rescued the Circuit from obscurity, and in doing so, it had raised some intriguing questions. There are precious few rallies now that cannot exist quite happily under a sponsor's name or a convenient national title, which conveys no more about the event than the title of a Grand Prix; sometimes, there is little else to say about it. In contrast, the Circuit of Ireland had once more become a rally that lived up to its name. The fact that it had to lower its status to do so calls into question the worth and the intention behind FISA's wooden restrictions on the length of major rallies. If the law permits a mere national rally to set a tougher challenge than a good many World Championship events, then the law is an ass. As a sport, rallying has thrived on the individual, not on formulae: the Monte Carlo Rally and the Paris-Dakar came to prominence because they caught the imagination and combined a sense of adventure with a challenge to the

car, not because they complied with some arbitrary set of rules hurriedly drafted by the old men in blazers in Paris.

It can be argued that the best years of the Paris-Dakar Rally were the days when works teams were largely absent. The Circuit started attracting works cars in the 1930s, and the UAC likes the idea of getting the big names back, which will never be easy when it clashes with the Safari, yet one wonders if it is even desirable. Perhaps the TT motor cycle races point the way forward. The fact that the Circuit has endured since 1931 suggests that it has a little of the magic that a great rally needs, and that the organisers would do better to concentrate on preserving that and letting the entries look after themselves. Sixty years after the first Circuit of Ireland, rallying sorely needs this anachronism.

THE PERFORMANCE.

This Calibra has just moved up a gear.

It's the new Turbo 4x4 version with a six speed gearbox unique in its class.

The extra cog is no gimmick. Without it you simply wouldn't appreciate the car's finely-tuned muscle-power.

Balancing the increased performance is a safer, more refined turbo system.

It cuts in swiftly at unusually low engine speeds, giving an immediate response when you want to overtake a slow-moving vehicle.

For the interior, a spot of power-dressing seemed appropriate.

All-black, all-leather heated seats. All matching the door panels, gear knob and steering wheel.

What isn't new about the seats is the now legendary amount of rear legroom.

As any car magazine will tell you, no other car of its type can match the Calibra for accommodation.

(One summed it up rather nicely, claiming it actually defies coupé law.*)

THE BEST SEATS.

Standard features include power steering, trip computer, CAT, deadlocking and alarm.

And a slinky, sophisticated SC804 radio cassette with six speakers. The system has an anti-theft removable display and the latest RDS EON cut-in travel information.

Finally, before launching our flagship, we took another long hard look at the Calibra's unmistakable, sleek styling.

Not that we wanted to change anything, of course. We just like looking at it.

For more details of either the Turbo, or the 8 or 16-valve version, telephone 0800 444200.

THE CALIBRA TURBO 4x4.

 **VAUXHALL**

Once driven, forever smitten.

Just one of the benefits of early retirement

The champion's boat. Unbeatable in every way. Speed. Style. Sophistication. Sunseeker International, three ranges of craft covering motoryachts, sportscruisers and high-performance offshore powerboats.

Sunseeker International (Boats) Limited
27 - 31 West Quay Road, Poole, Dorset BH15 1HX England
Telephone: 0202 675071 Facsimile: 0202 681646

WORLD CHAMPIONSHIP RALLIES

1992

MONTE CARLO RALLY

Didier Auriol denied that it had been an easy win, but without the vehemence drivers usually display on these occasions. It was impossible to deny that his second Monte Carlo victory had at least looked easy. As usual, the stages had been long and hard, the surface altering constantly — dry tarmac interspersed with water, ice and salt. Of course it hadn't been easy, but only the tyre fiasco on Sisteron-Thoard had prevented the Frenchman from running away from the opposition; Toyota and Ford were merely well beaten rather than humiliated.

For once, the winning driver was all but overshadowed by the car. It is taken as read that Auriol is exceptionally quick on tarmac and that the Delta has been an effective tarmac car ever since the Integrale replaced the HF 4x4. Rival teams had been braced for a further improvement from the latest variant — it even looked reminiscent of a Group B Delta S4 — but they were left open-mouthed at the Integrales' pace none the less. The tyres were the same, the engines hamstrung by the same turbo restrictors as everyone else's, yet the longer travel suspension had turned the nervous, twitchy Delta into a thoroughbred. It wasn't merely Auriol after all: Juha Kankkunen was driving with the assurance of a man born and bred in the Alps and, while Armin Schwarz and François Delecour could occasionally disrupt the Lancia monopoly at the top of the timesheets, they were offering a gesture of defiance rather than a serious challenge. Auriol admitted that he saw no need to take risks, saving the full-blooded attack for the dry stages. When Delecour blew his Cosworth's turbo on SS11, presenting the Lancia man with a lead of more than a minute over Sainz, the Jolly Club had as good as won the event, with a day and a night still to run.

The relaxed atmosphere at Sisteron had disappeared entirely at the overnight halt in Digne. Backed against the wall of the garage, the Michelin men could only shrug as an enraged Bortoletto fired questions at them. The mere suggestion of anything other than slicks had been scoffed at in Sisteron, but the four kilometres of snow through the woods on the Col de la Fontbelle had defeated all three of the Martini Racing cars, and now Sainz was in the lead. Auriol had not only lost two minutes, but wrecked the clutch. It was an uncharacteristic tactical error on the Italians' part, but one that the effectiveness of the new Delta minimised. Well aware that the latest Celica was in dire handling trouble on asphalt and that the new engine bordered on the lethargic, Sainz and Toyota sensed that trying to hold off Auriol was fruitless, and that it was only a matter of time before he regained the lead that was rightfully his.

The mix of dry conditions and roads Auriol knows intimately from his French Championship days provided the ideal platform for reeling in Sainz. Four fastest times in six stages pruned the Spaniard's lead to a paltry three seconds on returning to Monaco. Sainz's quickest time on the first run at the Col de Turini the following night forestalled the inevitable for a single stage, but then he was well aware that Auriol could pick his moment. An astounding new record on the Col de la Couillole put the matter beyond doubt and, while Delecour believed that he might have won but for persistent turbo problems, the Toyota men were under no illusions. Delecour's forlorn charge couldn't quite overhaul a contented Kankkunen and that, just as much as Auriol's victory, demonstrated Lancia's genius for extracting the utmost from a new car.

MONTE CARLO RALLY

Try as he might, François Delecour could only beat the Lancias occasionally on stages he knows like the back of his hand (above). A scattering of snow on the northernmost stages failed to loosen the Integrales' grip on the event (top left). Tommi Mäkinen did his reputation a power of good in the Nissan (centre), while Didier Auriol delivered the sort of confident performance that his rivals had feared.

Photo LAT

Photo Pascal Huit

SWEDISH RALLY

It was hard not to feel a trace of sympathy for Mats Jonsson. The laconic man from Forshaga, just north of Karlstad, has always been content to let his results speak for him. Overlooked and underrated, he has spent years being taken for granted by Opel and Toyota: good results that might have led to promotion for another driver were treated as no more than par for the course for Mats. The Swedish should have been his moment of glory, then — recognition at last that he bore comparison with the likes of Carlsson, Blomqvist and Waldegård. Instead, the press were making a fuss of the man he'd beaten fair and square into second place, Colin McRae.

The young Scot had upset pre-event predictions in no uncertain terms. At the age of 23, he had matched the best result ever recorded by a non-Nordic driver, quite apart from easily bettering anything achieved by a British driver in Sweden, and a Subaru competitor anywhere. That was the real cause of the fuss though. Second place was a remarkable feat, but the style had been as important as the result. It had not been won by driving a markedly superior car, nor by keeping going as others fell by the wayside, but on raw speed, and under some pressure purely to finish after his team-mate, Ari Vatanen, destroyed his Legacy on the first stage.

Third at the end of the first leg, the number seven Subaru speeded up as the route headed north-east to Falun and the snow deepened. Despite a gearbox that jumped out of gear, McRae was promoted to second when Sebastian Lindholm's Sierra broke a front drive-shaft and the centre differential on successive stages, and the fact that Stig Blomqvist and Markku Alén were breathing down his neck didn't bother him in the slightest. Blomqvist had had two punctures in the Nissan, but they did not account for the deficit; experimenting with transmission microchips and different makes of tyre failed to tip the balance, and he freely paid the Scot an immense compliment: in his view, McRae is the best British rally driver of all, better even than Paddy Hopkirk. Alén, meanwhile, complained bitterly of a lethargic engine, eventually forcing Toyota Sweden to ring TTE headquarters for advice.

At that point, McRae had put up stout opposition to Jonsson, without looking like anything more than a worthy runner-up. In the space of two stages, all that changed, for his performance as darkness fell raised the tantalising, nay extraordinary possibility that he might even win. Driving snow coincided with dusk, and McRae seized his opportunity. He cropped 29 seconds from the fleeing Toyota, halving Jonsson's lead in the process. It was a measured assault rather than a rush of blood to the head, since he backed off on the shorter stage before the overnight halt, allowing a surprised Jonsson to regain a second. Not known for advertising his feelings, the leader smiled and expressed his admiration.

Victory was too much to hope for: probing at the start of the next leg revealed that Jonsson is wide awake in the morning, and McRae's hopes dwindled on the longest stage of the rally, Likenäs. The Legacy lost power when the air intake was blocked by snow and, although he shared second fastest with Blomqvist, he had lost another six seconds when he had hoped to tear a chunk out of Jonsson's lead. Since the remaining stages were very much on the leader's territory, there wasn't much hope of pulling off another ambush as he had the night before.

As the finish neared, even the imperturbable Jonsson admitted to an attack of nerves, despite a Subaru puncture that removed the last chance of a shock victory. McRae was pleased, naturally, and yet a finely judged, points-scoring finish hadn't been quite what he wanted, no matter how sensational the result; leading the 1991 RAC Rally had been more of a thrill.

Photo Pascal Huit

Some felt that Colin McRae was driving too sideways, but there wasn't much else to criticise in the Scot's handling of the Subaru (top left). If Mats Jonsson was surprised he kept it to himself. However, it was no secret that he had to push the Toyota to the limit to secure his first home victory.

Snow gives the driver room to experiment. Lasse Lampi steers a conservative line in his Mitsubishi (left), whereas Markku Alén explores the outer limits of the Celica GT4 (below). Even Stig Blomqvist had to give best to McRae, although he still gave the Sunny its best World Championship result to that point.

Photo LAT

Marlboro

Portugal has been the setting for some of Miki Biasion's finest performances. Second place in the Mobil Cosworth ranked with any of his victories for Lancia. Andrea Aghini (right) was one of the sensations of the event on his first attempt at the rally, leading the first leg.

RALLY OF PORTUGAL

Juha Kankkunen was enjoying the joke. Smiling contentedly, he promised journalist after journalist that next year he would contest tarmac rallies only. It was sunny and springlike — the sort of day to make one glad to be alive — and the Finn was in a mood to appreciate these things. At the time, at the re-group in Gois, he was only fourth, but he knew that the situation could only improve when the rally turned to gravel the next morning. Andrea Aghini would almost certainly be less competitive on the loose, and who was to say that the runaway leader, François Delecour, could maintain the same pace in view of Ford's legion of mechanical failings over the preceding months? Moreover, Kankkunen's most formidable rival, Didier Auriol, was already on his way home after the third Martini Lancia had run a bearing.

Indeed, Kankkunen was relaxed throughout. He completed the first tarmac leg in fourth place and, as everyone had expected, remorselessly took the lead the following day. By the time the Jolly Club mechanics had adjusted the front anti-roll bar to cure the understeer, he had transformed an overnight deficit of 1 minute 14 seconds to Delecour into a 30- second lead over Aghini. The handling problem hadn't been readily apparent to an outsider, and nor were any of the others: clobbering a stone deranged the rear suspension, and a flying rock sliced through a brake pipe a stage later, midway through the third leg. Kankkunen could afford to make light of these upsets to a pleasant routine, in which he set fastest stage times more or less at will and smoothly pulled away from the dogfight for second between Carlos Sainz and Miki Biasion. The 1991 champion variously described his driving as 'normal', or even, as the finish neared, as 'road section'. As victories go, it was not only far from taxing, but achieved on an event that has never favoured him in the past. The novelty value of winning a rally with so much tarmac so easily was irresistible.

If Kankkunen's performance was assured, Biasion's was remarkable. Optimism had been a poor substitute for confidence for months at Ford and, while Delecour's command of the tarmac was good for morale, no one was placing money on the Sierras for the gravel. When Delecour's sump split on the first gravel stage and Biasion instantly ran into steering trouble, Boreham's worst fears looked on the point of being realised. By the end of the second leg, a determined Sainz had sliced Biasion's 1 minute 20 second cushion to barely 20 seconds, swiftly making amends for the Celica's dreadful performance on tarmac. Swapping places looked to be only a matter of time.

Biasion handled the situation with the coolness of a surgeon. While Sainz re-doubled his efforts, the placid Italian turned the rally into an extended test session, methodically assessing different dampers on one stage, a new differential on the next. To the Spaniard's intense frustration, the Ford man re-took second, having dropped to third for only one stage, and proceeded to amass a clear lead. To Sainz, the Cosworth's speed was as baffling as its reliability, granted that spares were thrown at the Mobil machine like confetti; even Arganil found no chink in the Sierra's armour. When a blown Toyota turbo finally put the issue beyond doubt, Sainz had already resigned himself to a sullen third. Ford could hardly claim to have troubled Lancia for any length of time, but it had bettered the Cosworth 4x4's World Championship record, and Biasion had silenced the doubters. Whereas Ford could draw satisfaction from a job well done, Toyota had to swallow the loss of crucial championship points and, to rub salt into the wound, to quell a damaging row between Sainz and Armin Schwarz when the latter crashed in his team-mate's dust, having caught the Spaniard when his turbo failed. While the Jolly Club celebrated, Toyota's disappointment was suffused with bitterness.

RALLY OF PORTUGAL

Toyota had plenty of food for thought, as a pensive Ove Andersson conceded. Carlos Sainz's best efforts (above) weren't enough to beat Ford, never mind Lancia. TTE had deployed all its resources as well (left). Ford had problems of its own, François Delecour retiring with a ruptured sump (centre left). Juha Kankkunen coolly waited for the gravel before giving the new Integrale its head (overleaf).

SAFARI RALLY

Call it luck, call it judgement, but the gambler's instinct stood Carlos Sainz in good stead. Enviously, the Lancia drivers reckoned the Spaniard had been lucky, thrashing the Toyota over the roughest Kenyan tracks almost as though this was a European sprint, yet somehow never breaking anything at a time or a place where it would cost him dearly. Any Safari winner is going to need a slice of good fortune but, so far as the Martini men were concerned, Sainz had developed an unusual knack of throwing double sixes.

Yet the winner had driven to a plan. Trusting the new Celica implicitly on its first Safari, he had decided to swallow his distaste for rallying in Africa and drive near enough flat out from the start. Luis Moya gave a clear signal of their intent by stating that there was no particular merit just in finishing a 1990s Safari, and that speed would tell. Sure enough, only one of the top 12 starters retired, and three of the first six finishers rolled — the tracking helicopters weren't for effect, but a reflection of the drivers' commitment. Sainz had spotted the trend and driven accordingly.

The first three legs were not expected to decide much provided the car held together, and the important thing was to be first on the road for the journey northwards to Eldoret and the daunting sections close to the Ugandan border. Nevertheless, things went according to plan and, by running first over the Mau Escarpment in still, dust-free air before dawn, Sainz doubled a slender seven-minute lead between Nairobi and Eldoret.

The Eldoret halt preceded the toughest leg of all — more than 1000 kilometres across northern Kenya, including an ascent of the Marich Pass — and yet the earlier belief that the Toyota must surely break had given way to a sense of resignation at Lancia. Sainz looked almost certain to get away with it, but luck had been combined with most of the aces. There was little to choose between the Integrale and the Celica on performance and the newer design held the upper hand, because it could be repaired more quickly. Faced with an unexpected rear shock absorber problem, the Jolly Club could only reduce suspension travel, while the drivers admitted that they had slowed down a fraction. Having made up two minutes on the opening sections after Eldoret, they dropped three making a precautionary shock absorber change at the top of the Marich Pass. When Sainz's turbo wastegate jammed, he continued to the re-group at Lake Baringo at barely diminished speed. TTE picked its moment, and coolly replaced the turbo, two struts and a driveshaft in 10 minutes, without penalty. Claudio Bortoletto shrugged and explained that the Celica was like a kit, whereas the Delta was not. In consequence, his drivers could hardly expect to take such liberties, while Martin Christie suggested that everyone might as well go back to Nairobi there and then.

Having wriggled out of the turbo crisis, Sainz replaced a leaking rear differential with a corresponding lack of drama. Then his hold on the lead slackened with the finish almost in sight. While the Jolly Club ordered the unfortunate Jorge Recalde to drop behind Juha Kankkunen, the rumours that the lead Celica's centre differential was on its last legs suddenly became fact. The transmission lasted as far as the tarmac, but it could not be counted upon to cope with a gentle run on a main road to Nairobi, and it was torn out and replaced the moment the car emerged from the Aberdare Hills. That scarcely tarnished a magnificent performance. For his part, Sainz pointed out that he was usually slower than Recalde on the roughest sections, and there was no need to say that he was the only works Toyota driver not to park his car on its roof at some point. One step closer to becoming the first driver to win every round of the World Championship and with a share of the series lead, the Spaniard was even prepared to contemplate returning to the Safari in future.

Juha Kankkunen (above) is keenly aware that the Safari has turned into a sprint, rolling to prove it on his way to second. Martin Christie (left) admires Juha Piironen's novel sun hat.

SAFARI RALLY

Dust is a constant hazard, especially after an accident. Mikael Ericsson found out the hard way (below left), requiring eye drops (below right) as he hauled his battered Celica to the finish through a haze of marram. Time control procedure still counts for something on the Safari: Juha Kankkunen (right) nonchalantly accepts his time card. Björn Waldegård was the only Lancia driver not to finish, his Delta destroyed in a flash fire. For the factory teams, the Safari has turned into a high speed race between car and helicopter (overleaf), Carlos Sainz holding the lead in this instance.

A face is worth a thousand words: François Delecour didn't need to spell out that keeping abreast of any of the Lancias required a superhuman effort. The Jolly Club men experienced contrasting fortunes, Didier Auriol winning by a handsome margin (top), while Andrea Aghini took to the island roads like a duck to water (centre). However, poor Philippe Bugalski (far right) required medical attention for an injured leg.

TOUR OF CORSICA

Didier Auriol seemed to be driven by something more than a healthy desire to succeed. Even when his lead had climbed beyond the minute mark and it was glaringly obvious that no one could sustain a genuine challenge, he hardly slackened his pace. It was only in part a sign of the faith he put in the Integrale. A passing mention of François Delecour's assessment of the position offered a clue to Auriol's tactics: when told that the Ford man reckoned that the difference between first and second was the factory Sierra's 30 bhp power deficit — a public hint that Ford had carried out precious little tarmac development in the previous 12 months — the leader snapped, 'He can think what he likes.'

As much as anything, Auriol was keen to silence Delecour. He conceded just one stage to his loquacious rival during the first leg but, while the northerner succeeded in matching him occasionally as the route wound across the island and northwards to Bastia, he didn't beat the flying Lancia again until the middle of the third leg, by which time even Auriol should surely have been satisfied with his lead. While Delecour was quite prepared to maintain the assault rather than accept the obvious, Auriol was just as keen to eliminate all traces of doubt. Having let the Ford driver claw back a paltry four seconds in two stages, he proceeded to gain another 12 on the remaining three prior to the overnight break in Calvi. This was a battle of wills as much as a battle for seconds and, if Auriol had his way, there would be no excuse for sympathetic articles in the French press implying that Delecour was the moral victor. Of course Auriol and Lancia alike needed the World Championship points, but there was pride at stake as much as points; this was the most dominant of Auriol's four wins in Corsica.

Even if Delecour had wanted to cruise to second, he didn't have the option until the latter stages of the third leg for, at the halfway point, a moment's relaxation would have demoted him from second to fourth: the Jolly Club juniors were exploiting their Deltas to full effect. Their performance rather than Auriol's demonstrated the bulbous Integrale's true superiority: while a driver of Auriol's calibre might be expected to shatter the opposition, few had imagined that the youngsters might outdistance the Pirelli-blighted Celicas, let alone worry Delecour like hounds after a stag. In the event, Andrea Aghini's startling times went largely to waste thanks to a messy excursion on Linguizzetta, soon after the start of the third leg, which even destroyed one of his Michelin ATS tyres. Corsica is not the kind of place where one leaves the road twice and gets away with it, and the second accident ensured that he only just beat an off-key Miki Biasion for sixth.

An ill-fitting seat, of all things, put Philippe Bugalski in such pain that he was obliged to settle for third. With extra cushioning, and a pain-killing injection in his leg, he was more than capable of fending off Sainz during the final leg, but the failure to overhaul Delecour may have cost him his place at Lancia. When its car is so dominant, the management feels able to ask a little more of its drivers.

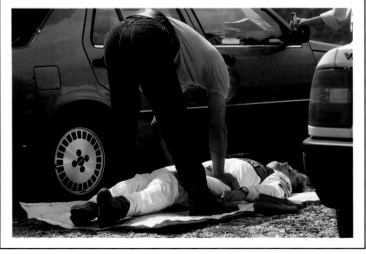

Photo Pascal Huit

ACROPOLIS RALLY

Claudio Bortoletto was in a generous mood, offering lunch to any journalist who'd made it down the long, rough gravel road section to the service point at Perivoli. It was cooler than it had been for a week at least and perfect weather for eating outside, but in practice the rally had long since turned into a picnic for the Jolly Club. By the time Didier Auriol had completed the first leg from Athens to Delphi — a five-stage loosener that wasn't expected to do much more than sort out seeding anomalies — he had as good as won. Indeed, the service area prior to the first overnight halt was the last point where questioning the effervescent Frenchman was a worthwhile exercise. It wasn't that he was unco-operative — far from it — merely that he felt able to ease off as early as stage seven, and there wasn't a great deal to talk about thereafter. His first all-gravel victory at World Championship level was singularly lacking in blood, sweat and tears.

Speculation that Lancia might actually be defeated in Greece never had been much more than wishful thinking, and the first leg soon injected a dose of reality: Auriol was presented with the kind of lead that, barring acts of God, would see him home to his third World Championship win in as many finishes. Carlos Sainz chose to retain the older suspension settings rather than the latest refinements preferred by his Toyota teammates, and completed the day a disappointing seventh, behind his colleagues, Miki Biasion, and the cheeky Colin McRae, never mind Auriol. His times the following day were much better, but still suggested that the suspension experiment had removed an element of doubt rather than robbed him of victory, even before his spectacular roll on Tarzan.

Realistically, Auriol had had more to fear from his Martini Racing companion, Juha Kankkunen. Characteristically, the Finn had started cautiously, easing the Delta into a trouble-free fifth after five stages. He was within striking distance of the leader, well placed on the road — neither sweeping the marbles for his rivals nor dodging too many boulders — and the car was in good fettle for the hard stages to come. True, the Integrale had cut out as he completed the fifth test, but nothing untoward could be found at the service point until he tried to re-start. Within sight of the time control, the Delta refused to fire. He was two minutes late by the time Juha Piironen got a time, and that earned them a minute's road penalty, demoting them to ninth. Kankkunen was honest enough to admit that he wasn't confident of beating Auriol in this form anyway, but the electronic failure had ensured that he couldn't even put his colleague under pressure.

Biasion confirmed Ford's revival by taking an accomplished third, holding second for much of the rally and fending off a determined challenge from an impressive McRae and the surviving Subaru. On his first Acropolis, the British Champion recorded more fastest times than anyone other than the Lancia drivers, and his pace on repeated stages gave a clear hint of what he will achieve when his experience matches his ability. Yet even his performance was overshadowed somewhat by the magnitude of the disaster that overtook TTE. Failing to finish best non-Lancia had become a fact of life for Köln in recent months, but hardly preparation for a massacre of 1989 proportions. This time, the Celicas were certainly no slower than the rest of the horde pursuing the Integrales, but notably less reliable, both Armin Schwarz and Markku Alén suffering wastegate problems, while Schwarz had to cope with a bout of transmission trouble during the second leg into the bargain. It wasn't mechanical fragility that obliged Toyota to rely on the Greek privateer, 'Jigger', for its World Championship points, however. All three of TTE's star performers contrived to roll and, as if having two scrap cars wasn't bad enough, there were photographs in magazines all over the world to prove it. Aside from the occasional support helicopter, there was nothing to disturb the Lancia picnic.

Didier Auriol was uncatchable in the Delta (top), Colin McRae unquenchable (right) in the Legacy, whereas François Delecour would have been quite content if the marshals had just left the car alone. Armin Schwarz had had more than enough trouble before he rolled the Celica.

ACROPOLIS RALLY

Carlos Sainz's roll (left) was only the start of a disastrous week for TTE. Jorge Recalde (below) was a good deal more circumspect, while Grégoire de Mevius drove brilliantly to win Group N for Nissan (below left). A large rock all but destroyed the Galant of one of the most formidable Acropolis performers, Kenneth Eriksson.

RALLY OF NEW ZEALAND

The long, remorselessly twisty Motu stages are two of the most demanding in the World Championship calendar, and their remoteness ensures that practice is usually restricted to a maximum of two runs through each. Inspired by Didier Auriol's 1991 records and a mere 43-second deficit to the leader, Carlos Sainz, Piero Liatti planned his attack for the high ridges above the vast Urutawa Forest. Unseasonably clear skies had contributed to patches of black ice on Motu One, and Piero was disappointed to drop 11 seconds to Sainz, particularly as Carlos himself was some 33 seconds off Auriol's time the previous year.

Liatti's hopes of an unlikely victory vanished for good on the next, however, when he slid wide on a slippery corner and clouted a rock hard with the ART Delta's left rear wheel. Whilst attempting to crab the remaining seven miles on a broken suspension arm and a twisted shock absorber, he went off again. Wheel tracks betrayed Sainz, revealing he had also left the road. Nevertheless, he had miraculously avoided the boulders that crippled his Italian challenger and, while the Spaniard charged into an unassailable lead, Liatti was left to struggle with a car that no longer handled like a 'Super Delta'.

Ultimately, Sainz made certain of the first big special stage win for the Celica 4WD and his personal New Zealand hat-trick but, after being harried mercilessly by the three-car Subaru team and then by Liatti, it was beyond doubt his least convincing Kiwi success. No wonder the local press called him 'the sad-eyed Spaniard'. Victory and the World Championship lead were of course a morale boost, yet only up to a point. Sainz's stage times made it plain that only some of the latest Toyota's suspension and transmission problems had been eliminated and, if Liatti's turn of speed in his private Integrale was any guide, the absence of the Martini squad was a godsend.

It took two-thirds of the event to persuade the Toyota to work. Even then, Sainz was in no danger of forgetting an early battering from the swift but unreliable Subarus, which had strengthened his resolve to carry out his own testing until the troublesome Celica 4WD displayed some of the poise round corners for which its predecessor was renowned.

Although Liatti's challenge lasted longest, the fiercest came from Subaru. With some justification, David Richards later described it as 'a win there for the taking', yet an event that had promised so much turned into an unprecedented disaster after just 15 of the 38 stages. By then, all the factory Subarus were out, all three sidelined by piston failures. Colin McRae had lasted only the opening five stages, and even those had been fraught with problems. 'Possum' Bourne had excited the locals by not only set-

Photo Linear

ting fastest time on the first stage, but maintaining his challenge for the lead until SS9. Ari Vatanen took over on the next stage but, as ominous puffs of blue smoke began to emerge from the exhaust, he knew the agony would be brief. A puncture cost him the lead after he had held it for three stages, but that was insignificant when the oil pressure fell to zero in Walker Bush.

Victory was most welcome, but it didn't inspire much confidence for the rest of Toyota's season to know that it had been achieved on reliability.

While Carlos Sainz (overleaf) was the New Zealand victor for the third year running, the Celica's first big stage rally success was only attained in the teeth of fierce opposition from a fired-up Piero Liatti in the ART Integrale (below). Ross Dunkerton was very much at home amidst the rolling scenery of North Island (left), his third place the best World Championship result for an Australian.

Photo Linear

RALLY OF ARGENTINA

Both Didier Auriol and Bernard Occelli were wide-eyed as they walked into the press tent, but not because Carlos Sainz or Toyota had sprung a surprise. The second leg had been going entirely to plan: they had extended their lead to over a minute and already the writing seemed to be on the wall for Toyota. Something totally unexpected, a bolt from the blue, looked to be Sainz's only hope of catching the Frenchmen, and he nearly got it on the last stage of the day, Yunca Suma-Alpachiri.

The crowd turned nasty when the stage was cancelled, because of mud and fog, and vented their spleen on the unfortunate Lancia. The crew were hemmed in as the car was pelted with rocks, and the windscreen and rear window were smashed. The situation became desperate when a piece of burning wood was pushed through the roof air-vent into the cockpit. Auriol began to barge his way through the crowd and had to drive for two kilometres before the torch could be removed, by which time it had badly damaged Occelli's seat. The rally had been forgotten as the survival instinct took over, and it was obvious the pair were just happy to have escaped a terrifying ordeal.

Less than 24 hours later, it had all been forgotten. There had been nothing else to upset their smooth progress to their fourth World Championship victory of the season. As Auriol's car was serviced before the last stage of the day, the little Frenchman explained to Lancia mechanics and spectating Argentinian farmers alike how he had tackled the previous stage. This was done in a series of jerky hand signals and rapid fire jokes. Occelli laughed, the mechanics laughed, the farmers smiled — his enthusiasm was infectious.

The celebrations had already begun with a day to go. Sainz had tried his final gambit on this stage and lost 25 seconds with a spin. One stage later the gap was a whisker under two minutes, and any likelihood of his stopping Auriol's charge to victory in South America had disappeared. The Spaniard had been at his most intense throughout the event, answering questions about the car very guardedly; yes, they were getting closer to Lancia, but they still had a little way to go. Of course, he was painfully aware of the advantage Lancia gained from Michelin's remarkable ATS tyres before he came to Argentina, but now some in the TTE camp fastened onto this as the only difference between the main protagonists. The recurrent theme of Sainz's rally was that his rival was able to cut the corners much tighter than he, Auriol seemingly unconcerned about punctures.

ATS did more than provide Auriol with a direct benefit. It indirectly hindered Sainz, who was often forced to swerve to avoid rocks the ditch-hooking Frenchman left strewn across the road. As soon as the Lancia driver grabbed the position of first on the road with a slender five-second advantage at the end of the first day, the uneasy Sainz embarked on an involuntary slalom. Sure enough, on the first stage that he was forced to run behind Auriol, he collected a puncture which cost him exactly a minute, a gap he was never able to reduce.

For the Argentinians, the battle for the lead was of no more than moderate interest. While Carlos Menem Junior may have been under no pressure from his Group N rivals, he had to handle the full glare of the media spotlight. There were times when he seemed to find it difficult to cope, driving much harder than necessary on the first day, clearly out to make an impression. He steadied himself thereafter, coping with a broken front differential and gearbox towards the end of the third leg before winning Group N.

The Toyota was closer this time, but not that close. Didier Auriol took Argentina by storm, recording his first win outside Europe.

RALLY OF ARGENTINA

Presidents were much in evidence in Argentina, FISA's Max Mosley observing proceedings with the Argentine leader, Carlos Menem (above), while the latter's son achieved a conclusive Group N victory in his Integrale (far right). Carlos Sainz and TTE had to be content with second once more (top right). Willy Lux experienced every co-driver's nightmare, an entire trip to South America wasted when he and Grégoire de Mevius arrived at the start too late.

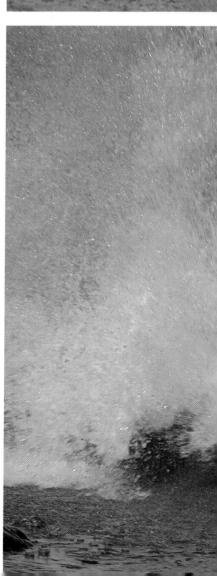

1000 LAKES RALLY

By the end of the event, Juha Kankkunen's irritation was undisguised. It was not a question of being beaten (although no professional driver likes to lose, especially a Finn on home ground), more the reception he was getting from the Finnish public. Too many people had expressed surprise that he couldn't beat Didier Auriol and, if the criticism was implied rather than stated, it was no less exasperating for that.

To most Finns, Carlos Sainz's 1990 victory was not just an extraordinary feat, but an aberration; perhaps non-Finns could win the 1000 Lakes, but there was no danger of their making a habit of it. Kankkunen was treated rather as though he were the World Snooker Champion facing an embarrassing defeat at the hands of a pub expert. It was useless to point out that Auriol had already won four World Championship rallies in 1992 and was clearly 'not bad'. Even after the rally, the headlines described it as a defeat for the Finn, not a victory for the Frenchman.

It was all too easy to overlook the strain on a man who betrayed no outward sign of being locked in a desperate struggle. There were no histrionics in service areas, not a mark on the car, yet no matter how hard he tried, Auriol withstood the pressure. If Kankkunen extracted a second on one stage, the leader could always regain four or five on the next, or the one after that.

The decisive phase was the start of the third leg: recognising that it was now or never, Kankkunen launched an all-out attack on the long, rollercoaster stages between Jyväskylä and Tampere, reasoning that if 75 mph average speeds and yumps like staircases didn't favour a Finn, nothing would. He was quickest on the longest stage of the rally, Ouninpohja, but only by a second. Auriol had weathered the storm, and had extended his lead to almost half a minute at the re-group in Tampere.

Kankkunen kept his thoughts to himself, as though he didn't want to face the inevitable, and one had to talk to the co-drivers to confirm the sneaking suspicion that the event was all but settled. Kankkunen had put body and soul into winning the 1000 Lakes, but it is hard for a triple World Champion to match the commitment of a man still seeking his first title. Having built up as good a knowledge of the stages as any Finn, Auriol could match or better Kankkunen's every move. If the Finns regarded this as a failure on Kankkunen's part rather than a testimony to Auriol's brilliance, his team-mate paid him an oblique compliment, describing the 1000 Lakes as his finest victory.

Lancia had not dominated the rally to the usual degree. Equipped with a greatly improved Celica, Markku Alén drove with such fire that TTE management began to wish that it had taken up Carlos Sainz's entry after all. While there was never much doubt that a Lancia would win, there was no question of the Jolly Club orchestrating the result either: Alén was far too close for that.

Subaru had something to celebrate besides, Ari Vatanen taking fourth place in the top Legacy, but the sensation of the rally was his team-mate, Colin McRae, who finished eighth. Few works drivers have got away with such a catalogue of accidents: a testing shunt that all but destroyed the car was merely a loosener. Two more accidents followed during the rally itself, never in a gear lower than fifth. By the end, the Prodrive men had worked out — with the help of television footage — that the indestructible Legacy had rolled 13 times in the course of the week. McRae had of course been extremely lucky, but he deserved a little adulation. Inspired by this almost Finnish display of courage and determination from a British driver and team, the spectators were even waving Union Jacks in the forests. Almost as much as Auriol's victory, that illustrated that the 1000 Lakes is no longer exclusively Finnish territory.

To finish first, you have to be French: Didier Auriol and Bernard Occelli celebrate their 1000 Lakes triumph with their Martini Racing colleagues, Juha Kankkunen and Juha Piironen. Colin McRae went in for a different sort of celebration (top right), miraculously completing his first 1000 Lakes at unabated speed in the remnants of his Subaru. Tommi Mäkinen was less fortunate, yet stunningly quick in a car that most commentators had written off (above). On this form (overleaf), Juha Kankkunen ought to have been unstoppable. It is the highest tribute to Auriol that he was not.

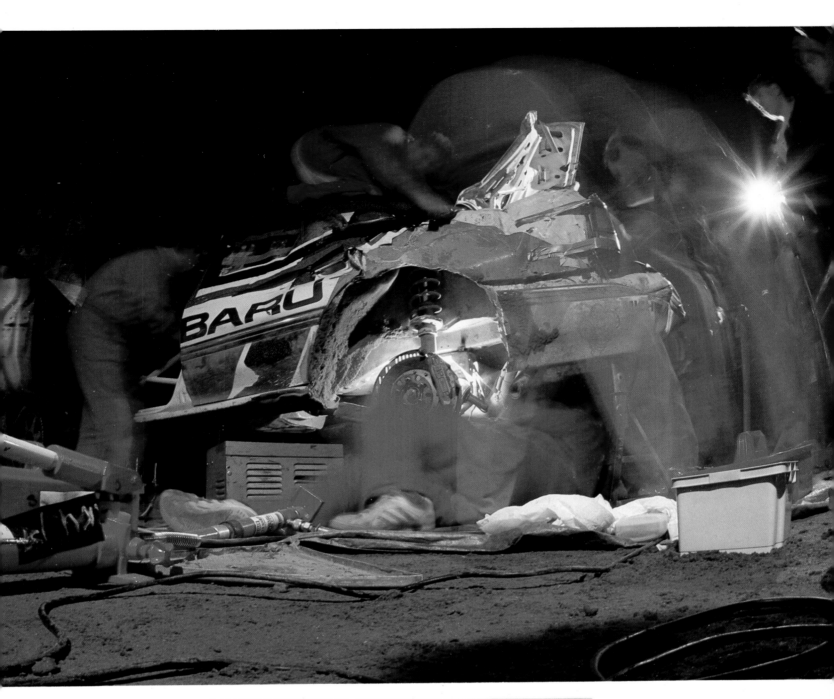

RALLY AUSTRALIA

It took Juha Kankkunen, the perennial runner-up, to bring home the scale of Didier Auriol's achievement. The jockey-sized Frenchman had just dominated the Rally Australia with his customary assurance, thereby winning his sixth World Championship rally of the season and surpassing Miki Biasion's record. Bearing in mind that Auriol appeared to be under no more stress than a taxi driver in a sleepy country town, and that the impending pressures of winning the world title left no visible mark, Kankkunen's words were the chief reminder that something momentous had taken place: he said that he had had his best season for years.

The world title was almost certainly headed elsewhere, and so far the Finn had taken only one victory, as opposed to four in 1991, but he was quite right. He had finished every rally he had started, none lower than third — the kind of results that most drivers can only dream of — and yet he was the man overshadowed at every turn. If this was his greatest run of success for years, what kind of superlative could be left for Auriol's season?

Kankkunen's audience needed no reminding that the Delta's brilliance could scarcely have given a top driver anything less, and yet it was strange that the victories hadn't been shared a little more evenly. The events of the previous four days provided a partial explanation. While Auriol had been the quickest driver once more, he had been a shade lucky on this occasion, and didn't mind admitting it. On roads as fast and treacherous as these, he pointed out, any driver needed some luck. In this case, Integrale number three had borne a charmed life. The first leg had been unusually demanding. The familiar variety of stages and the exceptionally slippery gravel that coats them had been combined with ceaseless rain that soon turned the tracks into a quagmire. Everyone had a story to tell: even Carlos Sainz clipped the bushes on Muresk, while Ari Vatanen nearly overshot a junction two stages later, and Kankkunen had bounced off a tree stump, wrecking the rear suspension and losing half a minute.

Auriol had been trying just as hard — he had been slightly faster than the others, as usual — and was no less prone to error. When asked for his version of events, Bernard Occelli grinned, tilting a hand in a theatrical, on-the-limit-of-adhesion gesture, as if to say that this was none of his doing. The difference was that Auriol's astounding bravery had paid off. He left the road three times on Helena 1 alone, knocked off two rear bumpers during the leg, and yet the only lasting damage on a rally where the trees sometimes grow on the road was a large dent in the rear door on Occelli's side. A day later, even that had been fixed.

As in Greece, an early problem had ensured that Kankkunen would offer no serious challenge unless Auriol faltered. There was no danger of that. Instead, the Finn had his work cut out to deal with the Japanese cars, fighting his way past Sainz and an electrifying Vatanen to take second, and then having to reel in Sainz again when he hit a rock hidden over a brow and demolished the Lancia's rear suspension once more, twisting the shell for good measure. Handed an unexpectedly generous 30-second lead after the first leg, Auriol had industriously doubled it the next day, and paced himself through the remaining day and a half of competition. The readiness to take risks and the ability to get away with them had paid off once again.

Sainz trailed in a close but well-beaten third, hampered by the differential problems that had blighted the Celica's progress for months. He had been lucky that Vatanen had broken his Subaru's gearbox early in the third leg. Until then, Ari had been the revelation of the event, belying the supposed need for first hand experience in Australia. As if that wasn't bad enough, there was a final affront for TTE: in a bid to influence senior management in Italy, Lancia had run its cars throughout at the higher 1993 minimum weight.

RALLY AUSTRALIA

What's a bit of rain and wind when you've got a decent hat? (above) Juha Kankkunen explains the importance of dodging the trees while the mechanics fix the rear suspension (top right). Ari Vatanen was in ebullient form in the Subaru, and should by rights have finished second if the transmission had lasted the distance.

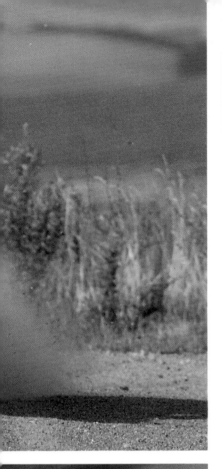

SANREMO RALLY

It was gone three o'clock in the morning, and of course Andrea Aghini would be delighted to answer some more questions. The language barrier could not hide the fact that he was relishing every moment. Yet while he had adapted to winning World Championship rallies and fielding press enquiries easily enough, the rest of the rallying world was still coming to terms with the shock. Didier Auriol's retirement on the first stage of the event had opened up a range of intriguing possibilities, but never this.

At first, there was no reason to suppose that there was anything unusual afoot. Certainly Aghini was quick on the opening tarmac stages, but then he had been just as impressive on asphalt in Portugal and Corsica, and there have been plenty of Italian drivers, from Tony Tognana to Fabrizio Tabaton, who have been fast on tarmac and faded as soon as the event moved to gravel. Even François Delecour wasn't disposed to match Aghini's pace on the slippery, treacherous stages in the mountains behind Carrara, but then he saw no reason to take such risks. He promised to step up the pace on the gravel the following day, and he had little need to spell out that Aghini would be no threat then.

Midway through the following afternoon, the Michelin technicians confessed their astonishment; they had never believed that the Jolly Club's junior recruit would be so quick on the loose. He was never faster than Juha Kankkunen, but he was rarely far behind either, and he was losing precious little ground to the works Fords. He was hardly identifiable as the man who had plummetted like a stone the moment he hit gravel in Portugal. The Michelin verdict was something of a revelation: if the outsiders collaborating most closely with Lancia, with stage times, compounds, weather conditions and test results to hand were surprised, it was no wonder that Aghini had taken everyone else unawares. Only Claudio Bortoletto seemed to feel that everything was going according to plan.

In the end, Kankkunen fought his way past. He would start the third and final leg first on the road — a mixed blessing in view of the dry conditions in Tuscany, which penalised him in a way that the damp tracks of Umbria had never hampered his team-mate — but the precise nature of the surface was no longer likely to make a difference to the outcome. Unless rain and fog descended over the Ligurian Alps that night, he knew that he would never hold off the Italian once the rally returned to asphalt, for Aghini was not only quick, but level-headed. There was every reason to suppose that he would not have won an all-gravel rally, and it might be argued that the double loop in Umbria had favoured the less experienced driver, but he had beaten all comers on the day. It was Kankkunen who had needed help from the weather.

While Aghini had his share of luck, severing an oil pipe within coasting distance of the end of the fourth stage and surviving a couple of spins on the gravel, he remained steady under fire until the rally was as good as won. On the last stage, with Kankkunen safely 40 seconds in arrears, he shot off the road on loose gravel and rippled the Integrale's flank against a fence. It had been the upstarts' rally, Kankkunen left to count his growing collection of second places, while at Ford, Miki Biasion was narrowly defeated by Delecour. Bump stop problems on the Italian's car could not disguise the fact that the Frenchman had become as dangerous an adversary on gravel as on asphalt.

In Italy, the Fiat group rules. Andrea Aghini led home the Lancias (top left), faring rather better than another tarmac expert driving a Delta, César Baroni. While Lancia made the headlines, Fiat quietly introduced the minimalist approach to rallying – the Cinquecento.

All **Photos** Pascal Huit

SANREMO RALLY

Shortening the odds: it's no use going the long way round if you want to succeed in Italy. Alex Fiorio (below left), and Miki Biasion (below right) put Lancia and Ford suspension through its paces respectively. Bruno Thiry made up for a trying season with the two-wheel drive Calibra by taking an excellent ninth place.

All **Photos** Pascal Huit

IVORY COAST RALLY

'Last year our lead was so big for so long that it was a bit of an anti-climax. This year we have driven flat out for two days and it feels better. We have driven every section like a special stage.' John Meadows, Kenjiro Shinozuka's British co-driver, was tired but happy after their second successive win on this tough, unpopular rally.

He had been neither of these things two days earlier while he stood by as the mechanics struggled to revive the crippled Galant. It had all been going to plan, with a 20-minute lead quickly established when the turbo blew approaching Abengourou. The half-hour lost changing the unit was no great worry, for in African rallying terms this is the blink of an eye, but when the car was fired up and it became obvious that the new turbo — which had remained unused in its box since the Safari — was far from healthy the crew felt the rally was slipping away. On the next competitive section the misaligned turbo impeller pressurised the engine and blew its lubricant out, forcing Kenjiro to wait for his chase car to come and by-pass the offending turbo. Over 90 minutes had been lost by the time an operational unit was fitted at Kregbe and, as far as Meadows was concerned, so was the rally.

Patrick Tauziac, the 1990 winner, was the chief beneficiary and he led until mid-way through the second day when his Galant's clutch packed up, allowing the Group N Nissan Sunny GTi-R of Grégoire de Mevius to head the field. Having survived for over 120 miles stuck in third gear, the amiable Belgian must have thought that he was on his way to the second World Rally Championship win for a Group N car when the temperature gauge went off the scale mid-way through the final day. The crew attempted to fill the radiator from a nearby stream only for the liquid to gush instantly from the exhaust pipe — a sure sign that the head gasket had given up the ghost. Moments before, Shinozuka had passed de Mevius on the road to reduce the gap between pursuer and pursued to less than 30 minutes, only for the Galant to lapse immediately onto three cylinders, a problem the crew thought was caused by a dropped valve. For the second time Kenjiro and John believed the rally was slipping from their grasp — but one should take nothing for granted on an African rally.

Success doesn't come easily in Africa. Easy winners on paper, Kenjiro Shinozuka and John Meadows were made to work hard for their second Ivory Coast victory for Mitsubishi (left). Bruno Thiry was delighted to bring his faithful Kadett home second (below), while Hiroshi Nishiyama fulfilled every privateer's dream by leading a World Championship in his Sunny GTi-R (bottom).

CATALONIA RALLY

At scrutineering, Carlos Sainz hadn't exactly radiated confidence. Certainly the viscous centre differential was a step forward, yet even now the Toyota's front tyres were lasting a maximum of 20 kilometres on tarmac. But some of the tarmac stages were more like 30 kilometres long! Sainz nodded; words would only have laboured the point. Under the circumstances, his opening charge had the impact of an electric shock. Claudio Bortoletto's immediate reaction to the Toyota's first stage time was that it must be a mistake. Perhaps, as François Delecour suggested, it was owed to the unique properties of Pirelli's thermal slick. It was not. TTE had used harder rubber from the start, and the times were just as astounding as the sun climbed and the roads grew drier.

The handling problem was still present, the front Pirellis down to the canvas by the end of the second stage as the understeer built up, but Sainz was unstoppable. He had a 40-second lead after six stages, and had more than doubled that by the close of the first leg. The ugly duckling Celica, the car no one in his right mind wanted to drive on tarmac, was the class of the field, while the Lancia drivers complained that the Integrales had lost their usual stability and bemoaned the lack of pre-event testing. Like a powerful but unfancied heavyweight, it looked as though TTE had connected with its first punch. A minute and 40 seconds would surely be too much for the Martini drivers to make up on the gravel.

Less than half a dozen stages later, the Toyota men had almost abandoned gloom in favour of resignation. Didier Auriol might have gone off the road and out of the running when the power steering failed, but Juha Kankkunen was making up ground hand over fist. The team calculated that the tall Finn was devouring Sainz's lead at the rate of 1.7 seconds per kilometre, which would give him victory by a margin nearly as great as Toyota's advantage the night before. Far from being the answer to all TTE's problems, the viscous differential had begun to look like a different blind alley. Sainz reported a crippling absence of lateral grip and, in contrast to the slicks, the HG35s were coming off the car almost unmarked. Australia had been no worse than this.

The Spaniard's conviction that he had the best settings after an exhaustive test session was unshakeable. Changing suspension and tyres two stages after the re-group in Cardona was an act of desperation. Miraculously, last year's shock absorbers and the old faithful ASGs worked like a charm. As the tracks became damper, smoother, and more slippery, the tide turned again. Toyota even beat Lancia on a stage. Generally, Kankkunen was still quicker, but the Delta's Michelin FBs were nothing like as effective as they had been during the day, and he was no longer catching Sainz quickly enough.

El Subira would be the acid test; 30.3 kilometres long, it was the first and longest stage of the last leg. Kankkunen had lopped 17 seconds from Sainz's lead on the same stage the day before, and required something similar if he was to pull off a victory that Lancia badly needed. In the event, the last-throw-of-the-dice alterations stood Toyota in good stead. Sainz lost a manageable eight seconds, and Kankkunen could only explain that now the Delta lacked grip; since just 70 kilometres of stages remained, Sainz's 50-second lead was safe, in spite of an 11th hour scare when someone noticed a split in the intercooler.

The impartiality of some of the finish marshals had been questioned, and Auriol would almost certainly have won if only he hadn't flown off on a yump into a right-hander, but the fact remained that the Jolly Club had been caught napping. The belief that TTE was a spent force for 1992 had been mistaken.

The rally hangs in the balance. Carlos Sainz (above) looks uneasy, while Didier Auriol drifts the Integrale into a fast left-hander over a bridge in hot pursuit.

The stress shows on Juha Kankkunen's features (left), as the World Championship swings tantalisingly within reach. Keenly aware that a finish was vital, the Finn bided his time on the asphalt (far left). Andrea Aghini was correspondingly wary of the gravel – not that it stopped him exploring the Delta's limits on hairpins.

RAC RALLY

While Carlos Sainz doggedly sounded a note of caution, as if talking of the World Championship might conjure up some misfortune as horrible as Didier Auriol's, Luis Moya was already outlining what he planned to do to a crate of whisky the following night. The co-driver had a point: they had survived Kielder in good shape, they had a useful if not impregnable lead over Juha Kankkunen, their most dangerous opponent — Auriol — was out of the rally, and just six stages remained. The unthinkable possibility that Sainz might become champion rather than one of the Lancia drivers had become odds-on, if not yet a certainty. Surely a hint at celebration was only a fraction premature.

Sainz had kept his belief that TTE's latest transmission and suspension changes gave him a chance to himself. Leading the first leg through the sodden parks of the Midlands had looked like a gesture of defiance, before the inevitable turning of the tables in the Welsh forests. Hadn't the Deltas been streets ahead on gravel in Catalonia? Even though he maintained his 40-second advantage over the Martini machines during the Welsh leg, Sainz refused to concede more than a sliver of satisfaction in public. It was beyond question that the Celica's handling was vastly improved and that Pirelli had the upper hand over Michelin on muddy, water-logged roads lashed by teeming rain; while the Toyotas were finally making good use of their rubber and Colin McRae exploited impossibly soft compounds to the full in his Subaru, the Michelin teams grumbled that they were making do with the same tyres that they had had for the 1000 Lakes and that they were hardly suitable for the prevailing conditions. Yet Sainz had remained acutely aware that Lancia invariably set the pace in Grizedale and that anything might happen in Kielder.

Sure enough, bright sunlight and a brisk, drying wind had set the scene for a counter-attack the next morning. Auriol halved the deficit in the Lake District, and the battle was finely balanced, 20 seconds separating the two, when the Frenchman's ignition slowed and then stranded him in Kielder, the Integrale a tantalising mile from the end of the stage. Kankkunen lost no further ground, but gained none either, and a puncture for the Finn on the final stage in Northumberland gave Sainz a little extra breathing space. The Jolly Club's notion that conditions might somehow turn in its favour in the north had been disabused. Kankkunen needed to produce something exceptional in Scotland to retrieve the situation and, when he skidded off early the next morning and broke a driveshaft, while driving without windscreen wipers, the rally was as good as settled. As Kankkunen redoubled his efforts in a successful bid to deprive Markku Alén of third on the final stage, Sainz was able to throttle back and drop a minute to the hitherto invincible Lancia.

It had been a thrilling yet brutal rally. This had been no occasion for honours to be shared. Sainz and Moya had exceeded the wildest expectations, but the losers were just as clearly defined and the disappointment was correspondingly bitter. There had been more than a World Championship at stake and, while Auriol came to terms with losing a crown that had seemed his for the taking two months previously, McRae had to accept a brake and transmission failure in Grizedale that destroyed his prospects of a first World Championship win and a prize of £100,000 from the rally sponsor, Lombard. For once, a British victory had been no fanciful dream, since McRae's level-headed showing in Wales had suggested that, on home soil, he had the speed to outrun the World Champion himself.

Carlos Sainz was the victor (above), Didier Auriol the vanquished (far left) on an event where neither teams nor drivers had the least margin for error. Andrea Aghini plunged into a wholly unfamiliar environment and emerged with some credit, bringing his Martini Delta home 10th.

RAC RALLY

*The head to head clash between
Colin McRae (above left) and
Malcolm Wilson (above right)
went in favour of the Scot and his
Subaru, although neither of the
leading British drivers had
much luck. Tommi Mäkinen
didn't have much luck either,
the Finn's works Nissan beset
by a string of punctures.
This suspension-bending
incident at Donington Park
only led to the first of many.*

RALLYE MONTE-CARLO 1992 1 1992

CLASSEMENT AND COMMUNE

FINALE

N

Castrol

St Jean-en-Royans
Valence
Crest
Die
Burzet
Vals le Bains
AUBENAS
Serres
Sisteron
DIGNE
ANNOT
Puget-Theniers
Nice
MONTE CARLO
Grasse
St Martin-Vesubie
Col de Turini
Beuil
Puget-Theniers
Levens
Escarene
Nice
MONTE CARLO

Bad Hombourg
Reims
PARIS
Lausanne
Sestrieres
Monaco
Barcelona

MONTE CARLO RALLY, 23-29 January. FIA World Rally Championship for Manufacturers, round 1. FIA World Rally Championship for Drivers, round 1.

Leading entries

1	Juha Kankkunen/ Juha Piironen	Lancia Delta HF Integrale Gr A
2	Carlos Sainz/ Luis Moya	Toyota Celica Turbo 4WD Gr A
3	Massimo Biasion/ Tiziano Siviero	Ford Sierra Cosworth 4x4 Gr A
4	Didier Auriol/ Bernard Occelli	Lancia Delta HF Integrale Gr A
5	Kenneth Eriksson/ Staffan Parmander	Mitsubishi Galant VR-4 Gr A
6	Armin Schwarz/ Arne Hertz	Toyota Celica Turbo 4WD Gr A
7	François Delecour/ Daniel Grataloup	Ford Sierra Cosworth 4x4 Gr A
8	François Chatriot/ Michel Périn	Nissan Sunny GTi-R Gr A
9	Timo Salonen/ Voitto Silander	Mitsubishi Galant VR-4 Gr A
10	Markku Alén/ Ilkka Kivimäki	Toyota Celica Turbo 4WD Gr A
11	Philippe Bugalski/ Denis Giraudet	Lancia Delta HF Integrale Gr A
12	Tommi Mäkinen/ Seppo Harjanne	Nissan Sunny GTi-R Gr A
17	Piergiorgio Bedini/ Dino Zamatta	Lancia Delta HF Integrale Gr N
18	Vladimir Berger/ Jiri Janacek	Skoda Favorit 136L Gr A
19	Christophe Spiliotis/ Isabelle Spiliotis	Ford Sierra Cosworth 4x4 Gr A
20	Pavel Sibera/ Petr Gross	Skoda Favorit 136L Gr A
21	Giovanni Manfrinato/ Claudio Condotta	Ford Sierra Cosworth 4x4 Gr N
23	Patrick Magaud/ Guylene Brun	Renault Clio 16S Gr A
24	Bertrand Balas/ Eric Laine	Lancia Delta HF Integrale Gr N

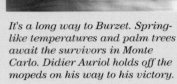

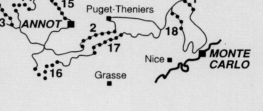

It's a long way to Burzet. Spring-like temperatures and palm trees await the survivors in Monte Carlo. Didier Auriol holds off the mopeds on his way to his victory.

Special stage times

SS 1. Col de Turini 1 (10.63 km)
1 A. Schwarz/A. Hertz (Toyota Celica Turbo 4WD) 7m 51s; 2 J. Kankkunen/J. Piironen (Lancia Delta HF Integrale) 7m 54s; 3 F. Delecour/D. Grataloup (Ford Sierra Cosworth 4x4) 7m 57s; 4 D. Auriol/B. Occelli (Lancia Delta HF Integrale), M. Alén/I. Kivimäki (Toyota Celica Turbo 4WD) 8m 01s; 6 C.Sainz/ L. Moya (Toyota Celica Turbo 4WD) 8m 09s.

SS 2. Pont des Miolans-St Auban (22.72 km)
1 Sainz/Moya (Toyota), Auriol/Occelli (Lancia) 14m 53s; 3 Schwarz/Hertz (Toyota) 14m 55s; 4 Kankkunen/Piironen (Lancia) 15m 00s; 5 Delecour/Grataloup (Ford) 15m 09s; 6 K. Eriksson/S. Parmander (Mitsubishi Galant VR-4) 15m 11s.

SS 3. Col du Corobin (19.60 km)
1 Kankkunen/Piironen (Lancia) 14m 25s; 2 Sainz/Moya (Toyota) 14m 28s; 3 Auriol/Occelli (Lancia), Schwarz/Hertz (Toyota) 14m 35s; 5 Delecour/Grataloup (Ford) 14m 41s; 6 Eriksson/Parmander (Mitsubishi) 14m 45s.

SS 4. Col de Perty (27.37 km)
1 Delecour/Grataloup (Ford) 18m 05s; 2 Auriol/Occelli (Lancia), Schwarz/Hertz (Toyota) 18m 25s; 4 Kankkunen/Piironen (Lancia) 18m 31s; 5 P. Bugalski/D. Giraudet (Lancia Delta HF Integrale) 18m 38s; 6 F. Chatriot/M. Périn (Nissan Sunny GTi-R) 18m 49s.

SS 5. St Nazaire le Desert (23.44 km)
1 Auriol/Occelli (Lancia) 15m 00s; 2 Kankkunen/Piironen (Lancia) 15m 04s; 3 Sainz/Moya (Toyota) 15m 07s; 4 Delecour/Grataloup (Ford) 15m 08s; 5 Bugalski/Giraudet (Lancia) 15m 18s; 6 Chatriot/Périn (Nissan) 15m 27s.

SS 6. Col de la Fayolle (35.97 km)
1 Auriol/Occelli (Lancia) 25m 36s; 2 Kankkunen/ Piironen (Lancia), Schwarz/Hertz (Toyota) 25m 43s; 4 Delecour/Grataloup (Ford) 25m 47s; 5 Sainz/Moya (Toyota) 25m 54s; 6 T. Mäkinen/S. Harjanne (Nissan Sunny GTi-R) 26m 17s.

SS 7. Burzet (41.41 km)
1 Delecour/Grataloup (Ford) 29m 19s; 2 Auriol/ Occelli (Lancia) 29m 30s; 3 Kankkunen/Piironen (Lancia) 29m 38s; 4 T. Salonen/V. Silander (Mitsubishi Galant VR-4) 29m 49s; 5 M. Biasion/T. Siviero (Ford Sierra Cosworth 4x4) 29m 53s; 6 Sainz/Moya (Toyota) 30m 00s.

SS 8. St Bonnet le Froid (12.24 km)
1 Kankkunen/Piironen (Lancia) 16m 49s; 2 Sainz/ Moya (Toyota), Salonen/Silander (Mitsubishi) 17m 10s; 4 Biasion/Siviero (Ford) 17m 20s; 5 Delecour/ Grataloup (Ford) 17m 27s; 6 Auriol/Occelli (Lancia) 17m 29s.

SS 9. Col du Marchand (32.76 km)
1 Auriol/Occelli (Lancia) 22m 23s; 2 Sainz/Moya (Toyota) 22m 46s; 3 Kankkunen/Piironen (Lancia) 22m 49s; 4 Delecour/Grataloup (Ford) 22m 56s; 5 Schwarz/Hertz (Toyota) 23m 12s; 6 Bugalski/ Giraudet (Lancia) 23m 21s.

SS 10. St Jean-en-Royans (25.44 km)
1 Schwarz/Hertz (Toyota) 13m 14s; 2 Auriol/Occelli (Lancia) 13m 22s; 3 Delecour/Grataloup (Ford) 13m 26s; 4 Kankkunen/Piironen (Lancia) 13m 30s; 5 Sainz/Moya (Toyota) 13m 31s; 6 Bugalski/Giraudet (Lancia) 13m 37s.

SS 11. Col de Saulce (30.38 km)
1 Schwarz/Hertz (Toyota) 20m 26s; 2 Sainz/Moya (Toyota) 20m 36s; 3 Auriol/Occelli (Lancia) 20m 38s; 4 Kankkunen/Piironen (Lancia) 20m 49s; 5 Chatriot/Périn (Nissan) 21m 07s; 6 Biasion/Siviero (Ford)

Finish lines

Ford had a good rally in **Group N**, the Monagasque couple **Christophe** and **Isabelle Spiliotis** leading home a trio of Sierra Cosworth 4x4s, but a rough time of it in Group A: disparaging remarks were attributed to both **François Delecour** and **Miki Biasion**, the latter after a string of power steering, brake and turbo failures that hampered his works Sierra seven stages running...**Philippe Bugalski** climbed to fifth in the third of the Martini Lancias after struggling with a faulty front differential for the first half of the rally ...**Kenneth Eriksson** crashed out of a rally for the first time in his professional career, smashing his Mitsubishi's front suspension on SS4...**François Chatriot** finished seventh in the best of the **Nissans**, hampered by a collapsed wheel bearing, but **Tommi Mäkinen** gave a good account of himself on his first Monte, and came close to beating Biasion...**Timo Salonen** brought the surviving Galant home in sixth place, but expressed disgust at Michelin's tyre recommendations...**Armin Schwarz** and **Markku Alén** both crashed, leaving **Sainz** to ensure that TTE got a finish.

Results

1	Didier Auriol/ Bernard Occelli	Lancia Delta HF Integrale	6h 54m 20s	Gr A
2	Carlos Sainz/ Luis Moya	Toyota Celica Turbo 4WD	6h 56m 25s	Gr A
3	Juha Kankkunen/ Juha Piironen	Lancia Delta HF Integrale	6h 57m 17s	Gr A
4	François Delecour/ Daniel Grataloup	Ford Sierra Cosworth 4x4	6h 59m 02s	Gr A
5	Philippe Bugalski/ Denis Giraudet	Lancia Delta HF Integrale	7h 04m 32s	Gr A
6	Timo Salonen/ Voitto Silander	Mitsubishi Galant VR-4	7h 05m 21s	Gr A
7	François Chatriot/ Michel Périn	Nissan Sunny GTi-R	7h 10m 47s	Gr A
8	Massimo Biasion/ Tiziano Siviero	Ford Sierra Cosworth 4x4	7h 11m 18s	Gr A
9	Tommi Mäkinen/ Seppo Harjanne	Nissan Sunny GTi-R	7h 12m 58s	Gr A
10	Christophe Spiliotis/ Isabelle Spiliotis	Ford Sierra Cosworth 4x4	7h 42m 41s	Gr N

147 starters, 86 finishers

Previous winners (since 1960)

1960	Walter Schock/Rolf Moll	Mercedes-Benz 220SE
1961	Maurice Martin/Robert Bateau	Panhard
1962	Eric Carlsson/Gunnar Haggbom	Saab 96
1963	Eric Carlsson/Gunnar Palm	Saab 96
1964	Paddy Hopkirk/Henry Liddon	Mini-Cooper S
1965	Timo Mäkinen/Paul Easter	Mini-Cooper S
1966	Pauli Toivonen/Ensio Mikander	Citroën DS21
1967	Rauno Aaltonen/Henry Liddon	Mini-Cooper S
1968	Vic Elford/David Stone	Porsche 911T
1969	Björn Waldegård/Lars Helmer	Porsche 911
1970	Björn Waldegård/Lars Helmer	Porsche 911T
1971	Ove Andersson/David Stone	Alpine Renault A110
1972	Sandro Munari/Mario Mannucci	Lancia Fulvia
1973	Jean-Claude Andruet/'Biche'	Alpine Renault A110
1975	Sandro Munari/Mario Mannucci	Lancia Stratos
1976	Sandro Munari/Silvio Maiga	Lancia Stratos
1977	Sandro Munari/Silvio Maiga	Lancia Stratos
1978	Jean-Pierre Nicolas/Vincent Laverne	Porsche 911 Carrera
1979	Bernard Darniche/Alain Mahé	Lancia Stratos
1980	Walter Röhrl/Christian Geistdörfer	Fiat 131 Abarth
1981	Jean Ragnotti/Jean-Marc Andrié	Renault 5 Turbo
1982	Walter Röhrl/Christian Geistdörfer	Opel Ascona 400
1983	Walter Röhrl/Christian Geistdörfer	Lancia Rally 037
1984	Walter Röhrl/Christian Geistdörfer	Audi Quattro A2
1985	Ari Vatanen/Terry Harryman	Peugeot 205 Turbo 16
1986	Henri Toivonen/Sergio Cresto	Lancia Delta S4
1987	Massimo Biasion/Tiziano Siviero	Lancia Delta HF 4x4
1988	Bruno Saby/Jean-François Fauchille	Lancia Delta HF 4x4
1989	Massimo Biasion/Tiziano Siviero	Lancia Delta HF Integrale
1990	Didier Auriol/Bernard Occelli	Lancia Delta HF Integrale
1991	Carlos Sainz/Luis Moya	Toyota Celica GT4

21m 11s.

SS 12. Sisteron-Thoard (36.87 km)
1 Schwarz/Hertz (Toyota) 26m 19s; 2 Sainz/Moya (Toyota) 26m 47s; 3 Salonen/Silander (Mitsubishi) 27m 21s; 4 Delecour/Grataloup (Ford) 27m 33s; 5 Mäkinen/Harjanne (Nissan) 27m 41s; 6 Bugalski/Giraudet (Lancia) 28m 52s.

SS 13. Malijai-Puimichel (12.32 km)
1 Auriol/Occelli (Lancia) 7m 54s; 2 Kankkunen/Piironen (Lancia) 7m 56s; 4 Sainz/Moya (Toyota), Schwarz/Hertz (Toyota) 8m 02s; 6 Biasion/Siviero (Ford) 8m 04s.

SS 14. Clumanc-Lambruisse (14.94 km)
1 Sainz/Moya (Toyota), Schwarz/Hertz (Toyota) 10m 02s; 3 Auriol/Occelli (Lancia) 10m 03s; 4 Bugalski/Giraudet (Lancia) 10m 07s; 5 Delecour/Grataloup (Ford) 10m 10s; 6 Kankkunen/Piironen (Lancia) 10m 13s.

SS 15. Col de la Colle St Michel (18.62 km)
1 Auriol/Occelli (Lancia) 11m 26s; 2 Schwarz/Hertz (Toyota), Delecour/Grataloup (Ford) 11m 29s; 4 Bugalski/Giraudet (Lancia) 11m 32s; 5 Sainz/Moya (Toyota) 11m 33s; 6 Kankkunen/Piironen (Lancia) 11m 38s.

SS 16. Trigance-Chateauvieux (27.57 km)
1 Sainz/Moya (Toyota) 15m 37s; 2 Auriol/Occelli (Lancia) 15m 39s; 3 Schwarz/Hertz (Toyota) 15m 40s; 4 Bugalski/Giraudet (Lancia) 15m 46s; 5 Chatriot/Périn (Nissan), Salonen/Silander (Mitsubishi) 16m 03s.

SS 17. Col de Bleine (33.52 km)
1 Auriol/Occelli (Lancia) 23m 04s; 2 Delecour/Grataloup (Ford) 23m 06s; 3 Bugalski/Giraudet (Lancia) 23m 15s; 4 Schwarz/Hertz (Toyota) 23m 21s; 5 Sainz/Moya (Lancia) 23m 26s; 6 Kankkunen/Piironen (Lancia) 23m 27s.

SS 18. Loda-Luceram (16.49 km)
1 Auriol/Occelli (Lancia) 12m 06s; 2 Delecour/Grataloup (Ford) 12m 12s; 3 Kankkunen/Piironen (Lancia), Bugalski/Giraudet (Lancia) 12m 16s; 5 Sainz/Moya (Toyota) 12m 18s; 6 Chatriot/Périn (Nissan) 12m 34s.

SS 19. Col de Turini 2 (22.21 km)
1 Sainz/Moya (Toyota) 16m 05s; 2 Auriol/Occelli (Lancia), Delecour/Grataloup (Ford) 16m 06s; 4 Kankkunen/Piironen (Lancia) 16m 14s; 5 Bugalski/Giraudet (Lancia) 16m 27s; 6 Chatriot/Périn (Nissan) 16m 44s.

SS 20. Col de la Couillole 1 (22.15 km)
1 Auriol/Occelli (Lancia) 13m 42s; 2 Delecour/Grataloup (Ford) 13m 44s; 3 Sainz/Moya (Toyota) 13m 51s; 4 Bugalski/Giraudet (Lancia) 13m 56s; 5 Biasion/Siviero (Ford) 14m 04s; 6 Kankkunen/Piironen (Lancia) 14m 05s.

SS 21. Col St Raphael-Tourette 1 (23.54 km)
1 Delecour/Grataloup (Ford) 16m 23s; 2 Auriol/Occelli (Lancia) 16m 36s; 3 Bugalski/Giraudet (Lan-

cia) 16m 40s; 4 Kankkunen/Piironen (Lancia) 16m 48s; 5 Sainz/Moya (Toyota), Chatriot/Périn (Nissan) 16m 49s.

SS 22. Utelle 1 (18.35 km)
1 Auriol/Occelli (Lancia) 14m 22s; 2 Delecour/Grataloup (Ford) 14m 27s; 3 Kankkunen/Piironen (Lancia) 14m 37s; 4 Sainz/Moya (Toyota) 14m 38s; 5 Biasion/Siviero (Ford) 14m 45s; 6 Chatriot/Périn (Nissan) 14m 53s.

SS 23. Col de Turini 3 (22.21 km)
Cancelled.

SS 24. Col de la Couillole 2 (22.15 km)
1 Auriol/Occelli (Lancia) 13m 29s; 2 Delecour/Grataloup (Ford) 13m 37s; 3 Kankkunen/Piironen (Lancia) 13m 44s; 4 Sainz/Moya (Toyota) 13m 55s; 5 Salonen/Silander (Mitsubishi) 13m 58s; 6 Chatriot/Périn (Nissan) 13m 59s.

SS 25. Col St Raphael-Tourette 2 (23.54 km)
1 Delecour/Grataloup (Ford) 16m 08s; 2 Auriol/Occelli (Lancia) 16m 22s; 3 Bugalski/Giraudet (Lancia) 16m 29s; 4 Kankkunen/Piironen (Lancia) 16m 30s; 5 Biasion/Siviero (Ford) 16m 40s; 6 Chatriot/Périn (Nissan) 16m 45s.

SS 26. Utelle 2 (18.35 km)
1 Delecour/Grataloup (Ford) 14m 14s; 2 Kankkunen/Piironen (Lancia) 14m 22s; 3 Auriol/Occelli (Lancia) 14m 23s; 4 Bugalski/Giraudet (Lancia) 14m 37s; 5 Sainz/Moya (Toyota) 14m 42s; 6 Salonen/Silander (Mitsubishi) 14m 50s.

Major retirements

Kenneth Eriksson/ Staffan Parmander	Mitsubishi Galant VR-4 SS 4	crashed
Markku Alén/ Ilkka Kivimäki	Toyota Celica Turbo 4WD SS 4	crashed
Patrick Magaud/ Guylene Brun	Renault Clio 16S SS 9	engine
Armin Schwarz/ Arne Hertz	Toyota Celica Turbo 4WD SS 15	crashed

FIA class winners

Group A
Over 2000 cc:	Auriol/Occelli (Lancia)
1300-2000 cc:	Jean-Marie Bezeulin/Jean Bourgoin (Peugeot 309 GTI 16v)
Up to 1300 cc:	Jacky Cesbron/Paul Giraud (Renault 4GTL)

Group N
Over 2000 cc:	Spiliotis/Spiliotis (Ford)
1600-2000 cc:	Michel Moreau/Thomas Lefebvre (Peugeot 309 GTI 16v)
1300-1600 cc:	Johan Bastiaens/Daniel Sonck (Honda Civic)
Up to 1300 cc:	Alain Pellerey/Daniel Pons (Citroën AX Sport)

Rally leaders

SS 1-4 Schwarz/Hertz (Toyota); **SS 5-11** Auriol/Occelli (Lancia); **SS 12-19** Sainz/Moya (Toyota); **SS 20-26** Auriol/Occelli (Lancia).

World Championship points

Drivers
1 Auriol 20; 2 Sainz 15; 3 Kankkunen 12; 4 Delecour 10; 5 Bugalski 8; 6 Salonen 6; 7 Chatriot 4; 8 Biasion 3; 9 Mäkinen 2; 10 Spiliotis 1.

Manufacturers
1 Lancia 20; 2 Toyota 17; 3 Ford 12; 4 Mitsubishi 8; 5 Nissan 6.

Route details

Leg 1
23/24 January: Starting from five departure points (Bad Hombourg, Barcelona, Lausanne, Reims and Sestrières) arriving at Monaco at 1740/24.

Leg 2
25 January: Starting from Monaco at 0700, finishing at Aubenas at 2005, including six special stages (139.73 km).

Leg 3
26/27 January: Starting from Aubenas at 0800/26, finishing at Monaco at 1848/27, following an overnight halt in Digne, including 12 special stages (316.06 km).

Leg 4
28/29 January: Starting and finishing at Monaco 1600/28-0809/29, including eight special stages (1 cancelled - 150.29 km).

Weather

Generally mild and dry, but with some snow and ice on high ground.

Special stage analysis

	1st	2nd	3rd	4th	5th	6th
Auriol/Occelli (Lancia)	11	7	4	1	-	-
Delecour/Grataloup (Ford)	5	7	2	4	4	-
Schwartz/Hertz (Toyota)	5	3	3	2	1	-
Sainz/Moya (Toyota)	4	5	2	3	7	2
Kankkunen/Piironen (Lancia)	2	5	5	-	7	4
Bugalski/Giraudet (Lancia)	-	1	4	5	3	3
Salonen/Silander (Mitsubishi)	-	1	1	1	2	1
Biasion/Siviero (Ford)	-	-	-	1	4	2
Alén/Kivimäki (Toyota)	-	-	-	1	-	-
Chatriot/Périn (Nissan)	-	-	-	-	3	7
Mäkinen/Harjanne (Nissan)	-	-	-	-	1	1
Eriksson/Parmander (Mitsubishi)	-	-	-	-	-	2

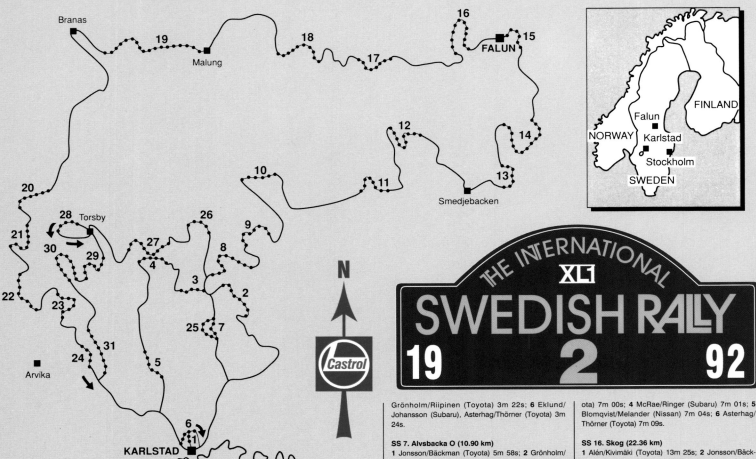

SWEDISH RALLY, 13-16 February. FIA World Rally
Championship for Drivers, round 2.

Leading entries

2	Markku Alén/	Toyota Celica GT4
	Ilkka Kivimäki	Gr A
3	Ari Vatanen/	Subaru Legacy RS
	Bruno Berglund	Gr A
4	Mats Jonsson/	Toyota Celica GT4
	Lars Bäckman	Gr A
5	Stig Blomqvist/	Nissan Sunny GTi-R
	Benny Melander	Gr A
7	Colin McRae/	Subaru Legacy RS
	Derek Ringer	Gr A
10	Björn Johansson/	Mazda 323 GT-X
	Anders Olsson	Gr A
11	Per Eklund/	Subaru Legacy RS
	Johnny Johansson	Gr A
12	Lasse Lampi/	Mitsubishi Galant VR-4
	Pentti Kuukkala	Gr A
13	Stig-Olov Walfridsson/	Mitsubishi Galant VR-4
	Gunnar Barth	Gr N
14	Mikael Sundström/	Lancia Delta HF Integrale
	Jakke Honkanen	Gr N
15	John Bosch/	Nissan Sunny GTi-R
	Peter Diekmann	Gr N
16	Leif Asterhag/	Toyota Celica GT4
	Tina Thörner	Gr N
17	Sebastian Lindholm/	Ford Sierra Cosworth 4x4
	Timo Hantunen	Gr N
18	Marcus Grönholm/	Toyota Celica GT4
	Ilkka Riipinen	Gr A
19	Harry Joki/	Peugeot 309GTI 16v
	Per Johansson	Gr A
20	Roger Ericsson/	Subaru Legacy RS
	Ola Carlsson	Gr N
21	Sven-Erik Eriksson/	Subaru Legacy RS
	Tommy Strom	Gr N
22	Kenneth Bäcklund/	Mitsubishi Galant VR-4
	Tord Andersson	Gr N
23	Sören Nilsson/	Mitsubishi Galant VR-4
	Per-Ove Persson	Gr N
24	Jarmo Kytölehto/	Mitsubishi Galant VR-4
	Kari Jokinen	Gr N

Special stage times

SS 1. I2 (2.04 km)
1 M. Jonsson/L. Bäckman (Toyota Celica GT4), S.
Blomqvist/B. Melander (Nissan Sunny GTi-R), M.
Alén/I. Kivimäki (Toyota Celica GT4) 1m 17s; 4 P.
Eklund/J. Johansson (Subaru Legacy RS), L. Lampi/
P. Kuukkala (Mitsubishi Galant VR-4), L. Asterhag/ T.
Thörner (Toyota Celica GT4), M. Grönholm/ I. Riip-
inen (Toyota Celica GT4) 1m 19s.

SS 2. Godåsen (26.24 km)
1 S. Lindholm/T. Hantunen (Ford Sierra Cosworth
4x4) 14m 02s; 2 C. McRae/D. Ringer (Subaru Legacy
RS) 14m 06s; 3 Jonsson/Bäckman (Toyota) 14m
07s; 4 S. Nilsson/P.-O. Persson (Mitsubishi Galant
VR-4) 14m 24s; 5 K. Bäcklund/T. Andersson (Mitsubishi Galant VR-4) 14m 27s; 6 Lampi/ Kuukkala
(Mitsubishi) 14m 30s.

SS 3. Skargen (6.92 km)
1 Jonsson/Bäckman (Toyota) 4m 12s; 2 Blomqvist/
Melander (Nissan), Lindholm/Hantunen (Ford) 4m
14s; 4 Alén/Kivimäki (Toyota) 4m 20s; 5 McRae/
Ringer (Subaru), Grönholm/Riipinen (Toyota) 4m
21s.

SS 4. Sagfallet (20.56 km)
1 Jonsson/Bäckman (Toyota) 12m 22s; 2
Blomqvist/Melander (Nissan) 12m 26s; 3 McRae/
Ringer (Subaru) 12m 35s; 4 Lindholm/Hantunen
(Ford) 12m 40s; 5 Grönholm/Riipinen (Toyota) 12m
41s; 6 Alén/Kivimäki (Toyota) 12m 43s.

SS 5. Kammersrud (11.87 km)
1 Alén/Kivimäki (Toyota) 6m 31s; 2 Jonsson/Bäckman (Toyota)
6m 34s; 3 Lindholm/Hantunen (Ford) 6m 35s; 4
McRae/Ringer (Subaru) 6m 41s; 5 Grönholm/ Riipinen (Toyota) 6m 42s; 6 Lampi/Kuukkala (Mitsubishi),
Blomqvist/Melander (Nissan) 6m 43s.

SS 6. Henstad (5.18 km)
1 Alén/Kivimäki (Toyota) 3m 15s; 2 Jonsson/Bäck-
man (Toyota) 3m 18s; 3 Blomqvist/Melander (Nissan) 3m 19s; 4 Lindholm/Hantunen (Ford) 3m 21s; 5
Grönholm/Riipinen (Toyota) 3m 22s; 6 Eklund/
Johansson (Subaru), Asterhag/Thörner (Toyota) 3m
24s.

SS 7. Alvsbacka O (10.90 km)
1 Jonsson/Bäckman (Toyota) 5m 58s; 2 Grönholm/
Riipinen (Toyota) 6m 04s; 3 Alén/Kivimäki (Toyota),
McRae/Ringer (Subaru) 6m 05s; 5 Lindholm/Han-
tunen (Ford) 6m 06s; 6 Asterhag/Thörner (Toyota)
6m 10s.

SS 8. Backa (29.35 km)
1 McRae/Ringer (Subaru) 16m 34s; 2 Jonsson/
Bäckman (Toyota) 16m 42s; 3 Grönholm/Riipinen
(Toyota) 16m 46s; 4 Blomqvist/Melander (Nissan)
16m 47s; 5 Asterhag/Thörner (Toyota) 16m 51s; 6
Alén/Kivimäki (Toyota) 16m 55s.

SS 9. Uddeholmshyttan (22.64 km)
1 Jonsson/Bäckman (Toyota) 12m 32s; 2 McRae/
Ringer (Subaru) 12m 33s; 3 Asterhag/Thörner (Toy-
ota) 12m 35s; 4 Alén/Kivimäki (Toyota) 12m 38s; 5
Grönholm/Riipinen (Toyota) 12m 45s; 6 Blomqvist/
Melander (Nissan) 12m 46s.

SS 10. Sågen (14.82 km)
1 Jonsson/Bäckman (Toyota) 8m 24s; 2 Blomqvist/
Melander (Nissan) 8m 25s; 3 Alén/Kivimäki (Toyota)
8m 30s; 4 McRae/Ringer (Subaru) 8m 32s; 5 Aster-
hag/Thörner (Toyota) 8m 35s; 6 Eklund/Johansson
(Subaru) 8m 46s.

SS 11. Telningsberg (20.71 km)
1 Jonsson/Bäckman (Toyota) 12m 17s; 2 McRae/
Ringer (Subaru) 12m 18s; 3 Blomqvist/Melander
(Nissan) 12m 19s; 4 Asterhag/Thörner (Toyota) 12m
22s; 5 Grönholm/Riipinen (Toyota) 12m 23s; 6 Alén/
Kivimäki (Toyota) 12m 27s.

SS 12. Nyhammar (24.53 km)
1 Blomqvist/Melander (Nissan) 13m 28s; 2 McRae/
Ringer (Subaru), Jonsson/Bäckman (Toyota) 13m
35s; 4 Alén/Kivimäki (Toyota) 13m 41s; 5 Asterhag/
Thörner (Toyota) 13m 42s; 6 Eklund/Johansson
(Subaru) 13m 53s.

SS 13. Vibberbo (27.05 km)
1 McRae/Ringer (Subaru) 16m 39s; 2 Jonsson/
Bäckman (Toyota) 16m 57s; 3 Alén/Kivimäki (Toy-
ota), Blomqvist/Melander (Nissan) 17m 06s; 5 Lampi/
Kuukkala (Mitsubishi) 17m 08s; 6 B. Johansson/A.
Olsson (Mazda 323 GT-X) 17m 21s.

SS 14. Nisshyttan (28.92 km)
1 McRae/Ringer (Subaru) 17m 29s; 2 Jonsson/
Bäckman (Toyota), Blomqvist/Melander (Nissan) 17m
40s; 4 Lampi/Kuukkala (Mitsubishi) 17m 55s; 5
Alén/Kivimäki (Toyota) 17m 57s; 6 Eklund/ Johansson (Subaru), Asterhag/Thörner (Toyota) 18m 16s.

SS 15. I13 (10.85 km)
1 Eklund/Johansson (Subaru) 6m 54s; 2 Alén/
Kivimäki (Toyota) 6m 55s; 3 Jonsson/Bäckman (Toy-
ota) 7m 00s; 4 McRae/Ringer (Subaru) 7m 01s; 5
Blomqvist/Melander (Nissan) 7m 04s; 6 Asterhag/
Thörner (Toyota) 7m 09s.

SS 16. Skog (22.36 km)
1 Alén/Kivimäki (Toyota) 13m 25s; 2 Jonsson/Bäck-
man (Toyota), Blomqvist/Melander (Nissan) 13m
27s; 4 McRae/Ringer (Subaru) 13m 30s; 5 Lampi/
Kuukkala (Mitsubishi) 13m 43s; 6 Asterhag /Thörner
(Toyota) 13m 47s.

SS 17. Djura (22.97 km)
1 Jonsson/Bäckman (Toyota) 12m 11s; 2 Blomqvist/
Melander (Nissan) 12m 14s; 3 Alén/Kivimäki (Toyota)
12m 15s; 4 McRae/Ringer (Subaru) 12m 17s; 5
Asterhag/Thörner (Toyota) 12m 24s; 6 Lampi/
Kuukkala (Mitsubishi) 12m 25s.

SS 18. Skalo (26.58 km)
1 McRae/Ringer (Subaru) 13m 48s; 2 Blomqvist/
Melander (Nissan) 13m 54s; 3 Jonsson/Bäckman
(Toyota) 13m 58s; 4 Alén/Kivimäki (Toyota) 13m 59s;
5 Asterhag/Thörner (Toyota) 14m 05s; 6 Lampi/
Kuukkala (Mitsubishi) 14m 13s.

SS 19. Likenas (42.81 km)
1 Jonsson/Bäckman (Toyota) 20m 45s; 2 McRae/
Ringer (Subaru), Blomqvist/Melander (Nissan) 20m
51s; 4 Alén/Kivimäki (Toyota) 21m 02s; 5 Asterhag/
Thörner (Toyota) 21m 15s; 6 Lampi/Kuukkala (Mitsubishi) 21m 35s.

SS 20. Svensk Andersberg (9.85 km)
1 Jonsson/Bäckman (Toyota) 6m 04s; 2 Alén/
Kivimäki (Toyota), Blomqvist/Melander (Nissan) 6m
05s; 4 McRae/Ringer (Subaru) 6m 11s; 5 Asterhag/
Thörner (Toyota) 6m 15s; 6 Eklund/Johansson 6m
17s (Subaru).

SS 21. Mitandersfors (13.03 km)
1 McRae/Ringer (Subaru) 8m 25s; 2 Jonsson/ Bäckman (Toyota) 8m 31s; 3 Alén/Kivimäki (Toyota) 8m
33s; 4 Asterhag/Thörner (Toyota) 8m 35s; 5
Blomqvist/Melander (Nissan) 8m 41s; 6 Lampi/
Kuukkala (Mitsubishi) 8m 45s.

SS 22. Axland (21.24 km)
1 Jonsson/Bäckman (Toyota) 10m 24s; 2 Alén/
Kivimäki (Toyota) 10m 26s; 3 McRae/Ringer (Subaru)
10m 29s; 4 Blomqvist/Melander (Nissan) 10m 31s; 5
Asterhag/Thörner (Toyota) 10m 33s; 6 Lampi/
Kuukkala (Mitsubishi) 10m 50s.

SS 23. Mangen (22.09 km)
1 Jonsson/Bäckman (Toyota) 13m 25s; 2 Alén/
Kivimäki (Toyota) 13m 28s; 3 Blomqvist/Melander
(Nissan), McRae/Ringer (Subaru) 13m 30s; 5 Lampi/
Kuukkala (Mitsubishi) 13m 40s; 6 Eklund/Johansson
(Subaru) 13m 46s.

SS 24. Tobyn (10.19 km)
1 Alén/Kivimäki (Toyota) 5m 25s; 2 Jonsson/ Bäckman (Toyota), Blomqvist/Melander (Nissan) 5m 30s;

4 McRae/Ringer (Subaru) 5m 32s; **5** Asterhag/
Thörner (Toyota) 5m 35s; **6** Eklund/Johansson (Subaru) 5m 37s.

SS 25. Alvsbacka V (11.67 km)
1 Alén/Kivimäki (Toyota), Blomqvist/Melander (Nissan) 6m 28s; **3** McRae/Ringer (Subaru) 6m 29s; **4** Jonsson/Bäckman (Toyota) 6m 31s; **5** Asterhag/
Thörner (Toyota) 6m 36s; **6** Eklund/Johansson (Subaru), Lampi/Kuukkala (Mitsubishi) 6m 41s.

SS 26. Malta (11.88 km)
1 Blomqvist/Melander (Nissan) 6m 20s; **2** Alén/
Kivimäki (Toyota), Jonsson/Bäckman (Toyota) 6m 23s; **4** McRae/Ringer (Subaru), Asterhag/Thörner (Toyota) 6m 24s; **6** Eklund/Johansson (Subaru) 6m 28s.

SS 27. Vargåsen (24.42 km)
1 Alén/Kivimäki (Toyota) 14m 24s; **2** Jonsson/ Bäckman (Toyota) 14m 25s; **3** McRae/Ringer (Subaru) 14m 27s; **4** Blomqvist/Melander (Nissan) 14m 29s; **5** Asterhag/Thörner (Toyota) 14m 38s; **6** Lampi/
Kuukkala (Mitsubishi), Eklund/Johansson (Subaru) 14m 51s.

SS 28. Skalla (8.67 km)
1 Jonsson/Bäckman (Toyota) 6m 37s; **2** Blomqvist/
Melander (Nissan) 6m 38s; **3** Alén/Kivimäki (Toyota) 6m 40s; **4** Eklund/Johansson (Subaru) 6m 42s; **5** Asterhag/Thörner (Toyota) 6m 48s; **6** Lampi/
Kuukkala (Mitsubishi) 6m 50s.

SS 29. Bjälverud (21.58 km)
1 Blomqvist/Melander (Nissan) 11m 19s; **2** Alén/
Kivimäki (Toyota) 11m 30s; **3** Jonsson/Bäckman (Toyota) 11m 33s; **4** McRae/Ringer (Subaru) 11m 39s; **5** Asterhag/Thörner (Toyota) 11m 44s; **6** Eklund/
Johansson (Subaru) 11m 55s.

SS 30. Lonnhojden (19.83 km)
1 Alén/Kivimäki (Toyota) 11m 09s; **2** McRae/Ringer (Subaru) 11m 17s; **3** Blomqvist/Melander (Nissan) 11m 23s; **4** Jonsson/Bäckman (Toyota), Eklund/
Johansson (Subaru) 11m 29s; **6** Asterhag/Thörner (Toyota) 11m 39s.

SS 31. Långjohanstorp (19.44 km):
1 Alén/Kivimäki (Toyota) 10m 10s; **2** McRae/Ringer (Subaru) 10m 14s; **3** Blomqvist/Melander (Nissan) 10m 28s; **4** Jonsson/Bäckman (Toyota) 10m 29s; **5** Asterhag/Thörner (Toyota) 10m 30s; **6** Eklund/
Johansson (Subaru) 10m 35s.

FIA class winners

Group A

Over 2000 cc:	Jonsson/Bäckman (Toyota)
1600-2000 cc:	Joki/Johansson (Peugeot)
1300-1600 cc:	Per Svan/Johan Olsson (Opel Corsa GSi)
Up to 1300 cc:	Jean-François Zumbihl/Daniel Rouche (Citroën AX Sport)

Group N

Over 2000 cc:	Nilsson/Persson (Mitsubishi)
1600-2000 cc:	Clemens Andersson/Raymond Eriksson (Opel Kadett GSi 16v)
1300-1600 cc:	Lars-Goran Andersson/Anders Wann (Opel Corsa GSi)
Up to 1300 cc:	Anders Soderberg/Karl-Arne Forsman (Suzuki Swift GTI)

Major retirements

Ari Vatanen/	Subaru Legacy RS	
Bruno Berglund	SS 1	rolled
Mikael Sundström/	Lancia Delta HF Integrale	
Jakke Honkanen	SS 6	centre diff
Sebastian Lindholm/	Ford Sierra Cosworth 4x4	
Timo Hantunen	SS 9	transmission
Stig-Olov Walfridsson/	Mitsubishi Galant VR-4	
Gunnar Barth	SS 10	rolled
John Bosch/	Nissan Sunny GTi-R	
Peter Diekmann	SS 10	gearbox
Marcus Grönholm/	Toyota Celica GT4	
Ilkka Riipinen	SS 11	engine
Kenneth Bäcklund/	Mitsubishi Galant VR-4	
Tord Andersson	SS 16	gearbox
Sven-Erik Eriksson/	Nissan Sunny GTi-R	
Tommy Strom	SS 26	crashed

Rally leaders

SS 1 Alén/Kivimäki (Toyota), Jonsson/Bäckman (Toyota), Blomqvist/Melander (Nissan); **SS 2** Lindholm/Hantunen (Ford); **SS 3** Jonsson/Bäckman (Toyota), Lindholm/Hantunen (Ford); **SS 4-31** Jonsson/Bäckman (Toyota).

World Championship points

Drivers
1 Auriol and Jonsson 20; **3** Sainz and McRae 15; **5**

Kankkunen and Blomqvist 12; **7** Delecour and Alén 10; **9** Bugalski and Asterhag 8.

Route details

Leg 1
13 February: Starting and finishing at Karlstad 1400-2035, including six special stages (72.81 km).
Leg 2
14 February: Starting from Karlstad at 0730, finishing at Falun at 1950, including nine special stages (189.77 km).
Leg 3
15 February: Starting from Falun at 0730, finishing at Karlstad at 1935, including nine special stages (191.12 km).
Leg 4
16 February: Starting and finishing at Karlstad at 0630-1440, including seven special stages (117.49 km).

Weather

Cold with snow and ice.

Special stage analysis

	1st	2nd	3rd	4th	5th	6th
Jonsson/Bäckman (Toyota)	14	10	4	3	-	-
Alén/Kivimäki (Toyota)	9	6	6	5	1	3
Blomqvist/Melander (Nissan)	5	11	6	3	2	2
McRae/Ringer (Subaru)	5	7	6	9	1	-
Lindholm/Hantunen (Ford)	1	1	1	2	1	-
Eklund/Johansson (Subaru)	1	-	-	3	-	12
Grönholm/Riipinen (Toyota)	-	1	1	1	6	-
Asterhag/Thörner (Toyota)	-	-	1	4	14	6
Lampi/Kuukkala (Mitsubishi)	-	-	-	2	3	10
Nilsson/Persson (Mitsubishi)	-	-	-	1	-	-
Bäcklund/Andersson (Mitsubishi)	-	-	-	-	1	-
Johansson/Olsson (Mazda)	-	-	-	-	-	1

There weren't many drivers ahead of the purple peril, Per Svan driving brilliantly in Opel Sweden's Corsa GSi.

Finish lines

The Sunne veteran, **Sören Nilsson**, ultimately made certain of Group N; his **Mitsubishi** Sweden colleagues were less fortunate, **Stig-Olov Walfridsson** rolling, while **Kenneth Bäcklund** broke his Galant's gearbox...Loose intercooler pipes hampered **Per Eklund**'s efforts in the **Camel Subaru**, but it took a power steering pump change to bring the Swede into contention...**Per Svan** was the top two-wheel drive runner and 11th overall in his Corsa GSi; it was also the highest placed European car...**Mikael Sundström** retired his Group N **Lancia** with a broken centre differential...**Marcus Grönholm**'s promising drive in a Toyota Finland Celica was curtailed by a blown engine...**Lasse Lampi** was neck and neck with **Leif Asterhag** until he went off into a snowbank for seven minutes on SS20...**Kjell Olofsson** and **Sven-Erik Eriksson** crashed their **Nissans** on the same stage during the final leg, handing second in Group N to **Jarmo Kytölehto**'s **Mitsubishi**.

Results

1	Mats Jonsson/	Toyota Celica GT4		
	Lars Bäckman	5h 24m 37s	Gr A	
2	Colin McRae/	Subaru Legacy RS		
	Derek Ringer	5h 25m 16s	Gr A	
3	Stig Blomqvist/	Nissan Sunny GTi-R		
	Benny Melander	5h 26m 09s	Gr A	
4	Markku Alén/	Toyota Celica GT4		
	Ilkka Kivimäki	5h 26m 25s	Gr A	
5	Leif Asterhag/	Toyota Celica GT4		
	Tina Thörner	5h 30m 53s	Gr A	
6	Per Eklund/	Subaru Legacy RS		
	Johnny Johansson	5h 35m 12s	Gr A	
7	Björn Johansson/	Mazda 323 GT-X		
	Anders Olsson	5h 38m 58s	Gr A	
8	Lasse Lampi/	Mitsubishi Galant VR-4		
	Pentti Kuukkala	5h 41m 51s	Gr A	
9	Sören Nilsson/	Mitsubishi Galant VR-4		
	Per-Ove Persson	5h 43m 22s	Gr N	
10	Jarmo Kytölehto/	Mitsubishi Galant VR-4		
	Kari Jokinen	5h 49m 29s	Gr A	

94 starters, 46 finishers

Previous winners

1960	Carl Magnus Skogh/Rolf Skogh	Saab 96
1961	Carl Magnus Skogh/Rolf Skogh	Saab 96
1962	Bengt Söderström/Rune Olsson	Mini-Cooper
1963	Berndt Jansson/Erik Petterson	Porsche S90
1964	Tom Trana/Gunnar Thermenius	Volvo 544
1965	Tom Trana/Gunnar Thermenius	Volvo 544
1966	Ake Andersson/Sven-Olof Svedberg	Saab 96
1967	Bengt Söderström/Gunnar Palm	
		Ford Lotus Cortina
1968	Björn Waldegård/Lars Helmer	Porsche 911T
1969	Björn Waldegård/Lars Helmer	Porsche 911S
1970	Björn Waldegård/Lars Helmer	Porsche 911S
1971	Stig Blomqvist/Arne Hertz	Saab 96 V4
1972	Stig Blomqvist/Arne Hertz	Saab 96 V4
1973	Stig Blomqvist/Arne Hertz	Saab 96 V4
1975	Björn Waldegård/Hans Thorszelius	
		Lancia Stratos
1976	Per Eklund/Björn Cederberg	Saab 96 V4
1977	Stig Blomqvist/Hans Sylvan	Saab 99 EMS
1978	Björn Waldegård/Hans Thorszelius	
		Ford Escort RS
1979	Stig Blomqvist/Björn Cederberg	Saab 99 Turbo
1980	Anders Kullang/Bruno Berglund	
		Opel Ascona 400
1981	Hannu Mikkola/Arne Hertz	Audi Quattro
1982	Stig Blomqvist/Björn Cederberg	Audi Quattro A1
1983	Hannu Mikkola/Arne Hertz	Audi Quattro A1
1984	Stig Blomqvist/Björn Cederberg	Audi Quattro A2
1985	Ari Vatanen/Terry Harryman	
		Peugeot 205 Turbo 16
1986	Juha Kankkunen/Juha Pironen	
		Peugeot 205 Turbo 16
1987	Timo Salonen/Seppo Harjanne	Mazda 323 Turbo
1988	Markku Alén/Ilkka Kivimäki	Lancia Delta HF Turbo
1989	Ingvar Carlsson/Per Carlsson	Mazda 323 Turbo
1991	Kenneth Eriksson/Staffan Parmander	
		Mitsubishi Galant VR-4

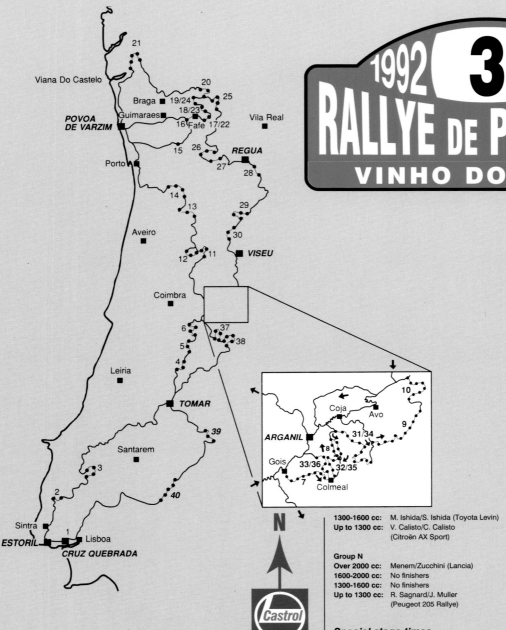

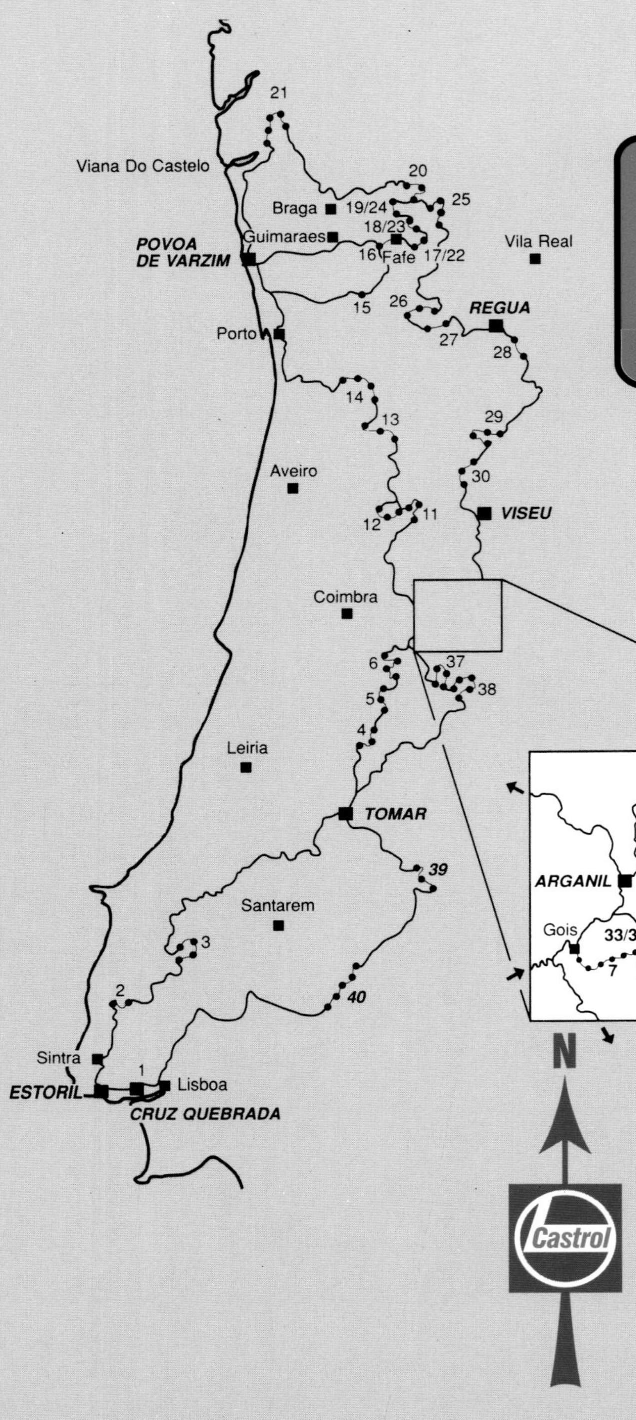
Viana Do Castelo
Braga
Guimaraes
POVOA DE VARZIM
Fafe
Vila Real
Porto
REGUA
Aveiro
VISEU
Coimbra
Leiria
TOMAR
Santarem
Sintra
ESTORIL
Lisboa
CRUZ QUEBRADA
Coja
Avo
ARGANIL
Gois
Colmeal
N
Castrol

1992
3
1992
RALLYE DE PORTUGAL
VINHO DO PORTO

RALLY OF PORTUGAL, 3-7 March. FIA World Rally Championship for Manufacturers, round 2. FIA World Rally Championship for Drivers, round 3.

Leading entries

1	Carlos Sainz/ Luis Moya	Toyota Celica Turbo 4WD Gr A
2	Didier Auriol/ Bernard Occelli	Lancia Delta HF Integrale Gr A
3	François Delecour/ Daniel Grataloup	Ford Sierra Cosworth 4x4 Gr A
4	Juha Kankkunen/ Juha Piironen	Lancia Delta HF Integrale Gr A
5	Armin Schwarz/ Arne Hertz	Toyota Celica Turbo 4WD Gr A
6	Kenneth Eriksson/ Staffan Parmander	Mitsubishi Galant VR-4 Gr A
7	Massimo Biasion/ Tiziano Siviero	Ford Sierra Cosworth 4x4 Gr A
8	Tommi Mäkinen/ Seppo Harjanne	Nissan Sunny GTi-R Gr A
9	Markku Alén/ Ilkka Kivimäki	Toyota Celica Turbo 4WD Gr A
10	Timo Salonen/ Voitto Silander	Mitsubishi Galant VR-4 Gr A
11	François Chatriot/ Michel Périn	Nissan Sunny GTi-R Gr A
12	Grégoire de Mevius/ Willy Lux	Nissan Sunny GTi-R Gr N
14	Piergiorgio Bedini/ Laurent Baggio	Lancia Delta HF Integrale Gr N
15	Fernando Capdevila/ Alfredo Rodriguez	Ford Sierra Cosworth 4x4m Gr N
16	Andrea Aghini/ Sauro Farnocchia	Lancia Delta HF Integrale Gr A
17	José Maria Bardolet/ Josep Autet	Ford Sierra Cosworth 4x4 Gr A
18	Mikael Sundström/ Jakke Honkanen	Lancia Delta HF Integrale Gr N
19	Mohammed Bin Sulayem/ Ronan Morgan	Ford Sierra Cosworth 4x4 Gr N
20	Carlos Menem/ Victor Zucchini	Lancia Delta HF Integrale Gr N
21	Kurt Gottlicher/ Otto Zwanzigleitner	Ford Sierra Cosworth 4x4 Gr N

FIA class winners

Group A

Over 2000 cc:	Kankkunen/Piironen (Lancia)
1600-2000 cc:	C. Macedo/M. Borges (Renault Clio 16S)
1300-1600 cc:	M. Ishida/S. Ishida (Toyota Levin)
Up to 1300 cc:	V. Calisto/C. Calisto (Citroën AX Sport)

Group N

Over 2000 cc:	Menem/Zucchini (Lancia)
1600-2000 cc:	No finishers
1300-1600 cc:	No finishers
Up to 1300 cc:	R. Sagnard/J. Muller (Peugeot 205 Rallye)

Special stage times

SS 1. Estadio (2.30 km)
1 M. Alén/I. Kivimäki (Toyota Celica Turbo 4WD) 1m 36s; **2** J. Kankkunen/J. Piironen (Lancia Delta HF Integrale), M. Biasion/T. Siviero (Ford Sierra Cosworth 4x4) 1m 38s; **4** C. Sainz/L. Moya (Toyota Celica Turbo 4WD), D. Auriol/B. Occelli (Lancia Delta HF Integrale), A. Schwarz/A. Hertz (Toyota Celica Turbo 4WD), K. Eriksson/S. Parmander (Mitsubishi Galant VR-4), F. Chatriot/M. Périn (Nissan Sunny GTi-R) 1m 39s.

SS 2. Gradil (9.00 km)
1 F. Delecour/D. Grataloup (Ford Sierra Cosworth 4x4) 4m 55s; **2** Kankkunen/Piironen (Lancia) 4m 58s; **3** Sainz/Moya (Toyota), Auriol/Occelli (Lancia), Alén/Kivimäki (Toyota) 4m 59s; **6** Schwarz/Hertz (Toyota), A. Aghini/S. Farnocchia (Lancia Delta HF Integrale) 5m 01s.

SS 3. Montejunto (9.50 km)
1 Auriol/Occelli (Lancia) 4m 59s; **2** Sainz/Moya (Toyota), Delecour/Grataloup (Ford) 5m 00s; **4** Kankkunen/Piironen (Lancia), Alén/Kivimäki (Toyota) 5m 01s; **6** Biasion/Siviero (Ford) 5m 03s.

SS 4. Figueiro dos Vinhos (20.40 km)
1 Delecour/Grataloup (Ford) 12m 17s; **2** Aghini/Farnocchia (Lancia) 12m 24s; **3** Biasion/Siviero (Ford) 12m 26s; **4** T. Salonen/V. Silander (Mitsubishi Galant VR-4) 12m 32s; **5** Kankkunen/Piironen (Lancia) 12m 33s; **6** Eriksson/Parmander (Mitsubishi) 12m 34s.

SS 5. Campelo (10.40 km)
1 Delecour/Grataloup (Ford) 6m 54s; **2** Biasion/Siviero (Ford) 6m 58s; **3** Alén/Kivimäki (Toyota), Aghini/Farnocchia (Lancia) 7m 01s; **5** Salonen/Silander (Mitsubishi) 7m 02s; **6** Sainz/Moya (Toyota), Schwarz/Hertz (Toyota) 7m 03s.

SS 6. Serra da Lousa (24.90 km)
1 Delecour/Grataloup (Ford) 14m 24s; **2** Aghini/Farnocchia (Lancia) 14m 30s; **3** Biasion/Siviero (Ford) 14m 34s; **4** Kankkunen/Piironen (Lancia) 14m 41s; **5** Schwarz/Hertz (Toyota) 14m 47s; **6** Sainz/Moya (Toyota), Alén/Kivimäki (Toyota) 14m 48s.

SS 7. Gois (17.90 km)
1 Delecour/Grataloup (Ford) 10m 38s; **2** Biasion/Siviero (Ford), Aghini/Farnocchia (Lancia) 10m 41s; **4** Kankkunen/Piironen (Lancia) 10m 46s; **5** Schwarz/Hertz (Toyota) 10m 48s; **6** Alén/Kivimäki (Toyota) 10m 49s.

SS 8. Arganil (12.60 km)
1 Kankkunen/Piironen (Lancia) 7m 53s; **2** Delecour/Grataloup (Ford) 7m 56s; **3** Aghini/Farnocchia (Lancia) 7m 58s; **4** Biasion/Siviero (Ford) 7m 59s; **5** Sainz/Moya (Toyota), Salonen/Silander (Mitsubishi), Eriksson/Parmander (Mitsubishi) 8m 07s.

SS 9. Piodao (18.80 km)
1 Aghini/Farnocchia (Lancia) 12m 16s; **2** Delecour/Grataloup (Ford), Kankkunen/Piironen (Lancia) 12m 20s; **4** Biasion/Siviero (Ford) 12m 22s; 5 Sainz/Moya (Toyota) 12m 31s; **6** Salonen/Silander (Mitsubishi) 12m 34s.

SS 10. Giao (14.10 km)
1 Aghini/Farnocchia (Lancia) 9m 05s; **2** Delecour/Grataloup (Ford), Kankkunen/Piironen (Lancia), Biasion/Siviero (Ford) 9m 10s; **5** Sainz/Moya (Toyota) 9m 15s; **6** Salonen/Silander (Mitsubishi) 9m 16s.

SS 11. Muna (9.30 km)
1 Sainz/Moya (Toyota) 5m 57s; **2** Biasion/Siviero (Ford) 5m 58s; **3** Delecour/Grataloup (Ford) 6m 00s; **4** Kankkunen/Piironen (Lancia) 6m 03s; **5** Schwarz/Hertz (Toyota), Aghini/Farnocchia (Lancia) 6m 04s.

SS 12. Caramulo (14.10 km)
1 Biasion/Siviero (Ford) 7m 56s; **2** Delecour/Grataloup (Ford) 7m 58s; **3** Sainz/Moya (Toyota), Aghini/Farnocchia (Lancia) 8m 01s; **5** Kankkunen/Piironen (Lancia) 8m 05s; **6** Schwarz/Hertz (Toyota) 8m 11s.

SS 13. Freita (24.10 km)
1 Kankkunen/Piironen (Lancia) 14m 38s; **2** Delecour/Grataloup (Ford) 14m 42s; **3** Aghini/Farnocchia (Lancia) 14m 44s; **4** Sainz/Moya (Toyota) 14m 48s; **5** Biasion/Siviero (Ford) 14m 50s; 6 Schwarz/Hertz (Toyota) 15m 12s.

SS 14. Arouca (22.20 km)
1 Delecour/Grataloup (Ford) 13m 23s; **2** Biasion/Siviero (Ford) 13m 32s; **3** Aghini/Farnocchia (Lancia) 13m 33s; **4** Kankkunen/Piironen (Lancia) 13m 41s; **5** Sainz/Moya (Toyota) 13m 44s; **6** Schwarz/Hertz (Toyota), Salonen/Silander (Mitsubishi) 13m 55s.

SS 15. Lousada (3.00 km)
1 Kankkunen/Piironen (Lancia), Schwarz/Hertz (Toyota), Alén/Kivimäki (Toyota) 2m 43s; **4** Sainz/ Moya (Toyota), Eriksson/Parmander (Mitsubishi) 2m 44s; **6** Aghini/Farnocchia (Lancia) 2m 46s.

SS 16. Veiga (5.80 km)
1 Alén/Kivimäki (Toyota) 3m 49s; **2** Sainz/Moya (Toyota) 3m 51s; **3** Kankkunen/Piironen (Lancia) 3m 52s; 4 Eriksson/Parmander (Mitsubishi) 3m 53s; **5** Schwarz/Hertz (Toyota), Chatriot/Périn (Nissan), Aghini/Farnocchia (Lancia) 3m 56s.

SS 17. Montim 1 (5.00 km)
1 Alén/Kivimäki (Toyota) 3m 53s; **2** Sainz/Moya (Toyota) 3m 55s; **3** Kankkunen/Piironen (Lancia),

Schwarz/Hertz (Toyota) 3m 56s; 5 Salonen/Silander (Mitsubishi), Eriksson/Parmander (Mitsubishi) 3m 57s.

SS 18. Lameirinha 1 (10.00 km)
1 Sainz/Moya (Toyota), Kankkunen/Piironen (Lancia) 6m 43s; 3 Alén/Kivimäki (Toyota) 6m 44s; 4 Eriksson/Parmander (Mitsubishi) 6m 45s; 5 Chatriot/Périn (Nissan) 6m 47s; 6 Schwarz/Hertz (Toyota) 6m 48s.

SS 19. Luilhas 1 (13.10 km)
1 Kankkunen/Piironen (Lancia) 9m 46s; 2 Salonen/Silander (Mitsubishi) 9m 47s; 3 Eriksson/Parmander (Mitsubishi), Alén/Kivimäki (Toyota) 9m 49s; 5 Sainz/Moya (Toyota) 9m 51s; 6 Schwarz/Hertz (Toyota) 9m 54s.

SS 20. Vieira do Minho (13.10 km)
1 Kankkunen/Piironen (Lancia) 9m 07s; 2 Alén/Kivimäki (Toyota) 9m 11s; 3 Schwarz/Hertz (Toyota) 9m 13s; 4 Eriksson/Parmander (Mitsubishi), Salonen/Silander (Mitsubishi) 9m 14s; 6 Sainz/Moya (Toyota) 9m 15s.

SS 21. Ponte de Lima (21.00 km)
1 Kankkunen/Piironen (Lancia) 15m 30s; 2 Sainz/Moya (Toyota), Salonen/Silander (Mitsubishi) 15m 38s; 4 Aghini/Farnocchia (Lancia) 15m 42s; 5 Schwarz/Hertz (Toyota), Biasion/Siviero (Ford) 15m 44s.

SS 22. Montim 2 (5.00 km)
1 Sainz/Moya (Toyota) 3m 51s; 2 Schwarz/Hertz (Toyota), Alén/Kivimäki (Toyota) 3m 52s; 4 Kankkunen/Piironen (Lancia) 3m 53s; 5 Eriksson/Parmander (Mitsubishi), Biasion/Siviero (Ford) 3m 55s.

SS 23. Lameirinha 2 (10.00 km)
1 Sainz/Moya (Toyota) 6m 30s; 2 Eriksson/Parmander (Mitsubishi) 6m 36s; 3 Schwarz/Hertz (Toyota), Alén/Kivimäki (Toyota) 6m 37s; 5 Kankkunen/Piironen (Lancia) 6m 38s; 6 Chatriot/Périn (Nissan) 6m 39s.

SS 24. Luilhas 2 (13.10 km)
1 Alén/Kivimäki (Toyota) 9m 37s; 2 Sainz/Moya (Toyota) 9m 39s; 3 Kankkunen/Piironen (Lancia) 9m 40s; 4 Eriksson/Parmander (Mitsubishi) 9m 42s; 5 Schwarz/Hertz (Toyota) 9m 47s; 6 Salonen/Silander (Mitsubishi), Chatriot/Périn (Nissan) 9m 48s.

SS 25. Cabeceiras de Basto (13.50 km)
1 Kankkunen/Piironen (Lancia) 8m 44s; 2 Salonen/Silander (Mitsubishi) 8m 47s; 3 Sainz/Moya (Toyota), Biasion/Siviero (Ford), Alén/Kivimäki (Toyota) 8m 48s; 6 Schwarz/Hertz (Toyota) 8m 54s.

SS 26. Carvalho de Rei (10.90 km)
1 Alén/Kivimäki (Toyota) 7m 34s; 2 Kankkunen/Piironen (Lancia) 7m 35s; 3 Sainz/Moya (Toyota), Biasion/Siviero (Ford) 7m 37s; 5 Eriksson/Parmander (Mitsubishi) 7m 38s; 6 Salonen/Silander (Mitsubishi) 7m 39s.

SS 27. Aboboreira (20.90 km)
1 Eriksson/Parmander (Mitsubishi) 14m 32s; 2 Sainz/Moya (Toyota) 14m 35s; 3 Kankkunen/Piironen (Lancia) 14m 36s; 4 Salonen/Silander (Mitsubishi) 14m 38s; 5 Biasion/Siviero (Ford) 14m 39s; 6 Aghini/Farnocchia (Lancia) 14m 46s.

SS 28. Armamar (9.30 km)
1 Biasion/Siviero (Ford) 6m 21s; 2 Kankkunen/Piironen (Lancia), Eriksson/Parmander (Mitsubishi) 6m 22s; 4 Sainz/Moya (Toyota), Schwarz/Hertz (Toyota) 6m 25s; 6 Alén/Kivimäki (Toyota) 6m 26s.

SS 29. Covelo de Paiva (15.40 km)
1 Kankkunen/Piironen (Lancia) 9m 19s; 2 Sainz/Moya (Toyota), Biasion/Siviero (Ford) 9m 21s; 4

Eriksson/Parmander (Mitsubishi) 9m 22s; 5 Schwarz/Hertz (Toyota) 9m 23s; 6 Alén/Kivimäki (Toyota) 9m 24s.

SS 30. Viseu (25.90 km)
1 Kankkunen/Piironen (Lancia) 16m 13s; 2 Salonen/Silander (Mitsubishi) 16m 14s; 3 Biasion/Siviero (Ford) 16m 15s; 4 Schwarz/Hertz (Toyota) 16m 21s; 5 Eriksson/Parmander (Mitsubishi) 16m 22s; 6 Aghini/Farnocchia (Lancia) 16m 26s.

SS 31. Arganil-Alqueve 1 (25.90 km)
1 Kankkunen/Piironen (Lancia) 18m 26s; 2 Biasion/Siviero (Ford) 18m 32s; 3 Salonen/Silander (Mitsubishi) 19m 01s; 4 Schwarz/Hertz (Toyota) 19m 08s; 5 Sainz/Moya (Toyota) 19m 11s; 6 Alén/Kivimäki (Toyota), Chatriot/Périn (Nissan) 19m 19s.

SS 32. Folques-Colmeal 1 (17.30 km)
1 Schwarz/Hertz (Toyota), Biasion/Siviero (Ford) 12m 51s; 3 Sainz/Moya (Toyota) 12m 57s; 4 Alén/Kivimäki (Toyota), Salonen/Silander (Mitsubishi) 12m 59s; 6 Kankkunen/Piironen (Lancia) 13m 01s.

SS 33. Linhares 1 (11.00 km)
1 Biasion/Siviero (Ford) 8m 31s; 2 Kankkunen/Piironen (Lancia) 8m 35s; 3 Schwarz/Hertz (Toyota), Salonen/Silander (Mitsubishi) 8m 37s; 5 Alén/Kivimäki (Toyota) 8m 40s; 6 Sainz/Moya (Toyota) 8m 41s.

SS 34. Arganil-Alqueve 2 (25.90 km)
1 Kankkunen/Piironen (Lancia) 18m 02s; 2 Schwarz/Hertz (Toyota), Biasion/Siviero (Ford) 18m 09s; 4 Sainz/Moya (Toyota) 18m 13s; 5 Alén/Kivimäki (Toyota) 18m 21s; 6 Salonen/Silander (Mitsubishi) 18m 24s.

SS 35. Folques-Colmeal 2 (17.30 km)
1 Schwarz/Hertz (Toyota) 12m 37s; 2 Kankkunen/Piironen (Lancia), Biasion/Siviero (Ford) 12m 42s; 4 Alén/Kivimäki (Toyota) 12m 44s; 5 Salonen/Silander (Mitsubishi) 12m 47s; 6 Alén/Kivimäki (Toyota) 12m 49s.

SS 36. Linhares 2 (11.00 km)
1 Schwarz/Hertz (Toyota) 8m 30s; 2 Kankkunen/Piironen (Lancia), Biasion/Siviero (Ford), Salonen/Silander (Mitsubishi) 8m 31s; 5 Alén/Kivimäki (Toyota) 8m 33s; 6 Sainz/Moya (Toyota) 8m 38s.

SS 37. Amoreira (15.90 km)
1 Alén/Kivimäki (Toyota) 12m 55s; 2 Kankkunen/Piironen (Lancia) 12m 56s; 3 Schwarz/Hertz (Toyota) 12m 59s; 4 Sainz/Moya (Toyota), Biasion/Siviero (Ford), Eriksson/Parmander (Mitsubishi) 13m 01s.

SS 38. Pampilhosa (12.90 km)
1 Kankkunen/Piironen (Lancia) 11m 08s; 2 Alén/Kivimäki (Toyota), Salonen/Silander (Mitsubishi) 11m 09s; 4 Biasion/Siviero (Ford) 11m 12s; 5 Chatriot/Périn (Nissan) 11m 41s; 6 J. Santos/C. Magalhaes (Toyota Celica GT4) 12m 16s.

SS 39. Abrantes (15.30 km)
1 Alén/Kivimäki (Toyota) 8m 18s; 2 Sainz/Moya (Toyota) 8m 19s; 3 Kankkunen/Piironen (Lancia) 8m 28s; 4 Biasion/Siviero (Ford) 8m 34s; 5 Chatriot/Périn (Nissan) 8m 56s; 6 F. Peres/R. Caldeira (Ford Sierra Cosworth 4x4) 9m 07s.

SS 40. Coruche (20.20 km)
1 Alén/Kivimäki (Toyota) 9m 24s; 2 Sainz/Moya (Toyota) 9m 33s; 3 Kankkunen/Piironen (Lancia) 9m 40s; 4 Biasion/Siviero (Ford) 9m 41s; 5 Chatriot/Périn (Nissan) 9m 53s; 6 Salonen/Silander (Mitsubishi) 10m 00s.

Major retirements

Didier Auriol/	Lancia Delta HF Integrale
Tiziano Siviero	SS 3	engine
Tommi Mäkinen/	Nissan Sunny GTi-R
Seppo Harjanne	SS 4	crashed
François Delecour/	Ford Sierra Cosworth 4x4
Daniel Grataloup	SS 15	holed sump
Mikael Sundström/	Lancia Delta HF Integrale
Jakke Honkanen	SS 27	lost a wheel
Andrea Aghini/	Lancia Delta HF Integrale
Sauro Farnocchia	SS 31	crashed
Kenneth Eriksson/	Mitsubishi Galant VR-4
Staffan Parmander	SS 31	crashed
Armin Schwarz/	Toyota Celica Turbo 4WD
Arne Hertz	SS 38	crashed

Rally leaders

SS 1 Alén/Kivimäki (Toyota); **SS 2** Alén/Kivimäki (Toyota), Delecour/Grataloup (Ford); **SS 3-14** Delecour/Grataloup (Ford); **SS 15-18** Aghini/Farnocchia (Lancia); **SS 19-40** Kankkunen/Piironen (Lancia).

World Championship points

Drivers
1 Kankkunen 32; 2 Sainz 27; 3 Alén, Auriol and Jonsson 20; 6 Biasion 18; 7 McRae 15; 8 Salonen 14; 9 Blomqvist 12; 10 Chatriot and Delecour 10.

Manufacturers
1 Lancia 40; 2 Toyota 31; 3 Ford 29; 4 Mitsubishi 18; 5 Nissan 14.

Route details

Leg 1
3/5 March: Starting from Cruz Quebrada Estadio Nacional 1500/3, finishing at Povoa de Varzim 0100/5, including 14 special stages (217.93 km).
Leg 2
5 March: Starting and finishing at Povoa de Varzim 1000-1915, including seven special stages (71.07 km).
Leg 3
6 March: Starting from Povoa de Varzim at 0700, finishing at Viseu at 1745, including nine special stages (124.08 km).
Leg 4
7 March: Starting from Viseu at 0400, finishing at Estoril at 2000, including 10 special stages (172.74 km).

Weather

Dry and mild apart from a foggy start to the final leg.

Special stage analysis

	1st	2nd	3rd	4th	5th	6th
Kankkunen/Piironen (Lancia)	13	10	6	6	3	1
Alén/Kivimäki (Toyota)	9	3	6	3	3	6
Delecour/Grataloup (Ford)	6	6	1	-	-	-
Biasion/Siviero (Ford)	4	11	5	6	4	1
Sainz/Moya (Toyota)	4	9	5	6	6	5
Schwarz/Hertz (Lancia)	4	2	5	4	7	8
Aghini/Farnocchia (Lancia)	2	3	5	1	4	-
Eriksson/Parmander (Mitsubishi)	1	2	1	8	5	1
Auriol/Occelli (Lancia)	1	-	1	1	-	-
Salonen/Silander (Mitsubishi)	-	6	2	4	7	2
Chatriot/Périn (Nissan)	-	-	-	1	5	3
Santos/Magalhaes (Toyota)	-	-	-	-	-	1
Peres/Caldeira (Ford)	-	-	-	-	-	1

Finish lines

Kenneth Eriksson had his second accident in as many rallies, rolling the lead **Mitsubishi** heavily in Arganil. Souvenir hunters all but stripped the car...**Markku Alén** overcame **Toyota** brake problems to deprive **Timo Salonen** of fourth, but only when the **Mitsubishi** man lost a rear wheel a stage from the finish...**Carlos Menem Junior** dominated the Group N category in his Top Run Delta Integrale... **Nissan** endured a dispiriting rally, **Tommi Mäkinen** crashing his **Sunny GTi-R** on SS4 when driving on a puncture, while **François Chatriot** fought back to sixth having lost 10 minutes on the same stage when he collected two front punctures simultaneously... **Mohammed Bin Sulayem** dropped six minutes in road penalties sorting out brake trouble in the first leg, and the Marlboro Team **Ford** driver spent the rest of the rally fighting his way through the dust left by slower cars, surviving a roll in the process...**Fernando Capdevila** led Group N in his Canary Islands **Cosworth** 4x4 until transmission trouble intervened...**Grégoire de Mevius** rolled his Group N Sunny GTi-R in Arganil.

Results

1	Juha Kankkunen/	Lancia Delta HF Integrale		
	Juha Piironen	6h 24m 37s	Gr A
2	Massimo Biasion/	Ford Sierra Cosworth 4x4	
	Tiziano Siviero	6h 26m 10s	Gr A
3	Carlos Sainz/	Toyota Celica Turbo 4WD	
	Luis Moya	6h 29m 36s	Gr A
4	Markku Alén/	Toyota Celica Turbo 4WD	
	Ilkka Kivimäki	6h 30m 09s	Gr A
5	Timo Salonen/	Mitsubishi Galant VR-4	
	Voitto Silander	6h 31m 16s	Gr A
6	François Chatriot/	Nissan Sunny GTi-R	
	Michel Périn	6h 45m 41s	Gr A
7	José Maria Bardolet/	Ford Sierra Cosworth 4x4	
	Josep Autet	6h 53m 55s	Gr A
8	Joaquim Santos/	Toyota Celica GT4	
	Carlos Magalhaes	7h 01m 20s	Gr A
9	Carlos Menem/	Lancia Delta HF Integrale	
	Victor Zucchini	7h 02m 47s	Gr N
10	José Miguel/	Ford Sierra Cosworth	
	Luis Lisboa	7h 14m 47s	Gr A

100 starters, 31 finishers

Previous winners

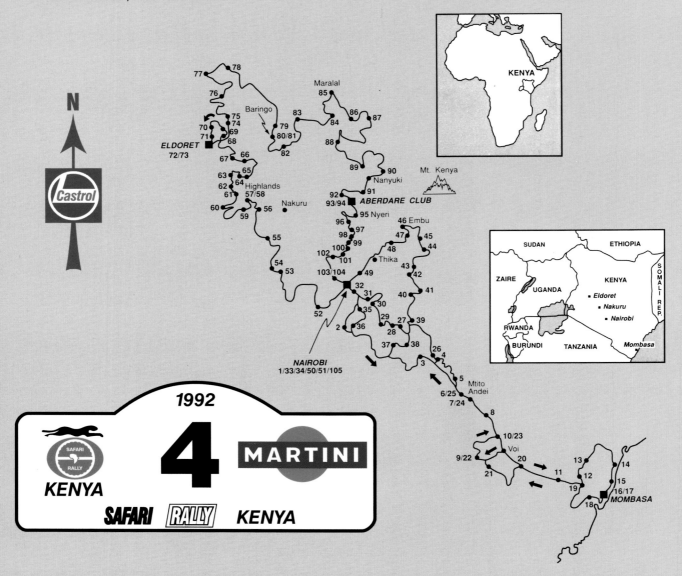

KENYA

1992

4

MARTINI

SAFARI RALLY KENYA

MARTINI SAFARI RALLY, 27 March-1 April. FIA World Rally Championship for Manufacturers, round 3. FIA World Rally Championship for Drivers, round 4.

Leading entries

1	Juha Kankkunen/	Lancia Delta HF Integrale
	Juha Piironen	Gr A
2	Mikael Ericsson/	Toyota Celica Turbo 4WD
	Nicky Grist	Gr A
3	Björn Waldegård/	Lancia Delta HF Integrale
	Fred Gallagher	Gr A
4	Rudi Stohl/	Audi 90 Quattro
	Peter Diekmann	Gr A
5	Jorge Recalde/	Lancia Delta HF Integrale
	Martin Christie	Gr A
6	Markku Alén/	Toyota Celica Turbo 4WD
	Ilkka Kivimäki	Gr A
7	Kenjiro Shinozuka/	Mitsubishi Galant VR-4
	John Meadows	Gr A
8	Carlos Sainz/	Toyota Celica Turbo 4WD
	Luis Moya	Gr A
9	Ian Duncan/	Toyota Celica GT4
	David Williamson	Gr A
10	Billy Rautenbach/	Toyota Celica GT4
	Surinder Thatti	Gr A
11	Per Eklund/	Subaru Legacy RS
	Johnny Johansson	Gr N
12	Patrick Njiru/	Subaru Legacy RS
	Ian Munro	Gr N
15	Marco Brighetti/	Daihatsu Charade GTti
	Abdul Sidi	Gr A
16	Azar Anwar/	Subaru Legacy RS
	Kul Sandhu	Gr A
17	Sarbi Rai/	Toyota Celica GT4
	Supee Soin	Gr A
18	Jonathan Toroitich/	Toyota Celica GT4
	Ibrahim Choge	Gr A
19	Jas Matharu/	Subaru Legacy RS
	Andy Nagi	Gr A
20	Guy Jack/	Daihatsu Charade GTti
	Dez-Page Morris	Gr A

21	Yasuhiro Iwase/ Sudhir Vinayak	Toyota Celica GT4 Gr N
22	Alfredo Tosca/ Roero Romanelli	Mazda 323 Turbo Gr N

Positions at end of each leg

Leg 1 – Nairobi-Shanzu

1	C. Sainz/L. Moya (Toyota Celica Turbo 4WD)	7m 00s
2	J. Recalde/M. Christie (Lancia Delta HF Integrale)	9m 00s
3	M. Alén/I. Kivimäki (Toyota Celica Turbo 4WD)	9m 00s
4	J. Kankkunen/J. Piironen (Lancia Delta HF Integrale)	10m 00s
5	B. Waldegård/F. Gallagher (Lancia Delta HF Integrale)	10m 00s
6	I. Duncan/D. Williamson (Toyota Celica GT4)	10m 00s

Leg 2 – Shanzu-Nairobi

1	Sainz/Moya (Toyota)	35m 00s
2	Recalde/Christie (Lancia)	42m 00s
3	Duncan/Williamson (Toyota)	51m 00s
4	Kankkunen/Piironen (Lancia)	53m 00s
5	Alén/Kivimäki (Toyota)	58m 00s
6	M. Ericsson/N. Grist (Toyota Celica Turbo 4WD)	1h 13m 00s

Leg 3 – Nairobi-Nairobi

1	Sainz/Moya (Toyota)	43m 00s
2	Recalde/Christie (Lancia)	50m 00s
3	Duncan/Williamson (Toyota)	1h 04m 00s
4	Kankkunen/Piironen (Lancia)	1h 10m 00s
5	Ericsson/Grist (Toyota)	1h 22m 00s
6	Alén/Kivimäki (Toyota)	1h 24m 00s

Leg 4 – Nairobi-Eldoret

1	Sainz/Moya (Toyota)	1h 19m 00s
2	Recalde/Christie (Lancia)	1h 34m 00s
3	Kankkunen/Piironen (Lancia)	2h 01m 00s
4	Ericsson/Grist (Toyota)	2h 30m 00s

5	Duncan/Williamson (Toyota)	2h 40m 00s
6	Alén/Kivimäki (Toyota)	2h 46m 00s

Leg 5 – Eldoret-Aberdare

1	Sainz/Moya (Toyota)	1h 59m 00s
2	Recalde/Christie (Lancia)	2h 27m 00s
3	Kankkunen/Piironen (Lancia)	2h 53m 00s
4	Ericsson/Grist (Toyota)	3h 33m 00s
5	Alén/Kivimäki (Toyota)	4h 27m 00s
6	Duncan/Williamson (Toyota)	5h 56m 00s

Leg 6 – Aberdare-Nairobi

1	Sainz/Moya (Toyota)	2h 35m 00s
2	Kankkunen/Piironen (Lancia)	3h 27m 00s
3	Recalde/Christie (Lancia)	3h 34m 00s
4	Ericsson/Grist (Toyota)	4h 13m 00s
5	Alén/Kivimäki (Toyota)	5h 40m 00s
6	Duncan/Williamson (Toyota)	6h 38m 00s

Major retirements

Björn Waldegård/ Fred Gallagher	Lancia Delta HF Integrale TC 26	fire

World Championship points

Drivers

1 Sainz and Kankkunen 47; **3** Alén 28; **4** Auriol and Jonsson 20; **6** Biasion 18; **7** McRae 15; **8** Blomqvist and Recalde 12; **10** Chatriot, Delecour and Eriksson 10.

Manufacturers

1 Lancia 57; **2** Toyota 51; **3** Ford 29; **4** Mitsubishi 20; **5** Nissan 14; **6** Subaru 11.

FIA class winners

Group A

Over 2000 cc:	Sainz/Moya (Toyota)
1600-2000 cc:	Brighetti/Sidi (Daihatsu)
1300-1600 cc:	No finishers

Up to 1300 cc:	Ashok Pattni/Zahid Mogul (Daihatsu Charade)

Group N

Over 2000 cc:	Njiru/Munro (Subaru)
1600-2000 cc:	No starters
1300-1600 cc:	No finishers
Up to 1300 cc:	No starters

Rally leaders

TC 1-13 Recalde/Christie (Lancia); **TC 14-24** Sainz/
Moya (Toyota); **TC 25** Recalde/Christie (Lancia); **TC
26-105** Sainz/Moya (Toyota).

Route details

Leg 1

27 March: Starting from Nairobi at 1100, finishing at Shanzu at 2025, including 14 timed sections (of which five competitive, 390.55 km).

Leg 2

28 March: Starting from Shanzu at 0900, finishing at Nairobi at 1744, including 15 timed sections (of which six competitive, 387.32 km).

Leg 3

29 March: Starting and finishing at Nairobi 0730-1417, including 16 timed sections (of which eight competitive, 442.91 km).

Leg 4

30 March: Starting from Nairobi at 0300, finishing at Eldoret at 1227, including 20 timed sections (of which eight competitive, 629.31 km).

Leg 5

31 March: Starting from Eldoret at 0200, finishing at Aberdare at 1557, including 19 timed sections (of which 11 competitive, 734.63 km).

Leg 6

1 April: Starting from Aberdare at 0500, finishing at Nairobi at 0940, including ten timed sections (of which six competitive, 242.37 km).

Weather

Hot and dry.

No rally driver has a following like Patrick Njiru's. The Kenyan made sure of a fine Group N win for Subaru.

Finish lines

Kenjiro Shinozuka was back in the top ten by the finish, but it had been hard going, as the works-supported **Mitsubishi** had required three head gasket changes, and had also caught fire twice, all before reaching Eldoret...**Björn Waldegård** took part in his first rally in a **Lancia** since 1976, but failed to finish, as his Delta burst into flames when it was being re-fuelled during the second leg...**Subaru** dominated Group N, **Patrick Njiru** leading home **Per Eklund** despite intercooler trouble...**Ian Duncan** was one of the stars of the show, splitting the works Lancias in the Esso/AVA **Celica** GT4 until the suspension collapsed a few miles from Suswa. Power steering trouble later on prevented him from beating any of the factory Toyotas...**Per Eklund** got so many punctures during the fifth leg that he had to radio Njiru for help: his team-mate left a wheel for him at a pre-determined point in mid-section, and said that he could have it provided thieves didn't get there first.

Results

1	Carlos Sainz/ Luis Moya	Toyota Celica Turbo 4WD 2h 35m 00s	Gr A
2	Juha Kankkunen/ Juha Piironen	Lancia Delta HF Integrale 3h 27m 00s	Gr A
3	Jorge Recalde/ Martin Christie	Lancia Delta HF Integrale 3h 34m 00s	Gr A
4	Mikael Ericsson/ Nicky Grist	Toyota Celica Turbo 4WD 4h 13m 00s	Gr A
5	Markku Alén/ Ilkka Kivimäki	Toyota Celica Turbo 4WD 5h 40m 00s	Gr A
6	Ian Duncan/ David Williamson	Toyota Celica GT4 6h 38m 00s	Gr A
7	Sarbi Rai/ Supee Soin	Toyota Celica GT4 8h 29m 00s	Gr A
8	Patrick Njiru/ Ian Munro	Subaru Legacy RS 8h 54m 00s	Gr N
9	Per Eklund/ Johnny Johansson	Subaru Legacy RS 9h 41m 00s	Gr N
10	Kenjiro Shinozuka/ John Meadows	Mitsubishi Galant VR-4 10h 30m 00s	Gr A

49 starters, 21 finishers

Previous winners (since 1959)

1959	Bill Fritschy/Jack Ellis	Mercedes-Benz 219
1960	Bill Fritschy/Jack Ellis	Mercedes-Benz 219
1961	Johnny Manuss/Bill Coleridge	Mercedes Benz 220E
1962	Tommy Fjastad/Bernard Schmider	VW1300
1963	Nick Norwicki/Paddy Cliff	Peugeot 404
1964	Peter Hughes/Bill Young	Ford Cortina GT
1965	Joginder Singh/Jaswant Singh	Volvo
1966	Bert Shankland/Chris Rothwell	Peugeot 404
1967	Bert Shankland/Chris Rothwell	Peugeot 404
1968	Nick Norwicki/Paddy Cliff	Peugeot 404
1969	Robin Hillyar/Jock Aird	Ford Taunus
1970	Edgar Herrmann/Hans Schuller	Datsun 160SSS
1971	Edgar Herrmann/Hans Schuller	Datsun 240Z
1972	Hannu Mikkola/Gunnar Palm	Ford Escort RS
1973	Shekhar Mehta/Lofty Drews	Datsun 240Z
1974	Joginder Singh/David Doig	Mitsubishi Colt Lancer
1975	Ove Andersson/Arne Hertz	Peugeot 504
1976	Joginder Singh/David Doig	Mitsubishi Colt Lancer
1977	Björn Waldegård/Hans Thorszelius	Ford Escort RS
1978	Jean-Pierre Nicolas/Jean-Claude Lefebvre	Peugeot 504
1979	Shekhar Mehta/Mike Doughty	Datsun 160J
1980	Shekhar Mehta/Mike Doughty	Datsun 160J
1981	Shekhar Mehta/Mike Doughty	Datsun Violet GT
1982	Shekhar Mehta/Mike Doughty	Datsun Violet GT
1983	Ari Vatanen/Terry Harryman	Opel Ascona 400
1984	Björn Waldegård/Hans Thorszelius	Toyota Celica Turbo
1985	Juha Kankkunen/Fred Gallagher	Toyota Celica Turbo
1986	Björn Waldegård/Fred Gallagher	Toyota Celica Turbo
1987	Hannu Mikkola/Arne Hertz	Audi 200 Quattro
1988	Massimo Biasion/Tiziano Siviero	Lancia Delta HF Integrale
1989	Massimo Biasion/Tiziano Siviero	Lancia Delta HF Integrale
1990	Björn Waldegård/Fred Gallagher	Toyota Celica GT4
1991	Juha Kankkunen/Juha Piironen	Lancia Delta HF Integrale

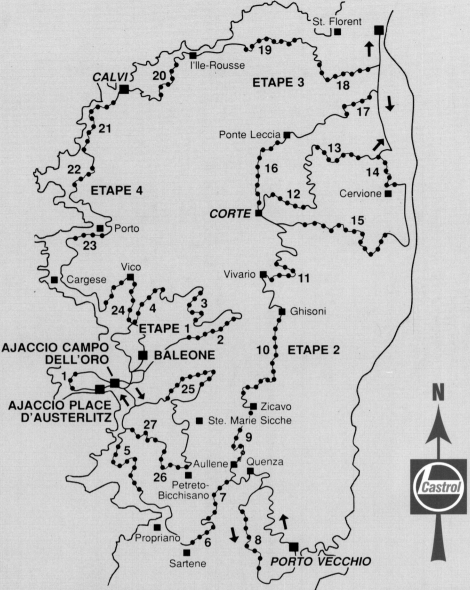

ETAPE 3

ETAPE 4

ETAPE 1

ETAPE 2

St. Florent

l'Ile-Rousse

CALVI

Ponte Leccia

Cervione

CORTE

Porto

Vico

Vivario

Cargese

Ghisoni

AJACCIO CAMPO
DELL'ORO

BALEONE

AJACCIO PLACE
D'AUSTERLITZ

Zicavo

Ste. Marie Sicche

Aullene   Quenza

Petreto-
Bicchisano

Propriano

Sartene

PORTO VECCHIO

N

Castrol

TOUR OF CORSICA, 3-6 May. FIA World Rally Championship for Manufacturers, round 4. FIA World Rally Championship for Drivers, round 5.

Leading entries

1	Carlo Sainz/ Luis Moya	Toyota Celica Turbo 4WD Gr A
2	Massimo Biasion/ Tiziano Siviero	Ford Sierra Cosworth 4x4 Gr A
3	Didier Auriol/ Bernard Occelli	Lancia Delta HF Integrale Gr A
4	Armin Schwarz/ Arne Hertz	Toyota Celica Turbo 4WD Gr A
6	François Delecour/ Daniel Grataloup	Ford Sierra Cosworth 4x4 Gr A
7	Philippe Bugalski/ Denis Giraudet	Lancia Delta HF Integrale Gr A
8	Piero Liatti/ Luciano Tedeschini	Lancia Delta HF Integrale Gr A
9	Alain Oreille/ Jean-Marc Andrié	Renault Clio 16S Gr A
10	Yves Loubet/ Jean-Paul Chiaroni	Citroën AX GTI Gr A
11	Fernando Capdevila/ Alfredo Rodriguez	Ford Sierra Cosworth 4x4 Gr N
12	Andrea Aghini/ Sauro Farnocchia	Lancia Delta HF Integrale Gr A
14	Bruno Thiry/ Stéphane Prévot	Opel Calibra Gr A
15	Jean Ragnotti/ Gilles Thimonier	Renault Clio 16s Gr A
16	Carlos Menem/ Victor Zucchini	Lancia Delta HF Integrale Gr N
17	Kurt Gottlicher/ Otto Zwanzigleitner	Ford Sierra Cosworth 4x4 Gr N
18	Giovanni Manfrinato/ Claudio Condotta	Ford Sierra Cosworth 4x4 Gr N
19	Jean-Pierre Manzagol/ Georges Monti	Renault 5GT Turbo Gr A
20	Patrick Bernardini/ Roch Demedardi	BMW M3 Gr A
21	Eric Mauffrey/ Hervé Sauvage	Renault Clio 16s Gr A
22	Fabien Doenlen/ Evelyne Merciol	Peugeot 309 GTI 16v Gr A

Special stage times

SS 1. Vignola-Capo di Feno (2.86 km)
1 D. Auriol/B. Occelli (Lancia Delta HF Integrale) 1m 46s; 2 A. Schwarz/A. Hertz (Toyota Celica Turbo 4WD), F. Delecour/D. Grataloup (Ford Sierra Cosworth 4x4), C. Sainz/L. Moya (Toyota Celica Turbo 4WD) 1m 47s; 5 M. Biasion/T. Siviero (Ford Sierra Cosworth 4x4), A. Aghini/S. Farnocchia (Lancia HF Integrale), P. Bugalski/D. Giraudet (Lancia Delta HF Integrale) 1m 48s.

SS 2. Carbuccia-Tavera (17.18 km)
1 Auriol/Occelli (Lancia), Delecour/Grataloup (Ford) 11m 51s; 3 Bugalski/Giraudet (Lancia) 11m 53s; 4 Aghini/Farnocchia (Lancia) 11m 56s; 5 Schwarz/Hertz (Toyota) 12m 01s; 6 Biasion/Siviero (Ford) 12m 05s.

SS 3. Suaricchio-Pont d'Azzana (22.19 km)
1 Auriol/Occelli (Lancia) 15m 41s; 2 Delecour/Grataloup (Ford) 15m 43s; 3 Bugalski/Giraudet (Lancia) 15m 47s; 4 Aghini/Farnocchia (Lancia) 15m 49s; 5 Sainz/Moya (Toyota), Schwarz/Hertz (Toyota) 15m 58s.

SS 4. Lopigna (22.45 km)
1 Delecour/Grataloup (Ford) 16m 09s; 2 Auriol/Occelli (Lancia) 16m 10s; 3 Bugalski/Giraudet (Lancia) 16m 21s; 4 Biasion/Siviero (Ford) 16m 24s; 5 Schwarz/Hertz (Toyota) 16m 25s; 6 Aghini/Farnocchia (Lancia) 16m 28s.

SS 5. Verghia-Pietra Rosa (26.55 km)
1 Auriol/Occelli (Lancia) 16m 40s; 2 Delecour/Grataloup (Ford) 16m 45s; 3 Schwarz/Hertz (Toyota) 16m 47s; 4 Sainz/Moya (Toyota) 16m 51s; 5 Bugalski/Giraudet (Lancia) 16m 56s; 6 Aghini/Farnocchia (Lancia) 17m 03s.

SS 6. Sartene-Surga (12.31 km)
1 Auriol/Occelli (Lancia) 7m 47s; 2 Delecour/Grataloup (Ford) 7m 49s; 3 Bugalski/Giraudet (Lancia) 7m 53s; 5 Aghini/Farnocchia (Lancia) 7m 55s; 6 Biasion/Siviero (Ford) 7m 56s.

SS 7. Zerubia (20.58 km)
1 Auriol/Occelli (Lancia), Delecour/Grataloup (Ford) 12m 24s; 3 Sainz/Moya (Toyota), Schwarz/Hertz (Toyota) 12m 27s; 5 Aghini/Farnocchia (Lancia) 12m 32s; 6 Bugalski/Giraudet (Lancia) 12m 35s.

SS 8. Levie-Sotta (26.00 km)
1 Auriol/Occelli (Lancia) 15m 27s; 2 Delecour/Grataloup (Ford) 15m 32s; 3 Bugalski/Giraudet (Lancia) 15m 40s; 4 Aghini/Farnocchia (Lancia) 15m 42s; 5 Schwarz/Hertz (Toyota) 15m 51s; 6 P. Liatti/L. Tedeschini (Lancia Delta HF Integrale) 15m 54s.

SS 9. Aullene-Zicavo (25.36 km)
1 Aghini/Farnocchia (Lancia) 16m 04s, 2 Auriol/Occelli (Lancia) 16m 07s; 3 Sainz/Moya (Toyota), Delecour/Grataloup (Ford) 16m 09s; 5 Bugalski/Giraudet (Lancia) 16m 10s; 6 Schwarz/Hertz (Toyota) 16m 13s.

SS 10. Col de Verde (40.30 km)
1 Auriol/Occelli (Lancia) 26m 58s; 2 Aghini/Farnocchia (Lancia) 27m 10s; 3 Delecour/Grataloup (Ford) 27m 12s; 4 Bugalski/Giraudet (Lancia) 27m 15s; 5 Sainz/Moya (Toyota) 27m 18s; 6 Schwarz/Hertz (Toyota) 27m 23s.

SS 11. Muracciole (16.38 km)
1 Auriol/Occelli (Lancia) 10m 01s; 2 Sainz/Moya (Toyota) 10m 04s; 3 Schwarz/Hertz (Toyota), Bugalski/Giraudet (Lancia), Aghini/Farnocchia (Lancia) 10m 05s; 6 Delecour/Grataloup (Ford) 10m 08s.

SS 12. Tralonca-Bustanico (15.02 km)
1 Auriol/Occelli (Lancia) 10m 38s; 2 Sainz/Moya (Toyota), Bugalski/Giraudet (Lancia) 10m 44s; 4 Delecour/Grataloup (Ford) 10m 50s; 5 Biasion/Siviero (Ford), Schwarz/Hertz (Toyota) 10m 52s.

SS 13. Morosaglia (24.18 km)
1 Auriol/Occelli (Lancia) 15m 31s; 2 Aghini/Farnocchia (Lancia) 15m 32s; 3 Bugalski/Giraudet (Lancia) 15m 39s; 4 Sainz/Moya (Toyota) 15m 42s; 5 Delecour/Grataloup (Ford) 15m 44ş; 6 Liatti/Tedeschini (Lancia) 15m 52s.

SS 14. Pont d'Acitaja-Mortete (25.43 km)
1 Auriol/Occelli (Lancia) 19m 26s; 2 Bugalski/Giraudet (Lancia) 19m 27s; 3 Aghini/Farnocchia (Lancia) 19m 32s; 4 Delecour/Grataloup (Ford) 19m 33s; 5 Biasion/Siviero (Ford) 19m 48s; 6 Schwarz/Hertz (Toyota) 19m 59s.

SS 15. Linguizzetta (44.81 km)
1 Auriol/Occelli (Lancia) 30m 08s; 2 Delecour/Grataloup (Ford) 30m 17s; 3 Bugalski/Giraudet (Lancia) 30m 22s; 4 Sainz/Moya (Toyota) 30m 26s; 5 Schwarz/Hertz (Toyota) 30m 30s; 6 Liatti/Tedeschini (Lancia) 30m 51s.

SS 16. Corte-Taverna (26.86 km)
1 Delecour/Grataloup (Ford) 15m 58s; 2 Auriol/Occelli (Lancia) 16m 01s; 3 Sainz/Moya (Toyota) 16m 03s; 4 Aghini/Farnocchia (Lancia) 16m 11s; 5 Bugalski/Giraudet (Lancia) 16m 14s; 6 Schwarz/Hertz (Toyota) 16m 15s.

SS 17. Barchetta-Borgo (17.18 km)
1 Delecour/Grataloup (Ford) 12m 18s; 2 Sainz/Moya (Toyota), Auriol/Occelli (Lancia) 12m 19s; 4 Aghini/Farnocchia (Lancia) 12m 24s; 5 Bugalski/Giraudet (Lancia) 12m 26s; 6 Schwarz/Hertz (Toyota) 12m 29s.

SS 18. Casatorra (25.24 km)
1 Auriol/Occelli (Lancia) 17m 11s; 2 Delecour/Grataloup (Ford) 17m 18s; 3 Sainz/Moya (Toyota) 17m 20s; 4 Aghini/Farnocchia (Lancia) 17m 23s; 5 Bugalski/Giraudet (Lancia) 17m 29s; 6 Schwarz/Hertz (Toyota) 17m 31s.

Group N had its fifth victor in as many rallies: this time it was a local head-master, **Jean-Marie Santoni**, driving a **Sierra Cosworth** 4x4...**Miki Biasion** had a miserable rally, complaining of handling problems and finishing a lacklustre seventh; the team insisted there was nothing wrong with the works Sierra...**Jean Ragnotti** won the two-wheel drive contest, leading a **Renault** sweep of the two-litre class and finishing ninth overall...**Fabien Doenlen** crashed his GCAP 309GTI...The disaster in the Furiani football stadium overshadowed the rally, and prompted the retirement of **Jean-Pierre Manzagol**: a relative of his co-driver, **Georges Monti**, was injured when the stand collapsed...**Fernando Capdevila** retired his Mike Taylor-run **Sierra Cosworth** with a broken drive flange...A persistent misfire hampered **Alain Oreille**'s efforts in the second works Clio, although he still finished 10th...**Christine Driano** took her first finish in Corsica as well as a class win in her works AX Sport. She said it meant much more to her than the ladies' prize.

Results

1	Didier Auriol/	Lancia Delta HF Integrale	
	Bernard Occelli	5h 34m 49s	Gr A
2	François Delecour/	Ford Sierra Cosworth 4x4	
	Daniel Grataloup	5h 36m 15s	Gr A
3	Philippe Bugalski/	Lancia Delta HF Integrale	
	Denis Giraudet	5h 38m 04s	Gr A
4	Carlos Sainz/	Toyota Celica Turbo 4WD	
	Luis Moya	5h 39m 22s	Gr A
5	Armin Schwarz/	Toyota Celica Turbo 4WD	
	Arne Hertz	5h 40m 42s	Gr A
6	Andrea Aghini/	Lancia Delta HF Integrale	
	Sauro Farnocchia	5h 42m 19s	Gr A
7	Massimo Biasion/	Ford Sierra Cosworth 4x4	
	Tiziano Siviero	5h 42m 21s	Gr A
8	Piero Liatti/	Lancia Delta HF Integrale	
	Luciano Tedeschini	5h 48m 42s	Gr A
9	Jean Ragnotti/	Renault Clio 16S	
	Gilles Thimonier	5h 55m 09s	Gr A
10	Alain Oreille/	Renault Clio 16S	
	Jean-Marc Andrié	6h 01m 03s	Gr A

104 starters, 46 finishers

Previous winners

1960	Walter Strahle/Herbert Linge	Porsche SC90
1961	René Trautmann/Jean-Claude Ogier	
		Citroën DS19
1962	Pierre Orsini/Jean-Baptiste Canonici	
		Renault Dauphine
1963	René Trautmann/Alexis Chabert	Citroën DS19
1964	Jean Vinatier/Roger Masson	Renault 8 Gordini
1965	Pierre Orsini/Jean-Baptiste Canonici	
		Renault 8 Gordini
1966	Jean-François Piot/Jean-François Jacob	
		Renault 8 Gordini
1967	Sandro Munari/Luciano Lombardini	
		Lancia Fulvia HF
1968	Jean-Claude Andruet/Maurice Gelin	
		Alpine Renault A110
1969	Gérard Larrousse/Maurice Gelin	Porsche 911R
1970	Bernard Darniche/Guy Demage	
		Alpine Renault A110
1972	Jean-Claude Andruet/"Biche"	Alpine Renault A110
1973	Jean-Pierre Nicolas/Michel Vial	
		Alpine Renault A110
1974	Jean-Claude Andruet/"Biche"	Lancia Stratos
1975	Bernard Darniche/Alain Mahé	Lancia Stratos
1976	Sandro Munari/Silvio Maiga	Lancia Stratos
1977	Bernard Darniche/Alain Mahé	Fiat 131 Abarth
1978	Bernard Darniche/Alain Mahé	Fiat 131 Abarth
1979	Bernard Darniche/Alain Mahé	Lancia Stratos
1980	Jean-Luc Thérier/Michel Vial	Porsche 911SC
1981	Bernard Darniche/Alain Mahé	Lancia Stratos
1982	Jean Ragnotti/Jean-Marc Andrié	
		Renault 5 Turbo
1983	Markku Alén/Ilkka Kivimäki	Lancia Rally 037
1984	Markku Alén/Ilkka Kivimäki	Lancia Rally 037
1985	Jean Ragnotti/Pierre Thimonier	
		Renault 5 Maxi Turbo
1986	Bruno Saby/Jean-François-Fauchille	
		Peugeot 205 Turbo 16
1987	Bernard Beguin/Jean-Jacques Lenne	BMW M3
1988	Didier Auriol/Bernard Occelli	
		Ford Sierra Cosworth
1989	Didier Auriol/Bernard Occelli	
		Lancia Delta HF Integrale
1990	Didier Auriol/Bernard Occelli	
		Lancia Delta HF Integrale
1991	Carlos Sainz/Luis Moya	Toyota Celica GT4

RALLYE DE FRANCE
36e TOUR DE CORSE
5
1992 1992

SS 19. Casta-Pietra Monetta (15.74 km)
1 Auriol/Occelli (Lancia) 10m 00s; 2 Aghini/Farnocchia (Lancia) 10m 01s; 3 Delecour/Grataloup (Ford) 10m 03s; 4 Bugalski/Giraudet (Lancia) 10m 08s; 5 Sainz/Moya (Toyota) 10m 10s; 6 Schwarz/Hertz (Toyota), Liatti/Tedeschini (Lancia) 10m 11s.

SS 20. Corbara-Montemaggiore (13.58 km)
1 Auriol/Occelli (Lancia) 8m 06s; 2 Delecour/Grataloup (Ford) 8m 08s; 3 Sainz/Moya (Toyota) 8m 09s; 4 Schwarz/Hertz (Toyota), Aghini/Farnocchia (Lancia) 8m 11s; 6 Bugalski/Giraudet (Lancia) 8m 13s.

SS 21. Notre Dame de la Serra (27.99 km)
1 Auriol/Occelli (Lancia) 16m 24s; 2 Delecour/Grataloup (Ford) 16m 26s; 3 Aghini/Farnocchia (Lancia) 16m 28s; 4 Bugalski/Giraudet (Lancia) 16m 32s; 5 Sainz/Moya (Toyota) 16m 41s; 6 Liatti/Tedeschini (Lancia) 16m 42s.

SS 22. Fango-Partinello (31.48 km)
1 Delecour/Grataloup (Ford) 21m 35s; 2 Auriol/Occelli (Lancia) 21m 37s; 3 Aghini/Farnocchia (Lancia) 21m 38s; 4 Bugalski/Giraudet (Lancia) 21m 48s; 5 Sainz/Moya (Toyota) 21m 53s; 6 Biasion/Siviero (Ford) 21m 54s.

SS 23. Porto-Piana (9.97 km)
1 Auriol/Occelli (Lancia), Delecour/Grataloup (Ford), Aghini/Farnocchia (Lancia) 6m 36s; 4 Bugalski/Giraudet (Lancia) 6m 39s; 5 Liatti/Tedeschini (Lancia) 6m 40s; 6 Sainz/Moya (Toyota) 6m 41s.

SS 24. Liamone-Ambiegna (43.93 km)
Cancelled.

SS 25. Suarella-Col de Marcuccio (25.21 km)
Cancelled.

SS 26. Bicchisano-Pila Canale (14.47 km)
Cancelled.

SS 27. Cognocoli (25.12 km)
Cancelled.

Major retirements

Carlos Menem/	Lancia Delta HF Integrale	
Victor Zucchini	SS 3	accident
Fernando Capdevila/	Ford Sierra Cosworth 4x4	
Alfredo Rodriguez	SS 7	turbo
Bruno Thiry/	Opel Calibra	
Stéphane Prévot	SS 10	halfshaft
Fabien Doenlen/	Peugeot 309 GTI 16v	
Evelyne Merciol	SS 15	accident

Rally leaders

SS 1-23 Auriol/Occelli (Lancia).

FIA Class Winners

Group A
Over 2000 cc: Auriol/Occelli (Lancia)
1600-2000 cc: Ragnotti/Thimonier (Renault)
1300-1600 cc: Patrick Magaud/Guylene Brun (Citroën AX GTI)
Up to 1300 cc: Christine Driano/Catherine François (Citroën AX Sport)

Group N
Over 2000 cc: Jean-Marie Santoni/Marcel Cesarini (Ford Sierra Cosworth)
1600-2000 cc: Georges Chiocca/Felix Paolini (Toyota Celica GT)
1300-1600cc: Hercul e Antonini/Pascale Seni (Peugeot 205 GTI)
Up to 1300 cc: Jean-Marc Sanchez/Marc Leonardi (Peugeot 205 GTI)

World Championship points

Drivers
1 Sainz 57; 2 Kankkunen 47; 3 Auriol 40; 4 Alén 28; 5 Delecour 25; 6 Biasion 22; 7 Jonsson and Bugalski 20; 9 McRae 15; 10 Salonen 14.

Manufacturers
1 Lancia 77; 2 Toyota 63; 3 Ford 46; 4 Mitsubishi 20; 5 Nissan 14; 6 Subaru 11; 7 Renault 2.

Route details

Leg 1
3 May: Starting and finishing from Ajaccio 1045-1445, including four stages (64.68 km).

Leg 2
4 May: Starting from Ajaccio at 0730, finishing at Bastia at 1830, including nine special stages (210.62 km).

Leg 3
5 May: Starting from Bastia at 0900, finishing at Calvi at 1800, including seven special stages (168.84 km).

Leg 4
6 May: Starting from Calvi at 0830, finishing at Ajaccio at 1630, including seven special stages (4 cancelled - 69.44 km).

Weather

Warm and dry throughout.

Special stage analysis

	1st	2nd	3rd	4th	5th	6th
Auriol/Occelli (Lancia)	18	5	-	-	-	-
Delecour/Grataloup (Ford)	7	9	3	2	1	1
Aghini/Farnocchia (Lancia)	2	3	4	7	3	2
Sainz/Moya (Toyota)	-	4	5	3	5	1
Bugalski/Giraudet (Lancia)	-	2	8	6	2	
Schwarz/Hertz (Toyota)	-	1	4	1	6	7
Biasion/Siviero (Ford)	-	-	-	1	3	3
Liatti/Tedeschini (Lancia)	-	-	-	-	1	6

6

39ᵒ ΡΑΛΛΥ ΑΚΡΟΠΟΛΙΣ

CYCLON · ΤΡΑΠΕΖΑ ΠΙΣΤΕΟΣ · ◈ INTERAMERICAN · HELM

N

Castrol

Karpenissi

Lamia

25/35

Delphi

Itea

Thiva

PELOPONNESE

Korinthus

Halkida

ATHENS

Lagonissi

Amfissa

ACROPOLIS RALLY, 31 May-3 June. FIA World Rally Championship for Manufacturers, round 5. FIA World Rally Championship for Drivers, round 6.

Leading entries

1	Juha Kankkunen/ Juha Piironen	Lancia Delta HF Integrale Gr A
2	Carlos Sainz/ Luis Moya	Toyota Celica Turbo 4WD Gr A
3	François Delecour/ Daniel Grataloup	Ford Sierra Cosworth 4x4 Gr A
4	Kenneth Eriksson/ Staffan Parmander	Mitsubishi Galant VR-4 Gr A
5	Ari Vatanen/ Bruno Berglund	Subaru Legacy RS Gr A
6	Didier Auriol/ Bernard Occelli	Lancia Delta HF Integrale Gr A
7	Markku Alén/ Ilkka Kivimäki	Toyota Celica Turbo 4WD Gr A
8	Massimo Biasion/ Tiziano Siviero	Ford Sierra Cosworth 4x4 Gr A
9	Colin McRae/ Derek Ringer	Subaru Legacy RS Gr A
10	Armin Schwarz/ Arne Hertz	Toyota Celica Turbo 4WD Gr A
11	Jorge Recalde/ Martin Christie	Lancia Delta HF Integrale Gr A
12	Alessandro Fiorio/ Vittorio Brambilla	Lancia Delta HF Integrale Gr A
14	Grégoire de Mevius/ Willy Lux	Nissan Sunny GTi-R Gr N
15	Fernando Capdevila/ Alfredo Rodriguez	Ford Sierra Cosworth 4x4 Gr N
16	Rudi Stohl/ Peter Diekmann	Audi 90 Quattro Gr A
17	'Jigger'/ Costas Stefanis	Toyota Celica GTA Gr A
18	Massimo Ercolani/ Mario Vimercati	Lancia Delta HF Integrale Gr N
19	'Stratassino'/ Tonia Pavli	Nissan Sunny GTi-R GrN
20	Mohammed Bin Sulayem/ Ronan Morgan	Ford Sierra Cosworth 4x4 Gr N
21	Manolis Panagiotopoulos/ Nikos Panou	Subaru Legacy RS Gr N

Special stage times

SS 1. Anavissos (4.47 km)
1 D. Auriol/B. Occelli (Lancia Delta HF Integrale) 3m 41s; **2** A. Schwarz/A. Hertz (Toyota Celica Turbo 4WD) 3m 42s; **3** J. Kankkunen/J. Piironen (Lancia Delta HF Integrale), M. Alén/I. Kivimäki (Toyota Celica Turbo 4WD), C. McRae/D. Ringer (Subaru Legacy RS) 3m 43s; **6** M. Biasion/T. Siviero (Ford Sierra Cosworth 4x4) 3m 45s.

SS 2. Mandra (10.84 km)
1 Auriol/Occelli (Lancia) 8m 38s; **2** McRae/Ringer (Subaru), Schwarz/Hertz (Toyota) 8m 42s; **4** Biasion/Siviero (Ford) 8m 44s; **5** Kankkunen/Piironen (Lancia), Alén/Kivimäki (Toyota) 8m 45s.

SS 3. Kineta (25.49 km)
1 Auriol/Occelli (Lancia) 17m 51s; **2** Biasion/Siviero (Ford) 17m 58s; **3** Schwarz/Hertz (Toyota) 18m 00s; **4** Alén/Kivimäki (Toyota) 18m 01s; **5** Kankkunen/Piironen (Lancia) 18m 06s; **6** McRae/Ringer (Subaru) 18m 10s.

SS 4. Harvati (12.58 km)
1 Auriol/Occelli (Lancia) 10m 12s; **2** Schwarz/Hertz (Toyota) 10m 21s; **3** Kankkunen/Piironen (Lancia) 10m 22s; **4** Alén/Kivimäki (Toyota) 10m 24s; **5** A. Vatanen/B. Berglund (Subaru Legacy RS), Biasion/Siviero (Ford) 10m 28s.

SS 5. Kitheronas (10.75 km)
1 Auriol/Occelli (Lancia) 7m 00s; **2** Alén/Kivimäki (Toyota) 7m 01s; **3** Schwarz/Hertz (Toyota) 7m 06s; **4** A. Fiorio/V. Brambilla (Lancia Delta HF Integrale) 7m 08s; **5** K. Eriksson/S. Parmander (Mitsubishi Galant VR-4) 7m 09s; **6** C. Sainz/L. Moya (Toyota Celica Turbo 4WD) 7m 10s.

SS 6. Hana Zagana 1 (18.19 km)
1 Kankkunen/Piironen (Lancia) 14m 33s; **2** F. Delecour/D. Grataloup (Ford Sierra Cosworth 4x4), Auriol/Occelli (Lancia) 14m 37s; **4** Sainz/Moya (Toyota), Vatanen/Berglund (Subaru) 14m 43s; **6** Biasion/Siviero (Ford), McRae/Ringer (Subaru), Fiorio/Brambilla (Lancia) 14m 56s.

SS 7. Pavliani 1 (14.86 km)
1 Auriol/Occelli (Lancia) 12m 42s; **2** Kankkunen/Piironen (Lancia), Delecour/Grataloup (Ford) 12m 50s; **4** McRae/Ringer (Subaru) 12m 52s; **5** Biasion/Siviero (Ford) 12m 53s; **6** Sainz/Moya (Toyota) 12m 56s.

SS 8. Arhani (8.32 km)
1 Kankkunen/Piironen (Lancia), Sainz/Moya (Toyota), Auriol/Occelli (Lancia) 6m 04s; **4** Delecour/Grataloup (Ford) 6m 05s; **5** Alén/Kivimäki (Toyota) 6m 06s; **6** Fiorio/Brambilla (Lancia) 6m 07s.

SS 9. Asvestis (11.16 km)
1 Kankkunen/Piironen (Lancia), Auriol/Occelli (Lancia) 7m 39s; **3** Biasion/Siviero (Ford) 7m 41s; **4** Sainz/Moya (Toyota), Alén/Kivimäki (Toyota) 7m 42s; **6** McRae/Ringer (Subaru) 7m 47s.

SS 10. Makrirahi (13.55 km)
1 Delecour/Grataloup (Ford) 7m 43s; **2** Sainz/Moya (Toyota) 7m 44s; **3** Kankkunen/Piironen (Lancia) 7m 47s; **4** Auriol/Occelli (Lancia) 7m 48s; **5** Biasion/Siviero (Ford) 7m 48s; **6** Fiorio/Brambilla (Lancia) 7m 49s.

SS 11. Anavra (13.33 km)
1 Sainz/Moya (Toyota) 8m 08s; **2** Delecour/Grataloup (Ford) 8m 09s; **3** Kankkunen/Piironen (Lancia), Auriol/Occelli (Lancia) 8m 10s; **5** Schwarz/ Hertz (Toyota) 8m 12s; **6** Biasion/Siviero (Ford) 8m 13s.

SS 12. Loutra Smokovou (8.99 km)
1 Alén/Kivimäki (Toyota) 5m 20s; **2** Kankkunen/Piironen (Lancia), Sainz/Moya (Toyota), Delecour/Grataloup (Ford) 5m 22s; **5** Auriol/Occelli (Lancia), Biasion/Siviero (Ford) 5m 23s.

SS 13. Rendina (27.31 km)
1 Auriol/Occelli (Lancia) 22m 52s; **2** Biasion/Siviero (Ford) 23m 04s; **3** Kankkunen/Piironen (Lancia) 23m 05s; **4** Delecour/Grataloup (Ford) 23m 37s; **5** McRae/Ringer (Subaru) 23m 38s; **6** Alén/Kivimäki (Toyota) 23m 56s.

SS 14. Dipotamia (11.07 km)
1 Kankkunen/Piironen (Lancia) 9m 15s; **2** Auriol/Occelli (Lancia) 9m 18s; **3** McRae/Ringer (Subaru) 9m 20s; **4** Delecour/Grataloup (Ford), Schwarz/Hertz (Toyota) 9m 23s; **6** Biasion/Siviero (Ford) 9m 27s.

SS 15. Domnista (15.45 km)
1 Kankkunen/Piironen (Lancia) 14m 15s; **2** Auriol/Occelli (Lancia) 14m 16s; **3** McRae/Ringer (Subaru) 14m 19s; **4** Delecour/Grataloup (Ford) 14m 20s; **5** Biasion/Siviero (Ford) 14m 21s; **6** Schwarz/Hertz (Toyota) 14m 27s.

SS 16. Krioneria (11.15 km)
1 Kankkunen/Piironen (Lancia), McRae/Ringer (Subaru) 10m 33s; **3** Biasion/Siviero (Ford) 10m 35s; **4** Auriol/Occelli (Lancia) 10m 36s; **5** Delecour/Grataloup (Ford), Schwarz/Hertz (Toyota) 10m 38s.

SS 17. Ano Hora (13.18 km)
1 Kankkunen/Piironen (Lancia) 9m 58s; **2** Delecour/Grataloup (Ford) 9m 59s; **3** McRae/Ringer (Subaru) 10m 02s; **4** Schwarz/Hertz (Toyota) 10m 03s; **5** Auriol/Occelli (Lancia) 10m 05s; **6** Biasion/Siviero (Ford) 10m 08s.

SS 18. Karoutes 1 (19.50 km)
1 Delecour/Grataloup (Ford) 12m 59s; **2** Kankkunen/Piironen (Lancia) 13m 09s; **3** Auriol/Occelli (Lancia), McRae/Ringer (Subaru), Schwarz/Hertz (Toyota) 13m 11s; **6** Biasion/Siviero (Ford) 13m 13s.

SS 19. Bauxites 1 (8.68 km)
1 Alén/Kivimäki (Toyota), Schwarz/Hertz (Toyota) 4m 30s; **3** Auriol/Occelli (Lancia), McRae/Ringer (Subaru) 4m 34s; **5** Delecour/Grataloup (Ford) 4m 35s; **6** Kankkunen/Piironen (Lancia), Biasion/Siviero (Ford) 4m 37s.

SS 20. Pente Oria 1 (19.09 km)
1 Kankkunen/Piironen (Lancia), McRae/Ringer (Subaru) 11m 59s; **3** Schwarz/Hertz (Toyota) 12m 00s; **4** Auriol/Occelli (Lancia), Biasion/Siviero (Ford) 12m 02s; **6** Delecour/Grataloup (Ford) 12m 23s.

SS 21. Prossilio 1 (9.30 km)
1 Kankkunen/Piironen (Lancia), Schwarz/Hertz (Toyota) 6m 09s; **3** Auriol/Occelli (Lancia) 16m 13s; **4** Alén/Kivimäki (Toyota) 16m 14s; **5** Delecour/ Grataloup (Ford), McRae/Ringer (Subaru) 6m 16s.

SS 22. Hani Zagana 2 (18.19 km)
1 McRae/Ringer (Subaru) 14m 20s; **2** Kankkunen/Piironen (Lancia) 14m 26s; **3** Auriol/Occelli (Lancia), Schwarz/Hertz (Toyota) 14m 29s ; **5** Biasion/Siviero (Ford) 14m 35s; **6** Delecour/Grataloup (Ford), Alén/Kivimäki (Toyota) 14m 36s.

SS 23. Pira (12.96 km)
1 McRae/Ringer (Subaru) 9m 09s; **2** Kankkunen/Piironen (Lancia) 9m 10s; **3** Auriol/Occelli (Lancia) 9m 11s; **4** Fiorio/Brambilla (Lancia) 9m 12s; **5** Alén/Kivimäki (Toyota) 9m 13s; **6** Biasion/Siviero (Ford) 9m 17s.

SS 24. Anatoli (9.29 km)
1 Schwarz/Hertz (Toyota) 8m 29s; **2** Kankkunen/Piironen (Lancia) 8m 30s; **3** Auriol/Occelli (Lancia) 8m 33s; **4** Biasion/Siviero (Ford), McRae/Ringer (Subaru) 8m 34s; **6** Alén/Kivimäki (Toyota) 8m 43s.

SS 25. Perivoli 1 (12.72 km)
1 Schwarz/Hertz (Toyota) 11m 14s; **2** Kankkunen/Piironen (Lancia) 11m 16s; **3** Auriol/Occelli (Lancia), McRae/Ringer (Subaru) 11m 18s; **5** Delecour/Grataloup (Ford), Fiorio/Brambilla (Lancia) 11m 21s.

SS 26. Gardiki 1 (22.87 km)
1 Auriol/Occelli (Lancia) 19m 17s; **2** Biasion/Siviero (Ford) 19m 24s; **3** Kankkunen/Piironen (Lancia) 19m 27s; **4** McRae/Ringer (Subaru) 19m 29s; **5** Delecour/Grataloup (Ford) 19m 37s; **6** Fiorio/Brambilla (Lancia) 19m 42s.

SS 27. Grameni Oxia 1 (11.46 km)
1 Kankkunen/Piironen (Lancia) 9m 32s; **2** Auriol/Occelli (Lancia) 9m 33s; **3** McRae/Ringer (Subaru) 9m 36s; **4** Fiorio/Brambilla (Lancia) 9m 42s; **5** Biasion/Siviero (Ford) 9m 43s; **6** Delecour/Grataloup (Ford) 9m 55s.

SS 28. Pentagi 1 (10.90 km)
1 McRae/Ringer (Subaru) 9m 57s; **2** Auriol/Occelli (Lancia) 10m 04s; **3** Kankkunen/Piironen (Lancia) 10m 05s; **4** Biasion/Siviero (Ford) 10m 10s; **5** Fiorio/Brambilla (Lancia) 10m 18s; **6** Delecour/Grataloup (Ford) 10m 19s.

SS 29. Diakopi (14.97 km)
1 McRae/Ringer (Subaru) 13m 28s; **2** Auriol/Occelli (Lancia) 13m 35s; **3** Kankkunen/Piironen (Lancia) 13m 39s; **4** Biasion/Siviero (Ford) 13m 42s; **5** Fiorio/Brambilla (Lancia) 13m 57s; **6** J. Recalde/M. Christie (Lancia Delta HF Integrale) 14m 01s.

SS 30. Koniakos (13.20 km)
1 McRae/Ringer (Subaru) 10m 49s; **2** Kankkunen/Piironen (Lancia), Auriol/Occelli (Lancia) 10m 50s; **4** Biasion/Siviero (Ford) 10m 55s; **5** Delecour/Grataloup (Ford) 11m 17s; **6** Recalde/Christie (Lancia) 11m 18s.

SS 31. Bauxites 2 (8.68 km)
1 Auriol/Occelli (Lancia) 4m 27s; **2** Biasion/Siviero (Ford) 4m 30s; **3** Kankkunen/Piironen (Lancia), McRae/Ringer (Subaru) 4m 31s; **5** Delecour/Grataloup (Ford) 4m 34s; **6** Fiorio/Brambilla (Lancia) 4m 35s.

SS 32. Pente Oria 2 (19.09 km)
1 Biasion/Siviero (Ford), McRae/Ringer (Subaru) 11m 56s; **3** Kankkunen/Piironen (Lancia) 12m 03s; **4** Auriol/Occelli (Lancia) 12m 05s; **5** Delecour/Grataloup (Ford) 12m 31s; **6** Recalde/Christie (Lancia) 12m 50s.

SS 33. Prossilio 2 (9.30 km)
1 Kankkunen/Piironen (Lancia) 6m 05s; **2** Biasion/Siviero (Ford) 6m 08s; **3** Auriol/Occelli (Lancia), McRae/Ringer (Subaru) 6m 10s; **5** Delecour/Grataloup (Ford) 6m 16s; **6** Recalde/ Christie (Lancia) 6m 29s.

SS 34. Pavliani 2 (14.86 km)
1 McRae/Ringer (Subaru) 12m 33s; **2** Auriol/Occelli (Lancia) 12m 38s; **3** Kankkunen/Piironen (Lancia) 12m 40s; **4** Biasion/Siviero (Ford) 12m 44s; **5** Delecour/Grataloup (Ford) 12m 47s; **6** Fiorio/Brambilla (Lancia) 12m 56s.

SS 35. Perivoli 2 (12.72 km)
1 Kankkunen/Piironen (Lancia), McRae/Ringer (Subaru) 11m 03s; **3** Auriol/Occelli (Lancia) 11m 05s; **4** Biasion/Siviero (Ford) 11m 07s; **5** Delecour/ Grataloup (Ford) 11m 12s; **6** Fiorio/Brambilla (Lancia) 11m 22s.

SS 36. Gardiki 2 (22.87 km)
1 McRae/Ringer (Subaru) 18m 46s; **2** Kankkunen/Piironen (Lancia) 18m 57s; **3** Biasion/Siviero (Ford) 18m 58s; **4** Auriol/Occelli (Lancia) 19m 03s; **5** Delecour/Grataloup (Ford) 19m 52s; **6** Recalde/ Christie (Lancia) 20m 20s.

SS 37. Grameni Oxia 2 (11.46 km)
1 Biasion/Siviero (Ford) 9m 26s; **2** Auriol/Occelli (Lancia) 9m 30s; **3** Kankkunen/Piironen (Lancia) 9m 31s; **4** McRae/Ringer (Subaru) 9m 55s; **5** Delecour/Grataloup (Ford), Recalde/Christie (Lancia) 10m 14s.

SS 38. Pendagi 2 (10.90 km)
1 Kankkunen/Piironen (Lancia) 9m 54s; **2** McRae/Ringer (Subaru) 9m 55s; **3** Auriol/Occelli (Lancia), Biasion/Siviero (Ford) 9m 59s; **5** Delecour/Grataloup (Ford) 10m 19s; **6** Recalde/Christie (Lancia) 10m 30s.

SS 39. Karoutes 2 (19.50 km)
1 Biasion/Siviero (Ford) 12m 57s; **2** Kankkunen/Piironen (Lancia), Auriol/Occelli (Lancia) 12m 58s; **4** McRae/Ringer (Subaru) 12m 59s; **5** Recalde/Christie (Lancia) 13m 54s; **6** 'Jigger'/C. Stefanis (Toyota Celica GT4) 14m 08s.

SS 40. Stiri (20.86 km)
1 Biasion/Siviero (Ford) 14m 20s; **2** Kankkunen/Piironen (Lancia) 14m 22s; **3** McRae/Ringer (Subaru) 14m 24s; **4** Auriol/Occelli (Lancia) 14m 31s; **5** Delecour/Grataloup (Ford) 14m 44s; **6** Recalde/ Christie (Lancia) 15m 14s.

FIA class winners

Group A	
Over 2000 cc:	Auriol/Occelli (Lancia)
1600-2000 cc:	'Leonidas'/Maria Korre Pavli (Renault Clio 16S)
1300-1600 cc:	Sergei Alyasov/Alexander Levitan (Lada Samara)
Up to 1300 cc:	Sotos Kokkinis/Stathis Mokkas (Peugeot 205 Rallye)
Group N	
Over 2000 cc:	de Mevius/Lux (Nissan)
1600-2000 cc:	No finishers
1300-1600 cc:	No finishers
Up to 1300 cc:	No finishers

Major retirements

Kenneth Eriksson/ Staffan Parmander	Mitsubishi Galant VR-4 SS 8	accident
Ari Vatanen/ Bruno Berglund	Subaru Legacy RS SS 12	engine
Carlos Sainz/ Luis Moya	Toyota Celica Turbo 4WD SS 13	accident
Mohammed Bin Sulayem/ Ronan Morgan	Ford Sierra Cosworth 4x4 SS 25	distributor
Markku Alén/ Ilkka Kivimäki	Toyota Celica Turbo 4WD SS 26	accident
Armin Schwarz/ Arne Hertz	Toyota Celica Turbo 4WD SS 26	accident

Rally leaders

SS 1-40 Auriol/Occelli (Lancia).

World Championship points

Drivers
1 Kankkunen 62; **2** Auriol 60; **3** Sainz 57; **4** Biasion 34; **5** Delecour 33; **6** Alén 28; **7** McRae 25; **8** Jonsson and Bugalski 20; **10** Recalde 18.

Manufacturers
1 Lancia 97; **2** Toyota 67; **3** Ford 61; **4** Subaru 23; **5** Mitsubishi 20; **6** Nissan 16; **7** Renault 2.

Route details

Leg 1
31 May: Starting from Athens at 0930, finishing at Delphi at 1930, including five special stages (64.36 km).
Leg 2
1 June: Starting and finishing at Delphi 07.30-1845, including 13 special stages (185.99 km).
Leg 3
2 June: Starting and finishing at Delphi 0730-1640, including 12 special stages (163.63 km).
Leg 4
3 June: Starting from Delphi at 0730, finishing at Athens at 2010, including 10 special stages (150.18 km).

Weather

Hot, dry and dusty.

Special stage analysis

	1st	2nd	3rd	4th	5th	6th
Kankkunen/Piironen (Lancia)	13	11	12	-	2	1
Auriol/Occelli (Lancia)	11	10	11	6	2	-
McRae/Ringer (Subaru)	11	2	11	5	2	3
Biasion/Siviero (Ford)	4	5	4	8	7	8
Schwarz/Hertz (Toyota)	4	2	6	2	1	1
Delecour/Grataloup (Ford)	2	5	-	4	15	4
Sainz/Moya (Toyota)	2	2	-	2	-	2
Alén/Kivimäki (Toyota)	2	1	1	4	3	3
Fiorio/Brambilla (Lancia)	-	-	-	3	3	7
Vatanen/Berglund (Subaru)	-	-	-	1	1	-
Recalde/Christie (Lancia)	-	-	-	-	2	7
Eriksson/Parmander (Mitsubishi)	-	-	-	-	1	-
'Jigger'/Stefanis (Toyota)	-	-	-	-	-	1

Finish lines

François Delecour was the last of the works drivers, taking fifth in the second Mobil **Cosworth** 4x4, having lost four minutes in a controversial incident at the start of SS9, when the start marshal apparently set off the plumbed-in fire extinguisher. The Frenchman lost two minutes waiting for the fumes to clear, and was then penalised two more minutes for failing to move off the start line within 20 seconds...**Grégoire de Mevius** beat off a fierce challenge from the Fords to win Group N in the Alcatel **Nissan**, pushing the Sunny to the limit downhill to compensate for the lack of power on the ascent...**Ari Vatanen** lost nearly four minutes when the works **Subaru**'s propshaft broke and savaged the gearbox, only to retire with a blown engine...**Alessandro Fiorio** was giving the factory drivers cause for concern in his private **Integrale**, but a variety of transmission maladies demoted him to seventh.

Results

1	Didier Auriol/ Bernard Occelli	Lancia Delta HF Integrale	7h 12m 08s	Gr A
2	Juha Kankkunen/ Juha Piironen	Lancia Delta HF Integrale	7h 13m 37s	Gr A
3	Massimo Biasion/ Tiziano Siviero	Ford Sierra Cosworth 4x4	7h 14m 33s	Gr A
4	Colin McRae/ Derek Ringer	Subaru Legacy RS	7h 16m 02s	Gr A
5	François Delecour/ Daniel Grataloup	Ford Sierra Cosworth 4x4	7h 27m 22s	Gr A
6	Jorge Recalde/ Martin Christie	Lancia Delta HF Integrale	7h 31m 58s	Gr A
7	Alessandro Fiorio/ Vittorio Brambilla	Lancia Delta HF Integrale	7h 44m 53s	Gr A
8	'Jigger'/ Costas Stefanis	Toyota Celica GT4	8h 00m 35s	Gr A
9	Grégoire de Mevius/ Willy Lux	Nissan Sunny GTi-R	8h 05m 11s	Gr N
10	Fernando Capdevila/ Alfredo Rodriguez	Ford Sierra Cosworth 4x4	8h 07m 40s	Gr N

84 starters, 41 finishers

Previous winners

1960	Walter Schock/Rolf Moll	Mercedes-Benz 220SE
1961	Erik Carlsson/Walter Carlsson	Saab 96
1962	Eugen Bohringer/Peter Lang	Mercedes-Benz 220SE
1963	Eugen Bohringer/Rolf Moll	Mercedes-Benz 300SE
1964	Tom Trana/Gunnar Thermenius	Volvo PV544
1965	Carl-Magnus Skogh/'Tandlakare'	Volvo 122S
1966	Bengt Söderstrom/Gunnar Palm	Ford Lotus Cortina
1967	Paddy Hopkirk/Ron Crellin	Mini-Cooper S
1968	Roger Clark/Jim Porter	Ford Escort TC
1969	Pauli Toivonen/Matti Kolari	Porsche 911S
1970	Jean-Luc Thérier/Marcel Callewaert	Alpine Renault A110
1971	Ove Andersson/Arne Hertz	Alpine Renault A110
1972	Håkan Lindberg/Helmut Eisendle	Fiat 124 Spyder
1973	Jean-Luc Thérier/Christian Delferrier	Alpine Renault A110
1975	Walter Röhrl/Jochen Berger	Opel Ascona
1976	Harry Kallström/Claes-Goran Andersson	Datsun 160J
1977	Björn Waldegård/Hans Thorszelius	Ford Escort RS1800
1978	Walter Röhrl/Christian Geistdörfer	Fiat 131 Abarth
1979	Björn Waldegård/Hans Thorszelius	Ford RS1800
1980	Ari Vatanen/David Richards	Ford Escort RS
1981	Ari Vatanen/David Richards	Ford Escort RS
1982	Michèle Mouton/Fabrizia Pons	Audi Quattro
1983	Walter Röhrl/Christian Geistdörfer	Lancia Rallye 037
1984	Stig Blomqvist/Björn Cederberg	Audi Quattro
1985	Timo Salonen/Seppo Harjanne	Peugeot 205 Turbo 16
1986	Juha Kankkunen/Juha Piironen	Peugeot 205 Turbo 16
1987	Markku Alén/Ilkka Kivimäki	Lancia Delta HF 4x4
1988	Massimo Biasion/Tiziano Siviero	Lancia Delta HF Integrale
1989	Massimo Biasion/Tiziano Siviero	Lancia Delta HF Integrale
1990	Carlos Sainz/Luis Moya	Toyota Celica GT4
1991	Juha Kankkunen/Juha Piironen	Lancia Delta HF Integrale

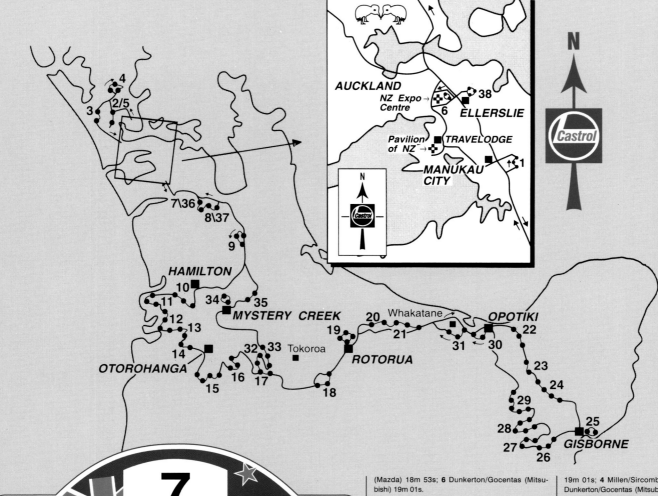

ROTHMANS
RALLY NEW ZEALAND
22ND ANNIVERSARY 1992

ROTHMANS RALLY OF NEW ZEALAND, 25-28 June.
FIA World Rally Championship for Drivers, round 7.

Leading entries

1	Carlos Sainz/ Luis Moya	Toyota Celica Turbo 4WD Gr A
2	Ari Vatanen/ Bruno Berglund	Subaru Legacy RS Gr A
3	Piero Liatti/ Luciano Tedeschini	Lancia Delta HF Integrale Gr A
4	Colin McRae/ Derek Ringer	Subaru Legacy RS Gr A
5	'Possum' Bourne/ Rodger Freeth	Subaru Legacy RS Gr A
6	Ross Dunkerton/ Fred Gocentas	Mitsubishi Galant VR-4 Gr A
7	Rod Millen/ Tony Sircombe	Mazda 323 GT-X Gr A
8	Neil Allport/ Jim Robb	Mazda 323 GT-X Gr A
9	Carlos Menem/ Victor Zucchini	Lancia Delta HF Integrale Gr A
10	Mohammed Bin Sulayem/ Ronan Morgan	Ford Sierra Cosworth Gr N 4x4
11	Mikael Sundström/ Jakke Honkanen	Lancia Delta HF Integrale Gr N
12	Ed Ordynski/ Harry Mansson	Mitsubishi Galant VR-4 Gr N
14	Ross Meekings/ Colin Smith	Toyota Celica GT4 Gr N
15	Kurt Gottlicher/ Otto Zwanzigleitner	Ford Sierra Cosworth 4x4 Gr N
16	Brian Stokes/ Jeff Judd	Ford Sierra Cosworth 4x4 Gr A
17	Joe McAndrew/ Bob Haldane	Subaru Legacy RS Gr A
18	Brian Watkin/ Gary Smith	Subaru Legacy RS Gr A
19	Ray Wilson/ Leo Bult	Mazda 323 GT-X Gr A
20	Frank Neale/ Philip Dodd	Toyota Celica GT4 Gr A
21	Gregg Taylor/ Peter Garnett	Mazda 323 4WD Gr A

Special stages times

SS 1. Totara Park (2.22 km)
1 P. Bourne/R. Freeth (Subaru Legacy RS) 1m 16s; 2 C. Sainz/L. Moya (Toyota Celica Turbo 4WD) 1m 17s; 3 A. Vatanen/B. Berglund (Subaru Legacy RS), P. Liatti/L. Tedeschini (Lancia Delta HF Integrale) 1m 18s; 5 C. McRae/D. Ringer (Subaru Legacy RS), R. Dunkerton/F. Gocentas (Mitsubishi Galant VR-4) 1m 19s.

SS 2. Riverhead Forest 1 (14.52 km)
1 Sainz/Moya (Toyota) 7m 22s; 2 McRae/Ringer (Subaru Legacy RS) 7m 31s; 3 Vatanen/Berglund (Subaru) 7m 32s; 4 Bourne/Freeth (Subaru) 7m 33s; 5 R. Millen/T. Sircombe (Mazda 323 GT-X) 7m 36s; 6 Liatti/Tedeschini (Lancia) 7m 45s.

SS 3. Kiwitahi (9.31 km)
1 Sainz/Moya (Toyota) 4m 47s; 2 Bourne/Freeth (Subaru) 4m 50s; 3 Vatanen/Berglund (Subaru), N. Allport/J. Robb (Mazda 323 GT-X) 4m 51s; 5 Liatti/Tedeschini (Lancia), Millen/Sircombe (Mazda) 4m 56s.

SS 4. Wainui Loop (30.35 km)
1 Liatti/Tedeschini (Lancia) 18m 38s; 2 Sainz/Moya (Toyota), Vatanen/Berglund (Subaru) 18m 44s; 4 Bourne/Freeth (Subaru) 18m 48s; 5 Allport/Robb (Mazda) 18m 53s; 6 Dunkerton/Gocentas (Mitsubishi) 19m 01s.

SS 5. Riverhead Forest 2 (14.52 km)
1 Sainz/Moya (Toyota) 7m 20s; 2 Vatanen/Berglund (Subaru), Bourne/Freeth (Subaru) 7m 22s; 4 Millen/Sircombe (Mazda) 7m 33s; 5 Liatti /Tedeschini (Lancia) 7m 39s; 6 Allport/Robb (Mazda) 7m 40s.

SS 6. Expo Centre (2.22 km)
1 Sainz/Moya (Toyota) 1m 21s; 2 Liatti/Tedeschini (Lancia) 1m 23s; 3 Bourne/Freeth (Subaru), Dunkerton/Gocentas (Mitsubishi) 1m 24s; 5 Vatanen/Berglund (Subaru), Millen/Sircombe (Mazda) 1m 25s.

SS 7. Maramarua West 1 (13.24 km)
1 Bourne/Freeth (Subaru) 7m 06s; 2 Millen/Sircombe (Mazda) 7m 12s; 3 Vatanen/Berglund (Subaru) 7m 15s; 4 Sainz/Moya (Toyota) 7m 17s; 5 Dunkerton/Gocentas (Mitsubishi) 7m 24s; 6 Liatti/Tedeschini (Lancia) 7m 42s.

SS 8. Maramarua Headquarters 1 (10.75 km)
1 Bourne/Freeth (Subaru) 6m 03s; 2 Vatanen/Berglund (Subaru) 6m 04s; 3 Sainz/Moya (Toyota) 6m 06s; 4 Millen/Sircombe (Mazda) 6m 07s; 5 Liatti/Tedeschini (Lancia) 6m 09s; 6 Dunkerton/Gocentas (Mitsubishi) 6m 11s.

SS 9. Waiti (12.25 km)
1 Liatti/Tedeschini (Lancia) 9m 04s; 2 Sainz/Moya (Toyota) 9m 08s; 3 Vatanen/Berglund (Subaru) 9m 09s; 4 Millen/Sircombe (Mazda) 9m 10s; 5 Allport/Robb (Mazda) 9m 17s; 6 J. McAndrew/B. Haldane (Subaru Legacy RS) 9m 20s.

SS 10. Waitetuna (16.70 km)
1 Vatanen/Berglund (Subaru) 9m 44s; 2 Liatti/Tedeschini (Lancia) 9m 46s; 3 Sainz/Moya (Toyota) 9m 51s; 4 Millen/Sircombe (Mazda) 9m 57s; 5 Allport/Robb (Mazda) 10m 01s; 6 Dunkerton/Gocentas (Mitsubishi), B. Stokes/J. Judd (Ford Sierra Cosworth 4x4) 10m 05s.

SS 11. Whaanga Coast (30.23 km)
1 Liatti/Tedeschini (Lancia) 23m 07s; 2 Vatanen/Berglund (Subaru) 23m 11s; 3 Millen/Sircombe (Mazda) 23m 15s; 4 Dunkerton/Gocentas (Mitsubishi) 23m 25s; 5 Stokes/Judd (Ford) 23m 39s; 6 Sainz/Moya (Toyota) 23m 41s.

SS 12. Bridal Veil (24.93 km)
1 Liatti/Tedeschini (Lancia) 18m 56s; 2 Vatanen/Berglund (Subaru) 18m 57s; 3 Sainz/Moya (Toyota) 19m 01s; 4 Millen/Sircombe (Mazda) 19m 11s; 5 Dunkerton/Gocentas (Mitsubishi) 19m 16s; 6 Allport/Robb (Mazda) 19m 30s.

SS 13. Okupata (16.33 km)
1 Liatti/Tedeschini (Lancia) 10m 58s; 2 Sainz/Moya (Toyota) 11m 03s; 3 Millen/Sircombe (Mazda) 11m 10s; 4 Dunkerton/Gocentas (Mitsubishi) 11m 12s; 5 Allport/Robb (Mazda) 11m 15s; 6 McAndrew/Haldane (Subaru) 11m 29s.

SS 14. Hautaru North (17.92 km)
1 Liatti/Tedeschini (Lancia) 14m 32s; 2 Vatanen/Berglund (Subaru) 14m 34s; 3 Sainz/Moya (Toyota), Millen/Sircombe (Mazda) 14m 42s; 5 Dunkerton/Gocentas (Mitsubishi) 14m 51s; 6 McAndrew/Haldane (Subaru) 14m 52s.

SS 15. Walker Bush (17.27 km)
1 Sainz/Moya (Toyota) 10m 45s; 2 Liatti/Tedeschini (Lancia) 10m 53s; 3 Millen/Sircombe (Mazda) 11m 08s; 4 Dunkerton/Gocentas (Mitsubishi) 11m 14s; 5 Allport/Robb (Mazda), McAndrew/Haldane (Subaru) 11m 15s.

SS 16. Hoddle Valley (10.14 km)
1 Sainz/Moya (Toyota) 6m 31s; 2 Liatti/Tedeschini (Lancia) 6m 39s; 3 Dunkerton/Gocentas (Mitsubishi) 6m 48s; 4 Millen/Sircombe (Mazda) 6m 53s; 5 McAndrew/Haldane (Subaru) 6m 55s; 6 Allport/Robb (Mazda) 6m 57s.

SS 17. Ngaroma (10.77 km)
1 Sainz/Moya (Toyota) 6m 52s; 2 Liatti/Tedeschini (Lancia) 6m 55s; 3 Dunkerton/Gocentas (Mitsubishi) 7m 11s; 4 Millen/Sircombe (Mazda) 7m 12s; 5 Allport/Robb (Mazda) 7m 17s; 6 McAndrew/Haldane (Subaru) 7m 23s.

SS 18. Maleme (14.57 km)
1 Sainz/Moya (Toyota) 7m 39s; 2 Liatti/Tedeschini (Lancia) 7m 43s; 3 Millen/Sircombe (Mazda) 7m 53s; 4 Dunkerton/Gocentas (Mitsubishi) 7m 59s; 5 McAndrew/Haldane (Subaru) 8m 00s; 6 Allport/Robb (Mazda) 8m 02s.

SS 19. Rotorua City (2.37 km)
1 Sainz/Moya (Toyota) 1m 29s; 2 Dunkerton/Gocentas (Mitsubishi) 1m 30s; 3 McAndrew/Haldane (Subaru) 1m 34s; 4 Millen/Sircombe (Mazda) 1m 35s; 5 Liatti/Tedeschini (Lancia) 1m 36s; 6 Allport/ Robb (Mazda) 1m 37s.

SS 20. Rotoehu (16.50 km)
1 Sainz/Moya (Toyota) 8m 52s; 2 Allport/Robb

(Mazda) 8m 54s; **3** Millen/Sircombe (Mazda) 8m 58s; **4** Liatti/Tedeschini (Lancia) 9m 01s; **5** Dunkerton/Gocentas (Mitsubishi) 9m 04s; **6** McAndrew/Haldane (Subaru) 9m 09s.

SS 21. Manawahe (24.75 km)
1 Sainz/Moya (Toyota) 17m 44s; **2** Liatti/Tedeschini (Lancia) 17m 50s; **3** Dunkerton/Gocentas (Mitsubishi) 18m 03s; **4** Millen/Sircombe (Mazda) 18m 09s; **5** M. Sundström/J. Honkanen (Lancia Delta HF Integrale) 18m 30s; **6** McAndrew/Haldane (Subaru) 18m 32s.

SS 22. Motu 1 (23.24 km)
1 Sainz/Moya (Toyota) 16m 30s; **2** Liatti/Tedeschini (Lancia) 16m 41s; **3** Dunkerton/Gocentas (Mitsubishi) 16m 45s; **4** Millen/Sircombe (Mazda) 16m 47s; **5** McAndrew/Haldane (Subaru) 17m 08s; **6** Sundström/Honkanen (Lancia) 17m 27s.

SS 23. Motu 2 (27.70 km)
1 Sainz/Moya (Toyota) 25m 34s; **2** Dunkerton/Gocentas (Mitsubishi) 26m 28s; **3** Liatti/Tedeschini (Lancia) 26m 45s; **4** Millen/Sircombe (Mazda) 26m 59s; **5** McAndrew/Haldane (Subaru) 27m 15s; **6** Sundström/Honkanen (Lancia) 27m 27s.

SS 24. Whakarau (33.54 km)
1 Sainz/Moya (Toyota) 24m 41s; **2** Dunkerton/Gocentas (Mitsubishi), Millen/Sircombe (Mazda) 25m 06s; **4** Liatti/Tedeschini (Lancia) 25m 30s; **5** K. Inoue/S. Hayashi (Mitsubishi Galant VR-4) 25m 47s; **6** McAndrew/Haldane (Subaru) 25m 51s.

SS 25. Kaiti Hill (2.11 km)
1 Sainz/Moya (Toyota) 1m 26s; **2** Liatti/Tedeschini (Lancia) 1m 29s; **3** Dunkerton/Gocentas (Mitsubishi) 1m 30s; **4** Millen/Sircombe (Mazda) 1m 32s; **5** McAndrew/Haldane (Subaru) 1m 36s; **6** Y. Fujimoto/H. Ichino (Nissan Sunny GTi-R) 1m 37s.

SS 26. Parikanapa 1 (25.84 km)
1 Sainz/Moya (Toyota) 18m 56s; **2** Millen/Sircombe (Mazda) 19m 01s; **3** Liatti/Tedeschini (Lancia) 19m 06s; **4** Dunkerton/Gocentas (Mitsubishi) 19m 19s; **5** Inoue/Hayashi (Mitsubishi) 19m 59s; **6** McAndrew/Haldane (Subaru) 20m 00s.

SS 27. Parikanapa 2 (18.75 km)
1 Sainz/Moya (Toyota) 12m 55s; **2** Liatti/Tedeschini (Lancia) 13m 06s; **3** Millen/Sircombe (Mazda) 13m 07s; **4** Dunkerton/Gocentas (Mitsubishi) 13m 12s; **5** McAndrew/Haldane (Subaru) 13m 47s; **6** Inoue/Hayashi (Mitsubishi) 13m 51s.

SS 28. Pehiri (30.22 km)
1 Sainz/Moya (Toyota) 17m 23s; **2** Liatti/Tedeschini (Lancia) 17m 49s; **3** Millen/Sircombe (Mazda) 17m 52s; **4** Dunkerton/Gocentas (Mitsubishi) 18m 05s; **5** McAndrew/Haldane (Subaru) 18m 36s; **6** Sundström/ Honkanen (Lancia) 18m 50s.

SS 29. Wharekopae (29.26 km)
1 Sainz/Moya (Toyota) 17m 59s; **2** Liatti/Tedeschini (Lancia) 18m 19s; **3** Millen/Sircombe (Mazda) 18m 27s; **4** Dunkerton/Gocentas (Mitsubishi) 18m 29s; **5** McAndrew/Haldane (Subaru) 19m 08s; **6** E. Ordynski/H. Mansson (Mitsubishi Galant VR4) 19m 21s.

SS 30. Old Creamery (8.27 km)
1 Sainz/Moya (Toyota) 5m 14s; **2** Dunkerton/Gocentas (Mitsubishi) 5m 17s; **3** Liatti/Tedeschini (Lancia) 5m 19s; **4** Millen/Sircombe (Mazda) 5m 22s; **5** McAndrew/Haldane (Subaru) 5m 26s; **6** Ordynski/Mansson (Mitsubishi) 5m 34s.

SS 31. Stanley (15.41 km)
1 Dunkerton/Gocentas (Mitsubishi) 11m 16s; **2** Sainz/Moya (Toyota), Liatti/Tedeschini (Lancia) 11m 25s; **4** Inoue/Hayashi (Mitsubishi) 11m 52s; **5** McAndrew/Haldane (Subaru) 11m 57s; Sundström/Honkanen (Lancia) 12m 00s.

SS 32. Taupaki (17.51 km)
1 Liatti/Tedeschini (Lancia) 12m 08s; **2** Sainz/Moya (Toyota), Dunkerton/Gocentas (Mitsubishi) 12m 13s; **4** Millen/Sircombe (Mazda) 12m 23s; **5** McAndrew/Haldane (Subaru) 12m 39s; **6** Inoue/Hayashi (Mitsubishi) 12m 43s.

SS 33. Hurimu (14.73 km)
1 Liatti/Tedeschini (Lancia) 5m 04s; **2** Dunkerton/Gocentas (Mitsubishi) 5m 05s; **3** Sainz/Moya (Toyota) 5m 08s; **4** Millen/Sircombe (Mazda) 5m 09s; **5** Inoue/Hayashi (Mitsubishi) 5m 13s; **6** McAndrew/Haldane (Subaru) 5m 14s.

SS 34. Mystery Creek (5.55 km)
1 Sainz/Moya (Toyota) 4m 33s; **2** Dunkerton/Gocentas (Mitsubishi), Millen/Sircombe (Mazda) 4m 34s; **4** Liatti/Tedeschini (Lancia) 4m 40s; **5** McAndrew/Haldane (Subaru), Inoue/Hayashi (Mitsubishi) 4m 47s.

SS 35. Maungakawa (8.11 km)
1 Sainz/Moya (Toyota) 5m 18s; **2** Liatti/Tedeschini (Lancia) 5m 21s; **3** Dunkerton/Gocentas (Mitsubishi) 5m 22s; **4** McAndrew/Haldane (Subaru) 5m 26s; **5** Inoue/Hayashi (Mitsubishi) 5m 33s; **6** Ordynski/Mansson (Mitsubishi) 5m 37s.

SS 36. Maramarua West 2 (13.24 km)
1 Sainz/Moya (Toyota) 7m 18s; **2** Liatti/Tedeschini (Lancia) 7m 31s; **3** McAndrew/Haldane (Subaru) 7m 36s; **4** Fujimoto/Ichino (Nissan) 7m 53s; **5** W. Orr/H. Orr (Subaru Legacy RS) 7m 55s; **6** Sundström/Honkanen (Lancia) 7m 56s.

SS 37. Maramarua Headquarters 2 (10.75 km)
1 Sainz/Moya (Toyota) 6m 03s; **2** Liatti/Tedeschini (Lancia) 6m 05s; **3** Dunkerton/Gocentas (Mitsubishi) 6m 29s; **4** R. Wilson/L. Bult (Mazda 323 GT-X), R. Jones/W. Churton (Mazda 323 GT-X) 6m 35s; **6** Sundström/Honkanen (Lancia) 6m 41s.

SS 38. Ellerslie Racecourse (2.90 km)
1 Sainz/Moya (Toyota), Liatti/Tedeschini (Lancia), Dunkerton/Gocentas (Mitsubishi) 2m 02s; **4** Inoue/Hayashi (Mitsubishi) 2m 08s; **5** K. Gottlicher/O. Zwanzigleitner (Ford Sierra Cosworth 4x4), S. Taguchi/C. Clarke (Mitsubishi Galant VR-4), C. Stallard/G. Jesse (Mitsubishi Galant VR-4) 2m 10s.

FIA class winners

Group A	
Over 2000 cc:	Sainz/Moya (Toyota)
1600-2000 cc:	Vanessa Slee/Sam Haldane (Daihatsu Charade GTti)
1300-1600 cc:	Richard McConnachie/Jeremy Tagg (Honda Civic)
Up to 1300 cc:	No starters
Group N	
Over 2000 cc:	Sundström/Honkaenen (Lancia)
1600-2000 cc:	No finishers
1300-1600 cc:	Aleksander Artemenko/Viktor Timovskiy (Lada Samara)
Up to 1300 cc:	Michael Simmonds/Alan Glen (Toyota Starlet)
Group B	
1300-1600 cc:	Dexter Dunlop/Keith McIlroy (Honda CRX)

Major retirements

Carlos Menem/	Lancia Delta HF Integrale	
Victor Zucchini	SS 2	accident
Colin McRae/	Subaru Legacy RS	
Derek Ringer	SS 5	engine
'Possum' Bourne/	Subaru Legacy RS	
Rodger Freeth	SS 9	engine
Brian Watkin/	Subaru Legacy RS	
Gary Smith	SS 12	electrics
Brian Stokes/	Ford Sierra Cosworth 4x4	
Jeff Judd	SS 13	rolled
Ari Vatanen/	Subaru Legacy RS	
Bruno Berglund	SS 15	engine
Mohammed Bin Sulayem/	Ford Sierra Cosworth 4x4	
Ronan Morgan	SS 20	driver illness
Neil Allport/	Mazda 323 GT-X	
Jim Robb	SS 21	accident
Rod Millen/	Mazda 323 GT-X	
Tony Sircombe	SS 35	engine
Joe McAndrew/	Subaru Legacy RS	
Bob Haldane	SS 36	engine

Rally leaders

SS 1 Bourne/Freeth (Subaru); **SS 2-10** Sainz/Moya (Toyota); **SS 11-13** Vatanen/Berglund (Subaru); **SS 14-38** Sainz/Moya (Toyota).

World Championship points

Drivers
1 Sainz 77; **2** Kankkunen 62; **3** Auriol 60; **4** Biasion 34; **5** Delecour 33; **6** Alén 28; **7** McRae 25; **8** Bugalski and Jonsson 20; **10** Liatti and Recalde 18.

Route details

Leg 1
25 June: Starting from Manukau at 1230, finishing at Auckland Travelodge at 2100, including six special stages (72.05 km).
Leg 2
26 June: Starting from Auckland Travelodge at 0800, finishing at Rotorua at 2130, including 13 special stages (194.59 km).
Leg 3
27 June: Starting and finishing from Rotorua 0700-2200, including 12 special stages (252.20 km).
Leg 4
28 June: Starting from Rotorua at 0700, finishing at Auckland Travelodge at 1635, including seven special stages (71.86 km).

Weather

Unseasonably warm and dry.

Special stage analysis

	1st	2nd	3rd	4th	5th	6th
Sainz/Moya (Toyota)	25	6	5	4	-	1
Liatti/Tedeschini (Lancia)	9	16	4	3	4	2
Bourne/Freeth (Subaru)	3	2	1	2	-	-
Dunkerton/Gocentas (Mitsubishi)	2	7	8	8	5	3
Vatanen/Berglund (Subaru)	1	6	5	-	1	-
Millen/Sircombe (Mazda)	-	4	8	8	5	3
Allport/Robb (Mazda)	-	1	1	-	6	5
McRae/Ringer (Subaru)	-	1	-	-	1	-
McAndrew/Haldane (Subaru)	-	-	2	1	13	9
Inoue/Hayashi (Mitsubishi)	-	-	-	2	5	2
Fujimoto/Ichino (Nissan)	-	-	-	1	-	1
Wilson/Bult (Mazda)	-	-	-	1	-	-
Jones/Churton (Mazda)	-	-	-	1	-	-
Sundström/Honkanen (Lancia)	-	-	-	-	1	6
Stokes/Judd (Ford)	-	-	-	-	1	1
Orr/Orr (Subaru)	-	-	-	-	1	-
Gottlicher/Zwanzigleitner (Ford)	-	-	-	-	1	-
Taguchi/Clarke (Mitsubishi)	-	-	-	-	1	-
Stallard/Jesse (Mitsubishi)	-	-	-	-	1	-
Ordynski/Mansson (Mitsubishi)	-	-	-	-	-	3

Changing to Lancia was good business for Mikael Sundström, who not only won Group N, but sold the car in New Zealand on the strength of it!

Finish lines

Ross Dunkerton became the first Australian driver to win a FISA A-seed after finishing third in his aged Ralliart Australia **Galant**....On his first visit to New Zealand, **Mikael Sundström** comfortably won Group N in his **Integrale**...**Ed Ordynski** finished one place behind in fifth after a battle with **Yoshio Fujimoto**'s Group N **Nissan** Sunny...**Carlos Menem Junior** squandered a clear Group N lead by putting his Top Run **Delta** off the road at the end of the first leg, avoiding a photographer standing in a ditch... **Mohammed Bin Sulayem** withdrew from the rally before the start of the final leg after being struck down with a painful stomach virus. He was a lowly 27th at the time in the MLP-tuned Marlboro **Cosworth** 4x4...**Will** and **Heather Orr**, the husband and wife partnership in a privately entered **Legacy**, were the highest placed New Zealand finishers in seventh...**Rod Millen** lost two minutes on the opening stage when the ignition cut-off switch turned itself off. He climbed back to fourth, only for the engine in his **Mazda** 323GT-X to expire three stages from the finish...**Neil Allport** was sixth when he slid his Falken-shod **Mazda** onto a bank on SS21...Other top local drivers who failed to finish included **Brian Watkins**, who crashed his Group N **Subaru** on SS12, and **Brian Stokes**, who put his Group A **Sierra** Cosworth 4x4 off the road three stages later ...**Samantha Haldane** became the youngest person to start a round of the World Rally Championship. At 17 years and 28 days, the Papakuru High School student navigated for Vanessa Slee in a **Daihatsu** Charade. The all-lady crew eventually finished first in class.

Results

1	Carlos Sainz/	Toyota Celica Turbo 4WD	
	Luis Moya	6h 36m 10s	Gr A
2	Piero Liatti/	Lancia Delta HF Integrale	
	Luciano Tedeschini	6h 40m 40s	Gr A
3	Ross Dunkerton/	Mitsubishi Galant VR-4	
	Fred Gocentas	6h 46m 22s	Gr A
4	Mikael Sundström/	Lancia Delta HF Integrale	
	Jakke Honkanen	7h 03m 12s	Gr N
5	Ed Ordynski/	Mitsubishi Galant VR-4	
	Harry Mansson	7h 06m 04s	Gr N
6	Yoshio Fujimoto/	Nissan Sunny GTi-R	
	Hakaru Ichino	7h 08m 36s	Gr N
7	Will Orr/	Subaru Legacy RS	
	Heather Orr	7h 12m 39s	Gr N
8	Seiichiro Taguchi/	Mitsubishi Galant VR-4	
	Chris Clarke	7h 13m 31s	Gr N
9	Barry Sexton/	Mazda 323 GT-X	
	Neil Cathcart	7h 14m 12s	Gr N
10	Craig Stallard/	Mitsubishi Galant VR-4	
	Graeme Jesse	7h 15m 16s	Gr N

76 starters, 41 finishers

Previous winners

1969	Grady Thompson/Rick Rimmer	Holden Monaro
1970	Paul Adams/Don Fenwick	BMW 2002
1971	Bruce Hodgson/Mike Mitchell	Ford Lotus Cortina
1972	Andrew Cowan/Jim Scott	Mini 1275GT
1973	Hannu Mikkola/Jim Porter	Ford Escort RS1600
1975	Mike Marshall/Arthur McWatt	Ford Escort RS1600
1976	Andrew Cowan/Jim Scott	Hillman Avenger
1977	Fulvio Bacchelli/Francesco Rosetti	Fiat 131 Abarth
1978	Russell Brookes/Chris Porter	Ford Escort RS
1979	Hannu Mikkola/Arne Hertz	Ford Escort RS
1980	Timo Salonen/Seppo Harjanne	Datsun 160J
1981	Jim Donald/Kevin Lancaster	Ford Escort RS
1982	Björn Waldegård/Hans Thorszelius	Toyota Celica Turbo
1983	Walter Röhrl/Christian Geistdörfer	Lancia Rally 037
1984	Stig Blomqvist/Björn Cederberg	Audi Quattro A2
1985	Timo Salonen/Seppo Harjanne	Peugeot 205 Turbo 16
1986	Juha Kankkunen/Juha Piironen	Peugeot 205 Turbo 16
1987	Franz Wittmann/Jorg Pettermann	Lancia Delta HF 4x4
1988	Josef Haider/Ferdinand Hinterleitner	Opel Kadett GSi
1989	Ingvar Carlsson/Per Carlsson	Mazda 323 Turbo 4x4
1990	Carlos Sainz/Luis Moya	Toyota Celica GT4
1991	Carlos Sainz/Luis Moya	Toyota Celica GT4

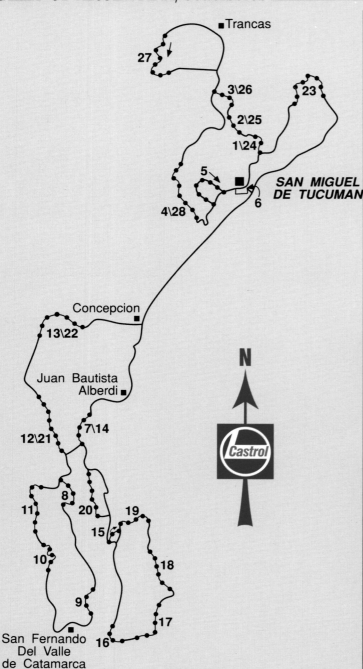

Trancas

27

3\26   23

2\25

1\24

5

SAN MIGUEL
DE TUCUMAN

4\28   6

N

Castrol

Concepcion

13\22

Juan Bautista
Alberdi

7\14

12\21

8

11   20   19

15

10   18

9

17

San Fernando   16
Del Valle
de Catamarca

RALLY OF ARGENTINA, 22-25 July. FIA World
Rally Championship for Manufacturers, round 6. FIA
World Rally Championship for Drivers, round 8.

Leading entries

1	Carlos Sainz/	Toyota Celica Turbo 4WD
	Luis Moya	Gr A
2	Jorge Recalde/	Lancia Delta HF Integrale
	Martin Christie	Gr A
3	Didier Auriol/	Lancia Delta HF Integrale
	Bernard Occelli	Gr A
4	Alessandro Fiorio/	Lancia Delta HF Integrale
	Vittorio Brambilla	Gr A
5	Rudi Stohl/	Audi 90 Quattro
	Peter Diekmann	Gr A
6	Grégoire de Mevius/	Nissan Sunny GTi-R
	Willy Lux	Gr N
7	Fernando Capdevila/	Ford Sierra Cosworth 4x4
	Alfredo Rodriguez	Gr N
8	Gustavo Trelles/	Lancia Delta HF Integrale
	Jorge Del Buono	Gr A
9	Carlos Menem/	Lancia Delta HF Integrale
	Victor Zucchini	Gr N
10	Gabriel Raies/	Renault 18 GTX
	José Maria Volta	Gr A
11	Sergio Secchi/	Renault 19
	Renato Russo	Gr A
12	Hugo Rosso/	Fiat Regatta 2000
	Fabio Macias	Gr A
14	Juan Raies/	Renault 18 GTX
	Rodolfo Ortiz	Gr A
15	Paulo Lemos/	VW Gol GTI
	Ricardo Costa	Gr A

16	Miguel Torras/	Renault 18 GTX
	Luis Maciel	Gr A
17	Jorge Bescham/	Fiat Regatta 2000
	José Garcia	Gr A
18	Daniel Rodriguez/	Renault 18 GTX
	Jorge Reartes	Gr A
19	Carlos Luaces/	VW Golf
	Maggi	Gr A
20	Hiroshi Nishiyama/	Nissan Sunny GTi-R
	Yoichi Yamazaki	Gr N
21	Alejandro Schmauk/	Alfa Romeo 33 16v
	Jaime Rojas	Gr N

Special stage times

SS 1. Timbo Viejo-El Cadillal 1 (8.07 km)
1 C. Sainz/L. Moya (Toyota Celica Turbo 4WD) 3m
24s; **2** D. Auriol/B.Occelli (Lancia Delta HF Integrale)
3m 28s; **3** A. Fiorio/V. Brambilla (Lancia Delta HF
Integrale) 3m 33s; **4** C. Menem/V. Zucchini (Lancia
Delta HF Integrale) 3m 35s; **5** J. Recalde/ M. Christie
(Lancia Delta HF Integrale) 3m 37s; **6** G. Trelles/J.
Del Buono (Lancia Delta HF Integrale) 3m 44s.

SS 2. El Cadillal-Cruce a Ticuchio 1 (18.17 km)
1 Auriol/Occelli (Lancia) 9m 11s; **2** Sainz/Moya (Toyota) 9m 12s; **3** Recalde/Christie (Lancia), Menem/
Zucchini (Lancia) 9m 34s; **5** Fiorio/Brambilla (Lancia)
9m 37s; **6** Trelles/Del Buono (Lancia) 9m 56s.

SS 3. Cruce a Ticuchio-Vipos 1 (15.50 km)
1 Auriol/Occelli (Lancia) 8m 53s; **2** Sainz/Moya (Toyota) 8m 56s; **3** Recalde/Christie (Lancia) 9m 15s; **4**
Fiorio/Brambilla (Lancia) 9m 20s; **5** Trelles/Del

Buono (Lancia) 9m 28s; **6** G. Raies/J.-M. Volta
(Renault 18 GTX) 10m 23s.

SS 4. Siambon-Lules 1 (31.92 km)
1 Auriol/Occelli (Lancia) 16m 30s; **2** Sainz/Moya
(Toyota) 16m 35s; **3** Fiorio/Brambilla (Lancia) 17m
10s; **4** Recalde/Christie (Lancia) 17m 14s; **5** Trelles/
Del Buono (Lancia) 17m 16s; **6** Menem/Zucchini
(Lancia) 18m 08s.

SS 5. San Pablo-San Javier (23.58 km)
Cancelled.

SS6. Tucuman Hipodromo (4.07 km)
1 Sainz/Moya (Toyota), Auriol/Occelli (Lancia) 2m
53s; **3** Recalde/Christie (Lancia) 2m 58s; **4** Fiorio/
Brambilla (Lancia), Menem/Zucchini (Lancia) 2m
59s; **6** R. Stohl/P. Diekmann (Audi 90 Quattro) 3m
10s.

SS 7. Dique Escaba-Las Heguerillas 1 (32.67 km)
1 Auriol/Occelli (Lancia) 19m 35s; **2** Fiorio/Brambilla
(Lancia) 20m 05s; **3** Recalde/Christie (Lancia) 20m
10s; **4** Trelles/Del Buono (Lancia) 20m 26s; **5** Sainz/

Moya (Toyota) 20m 35s; **6** Menem/Zucchini (Lancia)
21m 20s.

SS 8. Los Varela-Rodeo Grande (8.66 km)
1 Sainz/Moya (Toyota) 4m 24s; **2** Auriol/Occelli (Lancia) 4m 30s; **3** Recalde/Christie (Lancia) 4m 38s; **4**
Fiorio/Brambilla (Lancia) 4m 39s; **5** Trelles/Del
Buono (Lancia) 4m 41s; **6** Menem/Zucchini (Lancia)
5m 07s.

SS 9. Pomancillo-Collagasta (8.35 km)
1 Auriol/Occelli (Lancia) 5m 55s; **2** Sainz/Moya (Toyota) 5m 58s; **3** Recalde/Christie (Lancia), Trelles/ Del
Buono (Lancia) 6m 10s; **5** Fiorio/Brambilla (Lancia)
6m 11s; **6** Stohl/Diekmann (Audi) 6m 39s.

SS 10. Bella Vista-Las Aguitas (6.33 km)
1 Sainz/Moya (Toyota) 4m 37s; **2** Auriol/Occelli (Lancia) 4m 40s; **3** Trelles/Del Buono (Lancia) 4m 49s; **4**
Fiorio/Brambilla (Lancia), Recalde/Christie (Lancia)
4m 53s; **6** Menem/Zucchini (Lancia) 5m 21s.

SS 11. Rio Trancas-Humaya (32.76 km)
1 Auriol/Occelli (Lancia) 25m 21s; **2** Sainz/Moya

TUCAMAN   **8**   22 AL 25 DE JULIO

12° RALLY YPF ARGENTINA '92

YPF

(Toyota) 25m 31s; **3** Fiorio/Brambilla (Lancia) 26m 04s; **4** Trelles/Del Buono (Lancia) 26m 12s; **5** Recalde/Christie (Lancia) 26m 16s; **6** Menem/Zucchini (Lancia) 28m 05s.

SS 12. Singuil-Las Chacritas 1 (30.50 km)
1 Auriol/Occelli (Lancia) 23m 18s; **2** Sainz/Moya (Toyota) 23m 20s; **3** Trelles/Del Buono (Lancia) 24m 05s; **4** Fiorio/Brambilla (Lancia) 24m 09s; **5** Recalde/Christie (Lancia) 24m 15s; **6** Menem/Zucchini (Lancia) 26m 01s.

SS 13. Yunca Suma-Alpachiri 1 (29.56 km)
Cancelled.

SS 14. Dique Escaba-Las Heguilleras 2 (32.67 km)
1 Sainz/Moya (Toyota) 19m 32s; **2** Auriol/Occelli (Lancia) 19m 45s; **3** Fiorio/Brambilla (Lancia) 20m 03s; **4** Trelles/Del Buono (Lancia) 20m 11s; **5** Recalde/Christie (Lancia) 20m 18s; **6** Menem/Zucchini (Lancia) 21m 53s.

SS 15. La Merced-El Totoral (4.86 km)
1 Sainz/Moya (Toyota) 3m 09s; **2** Auriol/Occelli (Lancia) 3m 10s; **3** Recalde/Christie (Lancia) 3m 14s; **4** Fiorio/Brambilla (Lancia), Trelles/Del Buono (Lancia) 3m 16s; **6** Stohl/Diekmann (Audi) 3m 38s.

SS 16. El Portezuelo-La Cumbre (10.05 km)
1 Auriol/Occelli (Lancia) 8m 31s; **2** Sainz/Moya (Toyota) 8m 32s; **3** Trelles/Del Buono (Lancia) 8m 47s; **4** Recalde/Christie (Lancia), Fiorio/Brambilla (Lancia) 8m 52s; **6** Menem/Zucchini (Lancia) 9m 30s.

SS 17. La Cumbre-Tintagasta (32.73 km)
1 Auriol/Occelli (Lancia) 23m 54s; **2** Sainz/Moya (Toyota) 24m 16s; **3** Trelles/Del Buono (Lancia) 24m 54s; **4** Fiorio/Brambilla (Lancia) 25m 03s; **5** Stohl/Diekmann (Audi) 28m 30s; **6** Raies/Volta (Renault) 28m 40s.

SS 18. El Alto-Alijilan (28.84 km)
1 Auriol/Occelli (Lancia) 22m 41s; **2** Sainz/Moya (Toyota) 22m 54s; **3** Trelles/Del Buono (Lancia) 24m 22s; **4** Menem/Zucchini (Lancia) 27m 03s; **5** Stohl/Diekmann (Audi) 27m 06s; **6** Raies/Volta (Renault) 27m 14s.

SS 19. Dique Sumampa-El Durazno (7.49 km)
1 Sainz/Moya (Toyota) 4m 33s; **2** Auriol/Occelli (Lancia) 4m 34s; **3** Trelles/Del Buono (Lancia) 4m 49s; **4** Fiorio/Brambilla (Lancia) 5m 03s; **5** Stohl/Diekmann (Audi) 5m 24s; **6** Raies/Volta (Renault) 5m 27s.

SS 20. San Antonio-Balcosna (16.62 km)
1 Auriol/Occelli (Lancia) 10m 54s; **2** Sainz/Moya (Toyota) 11m 19s; **3** Trelles/Del Buono (Lancia) 11m 47s; **4** Fiorio/Brambilla (Lancia) 12m 28s; **5** Raies/Volta (Renault) 13m 19s; **6** Stohl/Diekmann (Audi) 13m 20s.

SS 21. Singuil-Las Chacritas 2 (30.50 km)
Cancelled.

SS 22. Yunca Suma-Alpachiri 2 (29.56 km)
Cancelled.

SS 23. Dique el Cajon-Villa Padre Monti (30.78 km)
1 Auriol/Occelli (Lancia) 17m 12s; **2** Sainz/Moya (Toyota) 17m 37s; **3** Fiorio/Brambilla (Lancia) 19m 18s; **4** Trelles/Del Buono (Lancia) 19m 25s; **5** Stohl/Diekmann (Audi) 20m 31s; **6** M. Torras/L. Maciel (Renault 18 GTX) 20m 56s.

SS 24. Timbo Viejo-El Cadillal 2 (8.07 km)
Cancelled.

SS 25 El Cadillal-Cruce a Ticuchio 2 (18.17 km)
1 Auriol/Occelli (Lancia) 9m 24s; **2** Sainz/Moya (Toyota) 9m 42s; **3** Fiorio/Brambilla (Lancia) 9m 47s; **4** Trelles/Del Buono (Lancia) 9m 48s; **5** Menem/Zucchini (Lancia) 10m 17s; **6** Raies/Volta (Renault) 10m 48s.

SS 26. Cruce a Ticuchio-Vipos 2 (15.50 km)
1 Sainz/Moya (Toyota) 9m 04s; **2** Auriol/Occelli (Lancia) 9m 16s; **3** Fiorio/Brambilla (Lancia) 9m 31s; **4** Trelles/Del Buono (Lancia) 9m 33s; **5** Raies/Volta (Renault) 10m 36s; **6** Torras/Maciel (Renault) 10m 44s.

SS 27. San Pedro-Las Juntas (31.40 km)
1 Sainz/Moya (Toyota) 16m 34s; **2** Auriol/Occelli (Lancia) 16m 44s; **3** Fiorio/Brambilla (Lancia) 17m 23s; **4** Trelles/Del Buono (Lancia) 17m 42s; **5** Menem/Zucchini (Lancia) 18m 33s; **6** Stohl/Diekmann (Audi) 19m 28s.

SS 28. Siambon-Lules 2 (31.92 km)
1 Auriol/Occelli (Lancia), Sainz/Moya (Toyota) 17m 07s; **3** Fiorio/Brambilla (Lancia) 17m 30s; **4** Trelles/Del Buono (Lancia) 17m 48s; **5** Menem/Zucchini (Lancia) 18m 34s; **6** Stohl/Diekmann (Audi) 19m 07s.

FIA class winners

Group A

Over 2000 cc:	Auriol/Occelli (Lancia)
1600-2000 cc:	Raies/Volta (Renault)
1300-1600 cc:	Juan Diaz Dian/José Arevalo (Fiat Regatta 85)
Up to 1300 cc:	No starters

Group N

Over 2000 cc:	Menem/Zucchini (Lancia)
1600-2000 cc:	Schmauk/Rojas (Alfa Romeo 33 16v)
1300-1600 cc:	No starters
Up to 1300 cc:	Carlos Menendez Behety/Juan Carlos Ferreyra (Suzuki Swift)

Major retirements

Grégoire de Mevius/ Willy Lux	Nissan Sunny GTi-R missed start
Fernando Capdevila/ Alfredo Rodriguez	Ford Sierra Cosworth 4x4 recce accident
Jorge Bescham/ José Garcia	Fiat Regatta 2000 SS 2
Jorge Recalde/ Martin Christie	Lancia Delta HF Integrale SS 17 accident
Hugo Rosso/ Fabio Macias	Fiat Regatta 2000 SS 23 engine

Rally leaders

SS 1-3 Sainz/Moya (Toyota); **SS 3** Sainz/Moya (Toyota), Auriol/Occelli (Lancia); **SS 4-28** Auriol/Occelli (Lancia).

World Championship points

Drivers
1 Sainz 92; **2** Auriol 80; **3** Kankkunen 62; **4** Biasion 34; **5** Delecour 33; **6** Alén 28; **7** McRae 25; **8** Bugalski and Jonsson 20; **10** Recalde and Liatti 18.

Manufacturers
1 Lancia 117; **2** Toyota 84; **3** Ford 60; **4** Nissan 30; **5** Subaru 23; **6** Mitsubishi 20; **7** Audi 10; **8** Renault Argentine 7; **9** Renault 2.

Weather

Cold and dry.

Route details

Leg 1
22 July: Starting and finishing from Tucuman 1100-1732, including six special stages (one cancelled-77.73 km).
Leg 2
23 July: Starting and finishing from Tucuman 0700-2000, including seven special stages (one cancelled-119.27 km).
Leg 3
24 July: Starting and finishing from Tucuman 0600-2016, including nine special stages (two cancelled-139.26 km).
Leg 4
25 July: Starting and finishing from Tucuman 0700-1605, including six special stages (one cancelled-127.77 km).

Special stage analysis

	1st	2nd	3rd	4th	5th	6th
Auriol/Occelli (Lancia)	15	8	-	-	-	-
Sainz/Moya (Toyota)	10	12	-	-	1	-
Fiorio/Brambilla (Lancia)	-	1	9	10	2	-
Trelles/Del Buono (Lancia)	-	-	8	9	3	2
Recalde/Christie (Lancia)	-	-	7	3	4	-
Menem/Zucchini (Lancia)	-	-	1	3	3	8
Stohl/Diekmann (Audi)	-	-	-	-	4	6
Raies/Volta (Renault)	-	-	-	-	2	5
Torras/Maciel (Renault)	-	-	-	-	-	2

Finish lines

Group N was virtually decided before the first stage started. **Fernando Capdevila** was involved in a recce accident, in which he broke his leg. To comply with FISA regulations, which require a crew to take part in a rally outside Europe to qualify for the Group N World Rally Championship, **Capdevila** sat in the passenger seat as his co-driver, **Alfredo Rodriguez**, drove over the starting ramp and promptly retired...**Grégoire de Mevius** was **leading the Group N Championship** before the start of the rally, but his co-driver, **Willy Lux**, made a very costly timing error, which saw the Belgian **Nissan** crew arrive too late to take the start...All this allowed **Carlos Menem Junior**, the son of the Argentinian President, to win Group N in his Lancia by finishing sixth...**Rudi Stohl** had a typically steady run in his **Audi** 90 Quattro and was able to hold off Menem by six seconds for fifth place, the latter recovering from time lost on the third leg with a broken front diff, gearbox problems and punctures...**Gabriel Raies** led the two-wheel drive brigade from start to finish in his **Renault** 18 GTX and finished seventh, but was nearly overhauled on the last stage by the similar car of **Miguel Torras** when he lost 90 seconds with a damaged piston...The Japanese driver **Hiroshi Nishiyama** finished ninth despite his **Nissan** Sunny GTi-R being without second gear for the whole of the last leg...The rally was blighted by cancelled stages and lost five tests in all, while teams were generally unhappy about the move from Cordoba to Tucuman.

Results

1	Didier Auriol/ Bernard Occelli	Lancia Delta HF Integrale 4h 47m 26s	Gr A
2	Carlos Sainz/ Luis Moya	Toyota Celica Turbo 4WD 4h 49m 44s	Gr A
3	Gustavo Trelles/ Jorge Del Buono	Lancia Delta HF Integrale 5h 01m 37s	Gr A
4	Alessandro Fiorio/ Vittorio Brambilla	Lancia Delta HF Integrale 5h 15m 19s	Gr A
5	Rudi Stohl/ Peter Diekmann	Audi 90 Quattro 5h 34m 33s	Gr A
6	Carlos Menem/ Victor Zucchini	Lancia Delta HF Integrale 5h 34m 39s	Gr N
7	Gabriel Raies/ José Maria Volta	Renault 18 GTX 5h 42m 24s	Gr A
8	Miguel Torras/ Luis Maciel	Renault 18 GTX 5h 43m 22s	Gr A
9	Hiroshi Nishiyama/ Yoichi Yamazaki	Nissan Sunny GTi-R 5h 56m 32s	Gr N
10	Walter D'Agostini/ Juan Turra	Renault 18 GTX 5h 57m 35s	Gr A

81 starters, 32 finishers

Previous winners

1979	Jean Guichet/Jean Todt	Peugeot 504
1980	Walter Röhrl/Christian Geistdörfer	Fiat 131 Abarth
1981	Guy Fréquelin/Jean Todt	Talbot Sunbeam Lotus
1983	Hannu Mikkola/Arne Hertz	Audi Quattro A1
1984	Stig Blomqvist/Björn Cederberg	Audi Quattro A2
1985	Timo Salonen/Seppo Harjanne	Peugeot 205 Turbo 16
1986	Massimo Biasion/Tiziano Siviero	Lancia Delta S4
1987	Massimo Biasion/Tiziano Siviero	Lancia Delta HF 4x4
1988	Jorge Recalde/Jorge Del Buono	Lancia Delta HF Integrale
1989	Mikael Ericsson/Claes Billstam	Lancia Delta HF Integrale
1990	Massimo Biasion/Tiziano Siviero	Lancia Delta HF Integrale
1991	Carlos Sainz/Luis Moya	Toyota Celica GT4

TTE looked to be on the right track in Argentina, Carlos Sainz leading briefly in the lone Celica 4WD.

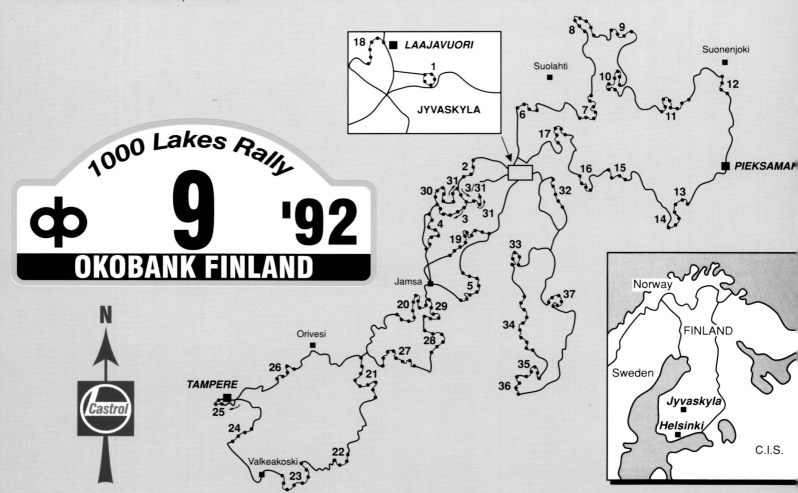

1000 LAKES RALLY, 27-30 August. FIA World Rally Championship for Manufacturers, round 7. FIA World Rally Championship for Drivers, round 9.

Leading entries

1	Juha Kankkunen/ Juha Piironen	Lancia Delta HF Integrale Gr A
3	Didier Auriol/ Bernard Occelli	Lancia Delta HF Integrale Gr A
4	Massimo Biasion/ Tiziano Siviero	Ford Sierra Cosworth 4x4 Gr A
5	Markku Alén/ Ilkka Kivimäki	Toyota Celica Turbo 4WD Gr A
6	Ari Vatanen/ Bruno Berglund	Subaru Legacy RS Gr A
7	Tommi Mäkinen/ Seppo Harjanne	Nissan Sunny GTi-R Gr A
8	François Delecour/ Daniel Grataloup	Ford Sierra Cosworth 4x4 Gr A
9	Colin McRae/ Derek Ringer	Subaru Legacy RS Gr A
10	Stig Blomqvist/ Benny Melander	Nissan Sunny GTi-R Gr A
11	Philippe Bugalski/ Denis Giraudet	Lancia Delta HF Integrale Gr N
12	Grégoire de Mevius/ Willy Lux	Nissan Sunny GTi-R Gr N
13	Mikael Sundström/ Jakke Honkanen	Nissan Sunny GTi-R Gr N
14	Lasse Lampi/ Pentti Kuukkala	Mitsubishi Galant VR-4 Gr A
15	Joukko Puhakka/ Keijo Eerola	Mitsubishi Galant VR-4 Gr N
16	Stig-Olov Walfridsson/ Gunnar Barth	Mitsubishi Galant VR-4 Gr N
17	Pavel Sibera/ Petr Gross	Skoda Favorit 136L
18	Giovanni Manfrinato/ Claudio Condotta	Ford Sierra Cosworth 4x4 Gr N
19	Vladimir Berger/ Jiri Janecek	Skoda Favorit 136L
20	Antero Laine/ Risto Virtanen	Toyota Celica Turbo 4WD Gr A
21	Marcus Grönholm/ Ilkka Riipinen	Toyota Celica Turbo 4WD Gr A

Special stage times

SS 1. Harju (2.72 km)
1 M. Alén/I. Kivimäki (Toyota Celica Turbo 4WD), M. Grönholm/I. Riipinen (Toyota Celica Turbo 4WD) 1m 57s; 3 A. Vatanen/B. Berglund (Subaru Legacy RS), C. McRae/D. Ringer (Subaru Legacy RS), S. Blomqvist/B. Melander (Nissan Sunny GTi-R) 1m 58s; 6 T. Mäkinen/S. Harjanne (Nissan Sunny GTi-R) 1m 59s.

SS 2. Kuohu (7.74 km)
1 D. Auriol/B. Occelli (Lancia Delta HF Integrale), Alén/Kivimäki (Toyota) 3m 52s; 3 J. Kankkunen/J. Piironen (Lancia Delta HF Integrale) 3m 53s; 4 Vatanen/Berglund (Subaru) 3m 55s; 5 Grönholm/Riipinen (Toyota) 3m 57s; 6 F. Delecour/D. Grataloup (Ford Sierra Cosworth 4x4), Blomqvist/Melander (Nissan) 3m 59s.

SS 3. Parkkola (22.48 km)
1 Kankkunen/Piironen (Lancia), Auriol/Occelli (Lancia) 11m 52s; 3 Vatanen/Berglund (Subaru) 11m 54s; 4 Alén/Kivimäki (Toyota) 11m 56s; 5 Delecour/Grataloup (Ford) 11m 59s; Mäkinen/Harjanne (Nissan) 12m 00s.

SS 4. Ehikki (14.64 km)
1 Auriol/Occelli (Lancia) 7m 16s; 2 Alén/Kivimäki (Toyota) 7m 19s; 3 Kankkunen/Piironen (Lancia) 7m 20s; 4 Vatanen/Berglund (Subaru) 7m 25s; 5 Delecour/Grataloup (Ford) 7m 26s; 6 Mäkinen/Harjanne (Nissan) 7m 27s.

SS 5. Vaheri (20.94 km)
1 Auriol/Occelli (Lancia) 10m 48s; 2 Vatanen/Berglund (Subaru) 10m 53s; 3 Kankkunen/Piironen (Lancia) 10m 54s; 4 Mäkinen/Harjanne (Nissan) 10m 59s; 5 Alén/Kivimäki (Toyota) 11m 00s; 6 Delecour/Grataloup (Ford) 11m 09s.

SS 6. Valkola (7.43 km)
1 Mäkinen/Harjanne (Nissan) 3m 30s; 2 Alén/Kivimäki (Toyota) 3m 34s; 3 Kankkunen/Piironen (Lancia) 3m 36s; 4 Auriol/Occelli (Lancia), Blomqvist/Melander (Nissan) 3m 37s; 5 S. Lindholm/ T. Hantunen (Ford Sierra Cosworth 4x4) 3m 40s.

SS 7. Lankamaa (16.01 km)
1 Kankkunen/Piironen (Lancia) 7m 49s; 2 Auriol/Occelli (Lancia) 7m 50s; 3 Vatanen/Berglund (Subaru) 7m 52s; 4 Alén/Kivimäki (Toyota), Mäkinen/Harjanne (Nissan) 7m 54s; 6 Blomqvist/Melander (Nissan) 8m 01s.

SS 8. Haapakyla (14.44 km)
1 Auriol/Occelli (Lancia) 7m 17s; 2 Alén/Kivimäki (Toyota), Mäkinen/Harjanne (Nissan) 7m 18s; 4 Kankkunen/Piironen (Lancia) 7m 21s; 5 Vatanen/Berglund (Subaru) 7m 24s; 6 Blomqvist/Melander (Nissan) 7m 25s.

SS 9. Jouhtikylä (13.16 km)
1 Kankkunen/Piironen (Lancia) 6m 39s; 2 Auriol/Occelli (Lancia), Mäkinen/Harjanne (Nissan) 6m 40s; 4 Vatanen/Berglund (Subaru) 6m 42s; 5 Alén/Kivimäki (Toyota) 6m 46s; 6 Blomqvist/Melander (Nissan) 6m 49s.

SS 10. Kalliokoski (20.26 km)
1 Alén/Kivimäki (Toyota) 9m 41s; 2 Auriol/Occelli (Lancia) 9m 42s; 3 Kankkunen/Piironen (Lancia) 9m 47s; 4 Vatanen/Berglund (Subaru) 9m 48s; 5 Blomqvist/Melander (Nissan) 9m 51s; 6 Lindholm/Hantunen (Ford) 9m 59s.

SS 11. Myhinpää (22.17 km)
1 Kankkunen/Piironen (Lancia), Vatanen/Berglund (Subaru) 10m 53s; 3 Auriol/Occelli (Lancia), Alén/Kivimäki (Toyota) 10m 54s; 5 Blomqvist/Melander (Nissan) 11m 07s; 6 Lindholm/Hantunen (Ford) 11m 11s.

SS 12. Mäkrä (6.17 km)
1 Auriol/Occelli (Lancia), Kankkunen/Piironen (Lancia) 3m 22s; 3 Alén/Kivimäki (Toyota), Vatanen/Berglund (Subaru) 3m 24s; 5 Blomqvist/Melander (Nissan) 3m 27s; 6 McRae/Ringer (Subaru) 3m 28s.

SS 13. Toikkala (9.53 km)
1 Auriol/Occelli (Lancia) 5m 07s; 2 Kankkunen/ Piironen (Lancia) 5m 09s; 3 Alén/Kivimäki (Toyota) 5m 10s; 4 Vatanen/Berglund (Subaru) 5m 15s; 5 McRae/Ringer (Subaru) 5m 16s; 6 M. Biasion/T. Siviero (Ford Sierra Cosworth 4x4), Blomqvist/Melander (Nissan) 5m 19s.

SS 14. Kutemajärvi (6.67 km)
1 Kankkunen/Piironen (Lancia) 3m 40s; 2 Vatanen/Berglund (Subaru) 3m 43s; 3 Blomqvist/Melander (Nissan), Alén/Kivimäki (Toyota) 3m 44s; 5 Lindholm/Hantunen (Ford), Auriol/Occelli (Lancia) 3m 47s.

SS 15. Haltulla (7.82 km)
1 Auriol/Occelli (Lancia) 4m 07s; 2 Kankkunen/Piiro-
nen (Lancia) 4m 10s; 3 Alén/Kivimäki (Toyota) 4m 11s; 4 Vatanen/Berglund (Subaru) 4m 12s; 5 Biasion/Siviero (Ford) 4m 16s; 6 McRae/Ringer (Subaru) 4m 17s.

SS 16. Ruuhimäki (7.28 km)
1 Auriol/Occelli (Lancia) 4m 02s; 2 Kankkunen/Piironen (Lancia) 4m 03s; 3 Alén/Kivimäki (Toyota) 4m 05s; 4 Vatanen/Berglund (Subaru) 4m 06s; 5 Biasion/Siviero (Ford) 4m 11s; 6 L. Lampi/P. Kuukkala (Mitsubishi Galant VR-4) 4m 13s.

SS 17. Laukaa (12.33 km)
1 Auriol/Occelli (Lancia) 6m 38s; 2 Kankkunen/Piironen (Lancia) 6m 40s; 3 Vatanen/Berglund (Subaru) 6m 42s; 4 Alén/Kivimäki (Toyota) 6m 44s; 5 Biasion/Siviero (Ford), Lindholm/Hantunen (Ford) 6m 50s.

SS 18. Laajavuori (3.54 km)
1 Auriol/Occelli (Lancia) 2m 09s; 2 Alén/Kivimäki (Toyota) 2m 11s; 3 Kankkunen/Piironen (Lancia), Biasion/Siviero (Ford) 2m 14s; 5 McRae/Ringer (Subaru), Lindholm/Hantunen (Ford) 2m 15s.

SS 19. Leustu (23.61 km)
1 Auriol/Occelli (Lancia), Kankkunen/Piironen (Lancia) 12m 20s; 3 Alén/Kivimäki (Toyota) 12m 22s; 4 Vatanen/Berglund (Subaru) 12m 23s; 5 McRae/Ringer (Subaru) 12m 33s; 6 Lindholm/Hantunen (Ford) 12m 38s.

SS 20. Ouninpohja (30.54 km)
1 Kankkunen/Piironen (Lancia) 15m 08s; 2 Auriol/Occelli (Lancia) 15m 09s; 3 Vatanen/Berglund (Subaru) 15m 17s; 5 Alén/Kivimäki (Toyota) 15m 20s; 6 Lampi/Kuukkala (Mitsubishi), McRae/Ringer (Subaru) 15m 29s.

SS 21. Västilä (21.42 km)
1 Auriol/Occelli (Lancia) 10m 03s; 2 Alén/Kivimäki (Toyota) 10m 04s; 3 Kankkunen/Piironen (Lancia) 10m 06s; 4 Vatanen/Berglund (Subaru) 10m 09s; 5 McRae/Ringer (Subaru) 10m 15s; 6 Lampi/Kuukkala (Mitsubishi) 10m 22s.

SS 22. Koivulahti (14.60 km)
1 Kankkunen/Piironen (Lancia) 7m 08s; 2 Auriol/Occelli (Lancia) 7m 09s; 3 Vatanen/Berglund (Subaru) 7m 11s; 4 Alén/Kivimäki (Toyota) 7m 15s; 5 Lindholm/Hantunen (Ford) 7m 19s; 6 McRae/Ringer (Subaru) 7m 20s.

SS 23. Uskila (22.48 km)
1 Auriol/Occelli (Lancia) 11m 05s; 2 Kankkunen/Piironen (Lancia) 11m 11s; 3 Alén/Kivimäki (Toyota) 11m 13s; 4 Vatanen/Berglund (Subaru) 11m 15s; 5 Lindholm/Hantunen (Ford) 11m 26s; 6 Lampi/Kuukkala (Mitsubishi) 11m 28s.

SS 24. Savo (8.34 km)
1 Alén/Kivimäki 4m 34s; 2 Kankkunen/Piironen (Lancia), Vatanen/Berglund (Subaru) 4m 36s; 4 Auriol/Occelli (Lancia) 4m 38s; 5 McRae/Ringer (Subaru) 4m 41s; 6 Lindholm/Hantunen (Ford) 4m 42s.

SS 25. Tampere (2.60 km)
1 Alén/Kivimäki (Toyota) 1m 56s; 2 Kankkunen/Piironen (Lancia), McRae/Ringer (Subaru), Vatanen/Berglund (Subaru), Lindholm/Hantunen (Ford) 1m 59s; 6 Auriol/Occelli (Lancia) 2m 00s.

SS 26. Siitima (14.70 km)
1 Auriol/Occelli (Lancia) 7m 37s; 2 Alén/Kivimäki (Toyota) 7m 38s; 3 Kankkunen/Piironen (Lancia) 7m 41s; 4 Vatanen/Berglund (Subaru) 7m 42s; 5 McRae/Ringer (Subaru) 7m 50s; 6 Lampi/Kuukkala (Mitsubishi) 7m 51s.

SS 27. Päijälä (23.29 km)
1 Auriol/Occelli (Lancia) 12m 47s; 2 Vatanen/Berglund (Subaru) 12m 51s; 3 Kankkunen/Piironen (Lancia) 12m 52s; 4 Alén/Kivimäki (Toyota) 12m 53s; 5 McRae/Ringer (Subaru) 13m 02s; 6 Lampi/Kuukkala (Mitsubishi) 13m 12s.

SS 28. Paateri (18.06 km)
1 Kankkunen/Piironen (Lancia), Auriol/Occelli (Lancia) 9m 36s; 3 Alén/Kivimäki (Toyota) 9m 39s; 4 Vatanen/Berglund (Subaru) 9m 42s; 5 Lindholm/Hantunen (Ford) 9m 51s; 6 Biasion/Siviero (Ford) 9m 54s.

SS 29. Hassi (14.69 km)
1 Auriol/Occelli (Lancia) 8m 10s; 2 Kankkunen/Piironen (Lancia) 8m 11s; 3 Alén/Kivimäki (Toyota) 8m 13s; 4 Vatanen/Berglund (Subaru) 8m 18s; 5 Lindholm/Hantunen (Ford) 8m 22s; 6 Biasion/Siviero (Ford) 8m 23s.

SS 30. Sahloinen (12.32 km)
1 Alén/Kivimäki (Toyota) 6m 35s; 2 Auriol/Occelli (Lancia) 6m 36s; 3 Kankkunen/Piironen (Lancia) 6m 38s; 4 Vatanen/Berglund (Subaru) 6m 39s; 5 Lampi/Kuukkala (Mitsubishi) 6m 50s; 6 Biasion/Siviero (Ford) 6m 51s.

SS 31. Surkee (21.29 km)
1 Auriol/Occelli (Lancia), Kankkunen/Piironen (Lancia) 11m 09s; 3 Vatanen/Berglund (Subaru) 11m 10s; 4 Alén/Kivimäki (Toyota) 11m 15s; 5 Lindholm/Hantunen (Ford) 11m 30s; 6 Biasion/Siviero (Ford) 11m 31s.

SS 32. Pitkäjärvi (7.25 km)
1 Auriol/Occelli (Lancia), Kankkunen/Piironen (Lancia) 3m 37s; 3 Vatanen/Berglund (Subaru) 3m 41s; 5 Alén/Kivimäki (Toyota) 3m 45s; 6 Biasion/Siviero (Ford), Lampi/Kuukkala (Mitsubishi), McRae/Ringer (Subaru) 3m 47s.

SS 33. Mutanen (13.33 km)
1 Kankkunen/Piironen (Lancia) 6m 57s; 2 Auriol/Occelli (Lancia) 6m 59s; 3 Alén/Kivimäki (Toyota) 7m 00s; 4 Vatanen/Berglund (Subaru) 7m 03s; 5 Biasion/Siviero (Ford) 7m 06s; 6 McRae/Ringer (Subaru), Lindholm/Hantunen (Ford) 7m 07s.

SS 34. Lempää (28.40 km)
1 Auriol/Occelli (Lancia) 14m 15s; 2 Kankkunen/Piironen (Lancia) 14m 22s; 3 Vatanen/Berglund (Subaru) 14m 29s; 4 Alén/Kivimäki (Toyota) 14m 37s; 5 Biasion/Siviero (Ford) 14m 38s; 6 Lindholm/Hantunen (Ford), Lampi/Kuukkala (Mitsubishi) 14m 50s.

SS 35. Ylemmäinen (11.61 km)
1 Kankkunen/Piironen (Lancia), Auriol/Occelli (Lancia) 6m 38s; 3 Vatanen/Berglund (Subaru) 6m 42s; 4 Alén/Kivimäki (Toyota) 6m 43s; 5 Lindholm/Hantunen (Ford) 6m 46s; 6 Biasion/Siviero (Ford) 6m 48s.

SS 36. Mynnilä (8.36 km)
1 Kankkunen/Piironen (Lancia), Vatanen/Berglund (Subaru) 4m 18s; 3 Alén/Kivimäki (Toyota) 4m 19s; 4 Auriol/Occelli (Lancia) 4m 20s; 5 Biasion/Siviero (Ford) 4m 24s; 6 Lindholm/Hantunen (Ford), McRae/Ringer (Subaru) 4m 25s.

SS 37. Vartiamäki (12.60 km)
1 Kankkunen/Piironen (Lancia) 7m 34s; 2 Vatanen/Berglund (Subaru) 7m 35s; 3 Auriol/Occelli (Lancia) 7m 36s; 4 McRae/Ringer (Subaru), Lindholm/Hantunen (Ford) 7m 39s; 6 Lampi/Kuukkala (Mitsubishi) 7m 41s.

FIA class winners

Group A
Over 2000 cc: Auriol/Occelli (Lancia)
1600-2000 cc: Kari Kytola/Ilkka Arrala (Opel Manta)
1300-1600 cc: Keijo Heikkila/Paavo Schukow (Alfa Romeo 33 4x4)
Up to 1300 cc: Sibera/Gross (Skoda)

Group N
Over 2000 cc: Kytölehto/Kapanen (Mitsubishi)
1600-2000 cc: Tapio Santala/Arto Bjorklund (VW Golf GTI 16v)
1300-1600 cc: Matti Tuominen/Veli Jantunen (Toyota Corolla GT)
Up to 1300 cc: Dick Sundman/Sven-Erik-Sandstrom (Suzuki Swift GTi)

Major retirements

Marcus Grönholm/ Ilkka Riipinen	Toyota Celica Turbo 4WD	SS5 accident
Giovanni Manfrinato/ Claudio Condotta	Ford Sierra Cosworth 4x4	SS7 accident
Tommi Mäkinen/ Seppo Harjanne	Nissan Sunny GTi-R	SS10 gearbox
François Delecour/ Daniel Grataloup	Ford Sierra Cosworth 4x4	SS11 accident
Stig Blomqvist/ Benny Melander	Nissan Sunny GTi-R	SS15 engine
Antero Laine/ Risto Virtanen	Toyota Celica Turbo 4WD	SS17 electrics
Joukko Puhakka/ Keijo Eerola	Mitsubishi Galant VR-4	SS19 gearbox
Stig-Olov Walfridsson/ Gunnar Barth	Mitsubishi Galant VR-4	SS28 engine
Mikael Sundström/ Jakke Honkanen	Nissan Sunny GTi-R	SS29 gearbox

Rally leaders

SS1 Alén/Kivimäki (Toyota) and Grönholm/Riipinen (Toyota); SS2 Alén/Kivimäki (Toyota); SS3-37 Auriol/Occelli (Lancia).

World Championship points

Drivers
1 Auriol 100; 2 Sainz 92; 3 Kankkunen 77; 4 Biasion 42; 5 Alén 40; 6 Delecour 33; 7 McRae 28; 8 Bugalski 22; 9 Jonsson 20; 10 Liatti and Recalde 18.

Manufacturers
1 Lancia 137; 2 Toyota 98; 3 Ford 70; 4 Subaru 35; 5 Nissan 33; 6 Mitsubishi 28; 7 Audi 10; 8 Renault Argentine 7; 9 Renault 2.

Route details

Leg 1
27 August: Starting and finishing from Laajavuori 1800-2310, including five special stages (68.52 km).
Leg 2
28 August: Starting and finishing from Laajavuori 0900-2100, including 13 special stages (146.81 km).
Leg 3
29 August: Starting and finishing from Laajavuori 0630-2120, including 13 special stages (227.94 km).
Leg 4
30 August: Starting and finishing from Laajavuori 0700-1345, including six special stages (81.55 km).

Weather

Cool and damp with some rain.

Special stage analysis

	1st	2nd	3rd	4th	5th	6th
Auriol/Occelli (Lancia)	22	7	2	3	1	1
Kankkunen/Piironen (Lancia)	16	9	10	1	-	-
Alén/Kivimäki (Toyota)	6	6	11	10	2	-
Vatanen/Berglund (Subaru)	2	6	11	14	1	-
Mäkinen/Harjanne (Nissan)	1	2	-	2	-	3
Grönholm/Riipinen (Toyota)	1	-	-	1	-	-
McRae/Ringer (Subaru)	-	1	1	2	10	5
Lindholm/Hantunen (Ford)	-	1	-	1	9	8
Blomqvist/Melander (Nissan)	-	-	2	1	3	5
Biasion/Siviero (Ford)	-	-	-	1	6	7
Lampi/Kuukkala (Mitsubishi)	-	-	-	-	3	7
Delecour/Grataloup (Ford)	-	-	-	-	2	2

Finish lines

François Delecour had been the best of the newcomers until he slid off on SS11 and broke the steering on his works **Sierra**...**Miki Biasion** drove faultlessly to finish fifth in his **Cosworth**, finding that all but seven stages had changed since he last contested the rally in 1989 ...**Jarmo Kytölehto** won Group N in his Teboil **Galant VR-4**, taking a decisive lead when **Mikael Sundström** broke his Camel **Nissan**'s engine...The works Nissans were sensationally fast. However, gearbox failure eliminated **Tommi Mäkinen** during the second leg, while **Stig Blomqvist**'s **Sunny** blew its engine later that day...Turbo problems ruined **Sebastian Lindholm**'s chances, the Finn having to be content with seventh in the Gordon Spooner **Cosworth**...If it wasn't for brake failure on the first and last stages of the third leg, **Lasse Lampi** might have beaten Miki Biasion for fifth in his ex-works **Galant**...**Marcus Grönholm**'s first run in a works car ended when he crashed his **Toyota** on the fifth stage...Under strict orders not to damage the car, **Philippe Bugalski** finished a steady ninth in the third Martini Racing **Integrale**...**Stig-Olov Walfridsson** retired his **Galant** with a blown engine.

Results

1	Didier Auriol/ Bernard Occelli	Lancia Delta HF Integrale 4h 32m 45s	Gr A
2	Juha Kankkunen/ Juha Piironen	Lancia Delta HF Integrale 4h 33m 25s	Gr A
3	Markku Alén/ Ilkka Kivimäki	Toyota Celica Turbo 4WD 4h 34m 44s	Gr A
4	Ari Vatanen/ Bruno Berglund	Subaru Legacy RS 4h 35m 17s	Gr A
5	Massimo Biasion/ Tiziano Siviero	Ford Sierra Cosworth 4x4 4h 41m 16s	Gr A
6	Lasse Lampi/ Pentti Kuukkala	Mitsubishi Galant VR-4 4h 42m 41s	Gr A
7	Sebastian Lindholm/ Timo Hantunen	Ford Sierra Cosworth 4x4 4h 43m 58s	Gr A
8	Colin McRae/ Derek Ringer	Subaru Legacy RS 4h 48m 30s	Gr A
9	Philippe Bugalski/ Denis Giraudet	Lancia Delta HF Integrale 4h 49m 40s	Gr A
10	Jarmo Kytölehto/ Arto Kapanen	Mitsubishi Galant VR-4 4h 57m 14s	Gr A

128 starters, 61 finishers

Previous winners (since 1965)

1965 Timo Mäkinen/Pekka Keskitalo — Mini-Cooper S
1966 Timo Mäkinen/Pekka Keskitalo — Mini-Cooper S
1967 Timo Mäkinen/Pekka Keskitalo — Mini-Cooper S
1968 Hannu Mikkola/Anssi Jarvi — Ford Escort TC
1969 Hannu Mikkola/Anssi Jarvi — Ford Escort TC
1970 Hannu Mikkola/Gunnar Palm — Ford Escort TC
1971 Stig Blomqvist/Arne Hertz — Saab 96 V4
1972 Simo Lampinen/Klaus Sohlberg — Saab 96 V4
1973 Timo Mäkinen/Henry Liddon — Ford Escort RS1600
1974 Hannu Mikkola/John Davenport — Ford Escort RS1600
1975 Hannu Mikkola/Atso Aho — Toyota Corolla
1976 Markku Alén/Ilkka Kivimäki — Fiat Abarth 131
1977 Kyosti Hamalainen/Marti Tiukkanen — Ford Escort RS
1978 Markku Alén/Ilkka Kivimäki — Fiat Abarth 131
1979 Markku Alén/Ilkka Kivimäki — Fiat Abarth 131
1980 Markku Alén/Ilkka Kivimäki — Fiat Abarth 131
1981 Ari Vatanen/David Richards — Ford Escort RS
1982 Hannu Mikkola/Arne Hertz — Audi Quattro
1983 Hannu Mikkola/Arne Hertz — Audi Quattro
1984 Ari Vatanen/Terry Harryman — Peugeot 205 Turbo 16
1985 Timo Salonen/Seppo Harjanne — Peugeot 205 Turbo 16
1986 Juha Kankkunen/Juha Piironen — Peugeot 205 Turbo 16
1987 Markku Alén/Ilkka Kivimäki — Lancia Delta HF 4x4
1988 Markku Alén/Ilkka Kivimäki — Lancia Delta HF Integrale
1989 Mikael Ericsson/Claes Billstam — Mitsubishi Galant VR-4
1990 Carlos Sainz/Luis Moya — Toyota Celica GT4
1991 Juha Kankkunen/Juha Piironen — Lancia Delta HF Integrale

Rain can increase grip on the unique back roads of Finland. Ari Vatanen pushes the Subaru to the limit on his way to his first finish of 1992.

RALLY AUSTRALIA, 19-22 September. FIA World Rally Championship for Manufacturers, round 8. FIA World Rally Championship for Drivers, round 10.

Leading entries

1	Juha Kankkunen/	Lancia Delta HF Integrale
	Juha Piironen	Gr A
2	Carlos Sainz/	Toyota Celica Turbo 4WD
	Luis Moya	Gr A
3	Didier Auriol/	Lancia Delta HF Integrale
	Bernard Occelli	Gr A
4	Ari Vatanen/	Subaru Legacy RS
	Bruno Berglund	Gr A
6	Ross Dunkerton/	Mitsubishi Galant VR-4
	Fred Gocentas	Gr A
7	Jorge Recalde/	Lancia Delta HF Integrale
	Martin Christie	Gr A
9	Rod Millen/	Mazda 323 GT-X
	Tony Sircombe	Gr A
10	'Possum' Bourne/	Subaru Legacy RS
	Rodger Freeth	Gr A
11	Ed Ordynski/	Mitsubishi Galant VR-4
	Mark Stacey	Gr N
12	Carlos Menem/	Lancia Delta HF Integrale
	Victor Zucchini	Gr A
13	Mohammed Bin	
	Sulayem/	Ford Sierra Cosworth
	Ronan Morgan	Gr N 4x4
14	Yoshio Fujimoto/	Nissan Sunny GTi-R
	Hakaru Ichino	Gr N
15	Kurt Gottlicher/	Ford Sierra Cosworth 4x4
	Josef Pointinger	Gr N
16	Jarmo Kytölehto/	Mitsubishi Galant VR-4
	Arto Kapanen	Gr N
17	Rob Herridge/	Subaru Legacy RS
	Chris Randell	Gr A
18	Greg Carr/	Lancia Delta HF Integrale
	Allen Oh .	Gr N
19	Kiyoshi Inoue/	Mitsubishi Galant VR-4
	Nakahara Yoshimasa	Gr N
20	Tolley Challis/	Mitsubishi Galant VR-4
	Rod Vanderstraaten	Gr N
21	Mario Panontin/	Toyota Celica GT4
	Mari Alessandrini	Gr N
22	Wayne Hoy/	Nissan Sunny GTi-R
	Andrew Bennett	Gr N

Special stage times

SS 1. Catchment Road (11.75 km)
1 D. Auriol/B. Occelli (Lancia Delta HF Integrale), J. Kankkunen/J. Piironen (Lancia Delta HF Integrale) 6m 32s; 3 A. Vatanen/B. Berglund (Subaru Legacy RS) 6m 36s; 4 C. Sainz/L. Moya (Toyota Celica Turbo 4WD) 6m 37s; 5 R. Dunkerton/F. Gocentas (Mitsubishi Galant VR-4) 6m 49s; 6 R. Millen/T. Sircombe (Mazda 323 GT-X) 6m 51s.

SS 2. Muresk 1 (6.81 km)
1 Sainz/Moya (Toyota) 3m 33s; 2 Auriol/Occelli (Lancia) 3m 36s; 3 P. Bourne/R. Freeth (Subaru Legacy RS) 3m 39s; 4 Kankkunen/Piironen (Lancia), Vatanen/Berglund (Subaru), Dunkerton/Gocentas (Mitsubishi) 3m 41s.

SS 3. York Railway (5.30 km)
1 Kankkunen/Piironen (Lancia), Sainz/Moya (Toyota) 2m 41s; 3 Auriol/Occelli (Lancia), Vatanen/Berglund (Subaru) 2m 42s; 5 Bourne/Freeth (Subaru) 2m 46s; 6 Dunkerton/Gocentas (Mitsubishi) 2m 48s.

SS 4. Muresk 2 (6.81 km)
1 Sainz/Moya (Toyota) 3m 44s; 2 Vatanen/Berglund (Subaru) 3m 46s; 3 Kankkunen/Piironen (Lancia), Auriol/Occelli (Lancia) 3m 47s; 5 Bourne/Freeth (Subaru) 3m 50s; 6 Dunkerton/Gocentas (Mitsubishi) 3m 52s.

SS 5. Helena 1 (30.05 km)
1 Auriol/Occelli (Lancia) 17m 18s; 2 Vatanen/Berglund (Subaru) 17m 26s; 3 Kankkunen/Piironen (Lancia) 17m 31s; 4 Sainz/Moya (Toyota) 17m 33s; 5 Bourne/Freeth (Subaru) 17m 49s; 6 Dunkerton/Gocentas (Mitsubishi), Millen/Sircombe (Mazda) 18m 01s.

SS 6. Atkins (4.42 km)
1 Auriol/Occelli (Lancia) 3m 10s; 2 Vatanen/Berglund (Subaru) 3m 14s; 3 Sainz/Moya (Toyota) 3m 15s; 4 Bourne/Freeth (Subaru) 3m 16s; 5 Millen/Sircombe (Mazda) 3m 18s; 6 J. Recalde/M. Christie (Lancia Delta HF Integrale) 3m 23s.

SS 7. Wellbucket (15.44 km)
1 Kankkunen/Piironen (Lancia) 9m 38s; 2 Auriol/Occelli (Lancia) 9m 42s; 3 Vatanen/Berglund (Subaru) 9m 43s; 4 Sainz/Moya (Toyota) 9m 46s; 5 Bourne/Freeth (Subaru) 10m 03s; 6 Millen/Sircombe (Mazda) 10m 04s.

SS 8. Helena 2 (30.05 km)
1 Auriol/Occelli (Lancia) 17m 36s; 2 Kankkunen/Piironen (Lancia) 17m 38s; 3 Sainz/Moya (Toyota), Vatanen/Berglund (Subaru) 17m 49s; 5 Millen/ Sircombe (Mazda) 18m 31s; 6 Bourne/Freeth (Subaru) 18m 33s.

SS 9. Langley Park 1 (2.00 km)
1 Kankkunen/Piironen (Lancia), Auriol/Occelli (Lancia) 1m 31s; 3 Vatanen/Berglund (Subaru) 1m 32s; 4 Dunkerton/Gocentas (Mitsubishi), Recalde/Christie (Lancia), Bourne/Freeth (Subaru) 1m 33s.

SS 10. Roller Coaster (5.61 km)
1 Kankkunen/Piironen (Lancia) 3m 07s; 2 Sainz/ Moya (Toyota), Auriol/Occelli (Lancia) 3m 13s; 4 Millen/Sircombe (Mazda) 3m 14s; 5 Dunkerton/ Gocentas (Mitsubishi) 3m 15s; 6 Recalde/Christie (Lancia), Bourne/Freeth (Subaru) 3m 18s.

SS 11. Murray Pines (20.35 km)
1 Auriol/Occelli (Lancia) 12m 40s; 2 Sainz/Moya (Toyota) 12m 50s; 3 Vatanen/Berglund (Subaru) 12m 57s; 4 Kankkunen/Piironen (Lancia) 13m 01s; 5 Bourne/Freeth (Subaru) 13m 12s; 6 Dunkerton/ Gocentas (Mitsubishi) 13m 23s.

SS 12. Bunnings South (16.08 km)
1 Auriol/Occelli (Lancia) 9m 25s; 2 Kankkunen/Piironen (Lancia) 9m 27s; 3 Vatanen/Berglund (Subaru) 9m 31s; 4 Sainz/Moya (Toyota) 9m 33s; 5 Bourne/Freeth (Subaru) 9m 53s; 6 Dunkerton/Gocentas (Mitsubishi) 10m 01s.

SS 13. Bunnings North (29.27 km)
1 Auriol/Occelli (Lancia) 15m 18s; 2 Kankkunen/Piironen (Lancia) 15m 20s; 3 Vatanen/Berglund (Subaru) 15m 21s; 4 Sainz/Moya (Toyota)15m 29s; 5 Bourne/Freeth (Subaru) 15m 59s; 6 Dunkerton/ Gocentas (Mitsubishi) 16m 07s.

SS 14. Bunnings West (36.67 km)
1 Vatanen/Berglund (Subaru) 20m 24s; 2 Auriol/ Occelli (Lancia) 20m 25s; 3 Kankkunen/Piironen (Lancia) 20m 28s; 4 Sainz/Moya (Toyota) 20m 45s; 5 Dunkerton/Gocentas (Mitsubishi) 21m 26s; 6 Recalde/Christie (Lancia) 21m 29s.

SS 15. Bunnings Central (6.96 km)
1 Kankkunen/Piironen (Lancia) 4m 21s; 2 Auriol/ Occelli (Lancia) 4m 22s; 3 Vatanen/Berglund (Subaru) 4m 23s; 4 Sainz/Moya (Toyota) 4m 26s; 5 Bourne/Freeth (Subaru) 4m 29s; 6 Recalde/Christie (Lancia) 4m 34s.

SS 16. Bunnings East (17.76 km)
1 Auriol/Occelli (Lancia) 10m 25s; 2 Kankkunen/ Piironen (Lancia) 10m 26s; 3 Vatanen/Berglund (Subaru) 10m 28s; 4 Sainz/Moya (Toyota) 10m 34s; 5 Bourne/Freeth (Subaru) 10m 46s; 6 Recalde/ Christie (Lancia) 10m 59s.

SS 17. TOS (15.67 km)
1 Kankkunen/Piironen (Lancia) 8m 22s; 2 Auriol/ Occelli (Lancia) 8m 23s; 3 Vatanen/Berglund (Subaru) 8m 26s; 4 Sainz/Moya (Toyota) 8m 37s; 5 Bourne/Freeth (Subaru) 8m 38s; 6 Dunkerton/ Gocentas (Mitsubishi) 8m 43s.

SS 18. Langley Park 2 (2.00 km)
1 Sainz/Moya (Toyota) 1m 28s; 2 Auriol/Occelli (Lancia) 1m 29s; 3 Kankkunen/Piironen (Lancia), Vatanen/Berglund (Subaru) 1m 30s; 5 Dunkerton/Gocentas (Mitsubishi), Bourne/Freeth (Subaru) 1m 31s.

SS 19. Myara (10.81 km)
1 Auriol/Occelli (Lancia) 6m 12s; 2 Kankkunen/Piironen (Lancia) 6m 14s; 3 Vatanen/Berglund (Subaru) 6m 18s; 4 Sainz/Moya (Toyota) 6m 24s; 5 Bourne/Freeth (Subaru) 6m 35s; 6 Recalde/Christie (Lancia) 6m 47s.

SS 20. Stirling West 1 (15.89 km)
1 Auriol/Occelli (Lancia) 9m 51s; 2 Kankkunen/Piironen (Lancia) 9m 54s; 3 Sainz/Moya (Toyota) 10m 03s; 4 Bourne/Freeth (Subaru) 10m 15s; 5 Dunkerton/Gocentas (Mitsubishi) 10m 30s; 6 Recalde/Christie (Lancia) 10m 33s.

SS 21. Stirling East (28.89 km)
1 Auriol/Occelli (Lancia) 16m 43s; 2 Kankkunen/Piironen (Lancia) 16m 47s; 3 Sainz/Moya (Toyota) 16m 55s; 4 Bourne/Freeth (Subaru) 17m 15s; 5 Recalde/Christie (Lancia) 17m 30s; 6 Dunkerton/Gocentas (Mitsubishi) 17m 32s.

SS 22. Brunswick (16.63 km)
1 Sainz/Moya (Toyota) 9m 39s; 2 Auriol/Occelli (Lancia) 9m 40s; 3 Kankkunen/Piironen (Lancia) 9m 41s; 4 Bourne/Freeth (Subaru) 9m 48s; 5 Dunkerton/Gocentas (Mitsubishi) 10m 02s; 6 Recalde/Christie (Lancia) 10m 03s.

SS 23. Wellington East (29.89 km)
1 Kankkunen/Piironen (Lancia) 17m 37s; 2 Auriol/Occelli (Lancia) 17m 41s; 3 Sainz/Moya (Toyota) 17m 47s; 4 Bourne/Freeth (Subaru) 18m 10s; 5 Recalde/Christie (Lancia) 18m 40s; 6 K. Inoue/N. Yoshimasa (Mitsubishi Galant VR-4) 19m 33s.

SS 24. Wellington West (21.90 km)
1 Auriol/Occelli (Lancia) 13m 22s; 2 Sainz/Moya (Toyota) 13m 35s; 3 Recalde/Christie (Lancia) 14m 22s; 4 Dunkerton/Gocentas (Mitsubishi) 14m 26s; 5 T. Challis/R. Vanderstraaten (Mitsubishi Galant VR-4) 14m 52s; 6 E. Ordynski/M. Stacey (Mitsubishi Galant VR-4) 14m 54s.

SS 25. Bunbury (2.97 km)
1 Auriol/Occelli (Lancia) 1m 55s; 2 Kankkunen/Piironen (Lancia), Sainz/Moya (Toyota) 1m 56s; 4 Recalde/Christie (Lancia) 1m 59s; 5 Bourne/Freeth (Subaru) 2m 00s; 6 Dunkerton/Gocentas (Mitsubishi) 2m 01s.

SS 26. Brunswick River (14.28 km)
1 Kankkunen/Piironen (Lancia), Sainz/Moya (Toyota) 8m 13s; 3 Auriol/Occelli (Lancia) 8m 14s; 4 Bourne/Freeth (Subaru) 8m 36s; 5 Dunkerton/Gocentas (Mitsubishi) 8m 41s; 6 Recalde/Christie (Lancia) 8m 47s.

SS 27. Stirling North (15.65 km)
1 Sainz/Moya (Toyota) 8m 45s; 2 Kankkunen/Piironen (Lancia) 8m 47s; 3 Auriol/Occelli (Lancia) 8m 55s; 4 Bourne/Freeth (Subaru) 9m 01s; 5 Dunkerton/Gocentas (Mitsubishi) 9m 16s; 6 Recalde/Christie (Lancia) 9m 24s.

SS 28. Stirling West 2 (15.89 km)
1 Kankkunen/Piironen (Lancia) 9m 43s; 2 Sainz/Moya (Toyota), Auriol/Occelli (Lancia) 9m 45s; 4 Bourne/Freeth (Subaru) 9m 58s; 5 Dunkerton/Gocentas (Mitsubishi) 10m 18s; 6 Recalde/Christie (Lancia) 10m 21s.

SS 29. Harvey Weir (8.19 km)
1 Kankkunen/Piironen (Lancia) 5m 02s; 2 Sainz/Moya (Toyota) 5m 04s; 3 Auriol/Occelli (Lancia) 5m 05s; 4 Bourne/Freeth (Subaru) 5m 09s; 5 Dunkerton/Gocentas (Mitsubishi) 5m 20s; 6 Recalde/Christie (Lancia) 5m 21s.

SS 30. Marrinup (10.49 km)
1 Kankkunen/Piironen (Lancia) 5m 55s; 2 Auriol/Occelli (Lancia) 6m 00s; 3 Sainz/Moya (Toyota) 6m 04s; 4 Bourne/Freeth (Subaru) 6m 20s; 5 Recalde/Christie (Lancia) 6m 37s; 6 Dunkerton/Gocentas (Mitsubishi) 6m 41s.

SS 31. Langley Park 3 (2.00 km)
1 Kankkunen/Piironen (Lancia) 1m 41s; 2 Auriol/Occelli (Lancia) 1m 42s; 3 Bourne/Freeth (Subaru) 1m 47s; 4 Dunkerton/Gocentas (Mitsubishi) 1m 48s; 5 Sainz/Moya (Toyota), Recalde/Christie (Lancia) 1m 51s.

SS 32. Swan Valley (11.69 km)
1 Kankkunen/Piironen (Lancia) 6m 43s; 2 Sainz/Moya (Toyota) 6m 47s; 3 Auriol/Occelli (Lancia) 6m 48s; 4 Dunkerton/Gocentas (Mitsubishi) 7m 10s; 5 Bourne/Freeth (Subaru) 7m 22s; 6 Recalde/Christie (Lancia) 7m 29s.

SS 33. Sawyers (5.91 km)
1 Kankkunen/Piironen (Lancia) 3m 19s; 2 Sainz/Moya (Toyota) 3m 20s; 3 Auriol/Occelli (Lancia) 3m 24s; 4 Bourne/Freeth (Subaru) 3m 30s; 5 Dunkerton/Gocentas (Mitsubishi) 3m 34s; 6 Recalde/Christie (Lancia) 3m 36s.

SS 34. Flynns (32.20 km)
1 Kankkunen/Piironen (Lancia) 19m 42s; 2 Sainz/Moya (Toyota) 19m 43s; 3 Auriol/Occelli (Lancia) 19m 47s; 4 Bourne/Freeth (Subaru) 20m 30s; 5 Dunkerton/Gocentas (Mitsubishi) 20m 56s; 6 Recalde/Christie (Lancia) 21m 15s.

SS 35. Beraking (30.34 km)
1 Kankkunen/Piironen (Lancia) 15m 51s; 2 Sainz/Moya (Toyota) 15m 58s; 3 Auriol/Occelli (Lancia) 16m 34s; 4 Bourne/Freeth (Subaru) 16m 40s; 5 Recalde/Christie (Lancia) 17m 39s; 6 Dunkerton/Gocentas (Mitsubishi) 17m 40s.

FIA class winners

Group A

Over 2000 cc:	Auriol/Occelli (Lancia)
1600-2000 cc:	David Strong/Bruce McKenzie (Daihatsu Charade GTti)
1300-1600 cc:	Michael Guest/David Green (Toyota Sprinter Levin)
Up to 1300 cc:	Russell Palmer/Roland Pickering (Suzuki Swift GTi)

Group N

Over 2000 cc:	Ordynski/Stacey (Mitsubishi)
1600-2000 cc:	Bob Nicoli/Dale Hynes (Daihatsu Charade GTti)
1300-1600 cc:	Wayne Bell/David Boddy (Hyundai Lantra)
Up to 1300 cc:	Ian Douglas/Brett Crawford (Suzuki Swift GTi)

Major retirements

Rob Herridge/ Chris Randell	Subaru Legacy RS	
Rod Millen/ Tony Sircombe	Mazda 323 GT-X	SS 9 steering rack
Carlos Menem/ Victor Zucchini	Lancia Delta HF Integrale	SS 11 accident
Ari Vatanen/ Bruno Berglund	Subaru Legacy RS	SS 11 accident
		SS 20 gearbox

Rally leaders

SS 1 Kankkunen/Piironen (Lancia), Auriol/Occelli (Lancia); SS 2-3 Auriol/Occelli (Lancia); SS 4 Sainz/Moya (Toyota); SS 5-35 Auriol/Occelli (Lancia).

World Championship points

Drivers
1 Auriol 120; 2 Sainz 104; 3 Kankkunen 92; 4 Biasion 42; 5 Alén 40; 6 Delecour 33; 7 Recalde and McRae 28; 9 Bugalski 22; 10 Dunkerton and Jonsson 20.

Manufacturers
1 Lancia 140 (157); 2 Toyota 108 (112); 3 Ford 70; 4 Subaru 43; 5 Mitsubishi 38; 6 Nissan 33; 7 Audi 10; 8 Renault Argentine 7; 9 Renault 2.

Route details

Leg 1
19 September: Starting and finishing in Perth 0930-2010, including nine special stages (112.63 km).

Leg 2
20 September: Starting and finishing in Perth 0700-1700, including nine special stages (153.07 km).

Leg 3
21 September: Starting and finishing in Perth 0600-2040, including 13 special stages (193.48 km).

Leg 4
22 September: Starting and finishing in Perth 0700-1215, including four special stages (80.14 km).

Weather

Cool throughout; very wet at first.

Special stage analysis

	1st	2nd	3rd	4th	5th	6th
Kankkunen/Piironen (Lancia)	17	9	5	2	–	–
Auriol/Occelli (Lancia)	14	12	9	–	–	–
Sainz/Moya (Toyota)	7	10	6	10	1	–
Vatanen/Berglund (Subaru)	1	3	13	1	–	–
Bourne/Freeth (Subaru)	–	–	2	14	12	3
Recalde/Christie (Lancia)	–	1	2	5	15	
Dunkerton/Gocentas (Mitsubishi)	–	–	5	12	11	
Millen/Sircombe (Mazda)	–	–	–	1	2	3
Challis/Vanderstraaten (Mitsubishi)	–	–	–	–	1	
Ordynski/Stacey (Mitsubishi)	–	–	–	–	–	1
Inoue/Yoshimasa (Mitsubishi)	–	–	–	–	–	1

Finish lines

Jorge Recalde stayed out of trouble to good effect, taking a well-judged fourth place in his Jolly Club-tended **Integrale**...**Ross Dunkerton** was the top Australian in fifth, losing touch with Recalde after puncturing two Yokohamas on the Ralliart Australia **Galant**...**Tony Sircombe** suffered broken ribs when **Rod Millen** crashed his **Mazda** soon after the start of the second leg...The Group N victor was **Ed Ordynski**, who also managed seventh overall in the P&O **Mitsubishi**...'Possum' **Bourne** lost 20 minutes when he clouted a rock that smashed his **Subaru's** front suspension and landed him in a ditch. Nevertheless, he still came sixth, recording his first World Championship finish in a Prodrive-built car...**Carlos Menem Junior** drove steadily at first, but then launched his Top Run **Integrale** into the trees, apparently when the steering broke...The New Zealander, **Dave Strong**, was the top two-wheel drive finisher, taking 16th overall and a class win in his Group A **Charade** GTti...**Mohammed Bin Sula-yem** ran as high as second in Group N in the Marlboro/MLP **Sierra**.

Results

1	Didier Auriol/ Bernard Occelli	Lancia Delta HF Integrale 5h 13m 12s	Gr A
2	Juha Kankkunen/ Juha Piironen	Lancia Delta HF Integrale 5h 14m 53s	Gr A
3	Carlos Sainz/ Luis Moya	Toyota Celica Turbo 4WD 5h 15m 16s	Gr A
4	Jorge Recalde/ Martin Christie	Lancia Delta HF Integrale 5h 32m 05s	Gr A
5	Ross Dunkerton/ Fred Gocentas	Mitsubishi Galant VR-4 5h 36m 15s	Gr A
6	'Possum' Bourne/ Rodger Freeth	Subaru Legacy RS 5h 46m 52s	Gr A
7	Ed Ordynski/ Mark Stacey	Mitsubishi Galant VR-4 5h 51m 39s	Gr N
8	Tolley Challis/ Rod Vanderstraaten	Mitsubishi Galant VR-4 5h 54m 26s	Gr N
9	Kiyoshi Inoue/ Nakahara Yoshimasa	Mitsubishi Galant VR-4 5h 54m 38s	Gr N
10	Craig Stallard/ Graeme Jesse	Mitsubishi Galant VR-4 6h 06m 37s	Gr N

97 starters, 60 finishers

Previous winners

1989 Juha Kankkunen/Juha Piironen Toyota Celica GT4
1990 Juha Kankkunen/Juha Piironen Lancia Delta HF Integrale
1991 Juha Kankkunen/Juha Piironen Lancia Delta HF Integrale

As a rule, 'Possum' Bourne has only to step into a Prodrive Subaru for something to go horribly wrong. The Rally Australia wasn't without its surprises, but at least he finished on this occasion.

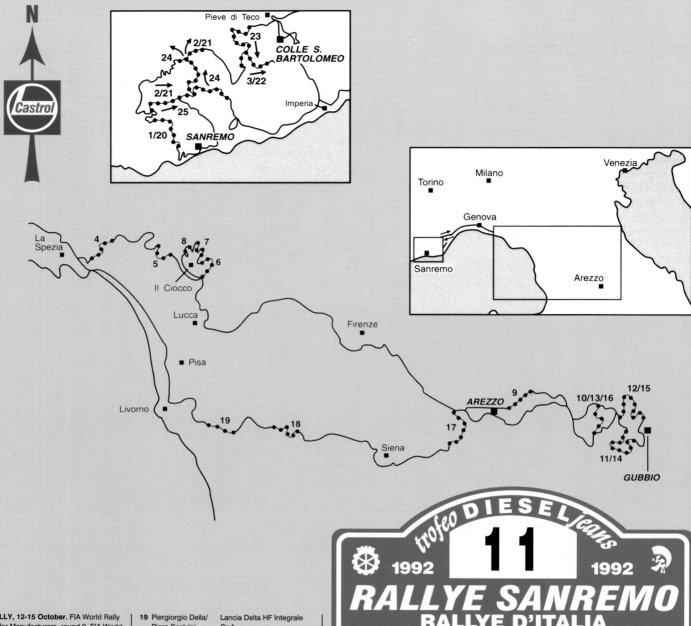

SANREMO RALLY, 12-15 October. FIA World Rally Championship for Manufacturers, round 9. FIA World Rally Championship for Drivers, round 11.

Leading entries

1	Juha Kankkunen/ Juha Piironen	Lancia Delta HF Integrale Gr A
2	Massimo Biasion/ Tiziano Siviero	Ford Sierra Cosworth 4x4 Gr A
3	Didier Auriol/ Bernard Occelli	Lancia Delta HF Integrale Gr A
4	François Delecour/ Daniel Grataloup	Ford Sierra Cosworth 4x4 Gr A
5	Andrea Aghini/ Sauro Farnocchia	Lancia Delta HF Integrale Gr A
6	Franco Cunico/ Steve Evangelisti	Ford Sierra Cosworth 4x4 Gr A
7	Piero Liatti/ Luciano Tedeschini	Lancia Delta HF Integrale Gr A
8	Alessandro Fiorio/ Vittorio Brambilla	Lancia Delta HF Integrale Gr A
10	Piergiorgio Bedini/ Luca Bonvicini	Lancia Delta HF Integrale Gr A
11	Bruno Thiry/ Stéphane Prévot	Opel Calibra Gr A
12	Giovanni Manfrinato/ Claudio Condotta	Ford Sierra Cosworth 4x4 Gr N
14	Mohammed Bin Sulayem/ Ronan Morgan	Ford Sierra Cosworth Gr N 4x4
15	Pavel Sibera/ Petr Gross	Skoda Favorit 136L
16	Vladimir Berger/ Miroslav Fanta	Skoda Favorit 136L Gr A
18	César Baroni/ Philippe David	Lancia Delta HF Integrale Gr A
19	Piergiorgio Deila/ Piero Scalvini	Lancia Delta HF Integrale Gr A
20	Gilberto Pianezzola/ Loris Roggia	Lancia Delta HF Integrale Gr A
21	Vanio Pasquali/ Francesco Mion	Lancia Delta HF Integrale Gr A
22	Gianluca Vita/ Lorenzo Dongara	Toyota Celica GT4 Gr A
23	Alessandro Fassina/ Massimo Chiapponi	Mazda 323 GT-X Gr N

Special stage times

SS 1. Coldirodi 1 (12.35 km)
1 A. Aghini/S. Farnocchia (Lancia Delta HF Integrale) 8m 14s; **2** F. Delecour/D. Grataloup (Ford Sierra Cosworth 4x4) 8m 17s; .3 M. Biasion/T. Siviero (Ford Sierra Cosworth 4x4) 8m 19s; **4** A. Fiorio/V. Brambilla (Lancia Delta HF Integrale) 8m 23s; **5** J. Kankkunen/ J. Piironen (Lancia Delta HF Integrale), F. Cunico/ S. Evangelisti (Ford Sierra Cosworth 4x4) 8m 24s.

SS 2. Monte Ceppo 1 (36.35 km)
1 Aghini/Farnocchia (Lancia) 25m 14s; **2** Delecour/ Grataloup (Ford) 25m 20s; **3** Kankkunen/Piironen (Lancia) 25m 45s; **4** P. Deila/P. Scalvini (Lancia HF Integrale) 25m 48s; **5** Biasion/Siviero (Ford) 25m 53s; **6** Fiorio/Brambilla (Lancia) 26m 07s.

SS 3. Colle d'Oggia 1 (15.66 km)
1 Delecour/Grataloup (Ford), Cunico/Evangelisti (Ford) 10m 51s; **3** Biasion/Siviero (Ford), Aghini/ Farnocchia (Lancia) 10m 53s; **5** Kankkunen/Piironen (Lancia) 10m 57s; **6** Fiorio/Brambilla (Lancia), C. Baroni/P. David (Lancia Delta HF Integrale), Deila/Scalvini (Lancia) 10m 59s.

SS 4. Castelnuovo Magra (21.79 km)
1 Aghini/Farnocchia (Lancia) 16m 11s; **2** Cunico/ Evangelisti (Ford) 16m 14s; **3** Delecour/Grataloup (Ford), Deila/Scalvini (Lancia) 16m 16s; **5** Biasion/ Siviero (Ford) 16m 18s; **6** Kankkunen/Piironen (Lancia) 16m 21s.

SS 5. Careggine (19.17 km)
1 Aghini/Farnocchia (Lancia) 12m 38s; **2** Delecour/ Grataloup (Ford) 12m 45s; **3** Cunico/Evangelisti (Ford) 12m 48s; **4** Deila/Scalvini (Lancia) 12m 52s; **5** Kankkunen/Piironen (Lancia) 12m 53s; **6** Baroni/ David (Lancia) 12m 55s.

SS 6. Tereglio (16.71 km)
1 Aghini/Farnocchia (Lancia) 12m 18s; **2** Delecour/ Grataloup (Ford) 12m 20s; **3** Kankkunen/Piironen (Lancia) 12m 23; **4** Cunico/Evangelisti (Ford) 12m 24s; **5** Biasion/Siviero (Ford) 12m 26s; **6** Deila/ Scalvini (Lancia) 12m 31s.

SS 7. Renaio (22.57 km)
1 Aghini/Farnocchia (Lancia) 17m 59s; **2** Kankkunen/Piironen (Lancia) 18m 09s; **3** Delecour/Grataloup (Ford) 18m 11s; **4** Biasion/Siviero (Ford) 18m 13s; **5** Cunico/Evangelisti (Ford) 18m 33s; **6** P. Liatti/L. Tedeschini (Lancia Delta HF Integrale) 20m 00s.

SS 8. Il Ciocco (3.12 km)
1 Kankkunen/Piironen (Lancia) 3m 03s; **2** Aghini/ Farnocchia (Lancia) 3m 07s; **3** Delecour/Grataloup (Ford) 3m 08s; **4** Cunico/Evangelisti (Ford), Deila/ Scalvini (Lancia) 3m 15s; **6** Liatti/Tedeschini (Lancia) 3m 16s.

SS 9. Alpe di Poti (15.09 km)
1 Kankkunen/Piironen (Lancia) 12m 56s; **2** Biasion/ Siviero (Ford) 13m 06s; **3** Aghini/Farnocchia (Lancia) 13m 10s; **4** Fiorio/Brambilla (Lancia) 13m 12s; **5** Liatti/Tedeschini (Lancia) 13m 14s; **6** Deila/Scalvini (Lancia) 13m 17s.

SS 10. Pieve de Saddi 1 (17.73 km)
1 Kankkunen/Piironen (Lancia) 11m 42s; **2** Delecour/ Grataloup (Ford) 11m 53s; **3** Biasion/Siviero (Ford) 11m 54s; **4** Aghini/Farnocchia (Lancia) 11m 55s; **5** Fiorio/Brambilla (Lancia) 11m 57s; **6** Liatti/Tedeschini (Lancia) 12m 01s.

SS 11. Nerbisci 1 (32.11 km)
1 Delecour/Grataloup (Ford) 21m 36s; **2** Kankkunen/ Piironen (Lancia) 21m 46s; **3** Aghini/Farnocchia (Lancia) 21m 48s; **4** Biasion/Siviero (Ford) 21m 53s; **5** Liatti/Tedeschini (Lancia) 22m 04s; **6** Deila/Scalvini (Lancia) 22m 12s.

SS 12. San Bartolomeo 1 (37.93 km)
1 Kankkunen/Piironen (Lancia) 27m 10s; **2** Aghini/ Farnocchia (Lancia) 27m 14s; **3** Biasion/Siviero (Ford) 27m 18s; **4** Delecour/Grataloup (Ford) 27m 19s; **5** Liatti/Tedeschini (Lancia) 27m 37s; **6** Fiorio/ Brambilla (Lancia) 27m 47s.

SS 13. Pieve de Saddi 2 (17.73 km)
1 Kankkunen/Piironen (Lancia) 11m 25s; 2 Biasion/ Siviero (Ford) 11m 33s; 3 Aghini/Farnocchia (Lancia) 11m 34s; 4 Delecour/Grataloup (Ford), Fiorio/Brambilla (Lancia) 11m 41s; 6 Liatti/Tedeschini (Lancia) 11m 43s.

SS 14. Nerbisci 2 (32.11 km)
1 Kankkunen/Piironen (Lancia) 21m 37s; 2 Biasion/ Siviero (Ford) 21m 39s; 3 Aghini/Farnocchia (Lancia) 21m 43s; 4 Fiorio/Brambilla (Lancia) 21m 46s; 5 Delecour/Grataloup (Ford) 21m 47s; 6 Liatti/Tedeschini (Lancia) 21m 51s.

SS 15. San Bartolomeo 2 (37.93 km)
1 Kankkunen/Piironen (Lancia) 26m 52s; 2 Delecour/ Grataloup (Ford) 27m 07s; 3 Biasion/Siviero (Ford) 27m 09s; 4 Aghini/Farnocchia (Lancia) 27m 10s; 5 Liatti/Tedeschini (Lancia) 27m 15s; 6 Fiorio/Brambilla (Lancia) 27m 18s.

SS 16. Pieve de Saddi 3 (17.73 km)
1 Kankkunen/Piironen (Lancia) 11m 28s; 2 Biasion/ Siviero (Ford) 11m 41s; 3 Aghini/Farnocchia (Lancia) 11m 45s; 4 Delecour/Grataloup (Ford) 11m 50s; 5 Fiorio/Brambilla (Lancia) 12m 00s; 6 Deila/Scalvini (Lancia) 12m 05s.

SS 17. Pergine (13.58 km)
1 Delecour/Grataloup (Ford) 9m 02s; 2 Biasion/ Siviero (Ford) 9m 08s; 3 Kankkunen/Piironen (Lancia) 9m 10s; 4 Aghini/Farnocchia (Lancia), Deila/ Scalvini (Lancia) 9m 13s; 6 Liatti/Tedeschini (Lancia) 9m 17s.

SS 18. Ulignano (15.52 km)
1 Biasion/Siviero (Ford) 10m 08s; 2 Delecour/Grataloup (Ford) 10m 10s; 3 Kankkunen/Piironen (Lancia) 10m 12s; 4 Aghini/Farnocchia (Lancia) 10m 15s; 5 Liatti/Tedeschini (Lancia) 10m 21s; 6 G. Pianezzola/L. Roggia (Lancia Delta HF Integrale) 10m 23s.

SS 19. Santa Luce (11.62 km)
1 Kankkunen/Piironen (Lancia) 9m 31s; 2 Delecour/ Grataloup (Ford) 9m 32s; 3 Biasion/Siviero (Ford), Aghini/Farnocchia (Lancia) 9m 35s; 5 Fiorio/Brambilla (Lancia), Deila/Scalvini (Lancia) 9m 45s.

SS 20. Coldirodi 2 (12.35 km)
1 Biasion/Siviero (Ford) 8m 10s; 2 Aghini/Farnocchia (Lancia) 8m 11s; 3 Delecour/Grataloup (Ford) 8m 13s; 4 Kankkunen/Piironen (Lancia) 8m 20s; 5 Fiorio/ Brambilla (Lancia), Deila/Scalvini (Lancia) 8m 24s.

SS 21. Monte Ceppo 2 (36.35 km)
1 Aghini/Farnocchia (Lancia) 25m 14s; 2 Kankkunen/ Piironen (Lancia) 25m 34s; 3 Delecour/Grataloup (Ford) 25m 35s; 4 Deila/Scalvini (Lancia) 25m 36s; 5 Biasion/Siviero (Ford) 25m 39s; 6 Pianezzola/Roggia (Lancia) 25m 59s.

SS 22. Colle d'Oggia 2 (15.66 km)
1 Delecour/Grataloup (Ford) 10m 54s; 2 Biasion/

Siviero (Ford) 10m 56s; 3 Aghini/Farnocchia (Lancia), Baroni/David (Lancia) 11m 02s; 5 Deila/Scalvini (Lancia) 11m 03s; 6 Kankkunen/Piironen (Lancia) 11m 04s.

SS 23. Rezzo (25.27 km)
1 Aghini/Farnocchia (Lancia) 18m 09s; 2 Biasion/ Siviero (Ford) 18m 14s; 3 Kankkunen/Piironen (Lancia) 18m 25s; 4 Delecour/Grataloup (Ford) 18m 28s; 5 Baroni/David (Lancia) 18m 34s; 6 Pianezzola/Roggia (Lancia) 18m 42s.

SS 24. Vignai (30.45 km)
Cancelled.

SS 25. Apricale-Baiardo (10.60 km)
1 Baroni/David (Lancia) 7m 35s; 2 Biasion/Siviero (Ford) 7m 36s; 3 Aghini/Farnocchia (Lancia) 7m 39s; 4 Delecour/Grataloup (Ford) 7m 41s; 5 Kankkunen/ Piironen (Lancia) 7m 44s; 6 Fiorio/Brambilla (Lancia) 7m 52s.

Major retirements

Didier Auriol/	Lancia Delta HF Integrale	
Bernard Occelli	SS 1	lost a wheel
Mohammed Bin Sulayem/	Ford Sierra Cosworth 4x4	
Ronan Morgan	SS 4	transmission
Franco Cunico/	Ford Sierra Cosworth 4x4	
Steve Evangelisti	SS 21	suspension
Piergiorgio Deila/	Lancia Delta HF Integrale	
Piero Scalvini	SS 23	accident

FIA class winners

Group A
Over 2000 cc: Aghini/Farnocchia (Lancia)
1600-2000 cc: Thiry/Prévot (Opel)
1300-1600 cc: Antonio Giambernardino/Ivano Benza (Peugeot 205 GTI)
Up to 1300 cc: Luigi Ottino/Gabriella Chicco (Peugeot 205 Rallye)

Group N
Over 2000 cc: Manfrinato/Condotta (Ford)
1300-2000 cc: Angelo Medeghini/Paolo Cecchini (Peugeot 309 GTI 16v)
Up to 1300 cc: Giovanni Panta/Mauro Mosca (Peugeot 205 Rallye)

Comic turn: the Italian television star, Giorgio Faletti, took the wheel of a Jolly Club Delta, and brought it to the finish into the bargain.

Rally leaders

SS 1-15 Aghini/Farnocchia (Lancia); SS 16-20 Kankkunen/Piironen (Lancia); SS 21-25 Aghini/ Farnocchia (Lancia).

Route details

Leg 1
12 October: Starting from Sanremo at 0700 and finishing at Arezzo at 2200, including eight special stages (147.72 km).

Leg 2
13 October: Starting and finishing in Arezzo 0700-1930, including eight special stages (218.36 km).

Leg 3
14/15 October: Starting from Arezzo at 0700/14 and finishing in Sanremo at 0110/15, including nine special stages (one cancelled - 140.95 km).

World Championship points

Drivers
1 Auriol 120; 2 Kankkunen 107; 3 Sainz 104; 4 Biasion 52; 5 Delecour 45; 6 Alén 40; 7 McRae and Recalde 28; 9 Aghini 26; 10 Liatti, Fiorio and Bugalski 22.

Manufacturers
1 Lancia 140 (177); 2 Toyota 108 (112); 3 Ford 84; 4 Subaru 43; 5 Mitsubishi 38; 6 Nissan 33; 7 Audi 10; 8 Renault Argentine 7; 9 Renault 2.

Weather

Cool and mainly dry with some showers.

Special stage analysis

	1st	2nd	3rd	4th	5th	6th
Kankkunen/Piironen (Lancia)	9	3	5	1	4	2
Aghini/Farnocchia (Lancia)	8	3	9	4	-	2
Delecour/Grataloup (Ford)	4	8	5	5	1	-
Biasion/Siviero (Ford)	2	8	6	2	4	-
Cunico/Evangelisti (Ford)	1	1	1	2	2	-
Baroni/David (Lancia)	1	-	1	-	1	2
Deila/Scalvini (Lancia)	-	-	1	5	3	5
Fiorio/Brambilla (Lancia)	-	-	-	4	4	5
Liatti/Tedeschini (Lancia)	-	-	-	-	5	6
Pianezzola/Roggia (Lancia)	-	-	-	-	-	3

Finish lines

A faulty wheel with no holes for the disc mounting bolts came off and caused **Didier Auriol**'s retirement on the first stage...Fuel pump trouble towards the end of the gravel couldn't deny **Alex Fiorio** fifth overall in his **Astra** Team Delta, making him best of the privateers...**Giovanni Manfrinato** recorded a comfortable Group N win in his Sierra **Cosworth** 4x4...**Piergiorgio Deila** became Italian Champion despite crashing his Nocentini **Delta** into a rockface, since **Franco Cunico**'s Tamoil Sierra had already succumbed to turbo, brake and, finally, suspension problems...**Bruno Thiry** brought the **Opel** Belgium Calibra home ninth, in spite of a lengthy gearbox change during the gravel leg...**Gilberto Pianezzola** scored his best World Championship result — sixth — in spite of rolling his Esso **Integrale** on SS15...The 1991 European Champion, **Piero Liatti**, could do no better than seventh in his ART **Delta**, thanks to an electronic problem during the first leg, and an alternator failure at night during the final leg.

Results

1	Andrea Aghini/	Lancia Delta HF Integrale	
	Sauro Farnocchia	5h 52m 11s	Gr A
2	Juha Kankkunen/	Lancia Delta HF Integrale	
	Juha Piironen	5h 52m 51s	Gr A
3	François Delecour/	Ford Sierra Cosworth 4x4	
	Daniel Grataloup	5h 53m 53s	Gr A
4	Massimo Biasion/	Ford Sierra Cosworth 4x4	
	Tiziano Siviero	5h 54m 06s	Gr A
5	Alessandro Fiorio/	Lancia Delta HF Integrale	
	Vittorio Brambilla	6h 00m 58s	Gr A
6	Gilberto Pianezzola/	Lancia Delta HF Integrale	
	Loris Roggia	6h 08m 13s	Gr A
7	Piero Liatti/	Lancia Delta HF Integrale	
	Luciano Tedeschini	6h 13m 28s	Gr A
8	César Baroni/	Lancia Delta HF Integrale	
	Philippe David	6h 15m 50s	Gr A
9	Bruno Thiry/	Opel Calibra	
	Stéphane Prévot	6h 37m 39s	Gr A
10	Giovanni Manfrinato/	Ford Sierra Cosworth 4x4	
	Claudio Condotta	6h 42m 18s	Gr N

102 starters, 41 finishers

Previous winners (since 1970)

1970 Jean-Luc Thérier/Marcel Callewaert
Renault Alpine A110
1971 Ove Andersson/Tony Nash Renault Alpine A110
1972 Amilcare Ballestrieri/Arnaldo Bernacchini
Lancia Fulvia
1973 Jean-Luc Thérier/Jacques Jaubert
Renault Alpine A110
1974 Sandro Munari/Mario Mannucci Lancia Stratos
1975 Björn Waldegård/Hans Thorszelius
Lancia Stratos
1976 Björn Waldegård/Hans Thorszelius
Lancia Stratos
1977 Jean-Claude Andruet/Christian Delferrier
Fiat 131 Abarth
1978 Markku Alén/Ilkka Kivimäki Lancia Stratos
1979 Tony Fassina/Mauro Mannini Lancia Stratos
1980 Walter Röhrl/Christian Geistdörfer Fiat 131 Abarth
1981 Michèle Mouton/Fabrizia Pons Audi Quattro A1
1982 Stig Blomqvist/Björn Cederberg Audi Quattro A2
1983 Markku Alén/Ilkka Kivimäki Lancia 037 Rallye
1984 Ari Vatanen/Terry Harryman
Peugeot 205 Turbo 16
1985 Walter Röhrl/Christian Geistdörfer
Audi Quattro Sport S1
1986 Markku Alén/Ilkka Kivimäki Lancia Delta S4
1987 Massimo Biasion/Tiziano Siviero
Lancia Delta HF Turbo
1988 Massimo Biasion/Tiziano Siviero
Lancia Delta HF Integrale
1989 Massimo Biasion/Tiziano Siviero
Lancia Delta HF Integrale
1990 Didier Auriol/Bernard Occelli
Lancia Delta HF Integrale
1991 Didier Auriol/Bernard Occelli
Lancia Delta HF Integrale

12

Rallye COTE D'IVOIRE - BANDAMA

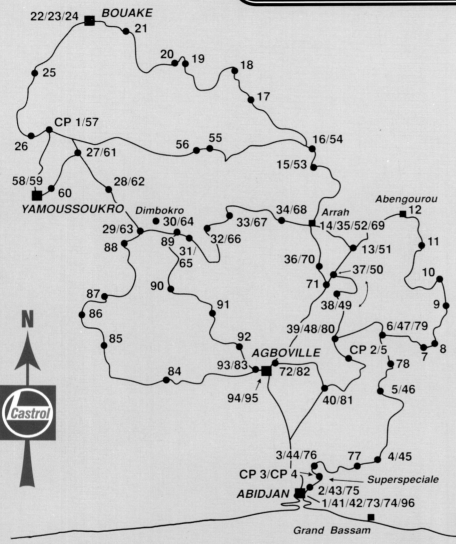

22/23/24 **BOUAKE**
21
20 19
25 18
17
CP 1/57
26 56 55 16/54
27/61 15/53
58/59 28/62
60 34/68 **Arrah** **Abengourou**
YAMOUSSOUKRO **Dimbokro** 33/67 14/35/52/69 12
29/63 30/64 13/51 11
88 89 32/66 36/70 37/50 10
31/65 71 9
90 38/49
87 39/48/80 6/47/79
86 91 **AGBOVILLE** CP 2/5 8
85 92 72/82 78 7
84 93/83 5/46
94/95 40/81
3/44/76 77 4/45
CP 3/CP 4 **Superspeciale**
ABIDJAN 2/43/75
1/41/42/73/74/96
Grand Bassam

N

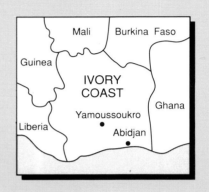

Mali | Burkina Faso
Guinea
IVORY COAST
Yamoussoukro
Liberia Ghana
Abidjan

IVORY COAST RALLY, 31 October-2 November.
FIA World Rally Championship for Drivers, round 12.

Leading entries

1	Kenjiro Shinozuka/ John Meadows	Mitsubishi Galant VR-4 Gr A
2	Patrick Tauziac/ Christian Boy	Mitsubishi Galant VR-4 Gr A
3	Rudi Stohl/ Peter Diekmann	Audi 90 Quattro Gr A
4	Grégoire de Mevius/ Willy Lux	Nissan Sunny GTi-R Gr N
5	Patrice Servant/ Thierry Brion	Audi 90 Quattro Gr A
6	Bruno Thiry/ Stéphane Prévot	Opel Kadett GSi Gr A
7	Adolphe Choteau/ Pierre Langlais	Toyota Corolla 16S Gr A
8	Kurt Gottlicher/ Jean-Jacques Lukas	Ford Sierra Cosworth 4x4 Gr N
10	Samir Assef/ Clement Konan	Toyota Celica GT4
11	Jean-Claude Dupuis/ Nathalie Copetti	Toyota Corolla 16S Gr A

Positions after superspecial (6.86 km)

1 K. Shinozuka/J. Meadows (Mitsubishi Galant VR-4) 5m 41s; **2** R. Stohl/P. Diekmann (Audi 90 Quattro) 5m 45s; **3** G. de Mevius/W. Lux (Nissan Sunny GTi-R) 5m 53s; **4** B. Thiry/S. Prévot (Opel Kadett GSi) 5m 59s; **5** P. Servant/T. Brion (Audi 90 Quattro) 6m 02s; **6** P. Tauziac/C. Boy (Mitsubishi Galant VR-4) 6m 03s.

Positions after each leg

Leg 1

1 Tauziac/Boy (Mitsubishi) 1h 37m 03s; **2** de Mevius/Lux (Nissan) 1h 41m 53s; **3** Servant/Brion

(Audi) 1h 51m 02s; **4** Thiry/Prévot (Opel) 2h 03m 59s; **5** S. Assef/C. Konan (Toyota Celica GT4) 2h 31m 27s; **6** H. Nishiyama/H. Yamaguchi (Nissan Sunny GTi-R) 2h 39m 07s.

Leg 2

1 de Mevius/Lux (Nissan) 3h 07m 53s; **2** Thiry/Prévot (Opel) 3h 34m 59s; **3** Shinozuka/Meadows (Mitsubishi) 3h 44m 41s; **4** Servant/Brion (Audi) 4h 07m 02s; **5** Nishiyama/Yamaguchi (Nissan) 4h 31m 07s; **6** Assef/Konan (Toyota) 6h 03m 27s.

FIA class winners

Group A

Over 2000 cc:	Shinozuka/Meadows (Mitsubishi)
1600-2000 cc:	Thiry/Prévot (Opel)
1300-1600 cc:	Occelli/Michel (Toyota)
Up to 1300 cc:	No starters

Group N

Over 2000 cc:	Nishiyama/Yamaguchi (Nissan)
1600-2000 cc:	No finishers
1300-1600 cc:	No finishers
Up to 1300 cc:	No finishers

Rally leaders

TC 1-11 Shinozuka/Meadows (Mitsubishi); **TC 12-49** Tauziac/Boy (Mitsubishi); **TC 50-85** de Mevius/Lux (Nissan); **TC 86-96** Shinozuka/Meadows (Mitsubishi).

Major retirements

Rudi Stohl/ Peter Diekmann	Audi 90 Quattro TC 18	rolled
Alain Lopes/ Jacky Delvaux	Opel Astra GSi TC 18	engine

Patrick Tauziac/ Christian Boy	Mitsubishi Galant VR-4 TC 54	clutch
Grégoire de Mevius/ Willy Lux	Nissan Sunny GTi-R engine	TC 86

World Championship points

1 Auriol 120; **2** Kankkunen 107; **3** Sainz 104; **4** Biasion 52; **5** Delecour 45; **6** Alén 40; **7** McRae and Recalde 28; **9** Aghini 26; **10** Liatti, Fiorio and Bugalski 22.

Route details

Leg 1

31 October/1 November: Starting and finishing in Abidjan 0900/31-0030/1, including one superspecial and 41 time controls (910.32 km).

Leg 2

1 November: Starting and finishing in Abidjan 1000-2330, including 32 time controls (724.44 km).

Leg 3

2 November: Starting and finishing in Abidjan 0900-2000, including 23 time controls (508.28 km).

Weather

Hot and humid with some thunderstorms.

For a while, it looked as though Grégoire de Mevius would take outright victory as well as the Group N Championship, only for the Belgian jinx to strike again.

Finish lines

Rudi Stohl and **Peter Diekmann** were lucky to emerge from their Audi 90 **Quattro** unhurt after suffering a fifth gear roll midway through the first day...Rudi's son **Manfred** rose from his hospital bed, where he had been suffering a fever, to take the start. However, he was still so ill that co-driver, **Kay Gerlach**, had to drive the **Quattro** as far as the Bouake regroup on the first day — he was eighth fastest on the superspecial...**Eija Jurvanen** and **Marjo Berglund** drove the Tusk Engineering's **Mitsubishi** Galant VR-4 chase car over the starting ramp to qualify for the Ladies' World Rally Championship...**Alain Lopes** gave the Opel Astra GSi its World Championship debut when **Bruno Thiry** decided to use the older Kadett GSi, and almost reached Bouake before its engine blew up ...**Hiroshi Nishiyama**'s fourth place was enough to give him the lead of the Group N World Rally Championship ...**Samir Assef** struggled with a two-wheel drive Toyota **Celica** GT4 for the second half of the rally and did well to finish fifth...**Guy Colsoul** lost almost five hours with recurrent rear suspension problems on his Mitsubishi Galant VR-4 ...The rally featured a much more compact route than in recent years with an increase in the double usage of competitive sections.

Results

1	Kenjiro Shinozuka/ John Meadows	Mitsubishi Galant VR-4 4h 09m 41s	Gr A
2	Bruno Thiry/ Stéphane Prévot	Opel Kadett GSi 5h 32m 59s	Gr A
3	Patrice Servant/ Thierry Brion	Audi 90 Quattro 5h 38m 02s	Gr A
4	Hiroshi Nishiyama/ Hisashi Yamaguchi	Nissan Sunny GTi-R 6h 24m 07s	Gr N
5	Samir Assef/ Clement Konan	Toyota Celica GT4 7h 42m 27s	Gr A
6	Alain Oudit/ Frédéric Spaak	Nissan Sunny GTi-R 7h 46m 36s	Gr N
7	Manfred Stohl/ Kay Gerlach	Audi 90 Quattro 8h 14m 19s	Gr A
8	Denis Occelli/ Franck Michel	Toyota Corolla 16S 8h 44m 44s	Gr A
9	Jean-Claude Dupuis/ Nathalie Copetti	Toyota Corolla 16S 8h 54m 49s	Gr A
10	Guy Colsoul/ Edy Paquay	Mitsubishi Galant VR-4 10h 42m 25s	Gr N

42 starters, 13 finishers

Previous winners

1969 Mark Gerenthon/Helen Gerenthon
Renault 8 Gordini
1970 Hans Schüller/Claes Billstam   Datsun 1800
1971 Bob Neyret/Jacques Terramorsi   Peugeot 504
1972 No finishers
1973 Edgar Herrmann/Hans Schüller   Datsun 180B
1974 Timo Mäkinen/Henry Liddon   Peugeot 504
1975 Bernard Consten/Gérard Flocon   Peugeot 504
1976 Timo Mäkinen/Henry Liddon
Peugeot 504 V6 Coupé
1977 Andrew Cowan/Johnstone Syer Mitsubishi Lancer
1978 Jean-Pierre Nicolas/Michel Gamet
Peugeot 504 V6 Coupé
1979 Hannu Mikkola/Arne Hertz
Mercedes-Benz 450 SLC
1980 Björn Waldegård/Hans Thorszelius
Mercedes-Benz 450 SLC
1981 Timo Salonen/Seppo Harjanne   Datsun Violet GT
1982 Walter Röhrl/Christian Geistdörfer
Opel Ascona 400
1983 Björn Waldegård/Hans Thorszelius
Toyota Celica Turbo
1984 Stig Blomqvist/Björn Cederberg
Audi Quattro Sport
1985 Juha Kankkunen/Fred Gallagher
Toyota Celica Turbo
1986 Björn Waldegård/Fred Gallagher
Toyota Celica Turbo
1987 Kenneth Eriksson/Peter Diekmann   VW Golf GTi
1988 Alain Ambrosino/Daniel le Saux   Nissan 200SX
1989 Alain Oreille/Michel Roissard   Renault 5GT Turbo
1990 Patrick Tauziac/Claude Papin
Mitsubishi Galant VR-4
1991 Kenjiro Shinozuka/John Meadows
Mitsubishi Galant VR-4

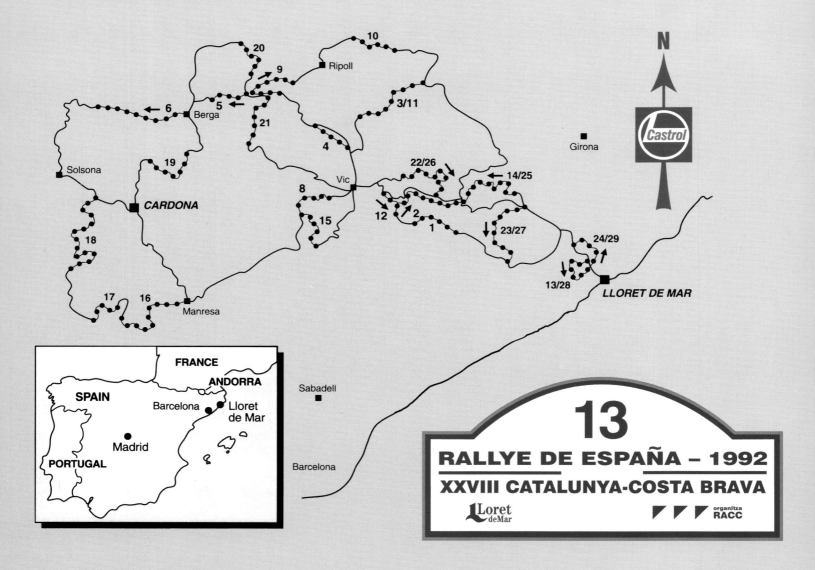

13
RALLYE DE ESPAÑA – 1992
XXVIII CATALUNYA-COSTA BRAVA

Lloret deMar ▼ ▼ ▼ organitza RACC

CATALONIA RALLY, 9-11 November. FIA World Rally Championship for Drivers, round 13.

Leading entries

1	Armin Schwarz/ Arne Hertz	Toyota Celica Turbo 4WD Gr A
2	François Delecour/ Daniel Grataloup	Ford Sierra Cosworth 4x4 Gr A
3	Didier Auriol/ Bernard Occelli	Lancia Delta HF Integrale Gr A
4	Carlos Sainz/ Luis Moya	Toyota Celica Turbo 4WD Gr A
5	Juha Kankkunen/ Juha Piironen	Lancia Delta HF Integrale Gr A
6	Alessandro Fiorio/ Vittorio Brambilla	Lancia Delta HF Integrale Gr A
7	Andrea Aghini/ Sauro Farnocchia	Lancia Delta HF Integrale Gr A
8	Gustavo Trelles/ Jorge Del Buono	Lancia Delta HF Integrale Gr A
9	Fernando Capdevila/ Alfredo Rodriguez	Ford Sierra Cosworth 4x4 Gr N
10	José-Marie Bardolet/ Josep Autet	Ford Sierra Cosworth 4x4 Gr A
11	José-Maria Ponce/ Juan Carlos Deniz	BMW M3 Gr A
12	Carlos Menem/ Victor Zucchini	Lancia Delta HF Integrale Gr N
14	Pavel Sibera/ Petr Gross	Skoda Favorit 136L
15	Vladimir Berger/ Miroslav Fanta	Skoda Favorit 136L
16	Mohammed Bin Sulayem/ Ronan Morgan	Ford Sierra Cosworth 4x4 Gr N
17	Pedro Diego/ Iciar Muguerza	Lancia Delta HF Integrale Gr A
18	Jesús Puras/ Alex Romani	Lancia Delta HF Integrale Gr A
19	Luis Climent/ José Munoz	Opel Corsa GSi Gr A
20	Capi Saiz/ Carlos Del Barrio	Peugeot 309 GTI 16v Gr A
21	Ignacio Lilly/ Mario Saguillo	Opel Corsa GSi Gr A

Special stage times

SS 1. Arbucies-Viladrau (16.17 km)
1 C. Sainz/L. Moya (Toyota Celica Turbo 4WD) 10m 28s; 2 A. Schwarz/A. Hertz (Toyota Celica Turbo 4WD) 10m 40s; 3 A. Aghini/S. Farnocchia (Lancia Delta HF Integrale) 10m 42s; 4 F. Delecour/D. Grataloup (Ford Sierra Cosworth 4x4) 10m 43s; 5 A. Fiorio/V. Brambilla (Lancia Delta HF Integrale) 10m 44s; 6 D. Auriol/B. Occelli (Lancia Delta HF Integrale) 10m 46s.

SS 2. L'Enclusa-Sant Hilari (27.45 km)
1 Sainz/Moya (Toyota) 17m 52s; 2 Schwarz/Hertz (Toyota), Aghini/Farnocchia (Lancia) 18m 03s; 4 Delecour/Grataloup (Ford) 18m 06s; 5 Auriol/Occelli (Lancia) 18m 08s; 6 J. Kankkunen/J. Piironen (Lancia Delta HF Integrale), J.-M. Bardolet/J. Autet (Ford Sierra Cosworth 4x4) 18m 12s.

SS 3. Coll de Bracons 1 (19.89 km)
1 Delecour/Grataloup (Ford) 12m 58s; 2 Schwarz/Hertz (Toyota) 13m 02s; 3 Aghini/Farnocchia (Lancia) 13m 04s; 4 Sainz/Moya (Toyota), Auriol/Occelli (Lancia) 13m 06s; 6 J. Puras/A. Romani (Lancia Delta HF Integrale) 13m 07s.

SS 4. La Trona (12.85 km)
1 Sainz/Moya (Toyota) 8m 25s; 2 Schwarz/Hertz (Toyota) 8m 34s; 3 Delecour/Grataloup (Ford) 8m 38s; 4 Puras/Romani (Lancia) 8m 39s; 5 Auriol/Occelli (Lancia) 8m 40s; 6 Aghini/Farnocchia (Lancia), Fiorio/Brambilla (Lancia) 8m 41s.

SS 5. Alpens-Vilada (21.23 km)
1 Sainz/Moya (Toyota) 13m 11s; 2 G. Trelles/J. Del Buono (Lancia Delta HF Integrale) 13m 14s; 3 Dele-

cour/Grataloup (Ford), Auriol/Occelli (Lancia) 13m 15s; 5 Schwarz/Hertz (Toyota), Aghini/Farnocchia (Lancia) 13m 17s.

SS 6. La Mina (17.16 km)
1 Sainz/Moya (Toyota) 9m 45s; 2 Auriol/Occelli (Lancia) 9m 49s; 3 Delecour/Grataloup (Ford) 9m 50s; 4 Schwarz/Hertz (Toyota) 9m 53s; 5 Fiorio/Brambilla (Lancia) 9m 55s; 6 Kankkunen/Piironen (Lancia), Aghini/Farnocchia (Lancia) 9m 57s.

SS 8. Santa Eulalia de Riuprimer (13.27 km)
1 Sainz/Moya (Toyota) 7m 27s; 2 Aghini/Farnocchia (Lancia) 7m 33s; 3 Delecour/Grataloup (Ford) 7m 34s; 4 Kankkunen/Piironen (Lancia) 7m 35s; 5 Auriol/Occelli (Lancia) 7m 37s; 6 Fiorio/Brambilla (Lancia) 7m 39s.

SS 9. Alpens-Les Lloses (21.91 km)
1 Auriol/Occelli (Lancia) 14m 18s; 2 Aghini/Farnocchia (Lancia), Kankkunen/Piironen (Lancia) 14m 20s; 4 Sainz/Moya (Toyota) 14m 22s; 5 Schwarz/Hertz (Toyota) 14m 26s; 6 Puras/Romani (Lancia) 14m 27s.

SS 10. Coll de Santigosa (10.60 km)
1 Sainz/Moya (Toyota) 7m 12s; 2 Kankkunen/Piironen (Lancia) 7m 16s; 3 Schwarz/Hertz (Toyota), Auriol/Occelli (Lancia), Bardolet/Autet (Ford), Puras/Romani (Lancia) 7m 23s.

SS 11. Coll de Bracons 2 (19.89 km)
1 Sainz/Moya (Toyota) 13m 01s; 2 Schwarz/Hertz (Toyota) 13m 14s; 3 Aghini/Farnocchia (Lancia) 13m 15s; 4 Auriol/Occelli (Lancia) 13m 17s; 5 Bardolet/Autet (Ford), Puras/Romani (Lancia) 13m 19s.

SS 12. Collsplana-Sant Hilari (26.11 km)
1 Sainz/Moya (Toyota) 17m 03s; 2 Aghini/Farnocchia (Lancia) 17m 17s; 3 Schwarz/Hertz (Toyota) 17m 21s; 4 Auriol/Occelli (Lancia), Bardolet/Autet (Ford) 17m 22s; 6 Kankkunen/Piironen (Lancia) 17m 26s.

SS 13. Lloret de Mar 1 (8.80 km)
1 Bardolet/Autet (Ford) 8m 30s; 2 Aghini/Farnocchia (Lancia) 8m 32s; 3 Sainz/Moya (Toyota), Fiorio/Brambilla (Lancia), Kankkunen/Piironen (Lancia) 8m 35s; 6 Schwarz/Hertz (Toyota) 8m 40s.

SS 14. El Subira 1 (30.32 km)
1 Kankkunen/Piironen (Lancia) 25m 29s; 2 Aghini/Farnocchia (Lancia) 25m 43s; 3 Sainz/Moya (Toyota) 25m 46s; 4 Bardolet/Autet (Ford) 25m 55s; 5 Fiorio/Brambilla (Lancia) 25m 57s; 6 Trelles/Del Buono (Lancia) 26m 19s.

SS 15. L'Estany (8.23 km)
1 Auriol/Occelli (Lancia) 5m 35s; 2 Kankkunen/Piironen (Lancia) 5m 36s; 3 Fiorio/Brambilla (Lancia) 5m 38s; 4 Sainz/Moya (Toyota), Aghini/Farnocchia (Lancia) 5m 42s; 6 Bardolet/Autet (Ford) 5m 44s.

SS 16. Rajadell-Castellfollit del Boix (21.05 km)
1 Kankkunen/Piironen (Lancia) 15m 19s; 2 Auriol/Occelli (Lancia) 15m 23s; 3 Sainz/Moya (Toyota) 15m 36s; 4 Fiorio/Brambilla (Lancia) 15m 37s; 5 Aghini/Farnocchia (Lancia) 15m 42s; 6 Schwarz/Hertz (Toyota) 15m 49s

SS 17. Prats de Rei (13.48 km)
1 Auriol/Occelli (Lancia) 7m 22s; 2 Fiorio/Brambilla (Lancia), Kankkunen/Piironen (Lancia) 7m 26s; 4 Sainz/Moya (Toyota) 7m 29s; 5 Schwarz/Hertz (Toyota) 7m 34s; 6 Aghini/Farnocchia (Lancia) 7m 37s.

SS 18. Pinos-Riner (31.51 km)
1 Kankkunen/Piironen (Lancia) 19m 37s; 2 Auriol/Occelli (Lancia) 19m 52s; 3 Sainz/Moya (Toyota) 19m 55s; 4 Fiorio/Brambilla (Lancia) 20m 03s; 5 Aghini/Farnocchia (Lancia) 20m 04s; 6 Schwarz/Hertz (Toyota) 20m 08s.

SS 19. Montmajor-Casserres (12.62 km)
1 Auriol/Occelli (Lancia) 8m 34s; 2 Kankkunen/Piironen (Lancia) 8m 35s; 3 Sainz/Moya (Toyota) 8m 42s;

4 Fiorio/Brambilla (Lancia) 8m 43s; 5 Aghini/Farnocchia (Lancia) 8m 46s; 6 Schwarz/Hertz (Toyota) 8m 48s.

SS 20. Sant Jaume de Frontanya (9.95 km)
1 Kankkunen/Piironen (Lancia) 8m 38s; 2 Sainz/Moya (Toyota) 8m 39s; 3 Auriol/Occelli (Lancia) 8m 41s; 4 Bardolet/Autet (Ford) 8m 44s; 5 Aghini/Farnocchia (Lancia) 8m 45s; 6 Schwarz/Hertz (Toyota) 8m 47s.

SS 21. Santa Maria de Merles (14.10 km)
1 Sainz/Moya (Toyota) 7m 21s; 2 Auriol/Occelli (Lancia), Fiorio/Brambilla (Lancia) 7m 27s; 4 Kankkunen/Piironen (Lancia) 7m 30s; 5 Schwarz/ Hertz (Toyota) 7m 32s; 6 Aghini/Farnocchia (Lancia) 7m 35s.

SS 22. Vilanova de Sau 1 (21.24 km)
1 Kankkunen/Piironen (Lancia) 19m 13s; 2 Sainz/Moya (Toyota) 19m 17s; 3 Aghini/Farnocchia (Lancia) 19m 22s; 4 Auriol/Occelli (Lancia) 19m 25s; 5 Bardolet/Autet (Ford) 19m 34s; 6 Puras/Romani (Lancia) 19m 41s.

SS 23. Santa Coloma-Sant Feliu 1 (27.95 km)
1 Kankkunen/Piironen (Lancia) 25m 33s; 2 Aghini/Farnocchia (Lancia) 25m 38s; 3 Auriol/Occelli (Lancia) 25m 40s; 4 Sainz/Moya (Toyota) 25m 46s; 5 Puras/Romani (Lancia) 26m 08s; 6 Fiorio/Brambilla (Lancia) 26m 13s.

SS 24. La Creu de Lloret 1 (12.78 km)
1 Aghini/Farnocchia (Lancia) 9m 20s; 2 Kankkunen/Piironen (Lancia) 9m 22s; 3 Sainz/Moya (Toyota) 9m 26s; 4 Auriol/Occelli (Lancia) 9m 28s; 5 Schwarz/Hertz (Toyota), Fiorio/Brambilla (Lancia), Puras/Romani (Lancia) 9m 40s.

SS 25. El Subira 2 (30.32 km)
1 Auriol/Occelli (Lancia) 25m 06s; 2 Aghini/Farnocchia (Lancia) 25m 18s; 3 Kankkunen/Piironen (Lancia) 25m 20s; 4 Sainz/Moya (Toyota) 25m 28s; 5 Fiorio/Brambilla (Lancia) 25m 40s; 6 Schwarz/Hertz (Toyota) 26m 02s.

SS 26. Vilanova de Sau 2 (21.24 km)
1 Auriol/Occelli (Lancia) 18m 37s; 2 Sainz/Moya (Toyota) 18m 50s; 3 Aghini/Farnocchia (Lancia) 18m 51s; 4 Kankkunen/Piironen (Lancia) 18m 54s; 5 Trelles/Del Buono (Lancia) 19m 04s; 6 Fiorio/ Brambilla (Lancia) 19m 07s.

SS 27. Santa Coloma-Sant Feliu 2 (27.95 km)
1 Auriol/Occelli (Lancia) 24m 30s; 2 Aghini/Farnocchia (Lancia) 24m 49s; 3 Kankkunen/Piironen (Lancia) 24m 53s; 4 Sainz/Moya (Toyota) 24m 59s; 5 Trelles/Del Buono (Lancia), Puras/Romani (Lancia) 25m 10s.

SS 28. Lloret de Mar 2 (8.80 km)
1 Auriol/Occelli (Lancia) 8m 21s; 2 Aghini/Farnocchia (Lancia) 8m 26s; 3 Kankkunen/Piironen (Lancia) 8m 27s; 4 Trelles/Del Buono (Lancia) 8m 31s; 5 Sainz/Moya (Toyota) 8m 36s; 6 Puras/Romani (Lancia) 8m 41s.

SS 29. La Creu de Lloret 2 (12.78 km)
1 Auriol/Occelli (Lancia) 8m 54s; 2 Aghini/Farnocchia (Lancia) 9m 02s; 3 Kankkunen/Piironen (Lancia) 9m 08s; 4 Puras/Romani (Lancia) 9m 09s; 5 Sainz/Moya (Toyota) 9m 14s; 6 Trelles/Del Buono (Lancia) 9m 26s.

FIA class winners

Group A

Over 2000 cc:	Sainz/Moya (Toyota)
1600-2000 cc:	No finishers
1300-1600 cc:	Climent/Munoz (Opel)
Up to 1300 cc:	Berger/Fanta (Skoda)

Group N

Over 2000 cc:	Bin Sulayem/Morgan (Ford)
1600-2000 cc:	D. Guixeras/J.-M. Falco (Peugeot 309 GTI 16v)
1300-1600 cc:	No finishers
Up to 1300 cc:	J. Azcona/J. Billmaier (Peugeot 205 Rallye)

Major retirements

Carlos Menem/ Victor Zucchini	Lancia Delta HF Integrale SS 2	accident
François Delecour/ Daniel Grataloup	Ford Sierra Cosworth 4x4 SS 10	accident
José-Maria Ponce/ Juan Carlos Deniz	BMW M3 SS 19	cracked sump
José-Maria Bardolet/ Josep Autet	Ford Sierra Cosworth 4x4 SS 24	propshaft

Rally leaders

SS 1-29 Sainz/Moya (Toyota).

Alex Fiorio has bounced back well following his abrupt departure from Ford, taking fourth in an Astra-tuned Integrale.

World Championship points

Drivers

1 Sainz 124; 2 Kankkunen 123; 3 Auriol 121; 4 Biasion 52; 5 Delecour 45; 6 Alén 40; 7 Aghini 38; 8 Fiorio 32; 9 McRae and Recalde 28.

Route details

Leg 1
9 November: Starting and finishing at Lloret de Mar 0800-2248, including 11 stages (SS7 was withdrawn before the start - 206.53 km).

Leg 2
10 November: Starting and finishing at Lloret de Mar 0800-2125, including 12 special stages (212.03 km).

Leg 3
11 November: Starting and finishing at Lloret de Mar 0900-1330, including five special stages (101.09 km)

Weather

Dry throughout

Special stage analysis

	1st	2nd	3rd	4th	5th	6th
Sainz/Moya (Toyota)	10	3	6	7	2	-
Auriol/Occelli (Lancia)	9	4	4	5	3	1
Kankkunen/Piironen (Lancia)	6	6	5	3	-	3
Aghini/Farnocchia (Lancia)	1	11	5	1	5	4
Delecour/Grataloup (Ford)	1	-	4	2	-	-
Bardolet/Autet (Ford)	1	-	1	3	2	2
Schwarz/Hertz (Toyota)	-	5	2	1	5	6
Fiorio/Brambilla (Lancia)	-	2	2	3	5	4
Trelles/Del Buono (Lancia)	-	1	-	1	2	2
Puras/Romani (Lancia)	-	-	1	2	4	4

Finish lines

Fernando Capdevila looked to have Group N firmly under control in his Mike Taylor-run Sierra until the last leg, when a faulty sensor dropped him to third...The beneficiaries were **Mohammed Bin Sulayem** and **Ronan Morgan** in the Mike Little version — some recompense for an unlucky season...**Didier Auriol** recorded some astounding times once the power steering was fixed after his off on SS13, just getting his Martini **Lancia** into the top ten by the finish...**Armin Schwarz** had an awful time on his final appearance for Toyota: the Xtrac **Celica** handled nothing like as well as **Sainz**'s viscous coupling car, and a differential problem combined with a faulty turbo to drop him to fifth at the finish...**Alex Fiorio** was fourth in the best Astra **Delta**, even though the seat came loose on SS5 and the windscreen washers failed later on...**François Delecour** crashed his works **Sierra** on a cautioned jump...**Christine Driano** lost the ladies' award to **Eija Jurvanen**'s **Cosworth** 4x4 by only two seconds in her works **Citroën** AX, and would probably have won it if the jack hadn't broken after she got a puncture on SS2...Transmission trouble blighted **Mia Bardolet**'s chances, the second works Sierra retiring with a broken propshaft ...**Carlos Menem** Junior's erratic season ended in another major accident in the Top Run Integrale...**José Maria Ponce**'s **BMW M3** succumbed to a cracked sump.

Results

1	Carlos Sainz/ Luis Moya	Toyota Celica Turbo 4WD	6h 21m 13s	Gr A
2	Juha Kankkunen/ Juha Piironen	Lancia Delta HF Integrale	6h 21m 49s	Gr A
3	Andrea Aghini/ Sauro Farnocchia	Lancia Delta HF Integrale	6h 22m 45s	Gr A
4	Alessandro Fiorio/ Vittorio Brambilla	Lancia Delta HF Integrale	6h 27m 39s	Gr A
5	Armin Schwarz/ Arne Hertz	Toyota Celica Turbo 4WD	6h 29m 43s	Gr A
6	Jesús Puras/ Alex Romani	Lancia Delta HF Integrale	6h 29m 45s	Gr A
7	Gustavo Trelles/ Jorge Del Buono	Lancia Delta HF Integrale	6h 31m 30s	Gr A
8	Pedro Diego/ Iciar Muguerza	Lancia Delta HF Integrale	6h 43m 30s	Gr A
9	Mohammed Bin Sulayem/ Ronan Morgan	Ford Sierra Cosworth 4x4	7h 02m 13s	Gr N
10	Didier Auriol/ Bernard Occelli	Lancia Delta HF Integrale	7h 12m 12s	Gr A

74 starters, 31 finishers

Previous winners (since 1980)

1980	Antonio Zanini/Jordi Sabater	Porsche 911SC
1981	Eugenio Ortiz/Guillermo Barreras	Renault 5 Turbo
1982	Antonio Zanini/Victor Sabater	Talbot Sunbeam Lotus
1983	Adartico Vudafieri/Tiziano Siviero	Lancia 037 Rallye
1984	Salvador Servia/Jordi Sabater	Opel Manta 400
1985	Fabrizio Tabaton/Luciano Tedeschinl	Lancia 037 Rally
1986	Fabrizio Tabaton/Luciano Tedeschini	Lancia Delta S4
1987	Dario Cerrato/Giuseppe Cerri	Lancia Delta HF
1988	Bruno Saby/Jean-François Fauchille	Lancia Delta HF
1989	Yves Loubet/Jean-Marc Andrié	Lancia Delta HF Integrale
1990	Dario Cerrato/Giuseppe Cerri	Lancia Delta HF Integrale
1991	Armin Schwarz/Arne Hertz	Toyota Celica GT4

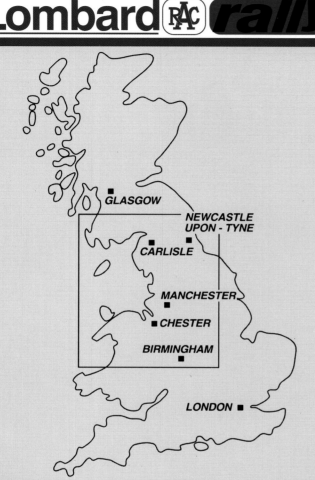

LOMBARD RAC RALLY, 22-25 November. FIA World Rally Championship for Manufacturers, round 10. FIA World Rally Championship for Drivers, round 14.

Leading entries

1	Juha Kankkunen/ Juha Piironen	Lancia Delta HF Integrale Gr A
2	Carlos Sainz/ Luis Moya	Toyota Celica Turbo 4WD Gr A
3	Massimo Biasion/ Tiziano Siviero	Ford Sierra Cosworth 4x4 Gr A
4	Colin McRae/ Derek Ringer	Subaru Legacy RS Gr A
5	Tommi Mäkinen/ Seppo Harjanne	Nissan Sunny GTi-R Gr A
6	Didier Auriol/ Bernard Occelli	Lancia Delta HF Integrale Gr A
7	Markku Alén/ Ilkka Kivimäki	Toyota Celica Turbo 4WD Gr A
8	Malcolm Wilson/ Bryan Thomas	Ford Sierra Cosworth 4x4 Gr A
9	Kenneth Eriksson/ Staffan Parmander	Mitsubishi Galant VR-4 Gr A
10	Ari Vatanen/ Bruno Berglund	Subaru Legacy RS Gr A
12	Stig Blomqvist/ Benny Melander	Nissan Sunny GTi-R Gr A
14	Grégoire de Mevius/ Willy Lux	Nissan Sunny GTi-R Gr N
15	Andrea Aghini/ Sauro Farnocchia	Lancia Delta HF Integrale Gr A
16	Fernando Capdevila/ Alfredo Rodriguez	Ford Sierra Cosworth 4x4 Gr N
18	Enrico Bertone/ Flavio Zanella	Lancia Delta HF Integrale Gr A
19	Lasse Lampi/ Pentti Kuukkala	Mitsubishi Galant VR-4 Gr A
20	Per Eklund/ Johnny Johansson	Subaru Legacy RS Gr A
21	Pavel Sibera/ Petr Gross	Skoda Favorit 136L Gr A
22	Vladimir Berger/ Miroslav Fanta	Skoda Favorit 136 L Gr A
24	Jarmo Kytölehto/ Voitto Silander	Mitsubishi Galant VR-4 Gr N

Special stage times

SS 1. Oulton Park 1 (5.07 km)
1 C. Sainz/L. Moya (Toyota Celica Turbo 4WD) 3m 18s; 2 C. McRae/D. Ringer (Subaru Legacy RS) 3m 24s; 3 M. Alén/I. Kivimäki (Toyota Celica Turbo 4WD), A. Vatanen/B. Berglund (Subaru Legacy RS) 3m 25s; 5 J. Kankkunen/J. Piironen (Lancia Delta HF Integrale), S. Blomqvist/B. Melander (Nissan Sunny GTi-R) 3m 27s.

SS 2. Weston Park (4.57 km)
1 Sainz/Moya (Toyota) 3m 15s; 2 McRae/Ringer (Subaru), Alén/Kivimäki (Toyota) 3m 18s; 4 T. Mäkinen/S. Harjanne (Nissan Sunny GTi-R), Vatanen/ Berglund (Subaru) 3m 19s; 6 D. Auriol/ B. Occelli (Lancia Delta HF Integrale) 3m 21s.

SS 3. Sutton Park (6.31 km)
1 M. Wilson/B. Thomas (Ford Sierra Cosworth 4x4) 3m 40s; 2 M. Biasion/T. Siviero (Ford Sierra Cosworth 4x4) 3m 41s; 3 Kankkunen/Piironen (Lancia) 3m 43s; 4 Mäkinen/Harjanne (Nissan) 3m 45s; 5 K. Eriksson/S. Parmander (Mitsubishi Galant VR-4), Blomqvist/Melander (Nissan) 3m 46s.

SS 4. Donington 1 (7.27 km)
1 Sainz/Moya (Toyota) 4m 24s; 2 Biasion/Siviero (Ford) 4m 28s; 3 Blomqvist/Melander (Nissan) 4m 29s; 4 Wilson/Thomas (Ford), Eriksson/Parmander (Mitsubishi) 4m 30s; 6 Alén/Kivimäki (Toyota) 4m 31s.

SS 5. Donington 2 (7.27 km)
1 McRae/Ringer (Subaru) 4m 22s; 2 Biasion/Siviero (Ford) 4m 23s; 3 Sainz/Moya (Toyota), Blomqvist/ Melander (Nissan) 4m 26s; 5 Kankkunen/Piironen (Lancia), Wilson/Thomas (Ford), Eriksson/Parmander (Mitsubishi) 4m 27s.

SS 6. Clumber 1 (6.94 km)
1 Alén/Kivimäki (Toyota) 3m 44s; 2 Sainz/Moya (Toyota) 3m 45s; 3 Biasion/Siviero (Ford) 3m 46s; 4 Wilson/Thomas (Ford) 3m 47s; 5 Blomqvist/Melander (Nissan) 3m 49s; 6 Kankkunen/Piironen (Lancia), Auriol/Occelli (Lancia) 3m 50s.

SS 7. Clumber 2 (6.94 km)
1 Biasion/Siviero (Ford), Alén/Kivimäki (Toyota) 3m 44s; 3 McRae/Ringer (Subaru), Auriol/Occelli (Lancia), Wilson/Thomas (Ford), Blomqvist/Melander (Nissan) 3m 45s.

SS 8. Chatsworth (8.64 km)
1 Kankkunen/Piironen (Lancia) 6m 23s; 2 McRae/Ringer (Subaru) 6m 25s; 3 Sainz/Moya (Toyota), Biasion/Siviero (Ford), Vatanen/Berglund (Subaru) 6m 30s; 6 Mäkinen/Harjanne (Nissan) 6m 31s.

SS 9. Oulton Park 2 (5.07 km)
1 Biasion/Siviero (Ford) 3m 31s; 2 Alén/Kivimäki (Toyota) 3m 32s; 3 Kankkunen/Piironen (Lancia), Sainz/Moya (Toyota) 3m 33s; 5 McRae/Ringer (Subaru) 3m 34s; 6 Blomqvist/Melander (Nissan) 3m 35s.

SS 10. Dyfnant (21.66 km)
1 Auriol/Occelli (Lancia) 13m 33s; 2 Kankkunen/Piironen (Lancia), McRae/Ringer (Subaru) 13m 35s; 4 Sainz/Moya (Toyota) 13m 37s; 5 Vatanen/Berglund (Subaru) 13m 41s; 6 Biasion/Siviero (Ford) 13m 46s.

SS 11. Myherin (32.94 km)
1 McRae/Ringer (Subaru) 19m 38s; 2 Sainz/Moya (Toyota), Wilson/Thomas (Ford) 19m 41s; 4 Auriol/ Occelli (Lancia) 19m 46s; 5 Vatanen/Berglund (Subaru) 19m 51s; 6 Alén/Kivimäki (Toyota) 19m 56s.

SS 12. Hafren (24.25 km)
1 McRae/Ringer (Subaru) 14m 54s; 2 Sainz/Moya (Toyota) 15m 02s; 3 Auriol/Occelli (Lancia) 15m 05s; 4 Kankkunen/Piironen (Lancia), Wilson/Thomas (Ford) 15m 07s; 6 Alén/Kivimäki (Toyota) 15m 10s.

SS 13. Pantperthog (15.14 km)
1 Sainz/Moya (Toyota) 7m 50s; 2 Auriol/Occelli (Lancia) 7m 51s; 3 McRae/Ringer (Subaru) 7m 52s; 4 Alén/Kivimäki (Toyota), Wilson/Thomas (Ford) 7m 53s; 6 Vatanen/Berglund (Subaru) 7m 55s.

SS 14. Dyfi Main (24.59 km)
1 McRae/Ringer (Subaru) 15m 01s; 2 Auriol/Occelli (Lancia) 15m 09s; 3 Sainz/Moya (Toyota) 15m 10s; 4 Wilson/Thomas (Ford) 15m 11s; 5 Alén/Kivimäki (Toyota) 15m 13s; 6 Kankkunen/Piironen (Lancia) 15m 14s.

SS 15. Gartheiniog (24.61 km)
1 McRae/Ringer (Subaru) 14m 06s; 2 Sainz/Moya (Toyota) 14m 13s; 3 Auriol/Occelli (Lancia) 14m 15s; 4 Alén/Kivimäki (Toyota), Wilson/Thomas (Ford) 14m 18s; 6 Kankkunen/Piironen (Lancia) 14m 22s.

SS 16. Penmachno South (13.37 km)
1 McRae/Ringer (Subaru), Wilson/Thomas (Ford) 7m 38s; 3 Kankkunen/Piironen (Lancia) 7m 40s; 4 Auriol/Occelli (Lancia), Vatanen/Berglund (Subaru) 7m 41s; 5 Sainz/Moya (Toyota) 7m 46s; 6 Biasion/ Siviero (Ford) 7m 47s.

SS 17. Penmachno North (11.35 km)
1 Biasion/Siviero (Ford), Wilson/Thomas (Ford) 6m 54s; 3 McRae/Ringer (Subaru), Auriol/Occelli (Lancia) 6m 55s; 5 Sainz/Moya (Toyota) 6m 56s; 6 Vatanen/Berglund (Subaru) 6m 57s.

SS 18. Brenig (9.78 km)
1 Alén/Kivimäki (Toyota) 5m 51s; 2 Vatanen/Berglund (Subaru) 5m 52s; 3 Auriol/Occelli (Lancia) 5m 54s; 4 Biasion/Siviero (Ford), McRae/Ringer (Subaru), Wilson/Thomas (Ford) 5m 55s.

SS 19. Clocaenog (19.25 km)
1 Vatanen/Berglund (Subaru) 10m 55s; 2 Sainz/Moya (Toyota) 10m 57s; 3 Kankkunen/Piironen (Lancia) 11m 02s; 4 Auriol/Occelli (Lancia) 11m 04s; 5 Alén/Kivimäki (Toyota) 11m 06s; 6 McRae/Ringer (Subaru) 11m 07s.

SS 20. Grizedale East. (7.19 km)
1 Sainz/Moya (Toyota) 4m 57s; 2 Vatanen/Berglund (Subaru) 5m 00s; 3 Kankkunen/Piironen (Lancia), Auriol/Occelli (Lancia) 5m 01s; 5 Mäkinen/Harjanne (Nissan) 5m 02s; 6 Alén/Kivimäki (Toyota) 5m 03s.

SS 21. Grizedale West (27.86 km)
1 Auriol/Occelli (Lancia) 18m 49s; 2 Vatanen/Berglund (Subaru) 19m 02s; 3 Kankkunen/Piironen (Lancia), Biasion/Siviero (Ford) 19m 08s; 5 Sainz/Moya (Toyota), Wilson/Thomas (Ford) 19m 13s.

SS 22. Comb (8.71 km)
1 Auriol/Occelli (Lancia) 5m 56s; 2 Alén/Kivimäki (Toyota) 5m 57s; 3 Sainz/Moya (Toyota) 5m 59s; 4 McRae/Ringer (Subaru), Wilson/Thomas (Ford) 6m 02s; 6 Mäkinen/Harjanne (Nissan) 6m 03s.

SS 23. Wythop (5.20 km)
1 Auriol/Occelli (Lancia), Wilson/Thomas (Ford) 3m 03s; 3 Alén/Kivimäki (Toyota) 3m 04s; 4 Sainz/Moya (Toyota) 3m 05s; 5 Kankkunen/Piironen (Lancia) 3m 06s; 6 McRae/Ringer (Subaru), Mäkinen (Nissan) 3m 07s.

SS 24. Kershope (33.03 km)
Cancelled.

SS 25. Wauchope (16.21 km)
1 Sainz/Moya (Toyota) 9m 00s; 2 Auriol/Occelli (Lancia), Vatanen/Berglund (Subaru) 9m 09s; 4 Kankkunen/Piironen (Lancia) 9m 11s; 5 McRae/Ringer (Subaru) 9m 13s; 6 Wilson/Thomas (Ford) 9m 15s.

SS 26. Broomylinn (27.63 km)
1 McRae/Ringer (Subaru) 16m 33s; 2 Kankkunen/Piironen (Lancia) 16m 41s; 3 Wilson/Thomas (Ford) 16m 46s; 4 Sainz/Moya (Toyota) 16m 48s; 5 Vatanen/Berglund (Subaru) 16m 50s; 6 Biasion/Siviero (Ford) 17m 01s.

SS 27. Pundershaw (42.90 km)
1 Kankkunen/Piironen (Lancia) 23m 31s; 2 Sainz/Moya (Toyota) 23m 34s; 3 McRae/Ringer (Subaru) 23m 35s; 4 Alén/Kivimäki (Toyota) 24m 18s; 5 Biasion/Siviero (Ford) 24m 20s; 6 Vatanen/ Berglund (Subaru) 24m 25s.

SS 28. Shepherdshield (20.68 km)
1 Vatanen/Berglund (Subaru) 11m 12s; 2 Sainz/Moya (Toyota) 11m 14s; 3 McRae/Ringer (Subaru) 11m 17s; 4 Kankkunen/Piironen (Lancia) 11m 24s; 5 Biasion/Siviero (Ford) 11m 31s; 6 Alén/ Kivimäki (Toyota) 11m 36s.

SS 29. Dalbeattie (12.34 km)
1 Wilson/Thomas (Ford) 8m 54s; 2 Mäkinen/Harjanne (Nissan) 8m 59s; 3 Vatanen/Berglund (Subaru)

9m 00s; 4 A. Aghini/S. Farnocchia (Lancia Delta HF Integrale) 9m 05s; 5 Alén/Kivimäki (Toyota) 9m 07s; 6 Sainz/Moya (Toyota) 9m 08s.

SS 30. Glengap (14.35 km)
1 McRae/Ringer (Subaru), Wilson/Thomas (Ford) 9m 05s; 3 Vatanen/Berglund (Subaru) 9m 08s; 4 Alén/Kivimäki (Toyota) 9m 14s; 5 Kankkunen/Piironen (Lancia) 9m 16s; 6 Sainz/Moya (Toyota) 9m 17s.

SS 31. Loch Derry (10.22 km)
1 Wilson/Thomas (Ford), Vatanen/Berglund (Subaru) 5m 53s; 3 Alén/Kivimäki (Toyota) 5m 58s; 4 Sainz/Moya (Toyota) 5m 59s; 5 Kankkunen/Piironen (Lancia) 6m 00s; 6 Biasion/Siviero (Ford), McRae/Ringer (Subaru) 6m 02s.

SS 32. Glentrool (10.44 km)
1 Vatanen/Berglund (Subaru) 16m 45s; 2 Wilson/Thomas (Ford) 16m 48s; 3 Sainz/Moya (Toyota) 16m 53s; 4 Kankkunen/Piironen (Lancia) 16m 55s; 5 Alén/Kivimäki (Toyota) 16m 58s; 6 Biasion/Siviero (Ford), McRae/Ringer (Subaru) 16m 59s.

SS 33. Loch Fleet (12.41 km)
1 Kankkunen/Piironen (Lancia) 14m 08s; 2 McRae/Ringer (Subaru) 14m 20s; 3 Wilson/Thomas (Ford) 14m 23s; 4 Biasion/Siviero (Ford), Vatanen/ Berglund (Subaru) 14m 28s; 6 Alén/Kivimäki (Toyota) 14m 30s.

SS 34. Ae (30.58 km)
1 Kankkunen/Piironen (Lancia) 18m 44s; 2 McRae/Ringer (Subaru) 18m 56s; 3 Mäkinen/Harjanne (Nissan) 18m 57s; 4 Biasion/Siviero (Ford) 19m 02s; 5 Alén/Kivimäki (Toyota) 19m 10s; 6 Eriksson/Parmander (Mitsubishi) 19m 12s.

FIA class winners

Group A
Over 2000 cc:	Sainz/Moya (Toyota)
1600-2000 cc:	Stephen Bennett/Duncan McMath (Peugeot 205 GTI)
1300-1600 cc:	Paul Griffiths/Jon Madoc-Jones (Toyota Corolla GTi)
Up to 1000 cc:	Sibera/Gross (Skoda)

Group N
Over 2000 cc:	Alister McRae/David Senior (Ford Sierra Cosworth 4x4)
1600-2000 cc:	Brendan Crealey/Nick Beech (Peugeot 309 GTI 16v)
1300-1600 cc:	Mike Williams/John Youd (Vauxhall Nova GSi)
Up to 1300 cc:	Bryan Shipp/David Moreton (Peugeot 205 Rallye)

Major retirements

Jarmo Kytölehto/ Voitto Silander	Mitsubishi Galant VR-4 SS 11	suspension
Fernando Capdevila/ Alfredo Rodriguez	Ford Sierra Cosworth 4x4 SS 21	front diff
Didier Auriol/ Bernard Occelli	Lancia Delta HF Integrale SS 26	engine
Stig Blomqvist/ Benny Melander	Nissan Sunny GTi-R SS 27	accident

Time stands still and even the weather ceases to matter when the world's best rally drivers make their annual visit to the forests: Markku Alén's lamps pick out the spectators lining the road.

Rally leaders

SS 1-14 Sainz/Moya (Toyota); SS 15-19 McRae/Ringer (Subaru); SS 20-34 Sainz/Moya (Toyota).

World Championship points

Drivers
1 Sainz 144; 2 Kankkunen 134; 3 Auriol 121; 4 Biasion 60; 5 Alén 50; 6 Delecour 45; 7 Aghini 39; 8 McRae 34; 9 Fiorio 32; 10 Recalde 28.

Manufacturers
1 Lancia 140 (191); 2 Toyota 116 (132); 3 Ford 94; 4 Subaru 60; 5 Mitsubishi 44; 6 Nissan 37; 7 Audi 10; 8 Renault Argentina 7; 9 Renault and GM Europe 2.

Route details

Leg 1
22 November: Starting and finishing in Chester 0645-1830, including nine special stages (58.08 km).
Leg 2
23 November: Starting and finishing in Chester 0500-1930, including 10 special stages (196.95 km).
Leg 3
24 November: Starting from Chester at 0700 and finishing at Carlisle at 20.45, including nine special stages (1 cancelled - 156.39 km).
Leg 4
25 November: Starting from Carlisle at 0545 and finishing at Chester at 20.00, including six special stages (123.37 km).

Weather

Wet and miserable with some very heavy downpours.

Special stage analysis

	1st	2nd	3rd	4th	5th	6th
McRae/Ringer (Subaru)	8	6	5	2	2	3
Wilson/Thomas (Ford)	7	2	3	8	2	1
Sainz/Moya (Toyota)	6	7	6	4	3	2
Vatanen/Berglund (Subaru)	4	4	4	3	3	3
Auriol/Occelli (Lancia)	4	3	6	3	-	3
Kankkunen/Piironen (Lancia)	4	2	6	4	5	3
Alén/Kivimäki (Toyota)	3	2	3	4	5	6
Biasion/Siviero (Ford)	3	3	3	3	2	4
Mäkinen/Harjanne (Nissan)	-	1	1	2	1	3
Blomqvist/Melander (Nissan)	-	-	3	-	2	3
Eriksson/Parmander (Mitsubishi)	-	-	-	1	2	1
Aghini/Farnocchia (Lancia)	-	-	1	-	-	-

Results

1	Carlos Sainz/ Luis Moya	Toyota Celica Turbo 4WD	5h 23m 06s	Gr A
2	Ari Vatanen/ Bruno Berglund	Subaru Legacy RS	5h 25m 22s	Gr A
3	Juha Kankkunen/ Juha Piironen	Lancia Delta HF Integrale	5h 25m 51s	Gr A
4	Markku Alén/ Ilkka Kivimäki	Toyoto Celica Turbo 4WD	5h 26m 35s	Gr A
5	Massimo Biasion/ Tiziano Siviero	Ford Sierra Cosworth 4x4	5h 26m 47s	Gr A
6	Colin McRae/ Derek Ringer	Subaru Legacy RS	5h 31m 14s	Gr A
7	Kenneth Eriksson/ Staffan Parmander	Mitsubishi Galant VR-4	5h 33m 26s	Gr A
8	Tommi Mäkinen/ Seppo Harjanne	Nissan Sunny GTi-R	5h 35m 07s	Gr A
9	Malcolm Wilson/ Bryan Thomas	Ford Sierra Cosworth 4x4	5h 35m 26s	Gr A
10	Andrea Aghini/ Sauro Farnocchia	Lancia Delta HF Integrale	5h 57m 58s	Gr A

156 starters, 102 finishers

Previous winners (since 1960)

1992

RESULTS

FIA WORLD RALLY CHAMPIONSHIP FOR DRIVERS

Round		1	2	3	4	5	6	7	8	9	10	11	12	13	14	Total
1	Carlos Sainz	15	-	12	20	10	-	20	15	-	12	-	-	20	20	**144**
2	Juha Kankkunen	12	-	20	15	-	15	-	-	15	15	15	-	15	12	**134**
3	Didier Auriol	20	-	-	-	20	20	-	20	20	20	-	-	1	-	**121**
4	Massimo Biasion	3	-	15	-	4	12	-	-	8	-	10	-	-	8	**60**
5	Markku Alén	-	10	10	8	-	-	-	-	12	-	-	-	-	10	**50**
6	François Delecour	10	-	-	-	15	8	-	-	-	-	12	-	-	-	**45**
7	Andrea Aghini	-	-	-	-	6	-	-	-	-	-	20	-	12	1	**39**
8	Colin McRae	-	15	-	-	-	10	-	-	3	-	-	-	-	6	**34**
9	Alessandro Fiorio	-	-	-	-	-	4	-	10	-	-	8	-	10	-	**32**
10	Jorge Recalde	-	-	-	12	-	6	-	-	-	10	-	-	-	-	**28**
11=	Philippe Bugalski	8	-	-	-	12	-	-	-	2	-	-	-	-	-	**22**
11=	Piero Liatti	-	-	-	-	3	-	15	-	-	-	4	-	-	-	**22**
13	Kenjiro Shinozuka	-	-	-	1	-	-	-	-	-	-	-	20	-	-	**21**
14=	Ross Dunkerton	-	-	-	-	-	-	12	-	-	8	-	-	-	-	**20**
14=	Mats Jonsson	-	20	-	-	-	-	-	-	-	-	-	-	-	-	**20**
16	Bruno Thiry	-	-	-	-	-	-	-	-	-	-	2	15	-	-	**17**
17=	Armin Schwarz	-	-	-	-	8	-	-	-	-	-	-	-	8	-	**16**
17=	Gustavo Trelles	-	-	-	-	-	-	-	12	-	-	-	-	4	-	**16**
19	Timo Salonen	6	-	8	-	-	-	-	-	-	-	-	-	-	-	**14**
20=	Stig Blomqvist	-	12	-	-	-	-	-	-	-	-	-	-	-	-	**12**
20=	Ed Ordynski	-	-	-	-	-	-	-	8	-	-	4	-	-	-	**12**
20=	Hiroshi Nishiyama	-	-	-	-	-	-	-	2	-	-	-	10	-	-	**12**
23=	Mikael Ericsson	-	-	-	10	-	-	-	-	-	-	-	-	-	-	**10**
23=	François Chatriot	4	-	6	-	-	-	-	-	-	-	-	-	-	-	**10**
23=	Mikael Sundström	-	-	-	-	-	-	10	-	-	-	-	-	-	-	**10**
26=	Leif Asterhag	-	8	-	-	-	-	-	-	-	-	-	-	-	-	**8**
26=	Rudi Stohl	-	-	-	-	-	-	-	8	-	-	-	-	-	-	**8**
26=	Per Eklund	-	6	-	2	-	-	-	-	-	-	-	-	-	-	**8**
26=	Carlos Menem	-	-	2	-	-	-	-	6	-	-	-	-	-	-	**8**
26=	Samir Assef	-	-	-	-	-	-	-	-	-	-	-	8	-	-	**8**

FIA WORLD RALLY CHAMPIONSHIP FOR GROUP N

Round		1	2	3	4	5	6	7	8	9	10	11	12	13	14	Total
1	Grégoire de Mevius	-	-	7	-	-	13	-	-	7	-	-	-	-	10	**37**
2	Hiroshi Nishiyama	-	-	-	5	-	-	-	10	-	-	-	13	-	-	**28**
3	Carlos Menem	-	-	13	-	-	-	-	13	-	-	-	-	-	-	**26**
4=	Jarmo Kytölehto	-	10	-	-	-	-	-	-	13	-	-	-	-	-	**23**
4=	Ed Ordynski	-	-	-	-	-	-	10	-	-	13	-	-	-	-	**23**
6	Fernando Capdevila	-	-	4	-	-	10	-	-	-	-	-	-	8	-	**22**
7	Giovanni Manfrinato	-	-	-	-	5	-	-	-	-	-	13	-	-	-	**18**
8	Mohammed Bin Sulayem	-	-	-	-	-	-	2	-	-	-	-	-	13	-	**15**
9=	Christophe Spiliotis	13	-	-	-	-	-	-	-	-	-	-	-	-	-	**13**
9=	Soren Nilsson	-	13	-	-	-	-	-	-	-	-	-	-	-	-	**13**
9=	Patrick Njiru	-	-	-	13	-	-	-	-	-	-	-	-	-	-	**13**
9=	Jean-Marie Santoni	-	-	-	-	13	-	-	-	-	-	-	-	-	-	**13**
9=	Mikael Sundström	-	-	-	-	-	-	13	-	-	-	-	-	-	-	**13**
9=	Alister McRae	-	-	-	-	-	-	-	-	-	-	-	-	-	13	**13**

Key to rounds: 1 Monte Carlo; 2 Swedish; 3 Portugal; 4 Safari; 5 Corsica; 6 Acropolis; 7 New Zealand; 8 Argentina; 9 1000 Lakes; 10 Australia; 11 Sanremo; 12 Ivory Coast; 13 Catalonia; 14 RAC.

FIA WORLD RALLY CHAMPIONSHIP FOR MANUFACTURERS

Round		1	2	3	4	5	6	7	8	9	10	Total	
1	**Lancia**	20	20	(17)	20	20	20	20	20	(20)	(14)	**140**	(191)
2	**Toyota**	17	14	20	(12)	(4)	17	14	14	-	20	**116**	(132)
3	**Ford**	12	17	-	17	14	-	10	-	14	10	**94**	
4	**Subaru**	-	-	11	-	12	-	12	8	-	17	**60**	
5	**Mitsubishi**	8	10	2	-	-	-	8	10	-	6	**44**	
6	**Nissan**	6	8	-	-	10	9	-	-	-	4	**37**	
7	**Audi**	-	-	-	-	-	10	-	-	-	-	**10**	
8	**Renault Argentina**	-	-	-	-	-	7	-	-	-	-	**7**	
9=	**Renault**	-	-	-	2	-	-	-	-	-	-	**2**	
9=	**GM Europe**	-	-	-	-	-	-	-	-	2	-	**2**	

Key to rounds: 1 Monte Carlo; **2** Portugal; **3** Safari; **4** Corsica; **5** Acropolis; **6** Argentina; **7** 1000 Lakes; **8** Australia; **9** Sanremo; **10** RAC.

Ford had its best World Championship season in years, the Sierras becoming solid top three finishers. Curiously, they did less well on home ground, despite Malcolm Wilson's best efforts.

1992
RALLY CAR SPECIFICATIONS

Toyota Celica Turbo 4WD

Opel/Vauxhall Calibra 16v

Renault Clio 16v

Car	Opel/Vauxhall Calibra 16v	Toyota Celica Turbo 4WD	Renault Clio 16v
Team Manager	Motor Sport Developments Ltd	Ove Andersson	Patrick Landon
Chief Engineer	David Whitehead	Dieter Bulling	Gilles Lallement
Sponsor/s	Michelin, De Carbon	Repsol, Marlboro	Elf, Michelin, Diac, Philips Car Stereo
Engine			
Cylinders	4 in-line	4 in-line	4 in-line
Mounts	Transverse/front	Transverse/front	Transverse/front
Capacity	1998 cc	1988 cc	1790 cc
Bore & stroke	86.0 x 86.0 mm	86 x 86 mm	82.6 x 83.5 mm
Compression ratio	11.8:1	8.5:1	12:1
Valves/camshafts	16/DOHC	16/4	16/DOHC
Fuel system	MBE electronic injection	Nippondenso electronic injection	Sodemo Sytel electronic injection
Turbocharger	—	Toyota CT26	—
Max. power	225 bhp @ 7500 rpm	299 bhp @ 5600 rpm	200 bhp @ 7200 rpm
Max. torque	230 N/m @ 5500 rpm	460 Nm @ 4000 rpm	21 kg/m @ 6200 rpm
Oil contract	Mobil	Repsol	Elf
Transmission			
Gearbox	GM/Xtrac 6-speed	Xtrac 6-speed	6-speed
Drive type	2WD (front)	4WD	2WD (front)
Clutch/differentials	AP single-plate	Xtrac diffs with hydraulic control/FF Developments viscous coupling	Tilton single-plate
Chassis			
Steering	Rack and pinion power assisted	Rack and pinion assisted	Rack and pinion assisted
Front suspension	McPherson strut (De Carbon dampers)	McPherson strut with Bilstein shock absorbers	McPherson strut aluminium hub carriers, Bilstein dampers
Rear suspension	Independent trailing arms (De Carbon dampers)	McPherson strut with Bilstein shock absorbers	Trailing arms, torsion bars, extra anti-roll bar, Bilstein dampers
Wheel rim widths	6.0 x 15 in./7.5 x 17 in. (OZ Racing)	6–8 x 15–17 in.	7.25 x 16 in. Speedline
Tyres	Michelin	Pirelli	Michelin
Front brakes	295 x 28 mm and 325 x 28 mm (6 pot)	Ventilated discs	315 mm ventilated discs, 4-pot caliper
Rear brakes	254 x 21 mm (2 pot)	Ventilated discs	254 mm ventilated discs, 2-pot caliper
Dimensions			
Overall length	4492 mm	4410 mm	3728 mm
Overall width	1688 mm	1745 mm	1645 mm
Height	1520 mm	1300 mm	1365 mm
Wheelbase	2600 mm	2545 mm	2472 mm
Weight	1100 kg	1130 kg	880 kg
Front track	1446 mm	1510 mm	1372 mm
Rear track	1426 mm	1510 mm	1351 mm
Body	3-door steel	3-door steel	3-door steel

Ford Sierra RS Cosworth 4x4

Mitsubishi Galant VR-4

Lancia Delta HF Integrale

Car	Ford Sierra RS Cosworth 4x4	Lancia Delta HF Integrale	Mitsubishi Galant VR-4
Team Manager	Colin Dobinson	Claudio Bortoletto	Andrew Cowan
Chief Engineer	Philip Dunabin	Vittorio Roberti	Roland Lloyd
Sponsor/s	Mobil, Autoglass	Martini Racing	Mitsubishi Oil, Michelin, PIAA, Sabelt, Bilstein
Engine			
Cylinders	4 in-line	4 in-line	4 in-line
Mounts	Front, north-south	Transverse/front	Transverse/front
Capacity	1998 cc	1995 cc	1997 cc
Bore & stroke	90.8 x 77.0 mm	84 x 90 mm	85.0 x 88.0 mm
Compression ratio	7.2:1	—	8.5:1
Valves/camshafts	16/DOHC	16/DOHC	16/DOHC
Fuel system	Weber/Marelli electronic injection and ignition	Digital IAW-Weber electronic injection	Electronic injection
Turbocharger	Garrett TB03	Garrett T3, air to air intercooler	Mitsubishi
Max. power	300 bhp @ 6500 rpm	295 bhp @ 7000 rpm	298 bhp
Max. torque	400 Nm @ 4500 rpm	43 kg/m @ 4500 rpm	42 kg/m
Oil contract	Mobil	Fiat Lubrificanti/Selenia	Mitsubishi Oil
Transmission			
Gearbox	Ford MS90 7-speed, non-synchromesh	6-speed	6-speed
Drive type	4WD	4WD, central self-locking torque split	4WD
Clutch/differentials	AP 7.25 twin-plate/VC	2-plate, ZF plate-type front and rear differentials	single-plate/VC and plate diff. options
Chassis			
Steering	Rack and pinion (assisted)	Rack and pinion (assisted)	Rack and pinion (assisted), 4WS
Front suspension	McPherson compression/ strut with TCA	McPherson strut, lower wishbone, anti–roll bar	McPherson strut
Rear suspension	Semi-trailing arm with coil over springs and dampers	McPherson strut, transverse link, anti–roll bar	Independent double wishbone with trailing arms
Wheel rim widths	6–8 x 16–17 in.	9 x 16/17 in. (asp), 5.5/7 x 15/16 in. (grav)	5.0/6.0/7.0/8.0 x 16 in., 9.0 x 17 in.
Tyres	Michelin	Michelin	Michelin
Front brakes	315-355 x 28 mm with 4-pot AP caliper	282/313/332 mm ventilated discs	4- or 6-pot caliper, ventilated discs
Rear brakes	285 x 28 mm with 4-pot AP caliper	282 mm ventilated discs	4- or 6-pot caliper, ventilated discs
Dimensions			
Overall length	4498 mm	3900 mm	4560 mm
Overall width	1697 mm	1770 mm	1695 mm
Height	1420 mm	1360 mm	1440 mm
Wheelbase	2625 mm	2480 mm	2600 mm
Weight	1190 kg	1100 kg	1200 kg
Front track	1464 mm	1566 mm	1400 mm
Rear track	1480 mm	1526 mm	1450 mm
Body	unitary 4-door steel	5-door steel	4-door steel

Nissan Sunny GTi-R

Peugeot 309 GTI 16v

Subaru Legacy RS

Car	Nissan Sunny GTi-R	Peugeot 309 GTI 16v	Subaru Legacy RS
Team Manager	Dave Whittock	Mick Linford	David Richards
Chief Engineer	Dave Gray	Chris Gradon	David Lapworth
Sponsor/s	JECS, Castrol, Dunlop	Shell, Dunlop, Hella, Bilstein, Sabelt	Rothmans
Engine			
Cylinders	4 in-line	4 in-line	Flat-4
Mounts	Transverse/front	Transverse/front	Front, in-line
Capacity	1998 cc	1927 cc	1994 cc
Bore & stroke	86 0 x 86.0 mm	83 5 x 88.0 rnm	92.6 x 75.0 mm
Compression ratio	8.2:1	11.5:1	8:1
Valves/camshafts	16/DOHC	16/DOHC	16/4
Fuel system	JECS 'L' Jetronic	Zytek electronic injection	Subaru
Turbocharger	Garrett	—	IHI
Max. power	300 bhp @ 6400 rpm	210 bhp	295 bhp @ 6400 rpm
Max. torque	over 35 kg/m @ 4800 rpm	21.5 kg/m @ 6000 rpm	320 Nm
Oil contract	Castrol	Shell	BP
Transmission			
Gearbox	6-speed	Peugeot BE3 6-speed	6-speed
Drive type	Electronic torque split 4WD	2WD (front)	4WD
Clutch/differentials	AP twin-plate	AP single-plate cerametallic clutch	AP carbon, Prodrive diffs with hydraulic control
Chassis			
Steering	Rack and pinion	Rack and pinion (assisted)	Rack and pinion
Front suspension	McPherson strut (Kayaba dampers)	Independent McPherson strut Bilstein dampers	Struts with TCA
Rear suspension	Parallel link strut (Kayaba dampers)	Torsion bars, Bilstein dampers	Struts with lateral and triangle links
Wheel rim widths	6.0 x 15 in./7.0/8.0 x 16 in.	Speedline/Revolution 6.0/7.0 x 15 in.	7.0 x 16 in. (grav), 18.0 x 17 in. (asp)
Tyres	Dunlop	Dunlop	Michelin/Pirelli
Front brakes	Ventilated discs	315 mm ventilated discs	AP 330–355 x 32 mm ventilated discs
Rear brakes	Ventilated discs	264 mm solid discs	AP 304 x 28 mm ventilated discs
Dimensions			
Overall length	3975 mm	4050 mm	4150 mm
Overall width	1695 mm	1650 mm	1705 mm
Height	1400 mm	1380 mm	1325 mm
Wheelbase	2430 mm	2470 mm	2580 mm
Weight	1140 kg	880 kg	1150 kg
Front track	1445 mm	1410 mm	1450 mm
Rear track	1435 mm	1380 mm	1450 mm
Body	3-door steel	3-door steel	4-door steel

An appreciation

Robin Turvey

by David Williams

It came as a surprise to find out that Robin Turvey was 62. He never looked it, and his outlook on life never reflected it. At his funeral, someone said that he would probably have liked to have died as he did, playing squash. Even close friends were astonished to hear him recall fire-watching during the Second World War.

One never questioned his age, because he never forced his years of experience and his considerable achievements down one's throat. His modesty was unfailing: anyone wanting to find out about works Tigers and Tulip Rallies had to ask. Robin mixed easily with a younger generation, some of whom had no first hand experience of road rallies, never mind the endurance events of the 1960s. On his final appearance for Vauxhall, on the 24 Hours of Ieper last June, he shared a Carlton chase car with Mark Higgins, who was young enough to have been his grandson.

Robin started rallying as a driver in 1953, but soon changed seats and earned a fine reputation as a meticulous and unflappable navigator. He made his first international appearance on the 1961 RAC, co-driving Tiny Lewis, and then joined the Rootes factory team, initially in Sunbeam Rapiers. However, he contested more events in the formidable 4.2-litre Tigers than any other works co-driver, guiding Andrew Cowan to an impressive top 15 result through the blizzards of the 1965 Monte, and then taking third place on the 1966 Tulip with Peter Harper.

Subsequently, he navigated works Imps, Fiat 124s and Opel Asconas, teaming up with anyone from Tony Fall to Brian Culcheth; he was second on the 1973 Acropolis with Rauno Aaltonen in a factory 124 Spider. He threw in his lot with Opel in 1974, by which time he had already established a reputation as an exceptional service co-ordinator, playing a significant part in Lancia's victories on the RAC Rally with Harry Kallstrom and the Fulvias. In addition to working with Jochen Berger at Opel in Germany, he became a key member of Dealer Opel Team in Britain. It was a small operation at first, but Robin's thorough preparation ensured that it was as effective as any of its rivals, and Jim McRae's Open Championship triumphs owed a great deal to faultless service planning; there was no such thing as a missed service point.

Robin set new standards in a field that even the biggest factories were liable to neglect, and most works teams now owe something to his influence and methods. He achieved results through exhaustive planning and, while his rivals dashed around dealing with last minute crises, he could be found enjoying a quiet drink at the bar. He had covered every contingency before leaving Weston-super-Mare — semi-works teams would get a copy of the service schedule as a matter of course, and journalists were also provided for as though they were his sole responsibility. In many ways, he resembled Henry Liddon. Courteous and softly spoken, he relied on a remarkable memory, an effortless talent as a fixer, and a gift for remaining unruffled in the face of intense pressure. Like Henry, his success stemmed from attention to detail rather than acting as a martinet. Moreover, his opponents were happy to admit that he was always ready to help.

Remarkably, he spent 39 years in rallying, much of it at a factory level, without once becoming a professional. After a spell at the Admiralty in Bath, he joined the south-western electricity board as a surveyor, and somehow managed to combine a full-time job with a time-consuming hobby. In acting as a professional, he proved himself to be an extraordinarily gifted amateur.

OLD WINE SEEKS NEW BOTTLE?

By Paul Evans, Assistant Rallies Editor, Motoring News

Time is a great healer. Perhaps memories of the 1992 Mobil 1/ *Top Gear* British Rally Championship will, like claret, become better as the years pass. It will never be considered a fine vintage, but at least the taste of vinegar that sometimes prevailed during the season may diminish.

With 112 registered contenders, the premier British series suffered proportionately less from a decline in entries than international championships on the continent, and at national level, particularly in the Mintex National Series and single make championships like the Peugeot Challenge — which alone mustered over 100 registered drivers — British rallying did a good deal better. However, it was only natural that the highest and therefore most expensive level bore the brunt of the decline in the present economic cli-

Photo Gavin Lodge

mate, although it is fair to say that some of the events looked poor value for money into the bargain.

Despite the number of crews registered, no more than half regularly took part in rallies and, since clubs usually needed over 60 cars to meet the costs incurred in running an international, two major events, the De Lacy and Welsh International Rallies, were cancelled. Three of the survivors, namely the Vauxhall Sport Rally (which as its name suggests had a manufacturer backing it) and the Scottish and Manx Rallies (which had the local tourist board and district council support), were well financed, whereas the remainder, the Pirelli (Cumbria), Elbow Inn Ulster and Elonex Rallies survived after finding limited backing at the 11th hour, although Northern Ireland MC

had committed itself to running the Ulster come what may. Given the economic situation, there is a good deal of justice in saying that the events were too expensive to run and directed at people who could not afford to contest them. Riding out a turbulent sea was the main priority, and the survivors deserve nothing less than calmer waters in 1993.

Already, time has healed the disappointment of the first round cancellation, as the new champion steals the attention. People involved in the 1992 British Championship, be they officials or spectators, will reflect on the year they were privileged to see Colin McRae reach new standards of excellence. Retaining his British title was done with ease but, despite the lack of competition, with total commitment and professionalism.

McRae's second British crown removed traces of doubt rather than staking his claim to be considered a top class driver. Disposing of the opposition was usually done on the first stage and, even though he spent a considerable proportion of the season driving well within his capabilities, he set fastest times on 92 of the 112 special stages that made up the 1992 series! After the first stage of the Vauxhall Sport Rally, his lead was 19s; on the Pirelli International it was 39s; on the Scottish it was just three seconds (although it was only a 2.41-mile blast around Knockhill, and after the first forest stage he was 38s ahead of the field); the Ulster, the Manx International and the Elonex all commenced with short stages, although that didn't prevent him from gaining a three-second lead

on each, which was generally more than a second per mile. Apart from Tommi Mäkinen, who pushed him extremely hard on the last event, and Bertie Fisher for a brief, remarkable spell on the Isle of Man, McRae was never seen again.

Colin had new pressures to face, however. Maintaining concentration was a constant challenge, and sometimes he felt that his success was barely welcomed. 'People are just waiting, some would love for me to make a mistake and go off the road,' he sighed during the Manx. If there was such a feeling, it was not because he is disliked — on the contrary — but in the vain hope that a slight error might turn a procession into a contest. It was the press grasping at straws, searching for exciting stories which didn't exist at

162

the head of the field. Finding a thought-provoking question to ask Colin was sometimes difficult. For instance, what do you ask a chap who is leading the Manx International Rally by almost seven minutes? Any problems? just didn't seem appropriate.

'After we finished second in Sweden at the beginning of the year, everyone expected us to be miles in front in the British Championship. We'd won the rallies before we'd even started,' admitted McRae. 'That does put a bit of pressure on you, because you know you should win the rallies — you've got the equipment and you've got the team there to win — but all you need to do is make one small mistake. Quite often when you're only driving at 90 per cent you can make a mistake a lot easier than when you're driving at 100 per cent. Concentration lapses a

event by almost four and a half minutes regardless. Only once, on the Manx International, did his concentration really slip, allowing Fisher the honour of becoming the only man other than McRae to lead a round of the British Championship until that point. It lasted precisely one stage before the status quo was restored. A severe talking to from the Prodrive management, who reminded Colin that he was on the Isle of Man to win and not to play with the opposition — or to give reporters something to write about — was enough and a blistering run over the remaining 24 stages enabled him to carve out a seven-minute victory margin. It also presented him with the title with one round remaining.

Only Nissan used the Elonex Rally to test for the Lombard RAC, and in the form of Tommi Mäkinen

very nature of the sport, where drivers are required to perform in a variety of slippery and unpredictable conditions means that no driver can be infallible. Nevertheless, McRae came of age in 1992, relinquishing his tendency to have unpressured accidents and becoming a tactician behind the wheel, at least when Mobil points were at stake. It's sometimes easy to overlook the fact that he's still only 24 years of age, and that David Richards took a chance with Prodrive's reputation by gambling on the young Scot in the first place.

Whereas Dave Campion ran the UK programme in 1991, John Spiller took over in 1992. His job was also harder than most gave him credit for, as driver motivation was sometimes in danger. Complacency can be as disastrous as brake failure, and when the need arose, as on the

Black's SBG concern, which ran the Shell Scholarship Sierra driven by Alister McRae, were private rather than factory operations. There were other competitors determined to make the new-look championship work, yet organisers of each of the six events must have spent many a sleepless night wondering if their particular event was going to attract enough entries to break even.

There was one organisation, however, which although it had a direct interest in the series, woefully lacked the commitment which others were seeking. When the RACMSA refuses to let its British Rally Championship Co-ordinator, Steve Fellows, attend important championship meetings, what hope has anyone else of obtaining information that could promote the series? One Clerk of the Course even described the MSA as being 'actively unhelpful' in 1992.

Photo Gavin Lodge

The brothers took the British Championship by storm in 1992: Colin McRae (left) became the first driver to achieve a 100 per cent record in the series, winning as he pleased for Subaru, while Alister dominated Group N in the Shell Scholarship Sierra.

wee bit and things can go wrong; there's a lot of pressure there to win.'

There were a few hiccoughs, but McRae's hold on the lead was such that they rarely carried any significance. When he drove eight miles through Dyfi on the Vauxhall Sport Rally with a rear puncture he still set fastest time. When the head gasket on his Rothmans Subaru had to be replaced during the final leg of the Perth Scottish Rally, he won the

offered McRae his strongest challenge all season. The Subaru team was using the overnight event in mid-Wales for pre-RAC testing as well, throwing different Pirellis at the car no matter what the optimum tyre choice for the stage. It was a close battle, which Mäkinen led for a while, although after a charge through the final two stages at Weston Park, Colin clinched victory by just two seconds. It was the first time a driver had won all the rounds of the British Championship in the same year, and that remarkable achievement is no less than his outstanding efforts in 1992 deserved.

It was a team effort of course, and the team that McRae joined two years ago has been instrumental in developing this naturally talented rebel into a professional driver. The

Manx, he could turn a lacklustre effort into a scintillating display of brilliance, while the rest of the time he played down the extent of his driver's domination. Despite the lack of serious opposition, Prodrive's professionalism never wavered one iota. It was on show to the British public every time it left its factory in Banbury, and its exhibition was a credit to the sport. Even the team's major sponsor was enthusiastically present on all but the final event, the Rothmans promotional team giving the championship some badly needed razzamatazz.

Prodrive was especially conspicuous as one of the few professional teams committed to the series. Most of the others, including Mike Little Preparations, which ran Louise Aitken-Walker's Cosworth, and Steve

The gulf between competitors and the RAC has seldom been so wide, and only the governing body of British motor sport is to blame for that. When the Chief Executive prefers to attend the Oxford v. Cambridge Boat Race instead of the Pirelli International Rally — a new event to the series, which was run by the RACMSA's own Lombard RAC Rally route co-ordinator in the teeth of severe financial problems — it's an insult to everybody. Having a keen interest in rowing is no excuse.

The ripples emanating from Colnbrook, because of the MSA's slow response to addressing the championship's problems, never diminished. While no one expected the RAC to act as a charity and throw money at hard-up organisers like confetti, one questions the need for the cancellation of the De Lacy and Welsh Rallies. It is common knowledge that the MSA has a substantial contingency fund. When this fund allegedly stands at over £1 million, one wonders why it chose to let two of Britain's best known rallies die instead of injecting a small percentage in the form of emergency aid. Why wasn't a minute portion of it used to encourage foreign crews to tackle the events? After all, it is the only rally championship the MSA runs directly.

The championship received a healthy boost when Patrick Snijers came over for the Manx, while that and the Ulster benefited from the extra entries chasing the popular Dunlop Tarmac Championship. Apart from the NME-tuned Sunny GTi-R on the Elonex Rally, McRae was rarely threatened by good quality Group A machinery on anything but asphalt rallies.

It looks as if the Lanark driver will have a bright future in rallying, but it's a tough world out there — just ask David Llewellin, who also won the title two years in succession. Much depends on skill, and a great deal on being in the right place at the right time. At least the former is something that can be developed, and so (to a certain level) can the talented youth that the British Championship highlighted in 1992. The format of the new Lombard Junior Championship, where the winner would be in an under 1600 cc Group A car, wasn't exactly designed to encourage a modestly financed under-25-year-old to compete, but it did bring together two exceptionally good drivers. Both were in works-supported cars, a fact that immediately banished all but a handful of their 24 rivals for the Junior award to the ranks of the also rans. The one possible exception was the promising northern Vauxhall man, Richard Forster. Inevitably, the privateers were often overlooked.

Jon Milner is well known for his aggressive style in his Shell/Simpson Salvage Peugeot 205GTI, but a new, mature Milner emerged as the season progressed. His rapid transformation from rallycross to rallying received an additional boost beyond the £10,000 cheque and the Junior title, when he was unanimously voted the 1993 Shell Rally Scholar.

His arch rival for the Junior Championship, Mark Higgins, enjoyed his first season with the Vauxhall Dealer Sport team and quickly adapted to the works Nova GSi. He finished in the top ten no fewer than four times, with his best result — fifth — coming on the final round. By the end of the year the experience gained from working with a professional team was certainly paying off, even if his budget was spent and only just enough money could be scraped together to contest the Elonex; the days when General Motors formed the backbone of the British Championship are becoming a distant memory.

Milner and Higgins were neck and neck until one of the two — Higgins — dropped a score. The young Isle of Man driver will always remem-

ber the first time he rolled a car in competition, as will the Vauxhall mechanics who had to repair the battered Nova after it had been somersaulted six times into a field on only the second stage of the Ulster Rally. That adopted Manxman, Tony Pond, once said : 'To be a world class driver you have to have world class accidents.' The Manx philosophy survives.

Undoubtedly, the best battle in the series was reserved for Group N, as the expense of running a top Group A car reached crippling levels. Five different manufacturers were represented amongst the ten showroom specification cars seeded in the top 20 of the Vauxhall Sport Rally. The initial list contained the defending Group N British Champion, Mika Sohlberg (Mitsubishi Galant), a former National Rally Champion, Graham Middleton (Toyota Celica 4WD), the reigning Peugeot Challenge Champion, Richard Burns (Subaru Legacy), the Group N winner of the previous year's Lombard RAC Rally, Robbie Head (Ford Sierra Cosworth 4x4) and the spectacular Scot, Dominic Buckley Junior (Mazda 323GT-X).

It would be a struggle to find a better gathering of drivers to contest a Group N class anywhere in the world, but it quickly degenerated into a two-way battle between Louise Aitken-Walker and Alister McRae. The cancellation of two early rounds of the championship meant that all the remaining scores would count. Disappointing results, or worse still retirement on the Vauxhall Sport and Pirelli Internationals caused several of their rivals to disappear. The cost of pursuing an international series kept Head out of title contention for one, and Sohlberg soon realised there was better value for money to be had in his native Finland. Transmission problems sent Burns OTL on the first round and immediately tilted his programme towards a successful attempt at the Mintex Series, Buckley spent almost as much of 1992 in Indonesia and Malaysia as he did in Britain, while Middleton gave up rallying to build a golf course in France. The British Championship could ill afford to lose such competitors, and suffered accordingly.

None the less, Group N remained the most exciting contest in the series, with the battle of the Scots only being resolved on the final round. The former World Ladies Rally Champion looked set to win the title in the MLP-prepared 'green' Sierra (which had a special development Cosworth engine and ran with a catalytic converter) after McRae crashed out of the Ulster. However, after Louise retired on the last stage of the Manx with a broken clutch, all McRae had to do was complete the final round to be assured of the title.

The McRae double was achieved through a finely judged performance by Alister in the Shell Scholarship car. The Ulster accident, when he was outwitted by a treacherously slippery patch of tarmac, was the only mishap in a magnificent season, which proved that, given a reliable car, he is one of the most promising

Jonny Milner (left) triumphed in a hard-fought battle for the Lombard Junior title, the Peugeot man beating Mark Higgins's Nova. Trevor Smith was Ford's front runner in his customer specification, five-speed Cosworth, albeit no match for the factory Subaru (below left).
The championship was enlivened by the occasional appearance of a number of visitors with powerful Group A machinery. Rob Barry (below) did his reputation a power of good with fifth place on the Ulster in his Sierra 4x4, while Frank Meagher (previous page) was generally the quickest two-wheel drive runner in his well-used Sierra Cosworth, seen in action on the Isle of Man.

Photo Gavin Lodge

young drivers in Britain. It couldn't have been a greater contrast to his soul-destroying experiences with his Nova GSi in 1991.

It was a swansong season for Aitken-Walker, who announced her retirement from competitive driving prior to the final round. She was proud that the 'young bucks', as she called the generation of upwardly mobile young drivers considered her as a yardstick, constantly comparing her times to their own. She also discovered that, more often than not, their stage times were better than hers and, after an award-winning 14-year career, she decided to quit while she was still one of the front runners. Even though the title eluded her, she was the only driver to challenge McRae throughout the season. British rallying will be considerably poorer without her.

There were other notable performances from the not-so-young bucks, particularly Trevor Smith.

'There's life in the old dog yet,' the former Mintex and BTRDA Champion announced at the end of the final round, delighted to have beaten Alister McRae to the runner's-up position in the championship. Although the Clausthaler Cosworth he drove all season was his 1991 Mintex Championship-winning Group A car, the advance to the premier division was a difficult one. Despite running on a limited budget, the Hendy Ford team always turned out an immaculate machine, although spare parts were regarded as an expensive luxury. Nevertheless, it persevered, and Smith, without ever looking like challenging McRae, achieved what he set out to do and became the best of the rest.

Kenny McKinstry started the season with sixth on the Vauxhall Sport and a brilliant second on the Pirelli in his ex-Prodrive Subaru. However, Kaliber wanted him to concentrate on the Dunlop Tarmac Championship and, as his

sponsor was paying the bills, it also called the shots. Similarly, the likes of Bertie Fisher, Frank Meagher and David Greer only appeared on the Ulster and Manx Rallies, purely because they were in the Tarmac Championship calendar as well; despite the pre-event anticipation, they were no match for Colin McRae.

Whether we will see any significant change in 1993 is open to debate, but at least the MSA has put its trust in somebody who is not only passionate about the sport, but listens to competitors and officials and may be able to enforce their recommendations. Even before John Horton signed the contract to become the 1993 Mobil 1/*Top Gear* British Championship Manager, the MSA signed a 'non-interference clause', promising not to meddle in the day-to-day running of the series. Provided someone else is given a free hand, that at least is a step in the right direction.

Photo Gavin Lodge

VAUXHALL SPORT INTERNATIONAL RALLY, 21 March. Mobil 1/*Top Gear* British Rally Championship, round 1.

1	Colin McRae/ Derek Ringer	Subaru Legacy RS	1h 23m 25s	Gr A
2	Trevor Smith/ Roger Jones	Ford Sierra Cosworth 4x4	1h 28m 23s	Gr A
3	Gwyndaf Evans/ Howard Davies	Ford Sierra Cosworth 4x4	1h 28m 58s	Gr A
4	Alister McRae/ Dave Senior	Ford Sierra Cosworth 4x4	1h 29m 11s	Gr N
5	Robbie Head/ Campbell Roy	Ford Sierra Cosworth 4x4	1h 29m 12s	Gr N
6	Kenny McKinstry/ Robbie Philpott	Subaru Legacy RS	1h 30m 27s	Gr A
7	Louise Aitken-Walker/ Tina Thörner	Ford Sierra Cosworth 4x4	1h 31m 46s	Gr N
8	Mika Sohlberg/ Steve Turvey	Mitsubishi Galant VR-4	1h 32m 03s	Gr N
9	Raymond Munro/ Neil Ewing	Ford Sierra Cosworth 4x4	1h 32m 15s	Gr A
10	Mick Jones/ Dilwyn Llewellin	Mitsubishi Galant VR-4	1h 34m 09s	Gr N

PIRELLI INTERNATIONAL RALLY, 4 April. Mobil 1/*Top Gear* British Rally Championship, round 2.

1	Colin McRae/ Derek Ringer	Subaru Legacy RS	1h 11m 14s	Gr A
2	Kenny McKinstry/ Robbie Philpott	Subaru Legacy RS	1h 16m 06s	Gr A
3	Alister McRae/ Dave Senior	Ford Sierra Cosworth 4x4	1h 16m 31s	Gr N
4	Raymond Munro/ Neil Ewing	Ford Sierra Cosworth 4x4	1h 18m 27s	Gr A
5	Louise Aitken-Walker/ Tina Thörner	Ford Sierra Cosworth 4x4	1h 18m 51s	Gr N
6	Trevor Smith/ Roger Jones	Ford Sierra Cosworth 4x4	1h 19m 47s	Gr A
7	Paul Dyas/ Stuart Derry	Ford Sierra Cosworth 4x4	1h 19m 50s	Gr A
8	Mark Higgins/ Cliff Simmons	Vauxhall Nova GSi	1h 20m 37s	Gr A
9	Mick Jones/ Dilwyn Llewellyn	Mitsubishi Galant VR-4	1h 20m 42s	Gr N
10	Andrew Hudson/ Jim Stairs	Ford Sierra XR4x4	1h 21m 49s	Gr A

PERTH SCOTTISH RALLY, 12-14 June. Mobil 1/*Top Gear* British Rally Championship, round 3.

1	Colin McRae/ Derek Ringer	Subaru Legacy RS	2h 32m 00s	Gr A
2	Alister McRae/ Dave Senior	Ford Sierra Cosworth 4x4	2h 36m 29s	Gr N
3	Robbie Head/ Campbell Roy	Ford Sierra Cosworth 4x4	2h 36m 47s	Gr N
4	Jimmy McRae/ Dougie Paterson	Ford Sierra Cosworth 4x4	2h 36m 51s	Gr A
5	Louise Aitken-Walker/ Tina Thörner	Ford Sierra Cosworth 4x4	2h 43m 42s	Gr N
6	Trevor Smith/ Roger Jones	Ford Sierra Cosworth 4x4	2h 46m 41s	Gr A
7	Paul Dyas/ Stuart Derry	Ford Sierra Cosworth 4x4	2h 46m 48s	Gr A
8	Mark Higgins/ Cliff Simmons	Vauxhall Nova GSi	2h 47m 25s	Gr A
9	Jonny Milner/ Chris Wood	Peugeot 205 GTI	2h 48m 13s	Gr A
10	Richard Burns/ Robert Reid	Subaru Legacy RS	2h 48m 37s	Gr N

THE ELBOW ULSTER RALLY, 31 July-1 August. Mobil 1/*Top Gear* British Rally Championship, round 4.

1	Colin McRae/ Derek Ringer	Subaru Legacy RS	2h 56m 59s	Gr A
2	David Greer/ Michael Reid	Ford Sierra RS Cosworth	3h 08m 13s	Gr A
3	Frank Meagher/ Micheal Maher	Ford Sierra RS Cosworth	3h 09m 01s	Gr A
4	Dave Metcalfe/ Ian Grindrod	Vauxhall Nova GSi	3h 09m 42s	Gr A
5	Rob Barry/ Allan Whittaker	Ford Sierra Cosworth 4x4	3h 15m 00s	Gr A
6	Louise Aitken-Walker/ Tina Thörner	Ford Sierra Cosworth 4x4	3h 16m 34s	Gr N
7	Trevor Smith/ Roger Jones	Ford Sierra Cosworth 4x4	3h 17m 06s	Gr A
8	Trevor Cathers/ Gordon Noble	Ford Sierra Cosworth 4x4	3h 18m 51s	Gr N
9	Jonny Milner/ Chris Wood	Peugeot 205 GTI	3h 19m 19s	Gr A
10	Paul Dyas/ Stuart Derry	Ford Sierra Cosworth 4x4	3h 21m 11s	Gr N

MANX INTERNATIONAL RALLY, 8-11 September. Mobil 1/*Top Gear* British Rally Championship, round 5.

1	Colin McRae/ Derek Ringer	Subaru Legacy RS	3h 45m 56s	Gr A
2	Bertie Fisher/ Rory Kennedy	Subaru Legacy RS	3h 52m 04s	Gr A
3	Kenny McKinstry/ Robbie Philpott	Subaru Legacy RS	3h 54m 29s	Gr A
4	Dave Metcalfe/ Ian Grindrod	Vauxhall Nova GSi	3h 58m 25s	Gr A
5	Frank Meagher/ Micheal Maher	Ford Sierra RS Cosworth	4h 02m 55s	Gr A
6	Gary Leece/ Pauline Taylor	Ford Sierra Cosworth 4x4	4h 05m 35s	Gr A
7	Alister McRae/ Dave Senior	Ford Sierra Cosworth 4x4	4h 06m 19s	Gr N
8	Trevor Smith/ Roger Jones	Ford Sierra Cosworth 4x4	4h 06m 57s	Gr A
9	Mark Higgins/ Cliff Simmons	Vauxhall Nova GSi	4h 07m 09s	Gr A
10	Jonny Milner/ Chris Wood	Peugeot 205 GTI	4h 13m 57s	Gr A

ELONEX INTERNATIONAL RALLY, 24-25 October. Mobil 1/*Top Gear* British Rally Championship, round 6.

1	Colin McRae/ Derek Ringer	Subaru Legacy RS	1h 31m 24s	Gr A
2	Tommi Mäkinen/ Seppo Harjanne	Nissan Sunny GTiR	1h 31m 26s	Gr A
3	Trevor Smith/ Roger Jones	Ford Sierra Cosworth 4x4	1h 39m 19s	Gr A
4	Alister McRae/ Dave Senior	Ford Sierra Cosworth 4x4	1h 39m 29s	Gr N
5	Mark Higgins/ Cliff Simmons	Vauxhall Nova GSi	1h 41m 02s	Gr A
6	Louise Aitken-Walker/ Tina Thörner	Ford Sierra Cosworth 4x4	1h 42m 31s	Gr N
7	Jonny Milner/ Chris Wood	Peugeot 205 GTI	1h 46m 52s	Gr A
8	Mick Jones/ Neil Dashfield	Mitsubishi Galant VR-4	1h 47m 02s	Gr N
9	Steve Green/ Alan Thomas	Vauxhall Nova GSi	1h 47m 35s	Gr A
10	Richard Forster/ Robert Wilkinson	Vauxhall Nova GSi	1h 47m 47s	Gr A

Drivers (overall)

		1	2	3	4	5	6	Total
1	Colin McRae	25	25	25	25	25	25	150
2	Trevor Smith	22	17	18	20	19	22	118
3	Alister McRae	19	20	22	0	20	20	101
4	Louise Aitken-Walker	16	18	19	22	0	18	93
5	Jonny Milner	12	11	15	19	17	17	91
6	Mark Higgins	10	15	16	0	18	19	78
7	Paul Dyas	9	16	17	18	-	11	71
8	Kenny McKinstry	17	22	-	0	22	-	61
9	Mike Williams	3	0	11	16	12	8	50
10	Mick Jones	13	14	-	-	-	16	43
11	Scott Bradshaw	0	0	9	14	14	6	43
12	Stephen Green	1	6	0	17	0	15	39
13	Robbie Head	18	0	20	-	0	-	38
14	Richard Forster	11	0	0	0	13	14	38
15	Richard Burns	0	10	14	-	-	13	37
16	Raymond Munro	14	19	0	-	-	-	33
17	Richard Hemingway	0	7	12	0	-	12	31
18	Ian Calvin	0	4	10	0	15	-	29
19	Mika Sohlberg	15	9	0	-	-	-	24
20	Harry Cathcart	-	-	-	13	11	-	24

Drivers (Group N)

1	Alister McRae	25	25	25	0	25	25	125
2	Louise Aitken-Walker	20	22	20	25	0	22	109
3	Paul Dyas	18	20	19	22	-	20	99
4	Mike Williams	17	0	17	19	20	19	92
5	Scott Bradshaw	12	0	16	18	22	18	86
6	Stephen Green	16	17	0	20	0	0	53
7	Nigel Shield	14	16	0	0	19	0	49
8	Robbie Head	22	0	22	-	0	-	44
9	Robert Smith	11	14	-	18	-		43
10	Mika Sohlberg	19	18	0	-	-	-	37
11	Richard Burns	0	19	18	-	-	0	37

Class N1 (up to 1.3 litre Group N)

1	Clive Wheeler	12	-	-	-	15	27
2	Stuart Harrington	15	-	-	-	-	-	15

Class N2 (up to 1.6 litre Group N)

1	Mike Williams	15	0	15	12	15	15	72
2	Stephen Green	12	15	0	15	0	0	42
3	John Leckie	-	12	12	-	-	-	24

Class N3 (up to 2.0 litre Group N)

1	Scott Bradshaw	12	0	15	15	15	12	72
2	Nigel Shield	15	15	0	0	12	0	42
3	Robert Smith	10	12	-	10	-		32

Class N4 (over 2.0 litre Group N)

1	Alister McRae	15	15	15	0	15	15	75
2	Louise Aitken-Walker	10	12	10	15	0	12	59
3	Paul Dyas	8	10	9	12	-	10	49

Class A5 (up to 1.3 litre Group A)

1	Steve Wedgbury	15	0	0	15	-	15	45
2	Harry Cathcart	-	-	-	12	15	-	27

Class A6 (up to 1.6 litre Group A)

1	Jonny Milner	15	12	12	15	12	12	78
2	Mark Higgins	10	15	15	0	15	15	70
3	Ian Calvin	5	9	10	0	9	-	33

Class A7 (up to 2.0 litre Group A)

1	Bernt Kollevold	15	15	0	0	-	12	42
2	Richard Burns	0	0	0	-	-	15	15

Class A8 (over 2.0 litre Group A)

1	Colin McRae	15	15	15	15	15	15	90
2	Trevor Smith	12	9	12	12	10	12	67
3	Kenny McKinstry	9	12	-	0	12	-	33

Manufacturers (Group A)

1	Subaru	15	15	15	15	15	15	90
2	Ford	12	10	12	12	10	12	68
3	Vauxhall	6	8	10	0	9	10	43
4	Mitsubishi	7	7	0	0	-	9	23

Manufacturers (Group N)

1	Ford	15	15	15	15	15	15	90
2	Vauxhall	7	7	10	12	9	7	52
3	Mitsubishi	9	8	0	0	-	-	17
4	Subaru	0	9	8	0	-	-	17
5	Renault	-	6	0	0	10	0	16
6	Toyota	0	5	6	0	0	-	11

T he British National Championship can at last boast it has produced a winner who will no doubt progress to greater things. In recent years, Mintex (or second division) champions have either immediately retired, lapsed dramatically into obscurity, or struggled in another series. The last exception to that dismal statistic was Mark Lovell, who won the title in 1985 — and where is he now?

However, the seven-year itch has been broken by a naturally talented youngster who will, if there is any justice in this world, surpass Lovell's many titles. Nevertheless, one feels that the fact that Richard Burns never intended to tackle the full Mintex Series in 1992 is something the organisers will be keen not to bring up too often in future conversations.

Having been organised directly by the RACMSA for 17 highly successful years, Colnbrook handed over the running of the old National Championship to the Association of National Championship Rally Organisers for 1992. The MSA was naturally keen for its new look Mobil 1/*Top Gear* British Championship not only to flourish, but to regain the mantle of the most successful rally championship in the country — something the National Championship had largely dragged from it in recent years. It didn't make life easy for ANCRO when responsibilities were transferred for, not content with preventing the use of the title 'Championship', the RAC poached two of its best events — the Vauxhall Sport and Cumbria Rallies — and with it the ANCRO Chairman, Jim Jones, who was also Clerk of the Course for the former and naturally couldn't bat for both sides. Rod Parkin, the irrepressible force behind the Yorkshire round of the ANCRO contest, was a more than capable, and willing replacement, taking Chairmanship of ANCRO and the newly entitled Mintex National Rally Series — 'series' supposedly being a less important title than 'championship' in the eyes of the British motor sport authorities.

If it wasn't so good at what it does, ANCRO could be criticised for a lack of democracy in its ranks. The committee consists of representatives from each organising club and, unsurprisingly, they immediately re-elected each other's events into the 1992 calendar.

Personally, they're all good friends, and the I'll-scratch-your-back-if-you-scratch-mine syndrome is sometimes all too apparent. In fact, it can be no harder to join the freemasons than it is to join ANCRO, and it's tempting to suppose that the latter has a secret handshake.

As the Mintex and re-vamped British Championships were trying to attract a similar, ever depleting pool of competitors, the success of the former was reflected in the lack of entries in the international competition. While organisers of the Mintex Series urged competitors to send their entry forms in early to avoid disappointment, there was never anything approaching an oversubscribed entry for a round of the principal championship, and several events did not take place at all.

The MSA appeared to have underestimated ANCRO's strength, and although a few at Colnbrook were quietly delighted the Mintex Series was riding the recession so well, others were embarrassed by the comparative disaster the re-designed British Championship became.

Although the boundaries have changed since last year, many of the fundamental distinctions between the two championships remain. What made one series a success, and the other championship — well, let's be polite and just say less successful? The Mintex is somewhat cheaper to contest, since all the events are one-day affairs with no recce allowed, other than the Manx National. However, it still attracted a host of Group A cars, and drivers of good calibre such as Pete Doughty, David Mann, David Gillanders and Brian Bell. It's little surprise that the aforementioned drivers are also successful, middle-aged businessmen — people who are generally quite well off — and if you can afford to buy something like a Group A Sierra Cosworth 4x4 and spend £4000 on a bit of fun for a weekend, there must be more than financial considerations in foresaking a one-day international and doing a one-day national.

Furthermore, the majority of the midfield runners were in homologated cars, and few took up the option of driving Escorts and Sunbeams, for example, even though those venerable old stagers were welcome, provided they were powered by engines of under 2.5 litres of course. You'd expect the likes of David Pemberton (Opel Corsa), Grahame Standen (Toyota Corolla) and Chris Ruck (Vauxhall Astra GTE) — all Group A champions — to contest the British Championship and even the Group N class winners, such as Keith Wain (Nova), and John Lay (Corolla) wouldn't be out of their depth in the international series.

The entry fee wasn't the only inflated difference between the international and national market place. Recces not only mean time off work, but hotel bills and extra petrol. If value for money is what you're look-

THE BEST OF BOTH WORLDS

By Paul Evans, Assistant Rallies Editor, Motoring News

Photos: Gavin Lodge

ing for, the British Championship doesn't seem as cost effective as the national, and entries proved that the supposed prestige of doing an international didn't compensate for the increase in budget.

Pre-season self-promotion was another triumph for ANCRO, another disaster for the MSA. The former knew that, to survive, it must always remain one step ahead of the RACMSA's new series. While the British Championship was still being tentatively discussed back in the autumn of 1991, ANCRO had published a calendar of events, with dates, and a list of substantial bonus schemes. Shell Oils, Mintex and Dunlop had all announced their support and, while some rallies would accommodate the Vauxhall, Peugeot and Skoda Challenges, others would also run restricted and historic rallies to boost entries. The positive, cards-on-the-table, approach paid handsome dividends and, while the RAC dithered about the structure and format of its new look series, competitors and their sponsors were attracted by the ANCRO proposals.

Parkin and his associates seem to have a very straightforward approach to rallying, which for some reason isn't adopted universally. Organising a championship has great potential for being a logistical nightmare without looking for problems. They never lost sight of the fact that rallies are organised for competitors, not for organisers; they were never afraid to ask competitors what they wanted from a championship, nor to provide it.

There was, however, one controversial decision made by ANCRO that worried some at the beginning of the year. In its attempt to please everybody and keep restrictions to a mini-

mum, it wanted to invite everyone to its series, and by 'everyone' it included those who drive Metro 6R4s.

Provided a vehicle complied with the RACMSA technical regulations, a hybrid was as welcome as a homologated car. Being biased towards forestry events five to one, a Group 4 Escort or Manta 400 was unlikely to offer a serious challenge for the title, whereas a Metro 6R4 was a completely different proposition. Many argued that an out of date car winning a national series wouldn't be good for British rallying, especially as recent champions had driven homologated cars and been granted B-seeds by FISA.

Four of Rover's Group B supercars entered the first round, and although two led, Bill Barton was the top Metro driver in third at the end of the day. Not only were there two homologated cars in front of him, but one was a Group N car. Despite the power disadvantage, Burns dislodged Barton after an electrifying final stage charge through Wytch Farm in Dorset. The last 5.55 miles of the Mazda Car-Line Winter Rally proved that ANCRO had been right in allowing Metros to participate, for Burns and the Team Shell Subaru had taken 27 seconds off the Lincolnshire farmer. It was clear the Metro was suffering from its lack of recent development, and that the six-year-old Group B car could be outgunned by a well-driven 1992 'showroom' car — if the right driver was in the latter.

The Genesis Sport team had planned to enter its Subaru on the British Championship, while its effervescent team manager, David Williams, drove it on Mintex rounds. However, as the winner of the first round, Trevor Smith, had not registered for the Mintex series, Burns found himself at the top of the leaderboard, despite only entering the event to shake the new car down. Had the De Lacy Rally not been can-

Richard Burns and Robert Reid were easily the most consistent performers in the Mintex Series (left), proving that, in the right hands, even a Group N Subaru can outgun heavyweight Group B machinery such as Bill Barton's Metro 6R4 (above).

celled, it's unlikely Richard would have travelled to Bournemouth at all, but the temptation to continue was irresistible, and Williams sacrificed his seat for the remainder of the season.

Sacrifice is something with which the Genesis Sport boss has become synonymous in helping Burns over the past three years. Having taken him under his wing and guided him through the Peugeot Challenge, his fellow Craven MC clubman has virtually adopted Burns. Office and private life have been disrupted by the sheer enthusiasm Burns demands, and Williams gains more satisfaction from watching this young driver progress than driving himself these days. Why don't more ageing rally drivers do the same, he often asks? Why not indeed.

There's no doubt that Williams has changed Burns for the better, giving the shy lad from Reading the confidence he once drastically lacked. The team's close links with the works Subaru squad were maintained, and became obvious from a very early stage in the season. Prodrive's David Campion travelled to

Bournemouth on a free weekend to 'watch' the Mazda Car-Line Winter Rally, stating his presence around the Genesis Team at service halts was purely out of interest. Soon, however, Burns and his equally devoted and determined co-driver, Robert Reid, were employed to make gravel notes for Colin McRae and Ari Vatanen on World Championship events, giving them invaluable experience that has led to a full contract for 1993.

One can argue that Burns isn't over-endowed with natural talent, but if he lacks innate car control, he more than compensates for it in determination. Practice, from a very early age, has made him the formidable driver he is today, and although a blush is easily teased from those boyish cheeks, a Jekyll and Hyde transformation takes place when he gets behind the wheel. His gangling, schoolboy appearance hasn't won everybody's heart, and one well-known Fleet Street scribe often tells him he should be less of a wimp and tell journalists to 'Eff off' now and again. Richard prefers to cock a snook at his critics on the stages, however, for it's difficult to argue with the kind of times he consistently sets.

Inside the car, he exhibits great maturity and exudes calmness. He's not spectacular, but a Group N Subaru doesn't lend itself to being thrown about, as speed is scrubbed off a lot more efficiently than it is regained. His initiation to Group N in the Peugeot Challenge taught him to be smooth and fast, and he has nurtured the technique to good effect. Moreover, he rarely has an accident, and is extremely sympathetic on machinery — which is essential for success in a Group N car.

Like Prodrive in the British Championship, the Genesis squad was clearly the most professional team in the national series, with designer clothes and debriefings as important as stage times. Yet the team was good humoured, even self-deprecating, as well as professional. The Burns/Reid/Genesis Sport combination is reminiscent of the David Llewellin/Phil Short/Collins Motorsport partnership which worked so well in the Open Championship, the air of relaxation masking the tremendous amount of work and determination that goes on behind the scenes. As the results came in, relaxation was augmented by confidence.

The Manx National, the only tarmac and pace note rally in the series, was a test of how the Wallingford-based team reacted in a crisis. Leading the Series entering the Isle of Man, it was nothing but a disaster for Burns from start to finish. Early gearbox problems ruled out a good result and, having decided to continue for a bit of experience, the finale came a little sooner, and substantially more violently, than anticipated. Doughty's Cosworth had ground to a halt with electrical problems and, before he could alert the following car, Burns appeared, fully committed to a fast, blind corner, unaware that the Ford blocked the narrow lane. The 50 mph impact destroyed the front of the Subaru, and only the strength of the Legacy ensured the crew escaped injury.

By now Burns had given up his assault on the British Championship and was fully committed to the Mintex Series. The car was rebuilt for the Severn Valley, and he won his first national event with ease. A second on the following Kayel Graphics left him with a cautious cruise through the final round to be sure of the title. Trevor Smith had been in a similar position 12 months before and had been obliged to fight for the crown after spending time in a ditch, but Burns has a mature head on young shoulders and kept out of trouble. At 21, he became the youngest ever winner of the national championship, an honour Malcolm Wilson had held since he won the award as a fresh-faced 22-year-old in 1978.

Some potentially threatening Group A opposition fluttered in and out of the series, without posing much of a challenge. The former National Champion, Ian Roberton, made just one appearance in his Sierra Cosworth 4x4, Steve Hill also making a solitary foray in a Galant VR-4, while Chris Mellors and Doughty only scored on one round apiece from a limited number of starts. Life would have been considerably harder for Burns had more of his rivals persevered: even if their title aspirations had faltered early in the year, appearances on rallies later in the season might possibly have taken points away from the top

Group N runner, conceivably bunching the championship contestants.

Well before the end of the season, it was apparent that Bill Barton would be Richard's only realistic challenger, and even his chances had deteriorated drastically by the final round in Yorkshire. True, David Mann did still have a mathematical chance of lifting the title, but the world's fastest mushroom farmer was in the unenviable position of having to rely on the misfortunes of the two ahead if he wanted to steal the show.

Barton, the 1988 BTRDA Gold Star Champion, had been tempted out of retirement by the new rules which allowed Metro 6R4s and, despite a clean break from rallying for several seasons, he was immediately on the pace. Support from Jet Oils gave him the financial encouragement to return, and a copybook championship assault was progressing nicely until the Severn Valley. Both he and his co-driver, Don George, were lucky to escape from a horrific accident during which they rolled violently in Hafren. It naturally knocked the wind out of their sails, and they were more than happy with third on the following Kayel Graphics. The reverse let Burns off the hook, however, and victory on the final round could only assure them of the runners'-up spot.

A year's development enabled Mann's Darell Staniforth-prepared Toyota Celica to enjoy its best season since its metamorphosis from Group N to Group A. Minor prob-

lems, usually in the engine management department, had often ruined strong performances, but 1992 was different. Although victory would yet again elude him, David was always a threat, and second on the Granite City was the very least he deserved for his perseverance over two often trying seasons. The Artemis-backed GT4 came to grief on the Severn Valley, when a moment's lack of concentration from the driver saw it slither wide and roll onto its side, coming to rest with its roof against a tree.

Dust, sunlight or a combination of the two seem to be a traditional hazard on the mid-Wales event, and when Mann was later blinded by sunshine, the Celica smashed its steering as it cannoned in and out of various ditches on either side of Hafren.

It was certainly a turning point in the season for, with both Mann and Barton out on the same stage, Burns would never be seriously worried again. Mann's season ended with two strong performances, making certain of an honourable third.

With one score to drop out of six, and 10 bonus points for entering all events, consistency was important if a top finishing position was to be obtained. After a shaky start, Dougie Watson-Clark will reflect on 1992 with a good deal of satisfaction. The Carlisle Cosworth pilot had been absent from the national arena on a regular basis for some time, but with backing from ATS, he was very much his former self, finishing in the top

eight on the final four rallies.

Murray Grierson swapped his rear-wheel drive Metro-Hart for a more conventional all-wheel drive 6R4 on the Severn Valley, but two retirements mid-season not only denied him points, but a realistic chance of the title. The quiet gentleman from Dalbeattie excelled in the latter part of the season, taking to four-wheel drive like a Scot to whisky. On his first event in the ex-Donald Milne Metro, he finished second overall, but his title aspirations dwindled with gearbox failure on the Kayel Graphics. Second again in Yorkshire was compensation for his loyalty to the series, although he'll be disappointed with fifth, behind Watson-Clark, in the final points tally.

Indeed, there were many disappointments. Financial restraints and other priorities brought only brief touches of brilliance from the likes of David Gillanders, Raymond Munro, Maurice Flux, Alister McRae and Jon Milner.

Once again the national series attracted a broad array of competitors. It epitomised the fundamental spirit of any sporting event, bringing people from different backgrounds together in a battle of skill and courage. On paper, it's the ideal proving ground for young drivers who are serious about making a career in rallying, although it has never previously fulfilled its potential in that respect. Burns's title could change all that, but the younger, hungry generation might have drawn

a very different conclusion had Barton won the title in his Metro. Ultimately, ANCRO managed to run a contest that appealed to the well-heeled clubman and the ambitious rising star alike, yet the decision to let the 6R4s return almost backfired, and it needed an exceptional young man to change the image of the national series.

Both David Mann, driving his battered Celica with undimmed gusto (above), and Scotland's 6R4 expert, Murray Grierson (left) deserved awards for determination, whereas Steve Smith ploughed a lonely furrow with his Delta.

MINTEX NATIONAL RALLY SERIES RESULTS

MAZDA CAR-LINE WINTER RALLY, 25 January. Mintex National Rally Series, round 1.

1	Trevor Smith/	Ford Sierra Cosworth 4x4	
	Roger Jones	1h 11m 15s	Gr A
2	Richard Burns/	Subaru Legacy RS	
	Robert Reid	1h 12m 07s	Gr N
3	Bill Barton/	MG Metro 6R4	
	Don George	1h 12m 22s	Gr B
4	David Gillanders/	Ford Sierra Cosworth 4x4	
	Steve Turvey	1h 12m 44s	Gr A
5	David Mann/	Toyota Celica GT4	
	Ian Wray	1h 13m 23s	Gr A
6	Steve Hill/	Ford Sierra Cosworth 4x4	
	Brian Goff	1h 13m 27s	Gr N
7	Brian Bell/	Ford Sierra Cosworth 4x4	
	Richard Taylor	1h 13m 37s	Gr A
8	Ian Donaldson/	Ford Sierra Cosworth 4x4	
	Keith Wareham	1h 14m 03s	Gr A
9	Jon Milner/	Peugeot 309 GTI	
	Chris Wood	1h 14m 50s	Gr A
10	Raymond Munro/	Ford Sierra Cosworth 4x4	
	Neil Ewing	1h 15m 12s	Gr A

GRANITE CITY RALLY, 11 April. Mintex National Rally Series, round 2.

1	Alister McRae/	Ford Sierra Cosworth 4x4	
	Dave Senior	1h 18m 59s	Gr N
2	David Mann/	Toyota Celica GT4	
	Ian Wray	1h 19m 23s	Gr A
3	Robbie Head/	Ford Sierra Cosworth 4x4	
	Campbell Roy	1h 20m 19s	Gr N
4	David Gillanders/	Ford Sierra Cosworth 4x4	
	Howard Davies	1h 20m 43s	Gr A
5	Murray Grierson/	MG Metro-Hart	
	Stewart Merry	1h 20m 56s	Gr B
6	Bill Barton/	MG Metro 6R4	

	Don George	1h 21m 25s	Gr B
7	Jeremy Easson/	Ford Sierra Cosworth 4x4	
	Alun Cook	1h 22m 31s	Gr A
8	Richard Burns/	Subaru Legacy RS	
	Robert Reid	1h 23m 15s	Gr N
9	Maurice Flux/	MG Metro 6R4	
	Wreford Piper	1h 23m 22s	Gr B
10	Pete Doughty/	Ford Sierra Cosworth 4x4	
	Lyn Jenkins	1h 23m 40s	Gr A

COP-Y-CAT KONICA MANX NATIONAL RALLY, 16 May. Mintex National Rally Series, round 3.

1	Bertie Fisher/	Subaru Legacy RS	
	Rory Kennedy	1h 41m 17s	Gr A
2	John Price/	MG Metro 6R4	
	Mike Bowen	1h 43m 20s	Gr B
3	Gary Leece/	Ford Sierra Cosworth 4x4	
	Pauline Taylor	1h 45m 42s	Gr A
4	Alister McRae/	Ford Sierra Cosworth 4x4	
	Dave Senior	1h 46m 05s	Gr N
5	Bill Barton/	MG Metro 6R4	
	Don George	1h 46m 38s	Gr B
6	David Mann/	Toyota Celica GT4	
	Ian Wray	1h 47m 07s	Gr A
7	Dougie Watson-Clark/	Ford Sierra Cosworth 4x4	
	Ian Connelly	1h 47m 58s	Gr N
8	Chris Griffiths/	Opel Manta 400	
	Stephen Griffiths	1h 48m 32s	Gr B
9	Raymond Munro/	Ford Sierra Cosworth 4x4	
	Neil Ewing	1h 49m 02s	Gr A
10	Sean Farrell/	Ford Sierra Cosworth	
	Adrian Farrell	1h 49m 35s	Gr A

KERRIDGE SEVERN VALLEY, 20 June. Mintex National Rally Series, round 4.

1	Richard Burns/	Subaru Legacy RS	
	Robert Reid	1h 21m 56s	Gr N
2	Murray Grierson/	MG Metro 6R4	
	Stewart Merry	1h 23m 08s	Gr B
3	Jeremy Easson/	Ford Sierra Cosworth 4x4	
	Alun Cook	1h 23m 57s	Gr A
4	Brian Bell/	Ford Sierra Cosworth 4x4	
	Ryland James	1h 25m 45s	Gr A
5	Graham Middleton/	Celica 4WD Turbo	
	Phil Mills	1h 26m 07s	Gr N
6	Marcus Dodd/	Ford Sierra Cosworth 4x4	
	Stephen McAuley	1h 26m 25s	Gr A
7	Jan Churchill/	Porsche 911 Carrera	
	John Taylor	1h 27m 27s	Gr B
8	Dougie Watson-Clark/	Ford Sierra Cosworth 4x4	
	Ian Connelly	1h 27m 31s	Gr N

9	Neil Hiorns/	Ford Sierra Cosworth XR4x4	
	Tom Watson	1h 28m 07s	Gr A
10	Steve Smith/	Lancia Delta HF Integrale	
	Brian Hughes	1h 28m 25s	Gr A

KAYEL GRAPHICS RALLY, 8 August. Mintex National Rally Series, round 5.

1	Stephen Finlay/	Ford Sierra Cosworth 4x4	
	Dessie Wilson	1h 13m 24s	Gr A
2	Richard Burns/	Subaru Legacy RS	
	Robert Reid	1h 15m 16s	Gr N
3	Bill Barton/	MG Metro 6R4	
	Don George	1h 15m 25s	Gr B
4	Marcus Dodd/	Ford Sierra Cosworth 4x4	
	Stephen McAuley	1h 16m 06s	Gr A
5	David Mann/	Toyota Celica GT4	
	Ian Wray	1h 16m 14s	Gr A
6	Brian Bell/	Ford Sierra Cosworth 4x4	
	Phil Mills	1h 16m 23s	Gr A
7	Dougie Watson-Clark/	Ford Sierra Cosworth 4x4	
	Ian Connelly	1h 16m 47s	Gr A
8	Steve Smith/	Lancia Delta HF Integrale	
	Brian Hughes	1h 17m 17s	Gr A
9	Jeremy Easson/	Ford Sierra Cosworth 4x4	
	Alun Cook	1h 18m 55s	Gr A
10	Phill Jones/	Opel Manta	
	Andy Salisbury	1h 18m 57s	Gr B

RALLY CAR FOREST STAGES, 26 September. Mintex National Rally Series, round 6.

1	Bill Barton/	MG Metro 6R4	
	Don George	1h 04m 32s	Gr B
2	Murray Grierson/	MG Metro 6R4	
	Campbell Roy	1h 05m 06s	Gr B
3	Richard Burns/	Subaru Legacy RS	
	Robert Reid	1h 05m 40s	Gr N
4	David Mann/	Toyota Celica GT4	
	Ian Wray	1h 06m 17s	Gr A
5	Nigel Worswick/	Ford Sierra Cosworth 4x4	
	John Robinson	1h 06m 59s	Gr A
6	Charles Payne/	Ford Sierra Cosworth 4x4	
	Hugh Edwards	1h 07m 02s	Gr A
7	Chris Mellors/	Ford Sierra Cosworth 4x4	
	Reg Smith	1h 07m 03s	Gr A
8	Dougie Watson-Clark/	Ford Sierra Cosworth 4x4	
	Ian Connelly	1h 07m 03s	Gr N
9	Brian Lyall/	Ford Sierra Cosworth 4x4	
	Duncan McIntosh	1h 08m 00s	Gr A
10	Steve Petch/	Ford Sierra Cosworth 4x4	
	George Tindall	1h 08m 26s	Gr N

B=Bonus T=Total

Drivers (overall)

		1	2	3	4	5	6	B	T
1	Richard Burns	25	16	0	25	25	20	10	121
2	Bill Barton	22	18	22	0	22	25	10	119
3	David Mann	19	22	20	0	19	19	10	109
4	Dougie Watson-Clark	0	13	19	15	17	17	10	91
5	Murray Grierson	10	19	0	22	0	22	10	83
6	Brian Bell	17	-	-	19	18	14	-	68
7	Steve Smith	13	0	0	13	16	12	10	64
8	Phill Jones	0	6	16	0	14	13	10	59
9	Gordon Smith	7	11	0	12	11	8	10	59
10	Neil Hiorns	0	0	14	14	0	15	10	53
11	Jeremy Easson	0	17	-	20	15	-	-	52
12	Ken Jones	11	0	15	0	6	10	10	52
13	Alister McRae	-	25	25	-	-	-	-	50
14	Marcus Dodd	12	0	-	17	20	0	-	49
15	Raymond Munro	14	12	18	-	-	-	-	44
16	David Gillanders	20	20	0	-	-	-	-	40
17	Jan Churchill	-	-	-	16	13	11	-	40
18	Chris Ruck	6	1	11	11	0	0	10	39
19	Graham Middleton	0	0	17	18	-	0	0	35
20	Richard Archer	0	8	12	0	0	5	10	33

Drivers (Group N)

1	Richard Burns	25	22	0	25	25	25	10	132
2	Dougie Watson-Clark	0	20	22	19	20	22	10	113
3	Gordon Smith	19	19	0	18	19	18	10	103
4	Tony Phillips	17	16	16	16(14)	15	10		90
5	Richard Archer	16	17	17	13	0	16	10	89
6	Ken Jones	20	0	19	0	17	19	10	85
7	John Lay	-	14	15	15	15	12	-	71
8	David Shering	0	18	-	17	18	17	-	70
9	Marcus Dodd	22	0	-	20	22	0	-	64
10	Iain Scott	(3)	10	13	6	11	8	10	58

Drivers (Group A)

1	David Mann	22	25	25	0	25	25	10	132
2	David Pemberton	(7)	17	18	15	17	17	0	94
3	Chris Ruck	13	16	19	18	10	0	0	86
4	Steve Smith	15	0	0	19	22	19	0	85
5	Neil Hiorns	0	0	20	20	11	20	0	81
6	Kevin Williams	9	13	0	14	16	16	0	78
7	Trevor Godwin	6	14	14	11	12	0	0	67
8	David Howells	0	0	15	12	15	14	0	64
9	Jeremy Easson	0	20	-	25	20	-	-	65
10	John Greenhalgh	-	0	17	13	14	15	-	59

Drivers (Group B)

1	Bill Barton	25	22	25	0	25	25	0	132
2	Murray Grierson	22	25	0	25	0	22	0	104
3	Phill Jones	11	17	22	0	20	19	0	99
4	Stephen Cotton	18	11	20	20	14	0	0	93
5	Colin Knott	16	15	0	16	16	15	0	88
6	David Boden	0	12	17	13	12	13	0	77
7	Nigel Bramall	0	18	0	18	15	14	0	75
8	Roger Duckworth	0	16	-	17	18	17	-	68
9	Jan Churchill	-	-	-	22	19	18	-	59
10	Mark Aplin	13	-	18	0	13	11	-	55

THE QUIET REVOLUTION

By David Williams

I t is a fact universally acknowledged that the European Championship is Italian property. Occasionally, it might be won by an Italian driver in a non-Italian car, but it is essentially controlled from Turin. Long before rally car groups were distinguished by letters instead of numbers, the Lancia or Fiat candidate invariably took the prize, the winning driver is still usually an Italian, and one has to go back to 1980 to unearth the last victorious combination lacking an Italian element. On that occasion, Antonio Zanini's opponent was another Porsche driver, and the striking feature of Erwin Weber's

victory in 1992 was not its novelty value, but the fact that he beat off two separate challenges that had a fair measure of Abarth support. More even than being the first German to win the title since 1979, or the first driver to win it in a Japanese car, the way in which Ralliart Germany dealt with the Lancia challenge is what sticks in the mind.

At the start of the year, it was only too easy to be cynical about the Russelsheim team. It was all very well for an experienced Abarth satellite such as Grifone to miss the first high scoring event, the co-efficient 10 Garrigues Rally, for the devastat-

ing speed of the new 'Deltona' on the Monte and in Portugal had demonstrated that Lancia drivers could afford to give the opposition a head start. It was surely another matter entirely for a private team venturing onto foreign territory for the first time, even though it had an established reputation for turning out beautifully built cars. The German-constructed Galant VR-4 had not been ready. When it appeared briefly on the Costa Smeralda, it was all too easy to understand the delay. Realising that the Galant was none too competitive on asphalt, the team had embarked on an intensive tarmac

development programme. This hadn't consisted of playing with springs and shock absorbers. On the contrary, it had demanded an extensive re-design, including a new gearbox casing designed to lower the centre of gravity, and the adoption of the full Xtrac centre differential, complete with hydraulics, pumps and sensors, which Ralliart Europe had always rejected as too complicated. Moreover, Germany had never run anything more advanced than five-speed Galants in the past. Weber retired at the end of a forgettable first leg with gearbox failure, and the staid-looking Mitsubishi hadn't got anywhere near the best Lancias on the asphalt that made up the first day's competition.

The entire project sounded wildly over-ambitious. A number of manufacturers benefit from well-financed, enthusiastic importers' teams, but the Opel operations in Belgium and Spain, for instance, rely on proven British tuners such as Tim Ashton and Sydney Meeke, with good connections with the factory. There might be small adjustments to the cars for local terrain, but wholesale re-development is out of the question. As it happens, a surprising

Weber bounced back from the Sardinian fiasco to score a lucky win on the Zlatni Piassatzi, cruising home to demolish thin opposition once Grifone's man, Piero Longhi, had crashed while leading. There were still teething problems with the Galant, though, and the team bravely opted to miss the Antibes Rally while it sorted them out. At that point, in mid-May, there was no clear leader in the series, but pulling out was a risk nevertheless. Now that Grifone had finally laid its hands on the latest Integrales, the promising Longhi would surely capitalise on Ralliart

number of key components on the German Mitsubishi *did* come from Britain, including much of the suspension and brakes, but the project had nothing whatever to do with Ralliart Europe in Rugby. Weber's car was prepared to a German specification, not to Rugby's, and the team could benefit from a freedom that Mitsubishi's official operation was unable or unwilling to exploit. Most notably, it built its own engines, freeing itself of the usual Japanese caution in plotting boost pressure and ignition settings from which Lancia has profited so richly in the last five years.

Germany's weakness.

In the event, the 26-year-old Italian retired at Antibes with broken transmission and, by the beginning of August, Weber was as good as champion. The key successes were dominant victories in Poland and on home soil in Germany, but the most impressive had been a shattering display at Ieper. None of the Lancia drivers was expected to feature, but no one genuinely expected Weber to beat the Flemish experts, Patrick Snijers and Robert Droogmans, on roads they know like the backs of their hands. Ultimately, Snijers outran Fabrizio Tabaton in a thrilling

sprint for the line, but not before Weber had built up a convincing lead, despite Pirellis that weren't lasting well in an unusually warm Belgian summer. The locals were aghast. Underestimating Weber somewhat, they were in no doubt that the Galant's power and generous suspension travel were allowing it to pull away from the Cosworths, and Droogmans had succumbed to transmission problems before the Mitsubishi fell foul of a broken propshaft. In the end, having dropped to fourth, Weber crashed after the gearbox had also given trouble, but that did nothing to erase the memory of the invincible Belgians being given a thorough hiding on home ground; the Galant had been the car to beat. It had made the Sierra look old-fashioned, and it excelled on the kind of fast, bumpy tarmac where Lancia's drivers, if not the car, were at their weakest.

So far as Ralliart Germany was concerned, the car still needed further development. Weber hadn't expressed much confidence in its ability to win before either the Polish or Ieper, which only added to the shock impact when it looked likely to do just that. Sure enough, on winding, mountainous roads in Madeira, its weight and inferior throttle response meant that it was no match for the top Integrales, yet by then it hardly mattered. Weber could afford to bide his time, settle for a good points finish, and put the title beyond doubt with a gravel win in northern Greece on the ELPA. He had succeeded where the unfortunate Snijers has so often gambled and lost, and done so without much in the way of assistance from either Ralliart Europe or Japan.

It would be a little misleading to

Ralliart Germany achieved the unthinkable, making short work of the favoured Lancia teams. The Galant became as formidable on tarmac as on gravel, but much of the credit should go to Erwin Weber (above), a canny and versatile performer whatever the conditions.

say that the Germans had transformed the old Mitsubishi into a tarmac racer where the official team had singularly failed. Apart from the fact that the engine needed further refinement to work well on the twistiest roads, it was never exactly bullet-proof. Ieper showed that the transmission wasn't entirely to be trusted, and Weber was a shade lucky to finish in Madeira after the fan-belt jumped off on the longest stage of the rally and the engine boiled.

Nevertheless, it had been quite quick enough to beat cars developed on far higher budgets, and Weber had made the most of it. He may lack the sheer speed of the top World Championship performers, but he is an adaptable, level-headed driver with a breadth of experience from his days at Opel and Volkswagen. He suffered from none of the uneasiness on quick Belgian or Polish tarmac that afflicted the Lancia drivers, and that allowed him to exploit the Mitsubishi's strengths to the full. Ieper was the only blemish on his record as a driver — an important consideration in a year where driving errors played a significant part in the outcome. He certainly benefited from the weaknesses of the opposition, but this was a conclusive victory even so. As soon as he had won the Deutschland, he was able to make plans to contest the Paris–Peking

Photo Michael Chester

and ignore the last two co-efficient 20 rounds of the championship, the Manx and Cyprus Rallies. While it has become something of a tradition for the European Champion to skip those events, no one else has been able to drop them as early as July.

That in turn owed something to good planning on his team's part. Realising that he would probably be required for the cross-country trip, it had swiftly added the Hunsrück Rally to his programme. It kept him under pressure, contesting three different rallies in four weeks, but it brought another 200 points close to home on an event he knows well, which his opponents weren't likely to tackle.

Despite official denials, it is hard to see how German success — and on such a scale — can have been anything but an embarrassment to Ralliart Europe and to the Japanese. Embarrassment worked on two levels, though. Weber was one of a small number of competitors accused of using illegal fuel on the Deutschland, although only Droogmans was eventually excluded, the ex-works fuel exceeding the maximum lead content permitted by the European Community. Weber's points lead was more than sufficient to handle disqualification in any event, and Mitsubishi's cause was indirectly aided by FISA, which was much more interested in sweeping the matter under the carpet.

Yet the Integrale remained the car to beat. Anything that could bring César Baroni within reach of the title, or Tabaton within seconds of a win at Ieper had to possess a large measure of superiority over its opposition, and Lancia's failure to mop up the European series for the umpteenth time had a great deal more to do with drivers than machinery. One of the ironies of the season was that the firm that habitually

dominates the European Championship was unable to capitalise on a technical mastery that it hadn't possessed for five years.

A look at the results suggests that Mitsubishi's record was patchy, but it was nothing like as bad as its rivals'. Grifone was unlucky. Longhi — a pleasant, diffident man, with all the right credentials for a European Champion — crashed twice. Once would have been forgiveable, whereas the second was always going to make life difficult. In fact, it ruined his season. He injured his back (and his co-driver, Maurizio Imerito), when he piled the Esso Lancia into a tree in Poland at 70 mph. He wasn't fit enough for a co-efficient 20 round for another six weeks, until Madeira, and by then his chances of depriving Weber of the title were purely mathematical.

Perhaps Lancia was complacent where Longhi was concerned. Grifone comes some way down the Abarth pecking order and, considering the driver's meagre experience outside Italy, it ought to have entered an 'old', 16-valve Delta for Garrigues to give him as much match practice as possible. Equally, Lancia might have produced a 'Deltona' in time for the Costa Smeralda. Outclassed by the newer, wider Lancias, Longhi could do no better than fifth.

With hindsight, he never made up for a sluggish getaway. Even one 'away' win might have given his confidence the kind of boost it needed to take on a driver with Weber's experience. As it was, he always struggled to beat the German, until Madeira. By then, Weber had no need to do anything more demanding than finish in the first four, and Longhi's target had shifted: having beaten the 1991 Champion, Piero Liatti, on the Ralli della Lana (another of Italy's

European Championship qualifiers), he needed to beat, or at least challenge, Andrea Aghini in Madeira. The Jolly Club driver won by four minutes. Knowing a lost cause when it saw one, Grifone decided to concentrate on rallies at home.

Victory in Poland hadn't settled things there and then, because Weber then faced an attack from an unexpected quarter, from Baroni. The Sanremo-born Frenchman had intended to contest the French Championship in an Integrale HF run by Mauro Pregliasco's Astra team, albeit with one eye on the European series from the start. Like Bernard Darniche before him, good scores at home raised the possibility of greater successes abroad, and he swung his sights to the European Championship by entering Ieper the moment he won Antibes at a canter.

He was off the pace until the suspension was adapted to bumpy Belgian roads, whereupon he began setting times that might have given him victory had he started the rally at that speed. He took an encouraging third, but in practice his commitment to the European Championship was never more than half-hearted. He chose to contest the French Championship Rouergue Rally instead of the Deutschland, and one wonders if he would have tried Madeira if it wasn't for the generous start money for which the event is renowned. Even the French budget was raised on a hand to mouth basis, and European Championship funds were much harder to come by; he was evidently capable of seizing the European crown, yet doing so would have been opportunistic in the extreme.

Astra made tentative enquiries about the Manx, but abandoned them the moment Baroni launched the car off the road in Madeira. At

the time, his Pirellis had definitely had the edge over the other Lancias' Michelins, and he had been putting Aghini's understeering Martini car under some pressure. One only needs to examine the Jolly Club's World Championship record to judge that a Lancia was perfectly capable of winning the European title as well. The crucial differences were Ralliart Germany's organisation and Weber's cool professionalism.

Ultimately, the two Delta drivers not only scored fewer points between them than Weber did in total, but were well beaten by the experienced Pole, Marian Bublewicz, whose second place recalled the successes of other East European drivers, such as Attila Ferjancz, or Sobieslaw Zasada. There could be no better evidence of the Lancia drivers' humiliation.

Bublewicz owed his second place to those traditional props of the East European pretender, a good car — from the west, naturally — and a keen understanding of the co-efficient game. There was no sign of him on awkward rallies with fierce opposition, such as Ieper or Madeira. He was naturally in evidence on home ground and in Cyprus, though, landing a good points haul where his

RAS-powered Sierra Cosworth 4x4 could outpace slender opposition without demanding too much of the driver; it isn't often that the runner-up fails to win a single round of the championship. That said, there is some evidence that Bublewicz is a little more than a Marlboro billboard on legs, for he worried Droogmans for a while in Poland, before dropping back to finish a distant third after transmission problems intervened; although he finished second in Cyprus, the home performance was his most memorable result. He did not achieve his new eminence purely on reliability either: but for a

174

gearbox failure on the Deutschland, he would have finished even further ahead of Baroni. If anything, years of driving home-produced machinery have concealed his ability.

No European Championship review would be complete without Patrick Snijers, and the usual runner-up was a leading contender once again, even though sponsors' dictates officially confined him to Belgium. Winning at Ieper was of course the highlight of his season, but it symbolised the handicap he had to bear at the same time. At least in RAS customer tune, the Sierra Cosworth 4x4 was clearly well past its best. The Galant and the Deltas could outpoint it in every area between them, and in most on an individual basis. Of course the Sierra still has a generous wheelbase and a good engine, but it is badly short of suspension travel, it weighs too much, and it is strongly inclined to understeer. In a sense, Ieper was a rally that Weber lost rather than an event that Snijers won; all the signs had been there in Poland, and Ieper merely disproved the theory that Flemish local knowledge would compensate for the car's deficiencies.

The usual trip to Madeira was hampered by a drastic shortage of final result in any case. On the other hand, the Manx left no room for excuses. A thorough practice session and an RAS car should have enabled Snijers to make Colin McRae try at least. Instead, he was horribly mugged by the Subarus, and was struggling to keep up with the Ulster privateers, never mind McRae, when engine failure put him out of his misery.

Like his fellow-countryman, Robert Droogmans took advantage of Belgian Championship rules to squeeze some extra European Championship events into his programme, without conspicuous success. The Gordon Spooner-run seven-speed Ford was generally reliable, but Droogmans took a growing dislike to its handling. He complained incessantly of understeer, regardless of suspension settings or tyre make, persuading himself if not the team that the shell was flexing. But for the front differential failure, the former European Champion might well have won at Ieper. However, he never looked likely to do so anywhere else, and his points total was amassed largely from seconds and thirds. Under the circumstances, it was no surprise that his final score, as opposed to his results, was compara- Austrian Champion had signed up to drive a second Grifone Delta, looking rather out of his depth before rolling on the Costa Smeralda. He then had an appalling accident at Antibes, when it looked for a time as though he might be paralysed. Mercifully, the news later in the summer was much more encouraging, but there was no sign of him in action again for the rest of the year. Grifone's remaining appearances relied largely on the team boss, Tabaton. After finishing a close second in Belgium (when he told Snijers that the Belgian would have won easily if he had been driving an Integrale), the double European Champion announced his retirement after rolling on one of his favourite events, Madeira.

There were no rewards for the top two-wheel drive runner, Jean Ragnotti, who gained virtually all of his points from spectacular performances on home soil. After holding a top five place in the championship in the first half of the year, when most of the significant French events took place, he dropped out of the top ten, in spite of the fact that Renault had expressed a degree of interest in getting him amongst the leaders by sending him to Madeira in a Simon Racing Clio. On that occasion, a dis- Ieper and the top five on the Isle of Man, but even ran as high as fourth on the destructive gravel tracks of Cyprus, until a host of mechanical breakages ultimately stopped the long-suffering car within hours of the finish.

Despite the unexpected result, the European Championship is as badly in need of an overhaul as ever, and the failure of the two-wheel drive cars to do better doesn't alter the fact that they offer the best chance of giving it some purpose. There is the added impetus that a wholesale change could save national rallying throughout Europe from gradual extinction. FISA has been lamentably cautious in promoting 'Formula 2', failing to recognise that the European series provides the opportunity to experiment in a comparatively risk-free environment. Turning what is theoretically the number two championship into a real training formula might finally give it a sense of purpose, and lay the basis for expansion at the same time. The signs are that Renault for one would seize the opportunity to win the European title with both hands, and who is to say that other manufacturers might not follow suit? If the step seems overly radical, turning the

Photo Pascal Huit

Marian Bublewicz put in the best performance recorded by an East European driver for years in his Sierra Cosworth 4x4 (top left). Piero Liatti's hopes crumbled in mid-season (left) and, unexpectedly, the best Lancia driver was ultimately César Baroni, who launched his European Championship bid with an emphatic victory at Antibes.

suitable tyres which, although the team unhesitatingly blamed Pirelli, smacked of RAS's usual seat of the pants organisation. It is debatable that it made much difference to the ble with the likes of Andrea Aghini (who only contested two events, finishing a dutiful second to Auriol on the Costa Smeralda and easily winning in Madeira), and Bernard Béguin (who never ventured outside his native France). Snijers and Droogmans would probably agree that the Escort Cosworth cannot come a moment too soon, but they still did better than poor Longhi, who didn't even have the consolation of a FISA A-seeding.

If Longhi's season was bitterly disappointing, it was a distinct improvement on the unfortunate Christoph Dirtl's. The 28-year-old eased engine and some of the steepest stages in the world consigned him to the lower reaches of the leaderboard. The fact that even the 47-year-old Frenchman couldn't unsettle the massed ranks of the four-wheel drive cars can be attributed partly to Renault's preoccupation with the French Championship, partly to the fact that it didn't play the co-efficients game as seriously as Bublewicz.

Bruno Thiry fared no better in Opel Belgium's troublesome Calibra, and if anything, the two-wheel drive star was Dave Metcalfe, who not only got his 1600 Nova into the top ten at championship over to two-wheel drive cars, rather than outlawing four-wheel drive cars from the events themselves, might offer a suitably gentle transition. The European Championship has remained unpromoted, because it is neither a stepping stone to better things, nor even much of an end in itself. If it remains a far-flung contest, with a large number of important events on small, remote islands, it will continue to be expensive even if FISA insists that all championship contenders drive Trabants, yet an imaginative change to the vehicle regulations might cure many of its other failings at a stroke.

175

EUROPEAN CHAMPIONSHIP RESULTS

COSTA SMERALDA RALLY, 7-11 April, Italy.

1	Didier Auriol/	Lancia Delta HF Integrale	
	Bernard Occelli	4h 01m 39s	
2	Andrea Aghini/	Lancia Delta HF Integrale	
	Sauro Farnocchia	4h 04m 26s	
3	Gianfranco Cunico/	Ford Sierra Cosworth 4x4	
	Stefano Evangelisti	4h 06m 37s	
4	Piergiorgio Deila/	Lancia Delta HF Integrale	
	Pierangelo Scalvini	4h 10m 35s	
5	Piero Longhi/	Lancia Delta HF Integrale	
	Maurizio Imerito	4h 15m 04s	
6	Vanio Pasquali/	Lancia Delta HF Integrale	
	Francesco Mion	4h 21m 36s	
7	Bruno Bentivogli/	Ford Sierra Cosworth 4x4	
	Ilaria Hedinger	4h 38m 43s	
8	Carlo Galli/	Ford Sierra Cosworth 4x4	
	Pierluigi Adamoli	4h 41m 27s	
9	Gianni Fiora/	Renault Clio 16S	
	Claudio Manfe	4h 44m 43s	
10	Bruno Arntsen/	Opel Kadett GSi	
	Geir Kirkhorn	4h 46m 14s	

ZLATNI PIASSATZI RALLY, 9-10 May, Bulgaria.

1	Erwin Weber/	Mitsubishi Galant VR-4	
	Manfred Hiemer	3h 06m 21s	
2	Christoph Dirtl/	Lancia Delta HF Integrale	
	Jorg Pattermann	3h 12m 26s	
3	Marian Bublewicz/	Ford Sierra Cosworth 4x4	
	Grzegorz Gac	3h 16m 28s	
4	Laszlo Ranga/	Lancia Delta HF Integrale	
	Erno Buki	3h 20m 53s	
5	Georgi Petrov/	VW Golf GTI	
	Ivan Tonev	3h 32m 47s	
6	Viktor Shkolni/	Lada Samara	
	Sergei Gogunov	3h 32m 49s	
7	Tichomir Zlatkov/	Lada Samara	
	Konstanca Tomova	3h 35m 12s	
8	Sergei Alyasov/	Lada Samara	
	Alexander Levitan	3h 35m 33s	
9	Svetoslav Dotchkov/	Nissan Sunny GTi-R	
	Kalin Niadenov	3h 38m 41s	
10	Alexander Artemenko/	Lada Samara	
	Viktor Timovsky	3h 38m 50s	

ANTIBES RALLY, 22-24 May, France.

1	César Baroni/	Lancia Delta HF Integrale	
	Philippe David	4h 43m 44s	
2	Bernard Béguin/	Ford Sierra Cosworth 4x4	
	Jean-Paul Chiaroni	4h 46m 04s	
3	Jean Ragnotti/	Renault Clio 16S	
	Gilles Thimonier	4h 51m 57s	
4	Dominique de Meyer/	BMW M3	
	Patrick Ferre	4h 54m 00s	
5	Alain Oreille/	Renault Clio 16S	
	Jean-Marc Andrié	4h 55m 45s	
6	Eric Mauffrey/	Renault Clio 16S	
	Hervé Sauvage	5h 02m 22s	
7	Michael Gerber/	Toyota Celica GT4	
	Peter Thul	5h 04m 01s	
8	Yves Loubet/	Citroën AX GTi	
	Didier Breton	5h 05m 57s	
9	Jean-Hug Hazard/	Ford Sierra Cosworth 4x4	
	Bruno Brissard	5h 08m 21s	
10	Raymond Blanchi/	Ford Sierra Cosworth	
	Jean-Pierre Ramagli	5h 10m 15s	

POLISH RALLY, 6-7 June, Poland.

1	Erwin Weber/	Mitsubishi Galant VR-4	
	Manfred Hiemer	3h 39m 08s	
2	Robert Droogmans/	Ford Sierra Cosworth 4x4	
	Ronny Joosten	3h 42m 42s	
3	Marian Bublewicz/	Ford Sierra Cosworth 4x4	
	Ryszrd Zyszkowski	3h 50m 49s	
4	Jens Mulvad/	Toyota Celica Turbo 4WD	
	Freddy Pedersen	4h 02m 54s	
5	Kurt Gottlicher/	Ford Sierra Cosworth 4x4	
	Werner Jahrbacher	4h 05m 35s	
6	Hermann Gassner/	Mitsubishi Galant VR-4	
	Harald Brack	4h 07m 29s	
7	Kurt Victor/	BMW M3	
	Geert Derammelaere	4h 08m 46s	
8	Andrzej Koper/	VW Golf GTI	
	Macief Wislawski	4h 11m 09s	
9	Wieslaw Stec/	Mitsubishi Galant VR-4	
	Arthur Skorupa	4h 13m 32s	
10	Vital Budo/	Renault Clio 16S	
	André Malais	4h 15m 03s	

24 HOURS OF IEPER, 26-28 June, Belgium.

1	Patrick Snijers/	Ford Sierra Cosworth 4x4	
	Dany Colebunders	3h 41m 43s	
2	Fabrizio Tabaton/	Lancia Delta HF Integrale	
	Rafaele Caliro	3h 41m 47s	
3	César Baroni/	Lancia Delta HF Integrale	
	Philippe David	3h 45m 35s	
4	Omer Saelens/	Ford Sierra Cosworth 4x4	
	Jacques Castelein	3h 50m 06s	
5	Jim McRae/	Ford Sierra Cosworth 4x4	
	Rob Arthur	3h 54m 14s	
6	Bruno Thiry/	Opel Calibra	
	Stéphane Prévot	3h 57m 09s	
7	Grégoire de Mevius/	Nissan Sunny GTi-R	
	Willy Lux	3h 57m 09s	
8	Jean-Marie Milissen/	Ford Sierra Cosworth 4x4	
	Antoine Lekkerkerker	3h 58m 35s	
9	Dave Metcalfe/	Vauxhall Nova GSi	
	Ian Grindrod	3h 58m 50s	
10	Pierre Dumoulin/	Ford Sierra Cosworth 4x4	
	José Termote	4h 01m 48s	

DEUTSCHLAND RALLY, 17-19 July, Germany.

1	Erwin Weber/	Mitsubishi Galant VR-4	
	Manfred Hiemer	3h 37m 05s	
2	Michael Gerber/	Toyota Celica GT4	
	Peter Thul	3h 39m 34s	
3	Robert Droogmans/	Ford Sierra Cosworth 4x4	
	Ronny Joosten	3h 40m 31s	
4	Dieter Depping/	Ford Sierra Cosworth 4x4	
	Klaus Wendel	3h 44m 08s	
5	Mathias Moosleitner/	Toyota Celica Turbo 4WD	
	Regine Raush	3h 56m 52s	
6	Josef Sivik/	Lancia Delta HF Integrale	
	Miroslav Houst	4h 02m 12s	
7	Isolde Holderied/	Mitsubishi Galant VR-4	
	Monika Eckardt	4h 03m 44s	
8	Kurt Victor/	BMW M3	
	Geert Derammelaere	4h 04m 19s	
9	Stefan Schlesack/	Ford Sierra Cosworth 4x4	
	Dieter Schneppenheim	4h 05m 18s	
10	Josef Burkhard/	Ford Sierra Cosworth 4x4	
	Detlef Schaller	4h 06m 36s	

MADEIRA RALLY, 8-9 August, Portugal.

1	Andrea Aghini/	Lancia Delta HF Integrale	
	Sauro Farnocchia	3h 09m 53s	
2	Piero Longhi/	Lancia Delta HF Integrale	
	Maurizio Imerito	3h 13m 02s	
3	Patrick Snijers/	Ford Sierra Cosworth 4x4	
	Dany Colebunders	3h 15m 13s	
4	Erwin Weber/	Mitsubishi Galant VR-4	
	Manfred Hiemer	3h 15m 43s	
5	Ramon Ferreyros/	Lancia Delta HF Integrale	
	Rafaele Ynzenga	3h 16m 28s	
6	Robert Droogmans/	Ford Sierra Cosworth 4x4	
	Ronny Joosten	3h 17m 34s	
7	Joaquim Santos/	Toyota Celica GT4	
	Carlos Magalhaes	3h 22m 18s	
8	Jorge Bica/	Lancia Delta HF Integrale	
	Joaquim Capelo	3h 23m 52s	
9	Jean Ragnotti/	Renault Clio 16S	
	Gilles Thimonier	3h 26m 17s	
10	Vitor Sa/	Ford Sierra Cosworth 4x4	
	Ornecas Camacho	3h 30m 12s	

ELPA RALLY, 22-24 August, Greece.

1	Erwin Weber/	Mitsubishi Galant VR-4	
	Manfred Hiemer	4h 15m 29s	
2	Enrico Bertone/	Lancia Delta HF Integrale	
	Flavio Zanella	4h 16m 40s	
3	Marian Bublewicz/	Ford Sierra Cosworth 4x4	
	Grzegorz Gac	4h 17m 40s	
4	Mamdouh Khayat/	Ford Sierra Cosworth 4x4	
	David Nicholson	4h 24m 06s	
5	Serdar Bostanci/	Ford Sierra Cosworth 4x4	
	Cihat Gurkan	4h 26m 20s	
6	'Stratissimo'/	Nissan Sunny GTi-R	
	Tonia Pavli	4h 27m 44s	
7	Panagiotis Giagnissis/	Mazda 323 GT-X	
	George Kerantzakis	4h 35m 33s	
8	Josef Sivik/	Lancia Delta HF Integrale	
	Miroslav Houst	4h 38m 34s	
9	Sotiris Kokkinis/	Peugeot 205 Rallye	
	Stathis Mokkas	4h 38m 34s	
10	Sotiris Hatzitsopanis/	Mazda 323 GTX	
	Athanasia Polymerou	4h 40m 56s	

Grifone was the clear favourite for the title, but the Genoese team wasn't offered one of the latest Integrales until the spring and Liatti's luck deteriorated as soon as he was offered the ultimate Lancia.

MANX INTERNATIONAL RALLY, 8-11 September, United Kingdom.

1	Colin McRae/	Subaru Legacy RS	
	Derek Ringer	3h 45m 56s	
2	Bertie Fisher/	Subaru Legacy RS	
	Rory Kennedy	3h 52m 04s	
3	Kenny McKinstry/	Subaru Legacy RS	
	Robbie Philpott	3h 54m 29s	
4	Dave Metcalfe/	Vauxhall Nova GSi	
	Ian Grindrod	3h 58m 25s	
5	Frank Meagher/	Ford Sierra RS Cosworth	
	Micheal Maher	4h 02m 55s	
6	Gary Leece/	Ford Sierra Cosworth 4x4	
	Pauline Taylor	4h 05m 35s	
7	Alister McRae/	Ford Sierra Cosworth 4x4	
	Dave Senior	4h 06m 19s	
8	Trevor Smith/	Ford Sierra Cosworth 4x4	
	Roger Jones	4h 06m 57s	
9	Mark Higgins/	Vauxhall Nova GSi	
	Cliff Simmons	4h 07m 09s	
10	Jonny Milner/	Peugeot 205 GTI	
	Chris Wood	4h 13m 57s	

ROTHMANS CYPRUS RALLY, 25-27 September, Cyprus.

1	Alessandro Fiorio/	Lancian Delta HF Integrale	
	Vittorio Brambilla	6h 32m 43s	
2	Dimi Mavropoulos/	Ford Sierra Cosworth 4x4	
	Nicos Antoniades	6h 37m 15s	
3	Marian Bublewicz/	Ford Sierra Cosworth 4x4	
	Grzegorz Gac	6h 38m 57s	
4	Andreas Tsouloftas/	Lancia Delta HF Integrale	
	Andros Achilleous	6h 52m 47s	
5	Andreas Kalogeru/	Mitsubishi Galant VR-4	
	Andreas Christodoulides	6h 58m 02s	
6	Josef Sivik/	Lancia Delta HF Integrale	
	Miroslav Houst	7h 01m 39s	
7	Dinos Mashias/	Subaru Legacy RS	
	Nicos Panagides	7h 09m 06s	
8	Vladislav Shtykov/	Lada Samara	
	Yuri Baikov	7h 10m 34s	
9	Kypros Kyprianou/	Peugeot 309 GTI	
	Charalambos Anastasiou	7h 15m 22s	
10	Constantinos Georgalis/	Nissan Sunny GTi-R	
	Athos Kollitiris	7h 18m 46s	

EUROPEAN CHAMPIONSHIP STANDINGS:
1 Erwin Weber 2200; **2** Marian Bublewicz 1150; **3** César Baroni 850; **4** Patrick Snijers 740; **5** Bernard Béguin and Andrea Aghini 700; **7** Colin McRae and Alex Fiorio 600; **9** Michael Gerber 580; **10** Josek Sivik and Piero Longhi 560.

176